Women and Work in Premodern Europe

This book re-evaluates and extends understandings about how work was conceived and what it could entail for women in the premodern period in Europe from *c.* 1100 to *c.* 1800. It does this by building on the impressive growth in literature on women's working experiences, and by adopting new interpretive approaches that expand received assumptions about what constituted 'work' for women. While attention to the diversity of women's contributions to the economy has done much to make the breadth of women's experiences of labour visible, this volume takes a more expansive conceptual approach to the notion of work and considers the social and cultural dimensions in which activities were construed and valued as work. This interdisciplinary collection thus advances concepts of work that encompass cultural activities in addition to more traditional economic understandings of work as employment or labour for production. The chapters reconceptualise and explore work for women by asking how the working lives of historical women were enacted and represented, and they analyse relationships that shaped women's experiences of work across the European premodern period.

Merridee L. Bailey is a social and cultural historian of late medieval and early modern England. She is an Associate Member of the Faculty of History, University of Oxford.

Tania M. Colwell specialises in the socio-cultural history of late medieval France and England. She is a visiting fellow in the School of History at the Australian National University, and an Honorary Associate Investigator with the ARC Centre of Excellence for the History of Emotions.

Julie Hotchin is a religious and cultural historian of medieval Europe. She is a visiting fellow in the School of History at the Australian National University, and an Honorary Associate Investigator with the ARC Centre of Excellence for the History of Emotions.

Women and Work in Premodern Europe

Experiences, Relationships and Cultural Representation, *c.* 1100–1800

Edited by Merridee L. Bailey, Tania M. Colwell, and Julie Hotchin

Routledge
Taylor & Francis Group
LONDON AND NEW YORK

First published 2018
by Routledge
2 Park Square, Milton Park, Abingdon, Oxon OX14 4RN
605 Third Avenue, New York, NY 10017

First issued in paperback 2022

Routledge is an imprint of the Taylor & Francis Group, an informa business

British Library Cataloguing-in-Publication Data
A catalogue record for this book is available from the British Library

Library of Congress Cataloging-in-Publication Data
Names: Bailey, Merridee L., editor. | Colwell, Tania M., editor. |
Hotchin, Julie, editor.
Title: Women and work in premodern Europe : experiences, relationships and cultural representation, c. 1100–1800 / edited by Merridee L. Bailey, Tania M. Colwell, and Julie Hotchin.
Description: New York : Routledge, 2018. |
Includes bibliographical references and index. |
Identifiers: LCCN 2017059459 (print) | LCCN 2018002649 (ebook) |
ISBN 9781315475097 () | ISBN 9781138202023 (hbk)
Subjects: LCSH: Women–Europe–History–To 1500. | Women–History–Middle Ages, 500–1500. | Sexual division of labor–Europe–History–To 1500.
Classification: LCC HQ1147.E85 (ebook) |
LCC HQ1147.E85 W6545 2018 (print) | DDC 305.4094–dc23
LC record available at https://lccn.loc.gov/2017059459

ISBN 13: 978-1-03-240187-4 (pbk)
ISBN 13: 978-1-138-20202-3 (hbk)
ISBN 13: 978-1-315-47509-7 (ebk)

DOI: 10.4324/9781315475097

Typeset in Sabon
by Out of House Publishing

Contents

List of figures, maps, and tables

Figures

Maps

Tables

Notes on contributors

Merridee L. Bailey is a social and cultural historian of late medieval and early modern England. Her first book, *Socialising the Child in Late Medieval England* (2012; pbk 2018), explored morality and courtesy in late medieval socialising discourses for young people. Additionally, she has written articles and chapters on the history of book culture, religious history, the history of emotions, and law and emotions. She is currently writing a book on the religious and social value of meekness from the Middle Ages to the present.

Nicholas Dean Brodie is a historian and author based in Hobart, Tasmania. His PhD examined English vagrancy legislation, and he continues to research and publish on late medieval and early modern topics, as well as on the history of colonial Australasia. His last two books were *1787: The Lost Chapters of Australia's Beginnings* (2016) and *The Vandemonian War: The Secret History of Britain's Tasmanian Invasion* (2017).

E. Jane Burns recently retired as the Druscilla French Distinguished Professor of Women's and Gender Studies at the University of North Carolina, Chapel Hill. She is the author of numerous publications on gender and clothing including *Bodytalk: When Women Speak in Old French Literature* (1993), *Courtly Love Undressed: Reading Through Clothes in Medieval French Culture* (2002), and *Sea of Silk: A Textile Geography of Women's Work in Medieval French Literature* (2009). She is also the editor of a volume of essays entitled *Medieval Fabrications: Dress, Textiles, Clothwork and Other Cultural Imaginings* (2004).

Tania M. Colwell specialises in the social and cultural history of late medieval France and England. She is a visiting fellow in the School of History at the Australian National University, where she has lectured in medieval and early modern European history, and she is also an Honorary Associate Investigator with the ARC Centre of Excellence for the History of Emotions. She has published in the fields of manuscript and early book culture, gender, patronage, emotions, and the marvellous. Her current book projects investigate the manuscript transmission and reception of the French Mélusine romances and the emotions of intercultural encounter in early travel narratives.

Jeremy Goldberg has written extensively on a variety of overlapping social and cultural history topics around gender, family, childhood, and housing in later medieval England. He teaches at Centre for Medieval Studies and in the Department of History at the University of York.

Julie Hotchin is a religious and cultural historian of medieval Europe. She is a visiting fellow in the School of History at the Australian National University, and Honorary Associate Investigator with the ARC Centre of Excellence for the History of Emotions. She has published research on medieval religious women, aspects of manuscript culture, and devotion and emotion. She is co-editor, with Fiona J. Griffiths, of *Partners in Spirit: Women, Men and Religious Life in Germany, 1100–1500* (Brepols, 2014). Her current project examines gender and authority in late medieval monastic reform.

Diana Jeske completed her PhD at Monash University in 2015. Her thesis, *Experimenting with Intimacy in the Latin West, 1080–1180*, examined a variety of sources, primarily letter exchanges, in which medieval men and women constructed novel understandings of appropriate intimate relationships between the sexes. Prior to finishing her PhD, Diana completed a Master of Studies in Medieval History at the University of Oxford and a Bachelor of Arts (Honours) at Simon Fraser University. She currently works as a learning skills advisor for the Monash University Library, helping students develop the necessary academic skills to succeed in university study. She is co-editor of the *Companion to Medieval Letters and Letter Writing*, forthcoming from Brill.

Anne Montenach is Professor of Early Modern History at Aix-Marseille University (Aix Marseille Univ., CNRS, TELEMME, Aix-en-Provence, France). Dr Montenach defended her PhD at the European University Institute in Florence and her thesis was published as *L'économie du quotidien. Espaces et pratiques du commerce alimentaire à Lyon au XVIIe siècle* (2009). Following research on the early modern urban economy with a special emphasis on informal circulations and exchange, she has turned to working on female economic territories in early modern Europe and is identifying how women were pivotal to urban economies, both illicit and legitimate. She has recently published several articles and books including *Femmes, pouvoirs et contrebande dans les Alpes au XVIIIe siècle* (2017). She has co-edited with Deborah Simonton two collections of essays, *Gender in the European Town: Female Agency in the Urban Economy, 1640–1830* (2013) and *Luxury and Gender in European Towns, 1700–1914* (with Marjo Kaartinen, 2014), and is working with her as series editor on the Bloomsbury *Cultural History of Work* (2018).

She was also a section editor of *The Routledge History Handbook on Gender and the Urban Experience* (2017), edited by Deborah Simonton.

Sarah Randles is an honorary research fellow in the School of Historical and Philosophical Studies at the University of Melbourne, an adjunct researcher at the University of Tasmania, and was recently a postdoctoral fellow in the ARC Centre of Excellence for the History of Emotions. Her current research project explores the emotions of pilgrimage and sacred place, focusing on the relics and other aspects of material culture of Chartres Cathedral. She has also published on medieval and later textiles, the Arthurian legend, and on medievalism in Australian architecture.

Ariadne Schmidt is an assistant professor at the Institute for History at Leiden University. She is a social and economic historian working in the field of gender history. After she received her PhD from the University of Amsterdam, she was affiliated with the International Institute of Social History where she directed a research project on women's work in the early modern Northern Netherlands. In 2010 she came to Leiden University where she co-directed the research project on *Crime and Gender, 1600–1900: A Comparative Perspective*. She has published on the history of women's work, children's work, gender, labour ideologies, guilds, family history, the history of law, singles, and crime.

Ellen Thorington is an associate professor of French at Ball State University, where she has served since receiving her doctorate from Princeton University in 2003. Her research interests are in medieval poetics, short narrative, and the female voice; her work includes articles on Marie de France, Christine de Pizan, and Chrétien de Troyes among others. She co-edited *Dame Philology's Charrette: Approaching Medieval Textuality through Chrétien's* Lancelot (2012), and is currently working on a book project: *Proverbs and Old Wives' Fables: Women as Figures of Wisdom in Old and Middle French Literature*.

Acknowledgements

We would like to thank the many people who provided their support and encouragement as we prepared this volume for publication. Publication has been made possible by a grant from the Scouloudi Foundation in association with the Institute of Historical Research; the Australian National University's Gender Institute and the School of History in the College of Arts and Social Sciences provided valuable financial and material assistance at an early stage of the project's development. We're also grateful to Angela Woollacott, Carolyn Strange, and Constant Mews for their enthusiastic support for this project at its inception.

While it may not be usual practice to thank the individual authors of the chapters that appear, the editors would nonetheless like to thank each of them for their enthusiastic responses to our initial requests for contributions and for their commitment and engagement with the themes of the volume. Particular thanks go to Anne Laurence for providing valuable feedback on the volume's themes at a pivotal stage in its development. We are also grateful to the comments of the anonymous reviewers for their blind-peer review of the volume. Finally, our grateful thanks to our families for their endless support and encouragement.

1 Approaching women and work in premodern Europe

Merridee L. Bailey, Tania M. Colwell, and Julie Hotchin

> Because it hath pleased God to bless me with many children and so caused me to observe many things falling out to mothers and to their children, I thought good to open my minde concerning a speciall matter belonging to all childe-bearing women, seriously to consider of: and to manifest my minde the better, even to write of this matter, so farre as God shall please to direct me; in summe, the matter I meane, Is the duty of nursing due by mothers to their owne children.[1]

Elizabeth Clinton's perception of her duties as a woman in her 1622 advice manual, *The Countesse of Lincolnes nurserie*, carries with it important implications for contemporary understandings of women and work in premodern Europe. Clinton believed ('thought good') that sharing her observations and experiences with other mothers through the medium of literature was an important and socially valuable activity. This activity would instil Christian virtues both in mother and child, and, according to some commentators, expiate her inability to breastfeed her own children.[2] *The Countesse of Lincolnes nurserie* thus projects an impression of this noblewoman in which the roles of mother, author, and teacher are intertwined, a complex image which harks back to historical forebears, such as Dhuoda and Christine de Pizan.[3] Clinton's 'work', as with the work of the women discussed throughout the present collection of essays, holds many meanings. It is constituted by Clinton's lived experience as mother certainly, but embedded within it also was her understanding of herself and her (re)productive roles in relation to both God and her child-bearing peers, and of her conception of herself as a teacher and writer. We should pause to remind ourselves that each of these experiences formed part of Elizabeth Clinton's professed self-identity.

It is with a view to understanding and assessing the complexity of women's working lives that *Women and Work in Premodern Europe, c. 1100–1800* explores the interrelated perspectives of women's experiences of work; their working relationships with other women, men, and God; and the cultural representation of women's participation across various spheres of endeavour. This requires the integration of cultural, intellectual, and economic activities into the repertoire of what work means, and *did* mean, to women and men in the past. The temporal and geographic scope through which women and work are examined spans roughly 1100–1800 and covers a large expanse of western Europe, including Germany, France and the Netherlands, and England. Throughout the volume, premodern is used as an inclusive term that refers to the period ranging from the medieval through to the latter phase of the early modern era.[4] This volume has two aims: to demonstrate how a more encompassing concept of work extends to a variety of women's (and of course, men's) occupations beyond the purely economic, and to examine women's enterprising strategies to negotiate the parameters shaping their intellectual, cultural, emotional, and economic labours.

There is, of course, a danger with opening a volume that explores women's work with the example of Elizabeth Clinton. It may suggest that we still find it hard to separate women's work from childrearing and the domestic economy. Elizabeth's example may also more subtly reinforce the idea that elite women's work was often related to literary endeavour, which, despite the constraints of gender roles, was an accustomed activity for elite women to perform.[5] However, women *were* heavily involved in childrearing and in literary activities from the medieval to modern periods; to deny this would be to make the mistake of confusing historical reality with lazily made stereotypes, the latter of which is a genuine cause for concern and something feminist historians since the 1960s have worked hard to correct. As scholars of women's work in premodern Europe have increasingly shown, the domestic or family economy was only one of various possible domains of women's labour, and a woman's life cycle, while significant, did not determine all aspects of an individual's working life.[6] Elizabeth's decision to write about the duty, as she saw it, for mothers to nurse their children illustrates how her reproductive, intellectual, and emotional labours equally constituted work alongside occupations performed in return for remuneration. Collectively, the authors in this volume examine a more encompassing view of women's work which advances our understanding of women's experiences, the intricacies of their working relationships, and how women's working activities were represented in different cultural *milieux*.

Uncovering women's work: Methods and sources

Work is a category that is historically contingent and the meanings attributed to it in a given time and place reflect cultural values about those activities characterised as 'work'.[7] In line with our aim to reconceive the idea of 'work', a term discussed in greater detail in the next section, this volume extends current research that historicises changing ideas of work across the premodern period. This aim reflects our contemporary historical moment in which the nature of work and its crucial role in shaping identity is being redefined and expanded.[8] From the 1960s feminist scholars focused effort on expanding concepts of work in its economic sense to include women's unpaid domestic and reproductive labour in the home. Current articulations of labour are similarly being broadened by researchers in a range of social science disciplines to expand what is recognised as work to include emotional and cognitive effort, and other various 'immaterial' activities.[9] One significant development arising from the work of Sheilagh Ogilvie has been to identity occupations according to 'verb' descriptions rather than 'noun' descriptors.[10] Evidence of women's work is therefore expanded beyond occupational titles (for example, 'seamstress') to include more complex phrases which are found across a wide range of sources that reveal how women (and men) actually spent their time (for example, 'carrying bricks').[11] The chapters in this volume employ both noun and verb approaches to understanding women's work. For example, Sarah Randles' fine-grained discussion of terminology focuses on occupational titles, while the women described in the chapters by Nicholas Dean Brodie and Jeremy Goldberg hold no occupational titles but nevertheless clearly spent their time in particular ways to ensure their livelihoods.[12] By exploring the array of historical meanings attributed to work for and, importantly, by women themselves, the chapters in this volume re-evaluate concepts and experiences of work as sites of social, economic, and cultural production in which women's identities were created and performed.

Building on our aim to extend the concepts and language used to analyse historical women's working practices, our contributors examine how women's working experiences were intricately intertwined with larger forces that shaped their lives, such as legal constraints, familial demands and expectations, political circumstances, and social mores. This volume thus positions women's work both within and beyond established domestic and economic parameters. Collectively, the authors investigate the diverse range of activities that could constitute work for European women within social, cultural, and economic spheres and the relationships that shaped women's experiences of work. Through the critical elaboration of original case studies of women's work in given times and places, our collection adds to an emerging body of research into women's working lives that focuses attention on how women 'manipulated and negotiated the legal, social and cultural constraints placed upon their work (and their lives)'.[13] Contributors to this volume investigate the diversity of women's working activities, the intricacies of their interactions with other women and men, and how they negotiated the limits of authority or other constraints they encountered. The picture that emerges from these studies is one of 'enterprising' women. We employ the term here in the sense used by Daryl Hafter and Nina Kushner in their study of women and work in eighteenth-century France to reflect not only women's enterprise in the commercial sense, but more broadly to refer to the resourceful, creative, and imaginative ways in which women reacted and responded to their diverse circumstances.

Cumulatively, the chapters uncover common themes and patterns across the breadth of activities examined as work. Women's literary endeavours contributed significantly to the cultural and intellectual environments in which medieval women lived. E. Jane Burns examines the creative endeavours of the fictional women who inhabit the thirteenth-century French *chansons de toile* to explore how female cloth workers voice their experiences of love. In these *chansons*, the women sing laments while working, a practice which has a long tradition dating back to antiquity.[14] The capacity of women to create literary spaces as a means to work within existing patriarchal structures to pursue a range of productive endeavours is also examined by Diana Jeske and Ellen Thorington, who show us how women adopted and adapted literary conventions to shape culture and who self-consciously referred to writing as labour. Jeske explores these themes in her study of twelfth-century epistolary culture in the letter collection from the Bavarian abbey of Tegernsee, while Thorington addresses similar questions in her study of Christine de Pizan.

Turning to the topics of textile industries and domestic labour, Randles explores women's involvement in textile production in western Europe between the thirteenth and fifteenth centuries, while Jeremy Goldberg's contribution looks at the essential domestic and economic work of urban bourgeois wives in later medieval England. Both chapters deal with household activities. Randles examines the gendered nature of textile production, exploring how the materiality of the household created constraints and yet offered opportunities for women to participate in vital productive work. Randles' chapter also offers readers a wide-ranging survey of how the historiography around this topic has developed and effectively challenges assumptions that medieval textile production was the preserve of women only. Her chapter offers both original research into textile history as well as a vital synthesis of prevailing trends within the discipline. Goldberg also explores a range of documentary, literary, and visual sources to demonstrate the variety of activities recognised as women's 'household work', including domestic, sexual, and kinship work.

The extent to which women's work enabled them to assume positions of authority or leadership was often limited during this period, although women could exercise the authority of office in certain circumstances.[15] Julie Hotchin's study of the work of monastic governance focuses on one office in which women did exercise authority, that of abbess. Her analysis examines the relational nature of women's monastic leadership in late medieval Germany. She shows how the quality of nuns' interactions with clerical officials influenced the nature and scope of how women exercised authority and governed the monastery. Like Hotchin, Ariadne Schmidt examines female governance but in the urban setting of early modern Dutch towns. She explores the shared and yet distinct experiences of women seeking to fulfil different roles in civic and guild networks across Dutch cities. Her chapter also includes a fascinating discussion of women who sat on the board of the Gouda prison, illustrating how women deployed gender ideologies to assert their authority in their conflicted interactions with their male counterparts.

How women with limited opportunities made ends meet, or found themselves in situations that circumscribed action, is the subject of chapters by Brodie and Anne Montenach, and is an issue also raised in the chapter by Burns. Brodie's approach to beggary and vagabondage in Tudor England introduces concepts relating to the absence of work and the circumstances in which begging could be considered suitable 'work' in the absence of other gainful activity.[16] While an 'absence of (honest) work' to support oneself was deemed criminal, Montenach's analysis of the early modern Lyonnais textile trade demonstrates how a fiercely regulated industry forced some women (and men) into 'illicit work' (criminal endeavours) precisely to 'earn a living' in a conscionable manner. Here, Montenach's focus on female agency and the scope various women had to carve out a role for themselves, however illicit, to create work in these trades adds new insight into questions of female authority. Brodie and Montenach demonstrate that women expected to work to maintain themselves and avoid dependence on the community, demonstrating how economic exigency outweighed patriarchal constraints that limited women's work or restricted it to the home. Schmidt's chapter on the contested relationships in early modern Dutch guilds offers similar insights into how often women's involvement in trades was permitted or tolerated by the authorities, subject to individual circumstances and the nature of the activity in which they were involved. Collectively, the chapters encourage scholars to rethink modern assumptions about the culturally contingent meanings and understandings of legitimate and illegitimate work, the working relationships women formed, and the cultural value of their work in the premodern period.

The sources explored in *Women and Work* are unusually rich and wide-ranging, allowing the volume to demonstrate a range of methodological approaches to identifying and analysing women's work. Readers will uncover epistolary volumes, ego documents, and philosophical reflections; manuscript and art historical evidence; conduct literature, *chansons de toile*, and romance; monastic charters and narrative accounts; civic, guild, and parish records; probate inventories, court records, and statutory law. The diversity of sources brings to light a rich array of evidence concerning premodern attitudes towards, and the lived experiences of, women and work.

Many of the authors in this volume use institutional sources, for example from law courts and guilds, to understand the social, cultural, and legal expectations of how work was organised in a structural, formal, or normative sense. Goldberg, Montenach, and Schmidt all make use of similar sources which nevertheless originate from places as diverse as northern England, the Netherlands, and Lyon. By basing their analysis on comparable institutional documents, these scholars show how women variously negotiated, challenged, or inserted themselves into these structures across western Europe. Brodie turns to English legal records to provide rich evidence of how women interacted with structures that regulated work. His chapter illustrates the continual negotiation of cultural expectations that poor women ought to work and how this attitude informed legal and civic practices. Goldberg's sensitive use of both legal sources and literary material produces a nuanced discussion of the interrelations between norm and practice which shows what can be gained from interdisciplinary analysis for understanding cultural expectations and women's behaviour. Randles' critique of how the historiography of women's textile production has at times been informed by and reproduced gender ideologies presents a salutary lesson for researchers employing documentary and visual sources of women and textile work. Her analysis of different categories of sources, including documentary records, as well as visual, literary, and lexical evidence, provides insights into what activities men and women performed and the material circumstances that influenced this. Her close readings of context, especially concerning visual analysis, identifies the challenges inherent in interpreting evidence, and provides valuable methodological models for further work on these topics. Her chapter also offers a model of how practice-led research, and knowledge about how certain textile activities or tools would have been used, can refine and reshape our knowledge about women's activities.

Chapters in this volume collectively explore women's work across western Europe in order to promote discussions about women's working experiences which are attentive to regional differences and particularities but which also observe similarities across geographic, temporal, and cultural contexts. The cultural settings examined include religious, courtly, and urban environments. Hotchin's chapter focuses on the leadership of northern German religious women, while Jeske's chapter investigates Bavarian monastic literary culture. Thorington explores Christine de Pizan's professional work as a writer within the French courtly environment, while Burns likewise turns to medieval French literary culture to examine the dark underside of textile work in the *chansons de toile*. Several contributors examine facets of women's working lives within civic and urban contexts. The chapters by Montenach on the illicit work of eighteenth-century Lyon women and Schmidt's work on early modern Dutch women focus attention on women's interactions with guild and civic structures, with a keen eye on how pragmatic concerns of an urban community could support women's activities even when they countered gendered ideology. Randles' chapter integrates English and continental European sources to produce a richer picture of the gendered nature of medieval textile production. Goldberg's exploration of wives in English urban households shows why we need to understand all of the roles women took on in households in order to create a holistic image of their working experiences. Brodie's analysis of vagabondage and beggary across Tudor England restores female vagrants to the historical record. Each of the authors share the desire to reconceptualise and explore work for women in order to re-evaluate and extend understandings about how work was conceived and what it could entail.

Work and its meanings

The concept of work is imprecise, varies greatly over time, and is highly contested.[17] Moreover, different cultures and languages differ with respect to the activities that are encompassed by a label like 'work' and those that are not. Indeed, commentators of the history of the idea of work in Europe contend that even activities customarily understood as 'work' in an economic sense in modern Western societies need to be understood not as separate from but embedded within social, political, and religious dimensions of life.[18] As Jürgen Kocka observes in his historiographical overview of the history of the term, a general concept of work 'in the sense of a purposeful application of physical and mental forces in order to fulfil needs' emerged only slowly.[19] It is instructive, then, to turn briefly to the semantic history of the concept of work as it was understood in the medieval and early modern periods for what this reveals about the activities that have constituted work in the past and the evolution of the term as it is understood in post-industrial societies today.

From the perspective of social economic history, the terms work and labour are widely understood to be synonymous, yet many European languages contain two etymologically unrelated terms for what are now often thought of as similar activities. There was no unified view of what activities constituted work in medieval Europe, although vernacular cultures associated terms for work such as *work*, *ouvrer*, *werken* with material undertakings that produced some kind of artefact. On the other hand the meaning of labour, using terms such as *labour*, *travailler*, or *arbeiten*, was closely identified with physical effort, pain, and suffering as an immaterial endeavour.[20] Despite these philosophical distinctions, in practice the boundaries between the immaterial and material associations of labour and work blurred early on. For instance, some of the earliest uses of 'work' in English language sources (variously *weorc*, *werc*, *wirke*) show a wide range of meanings, including acts or deeds either individually performed or collectively enacted, tasks or functions needing to be carried out, or activities involving mental or physical effort.[21]

Medieval theological understandings of work also emphasised its significance in moral terms, with devotional and secular tracts referring to 'werkes of almus' and a 'werke of charitee', whereby the work in question expressed moral qualities and purpose.[22] The notion that humanity was condemned to labour primarily as a means to ensure subsistence as a consequence of the Fall lent the weight of moral force to physical effort.[23] However, labour was also valued as a means of avoiding the evils associated with idleness. Labour was further held to afflict the body, thereby restraining sexual appetites, and was considered to be a means of enacting compassion and achieving salvation.[24] For some theologians, labour thus aligned the labouring body with primarily spiritual and moral aims, rather than material gain (aside from that which was essential to live). Although there is no doubt that work was commonly used in medieval and early modern sources in relation to an activity which was productive, remunerative, and generally associated with actions relating to occupations and employment, at least in some premodern cultures, work extended beyond having associations with economic value to, at times, take on some of the moral overtones carried by the term labour.

It was primarily from the industrial period that work became more closely identified with remunerative activity and shifts in attitude that prioritised economic production. By 1800 the concept of work acquired the meaning with which we are most familiar today, becoming closer to the idea of 'labour' as working for subsistence and denoting earning for a living through some form of market-related activity, primarily but not solely for wages and salaries.[25] While this volume does not extend beyond 1800, it is worth being aware of the extent to which this latter concept of work now implicitly shapes so much of the contemporary thought and scholarship about work in all preceding periods.[26]

Despite the differentiated meanings associated with work over time, the most recent studies of historical women's work have tended to remain embedded within the economic model which regards work as a sanctioned commoditised activity directly linked to various modes of production. As a consequence, the question of work has primarily been investigated through the lens of economic and labour paradigms.[27] Within this framework, researchers are seeking to expand in innovative and important ways the activities that are understood as constituting work in this economic sense. In her project on English rural women's work, for instance, Jane Whittle adopts an expanded definition of work that recognises the contribution of activities undertaken to benefit others within the household as an element of broader economic well-being. She thus defines work as 'any activity that could be substituted with purchased goods or services', arguing that these too 'should be considered "productive" and part of the economy'.[28] Such research has importantly suggested that domestic chores, such as childcare, were more monetised than previously thought, an insight which complements Ruth Mazo Karras' observations underlining the significance of the domestic arena to the construction of the economy.[29] Much of this scholarship has been a response to a broader desire to make women's work 'visible', to find evidence of it in different archival sources, and to argue for women's economic contribution in non-traditional areas. This attention to the diversity of women's contributions to the economy has greatly expanded our knowledge of women's experiences of labour. The sheer breadth of our understandings of women's work across agricultural, domestic, and labour markets is testament to the success of these efforts.[30]

However, there is a risk that in overlooking premodern distinctions between notions of work and labour that we are occluding activities undertaken by women that did not have a perceptible relationship with a monetised economy. This is central to how ideas about gender are constructed. As Goldberg comments in his chapter, taking only a narrow view of work impoverishes our ability to understand the full extent of women's (and men's) lives in the past. Concepts of work that privilege a particular type of employed activity, even when this activity is shown to be broader and more visible than previously accepted, still disregard the actual activities of many women in troubling ways. For example, the term 'housewife' as it is understood today lacks the depth of occupations that formerly were attributed to it. The classical Greek *oikos* referred to the prudent economic and moral management of the household, the term from which we derive the concept of the oeconomy.[31] Although the importance of oeconomics in understanding how household management was once seen as analogous with the governance of the polity has been largely overlooked, medieval concepts of work embraced the idea of work as an effort or labour, inclusively defined to encompass spiritual and moral toil.

This collection aims to broaden existing scholarly approaches to work to incorporate the devotional, intellectual, and emotional elements that comprised much of the work carried out by women, as well as by men.[32] Studies of work informed by economic history approaches tend to marginalise the inherent nature of work as a cultural activity, an activity whose productive quality entailed the reproduction of social relations and values. As Patrick Joyce argues, to fully understand the meanings of work in a given historical context, we must look beyond the realm of economic activity to consider the social and cultural dimensions in which activities were construed and valued.[33] Moreover, as Karras suggests, the fact that an activity is not identified as an occupation or endeavour that we might consider being a form of work today does not mean that it should be excluded from our investigations.[34] Kocka's general concept of work as the 'purposeful application of physical or mental forces' in order to fulfil different needs is therefore a useful umbrella definition to capture what we mean by 'work', whether that need is material, cultural, or intellectual.[35]

In responding to this call for a more inclusive definition of work the chapters in this volume advance concepts of work that encompass cultural and spiritual activities, in addition to economic understandings of work as employment or labour for production. Chapters by Brodie and Montenach deploy work in terms that primarily relate women's actions to labour or economic production, or to the effects of its absence. Jeske, Hotchin, and Thorington reveal through their examination of literary and religious endeavours that work is also a term that is appropriate to describe activity involving mental effort and the production of cultural knowledge. Chapters by Burns, Goldberg, Randles, and Schmidt show how these cultural and economic aspects are intertwined and how women's labours had cultural value and crucial economic importance.

Existing and new paradigms for understanding women's work

Our volume's title, *Women and Work in Premodern Europe*, consciously acknowledges the seminal volumes of essays edited by Lindsey Charles and Lorna Duffin, and Barbara Hanawalt in the mid-1980s.[36] Contributors to these volumes initiated critical exploratory forays into women's participation in economic life in continental Europe or, more narrowly, England, as part of the second wave of feminist scholarship seeking to restore women to the historical record. Research over the ensuing three decades has shown that working women were ubiquitous in most premodern industries and that their labour was crucial to the survival and reproduction of the household at all levels of the social scale. Such work has stimulated an academic industry which, over the last three decades, has produced an extensive volume of research uncovering the breadth and depth of women's involvement across a spectrum of economic activities spanning urban and, to a lesser extent, rural communities across Europe from Ireland to Russia, and from Scandinavia to the Mediterranean.[37] Research has extended from the most recognised occupations of brewing and almost all aspects of the textile trades (both legal and illegal), to the crafts of various artisans such as pipe makers, chandlers, dyers, scribes and illuminators, and blacksmiths.[38]

Collectively, this important body of research has presented a kaleidoscope of evidence bringing to light women's involvement in many occupations across the premodern period. However, scholars widely agree that while the socio-historic circumstances framing women's working lives may have varied over time according to locale, social rank, and so on, a consistent feature of women's working experiences was the patriarchal framework which variably limited women's access to positions of authority and status. Labelled the 'new orthodoxy' by Rafe Blaufarb, this scholarly position acknowledges the significant work of earlier scholars such as Judith M. Bennett, Martha C. Howell, and Merry E. Wiesner-Hanks, who have done much to make medieval and early modern women's work visible and to understand the constraints restricting women's activities.[39] A new range of questions seeking to understand how women opened up opportunities or took advantage of their circumstances to create spaces in which they could work has been stimulated by this current research. Refocusing our questions in a way that recognises female agency across different fields of economic, intellectual, and domestic activity places women, their actions, and their aspirations at the centre of research. Thus, while we know the critical importance of women's labour to pre-industrial economies, we now need to think more deeply about how women negotiated prevailing structures and frequently restrictive personal circumstances to achieve their aims. How did women create spaces for themselves in which to build relationships which facilitated their pursuit of particular goals and fulfillment of their personal, familial, or social needs? Ultimately, the authors in this volume demonstrate how women creatively grasped opportunities and demonstrated enterprising behaviour across a range of occupations and fields of endeavour.

By centring attention on women's active negotiation of their institutional and personal circumstances, chapters in this collection bear out an important recent observation that women's agency and subordination were 'not mutually exclusive states':

> [O]ne possible way to move beyond the agency-subordination divide is to assume from the outset that patriarchal authority in early modern [and, we would add, medieval] Europe was limited by a variety of forces rather than to assume its rigidity and dominance. Thus, monolithic social norms and institutional structures are no longer the straw men against which women's activities are evaluated; rather, women's activities and responses themselves are the baseline for comparative analysis.[40]

Theresa Earenfight and Therese Martin have productively illustrated how ideas about women's power and agency could be explored by focusing on the creation and negotiation of relationships.[41] Developing this approach, authors in this volume highlight where women's relationships with men and with other women can be characterised as collaborative, interdependent, or mutually dependent. Instructive parallels with these three concepts—collaboration, mutual dependency, and interdependency—can be drawn from similar analytical approaches currently applied to medieval rulership, the exercise of joint aristocratic lordship, and interactions between men and women in religious life.[42] Just as terms such as agency offered a more nuanced approach in women's history to traditional notions of power across social ranks, and recent approaches in art history urge greater attention to women's participation in all aspects of the creative process, so too does the emphasis on relationships across the spectrum of mutual dependency, collaboration, or interdependency highlight how women found ways to assert their interests or to have their activities recognised or valued as legitimate, despite inequalities of power and access to economic resources.[43]

As Janine M. Lanza notes for the early modern period, women 'used their relationships to men, as daughters, wives and widows, as well as their skills, persistence and hard work, to open doors that might otherwise be closed to them'.[44] Lanza's observation about the capacity of women to navigate existing structures and relationships to participate actively in their worlds holds for women across the period; hence a key theme of the volume is the question of how and in what circumstances women negotiated structures that constrained or enabled them through their relationships.

Scholars attentive to women's agency recognise that the nature of women's experiences and their opportunities expanded and contracted according to local circumstance across the premodern period. Here, the question of change or continuity over time is particularly apt. As noted, one consistent feature of women's lives was their inferior *status* compared with men in most areas of life. For this reason, Bennett argues that rather than channelling research into chronological timeframes marked out by broad socio-institutional events, such as the consolidation of the universities, the Reformation, or emergent humanism, we must acknowledge the multiple chronologies of women's experiences, based variously on the specificity of location, time, social order, religion, ethnicity and so on.[45] Bennett prompts us to consider new periodisations based on women's histories, and to feel comfortable thinking about long-term continuities. Wiesner-Hanks, however, has highlighted how emphasising continuities could risk essentialising women's experiences, and that periodisation can illuminate change in women's historical positions, particularly during the early modern period.[46] As historians, turning away from questions of change or continuity over time is unsettling as there is a deep-seated desire to pinpoint when and why women's positions improved or declined and to make comparisons about women's overall status across periods.[47] Importantly, *Women and Work* does not suggest that the experiences of womanhood were constant across the period or that patterns of women's work developed in an even, continuous arc. Rather, it aims to trace the idiosyncratic dynamics shaping women's individual and collective participation within the premodern European world at particular times and to show the value of original case studies to deepen our knowledge about the diversity of premodern women's work and how this expands our understanding of concepts of work. We need to learn to study variation among women's experiences without positing a straightforward transformation in the social or economic status of women. In this way we can understand the possibility that the patriarchal institutions and structures within which women manoeuvred could shift and change without much altering the force of patriarchal power. Furthermore, we need to think about what women's history would look like if it were freed from the turning points and chronologies of traditional history.[48]

This in part explains our choice of the expansive term 'premodern' as the focus of this volume. Few investigations into the nature of historical women's working lives to date have encompassed the centuries prior to or beyond the imaginary temporal divide of 1500. Certainly, from a medievalist's perspective, Bennett's important study of English alewives, and Marjorie K. McIntosh's examination of English women's participation in the market economy, each trace fluctuations in the low relative value assigned to women's work from 1300 to around 1620.[49] Additionally, Howell's study of women's economic production in northern France spans the fourteenth into the mid-sixteenth century.[50] From an early modernist's perspective, studies more rarely glance back into the fifteenth century. While Wiesner's investigation into urban working women in Renaissance Germany occasionally turns back towards the 1400s,[51] more recent studies, such as Lanza's work on gender and the economy in early modern France or Micheline White's analysis of women and textual production in England at the same period, typically begin around 1500 or shortly thereafter.[52] With notable exceptions, including James Farr's studies of European artisans from 1300 into the twentieth century, Jane Humphries and Jacob Weisdorf's study of wage data between 1260 and 1850, and The Cambridge Group for the History of Population and Social Structure's study of Britain's occupational structure between 1379 and 1911, historical studies of work and workers more broadly have understandably shied away from a *longue durée* which encompasses significant structural, political, religious, and socio-economic change.[53]

Women and Work adopts a generous timeframe, spanning the period from *c.* 1100 to *c.* 1800. This broad chronological span challenges the artificial periodisation which posits a break from the medieval to the early modern era around 1500, a framework which continues to inform much contemporary scholarship on women and their experiences of work and, indeed, the shape of medieval and modern history itself.[54] By including essays that span western Europe between *c.* 1100 and *c.* 1800, this volume makes an important contribution to the ongoing scholarly reappraisal of this field at a key moment in its development. At one end of this scale, Jeske's study of the letters associated with the twelfth-century abbey of Tegernsee introduces us to the High Middle Ages, while chapters by Goldberg, Randles, Burns, Thorington, and Hotchin span the later Middle Ages of England, France, and Germany. Brodie's contribution centres upon Tudor England, while Schmidt explores early modern Netherlands. Our terminus is Montenach's study of eighteenth-century Lyon. Collectively, while all authors cautiously accept the basic premise that patriarchal structures were a consistent feature of the premodern world, *Women and Work*'s wide chronological scope encouraged contributors to attend to the specificities of women's working experiences in case studies free from grand narratives positing change based on events and circumstances which may, or may not, have materially or culturally impacted on the lives of all individuals in the premodern period.

Themes: Experiences, relationships, and cultural representation

These subtitles distinguish the volume from the existing body of work on women's working lives, stressing aspects of historical inquiry that reflect contemporary concerns with the construction of identity while building upon the broad tradition of earlier studies of women and work. Each theme is interlinked, illustrating how women's experiences were dependent on the relationships they formed with other women and men, and vice versa.

Experiences

In our collection, 'experiences' encompass historical women's lives and interpretation of circumstances, local examples, and case study approaches. In focusing their analyses on the experiences of premodern European women's work, contributors to *Women and Work* employ a range of methodological approaches to their evidence to uncover the lived materiality of women's lives. Our contributors acknowledge that the category of 'woman' is neither static nor unidimensional. Whether women were married, widowed, or single, living in urban or rural settings, their family background, access to training, and education all markedly shaped the economic and social opportunities available to them. There was wide variance too in the nature and scale of legal constraints and social customs that delineated women's economic and cultural opportunities by region, place, and period.[55] Individual personality and attributes also influenced how women reacted to the constraints they encountered and the degree to which they desired or were able to negotiate their circumstances. The chief dimension shaping women's working experiences, however, were their economic resources and ability to deploy them.

Elite women had access to greater material resources although, like their counterparts of lesser economic means, they also experienced legal, social, and familial constraints on their economic or cultural agency. Elite women usually married young and were often widowed at least once, which could grant them access to wealth in the form of property or other investments. As Goldberg's chapter outlines, the work of married women of the mercantile elite was centred on the household, encompassing a complex range of economic, administrative, sociable, and emotional labours integral to the success of the domestic economy. Such women could also perform an important role in the wider economy, managing their own business, investing capital in trade, or managing property.[56] The nuns examined by Hotchin were also drawn from patrician families of similar status. The abbess' work of monastic administration resembled in many respects a wife's responsibility to manage wealthy secular households. Nuns, like their married counterparts, also managed property, cultivated vital social and patronage networks, directed their convent and its *familia,* and ensured their households were fed and clothed. These material labours provided the economic means to sustain the spiritual work of their intercessory prayer.[57]

Women of elite social standing were best placed by virtue of their (relative) access to education, and their familial and patronage networks, to acquire the personal, literate, and cultural resources necessary to write. It comes as little surprise then, that the intellectual work by or attributed to women examined in this collection derives from erudite, courtly *milieux* in which certain women established a place for their intellectual energies and ethical instruction. Thorington traces the importance of Christine de Pizan's paternal, spousal, and royal networks, which facilitated opportunities for her to take the highly unusual step to establish herself as a female writer. The female epistolary voices analysed by Jeske show women exercising cultural agency as literary and artistic patrons, and participating in and shaping courtly traditions of intimate relationships.

Women of more middling economic means participated in business, commerce, sales, and business partnerships. The breadth of their activities differed from those of men in scale rather than type, and in the scope open to women to take a leading role. Several contributors extend our understanding of the importance of women's work within urban economies, highlighting the variety and extent of women's activities beyond the purely domestic. Goldberg gives examples of wealthier wives who managed their own businesses in brewing or as chandlers, whereas wives in households of lesser means earned income through piecework in the textile trades or by intermittent day work. Randles' chapter provides valuable evidence about the significance of women's access both to raw materials and the objects needed to make particular textiles, and how this influenced textile production and women's economic roles.

Current research into women's interactions with craft guilds focuses attention on the extent of women's involvement, and the fact that guilds did not uniformly or necessarily restrict women's participation.[58] Chapters by Goldberg, Montenach, and Schmidt take as standard the assumptions of women's involvement in guilds. The question the authors explore are therefore more nuanced—not were women involved, but how? In what capacity? How did they exploit loopholes, structures, or arrangements to carve out roles for themselves? What they have revealed is that women were involved at the margins, through illicit activity, or seeking to claim authority for themselves as widows to run the business, or they could be crucial to the functioning of a household including its workshop, in diverse ways as servants or family members who learned critical skills. Women and men of lesser status often encountered similar restrictions. Indeed, wives of masters may actually have had better access to certain guild privileges than some men.[59] These findings remind us of the 'discordance between regulation and reality', and how the legal frameworks of guilds 'were more about situating women and regulating their activities, rather than preventing them from operating businesses and working in workshops'.[60] Combined, these chapters offer valuable insights into the visibility and social recognition of the value of women's labour to pre-industrial societies and cultures.

Hard work for impoverished women, irrespective of their marital status, was a harsh reality. Although sources that shed light on the experiences of poor women are less numerous than for elite, mercantile, and artisan women, several contributors employ creative approaches to uncover aspects of how poor and marginalised women made ends meet by labouring, selling, pilfering, or begging. Even when they did secure work, wage rates for women remained about one half to three quarters below those paid to men. In addition, work in service and other wage labour was low in status.[61] As Jane Whittle has observed, 'A flexible workforce of poorly paid women benefited the wider economy, but the degree it benefited medieval women themselves is questionable.'[62] Several contributors examine how the activity of servants and other lower-status women provided labour that sustained the material wealth of elite households. Goldberg shows how a girl's progression through various forms of domestic service could equip her with the training and skills to one day manage her own household, as the wife of an artisan.

Burns' sensitive reading of the Old French *chansons de toile* suggests the dark history of coerced labour that underpinned silk production and importation from the east, and raises questions about the structural relations and mutual dependencies between elite households and low-status women workers in late thirteenth-century Paris.[63] Montenach turns attention to how the illicit trade in silk thread and fabric in Lyon provided impoverished women with a means for survival. Importantly, she notes how on occasion civic and guild officials dealt flexibly with women caught infringing guild regulations. Civic authorities recognised that offering women the means to maintain themselves, even if illegally, could be more beneficial than having them turn to poor relief. The experiences of marginal, vagrant women are brought to the fore in Brodie's analysis of the vagrancy laws in sixteenth-century England. Legal and civic records document poignant evidence of the harsh material reality of female beggars' existence and the strategies civic officials mustered to find them employment, often as domestic servants, to license them as beggars, or to expel them from town.

The contributors to *Women and Work* have effectively taken up the challenge to explore the experiences of premodern women's work using the women themselves as the point of departure for their analyses, rather than committing *a priori* to historiographical narratives in which masculine experience and structures are the norm.

Relationships

Understanding the relationships women formed with other women and with men is central to interpreting working experiences and offers a more complete picture of women's working lives. Contributors to this volume examine how women interacted with other women and men in diverse working circumstances.

Women participated in overlapping networks reflecting their multiple roles within the household, family, and work; analysis of how women utilised and participated in these networks reveals considerably more interdependence than has often been assumed. Scholars are increasingly sensitive to the idea that patriarchy is not unifying or univocal but allowed considerable scope for certain women to manoeuvre within certain parameters. A common thread to emerge from recent research is that women were not excluded from the workforce per se, but from positions of authority. Contributors to this volume assess the levels of authority women could make for themselves in flexible and imaginative ways: why were some women supported in positions of authority and in what circumstances? Here, authors focus on collaboration, interdependence, and mutual dependency. Such themes are pervasive irrespective of whether the context is economic, as in the chapters by Burns, Goldberg, Schmidt, and Montenach; legal, as in Brodie's chapter; or literary or spiritual, as in the studies by Hotchin, Jeske, and Thorington. As Wiesner also pointed out in her landmark study, men in positions of traditional civic and economic power were aware of the economic value, status, political and theoretical implications of women's work and the benefits that accrued from it, as were many women.[64]

The interdependent nature of women's social, emotional, and economic activities is brought to the fore in Goldberg's analysis of the sociable work required of late medieval English mercantile and artisanal wives. He draws on the concept of 'kinship' work to describe how the active cultivation of a household's kinship ties for the benefit of family and business was understood as the work of wives. Mercantile and artisanal households could acquire multiple benefits through women's social ties. Servants were often kin but could also be identified and employed through familial, trade, or business associations. Women's sociable contacts with family members and in their local neighbourhoods, as well as those developed through their own business ventures, could also prove financially productive in generating custom for business or in developing trusted relations that could lead to essential access to credit. Kinship work, therefore, Goldberg concludes, may have proven vital to the success of the household economy.

Women also functioned as intermediaries in local, urban networks of work, whether legal, informal, or illegal.[65] Montenach highlights how women's networks in the textile trade in eighteenth-century Lyon, created and maintained through acquaintance and word of mouth, were instrumental in enabling women to develop underground networks of women and men through which to distribute stolen silk thread. She shows how women's familiar knowledge of urban spaces, neighbourhoods, and their inhabitants proved vital to opening opportunities for women traders and the men and women who supplied them to foster the illegal trade in silk in Lyon. Women, sometimes wives of cloth merchants or poorer women, also acted as intermediaries to smuggle calico, utilising local and international networks of trade contacts to extend their reach. Successful networks to sustain these illegal activities depended, like their sanctioned household counterparts, on developing confidence and trust.

Women's relations of patronage and clientage could also be crucial in opening opportunities for work. Christine de Pizan, although unusual as a woman who supported her family through her writing and who secured royal patronage, offers an illustrative example of how familial relations and royal patronage enabled her to establish and manage a successful business after the death of her husband. Thorington outlines the development of the patronage relations between Christine and Queen Ysabel, seeing in their interactions a reciprocal working relationship. The queen promoted Christine's authorial work, lending it legitimacy and creating opportunities for financial reward, and Christine performed an advisory or counselling role for the queen, for the 'betterment of France', through her writing. Jeske's analysis of twelfth-century women's epistolary practices also illustrates women's ability to negotiate patronage networks to create and promote their cultural agency, demonstrating how letters both enacted and recorded the work of sociability through familial and patronal relations to influence literary and artistic commissions.

Women working together in similar occupations, whether through choice, proximity, or economic necessity, could also forge strong bonds of solidarity through which they promoted common interests. Montenach detects a culture of solidarity among economically precarious single women in particular in eighteenth-century Lyon. On occasion when women who traded in stolen silk threads were sought by authorities, the woman's neighbours and friends banded together to offer protection, claiming to authorities that they had no knowledge of her whereabouts. Brodie offers evidence that women in parish communities in sixteenth-century England worked together to raise money for charitable causes. Schmidt also examines how artisanal widows in Dutch cities banded together, on occasion with men, to petition civic governors to protect their right to manage their workshops. Such examples of women acting jointly to pursue common business interests invite questions about how they knew one another, how they prepared and prosecuted their petitions, the level of support and assistance provided by male counterparts, and also their evident self-understanding as female members of a professional occupation. These are valuable examples attesting to how women collaboratively deployed information and professional knowhow to pursue their goals.

Investigation into the interactions between women and men in this volume reinforce that these relations were multi-layered and more complex than familiar assumptions about gender and work often allow. Schmidt explores elements of collaboration in her discussion of the delicate balance between the rights of a widow to operate her workshop and the qualified journeyman on whom she relied to operate her business. The term she uses, 'mutual dependency', draws attention to the relational dimension of the circumstances shaping women's work by stressing the intersection of women's working experiences with those of men and other women. The concept of 'mutual dependency' can be productive as it underlines the relational and gendered nature of power inherent in women's working interactions. Schmidt and Montenach also illustrate how guild structures regulating work could operate to exclude women, but that in practice men recognised their value or contribution in some circumstances and showed flexibility to accommodate or promote female activities when they did not impinge on their own aims. The willingness of male officials to support women's activities as a going concern when their interests intersected is an important reminder that decisions affecting women could also be shaped by pragmatism rather than by gender ideology alone.

Cultural representation

A goal of the collection is to develop an encompassing view of work. Whereas experiences and relationships speak to the historical experience of working women, cultural representations of work alert us to the multiple ways in which societies employ images of work—visually or in text—to convey norms, expectations, and values about social and moral order.[66] As Gehard Jaritz puts it, visual representations of work convey a particular social group's values of 'the *right* work done by the *right* people at the *right* place and the *right* time and in the *right* way.'[67] Although depictions of people at work often contain the 'reality effect' through their finely detailed representation, images of work are never merely descriptive or intended to portray labour in isolation from other cultural meanings and values. Visual and literary sources of female work can offer valuable insights into how women's labour is perceived, although their representative value as interpretations of women's working experience needs to be carefully weighed. Contributors to this volume, notably Burns, Jeske, Randles, and Goldberg, engage with visual and literary representations of work in multiple ways, teasing out how particular images of women's work articulate gendered norms about women's role and place within premodern societies and suggesting how women may have negotiated these expectations in practice.

These themes are brought to the fore in a compelling way in the imagery of a woman spinning with distaff and spindle. This represents the archetypal premodern image of women's work through which a multiplicity of cultural values about social order, gender relations, and the essential nature of womanhood were expressed. The fourteenth-century proverb 'When Adam delved and Eve span / Who was then the gentleman?', with which Randles opens her chapter has a long history in mediating ideas about late medieval social relations. Moreover, as Catherine Batt has argued, this phrase also crystallises women's role as spinners, through which Eve and her distaff function primarily to affirm Adam as the tiller of the soil.[68] Depictions of Eve or the Virgin spinning such as those discussed by Randles conveyed ideals of medieval womanhood and raise questions about the relationship between image and material practice, and how we are to interpret its meaning. The iconography of producing textiles ignores the material circumstances in which this activity was performed by historical women and, as Randles demonstrates, men as well. Her analysis of textile trades in medieval Europe offers striking evidence of the extent of men's involvement while also illustrating how activities in textile production were gendered. She concludes that looking at representations of textile production in any single medium tends to distort the way in which it was gendered, and that therefore an interdisciplinary approach that looks at different media and the circumstances in which the representation was produced gives a more accurate picture.

Goldberg is similarly attentive to the relation between representation and historical practice; he employs a variety of literary texts that suggest the nature and scale of a late-medieval bourgeois housewife's role and responsibilities. As he observes, texts such as conduct literature do not offer a simple reading of social practice; however when read against other documentary evidence they can suggest a cultural expectation about the activities a housewife was expected and required to perform and in what manner.

The depiction of two elaborately attired women labouring at a construction site on the cover of this volume itself offers a striking example of the interplay of meanings between material and immaterial labour, and physical and intellectual work, which lies at the heart of this collection. The two women on the right are shown constructing the foundations of a building depicting the allegorical opening of Christine de Pizan's *City of Ladies*.[69] Christine describes how, at a moment when she felt overcome with grief and frustration at the ceaseless literary critique of women, she sees in a vision the figures of three female virtues, Reason, Rectitude, and Justice, who offer to assist her to construct a city of virtuous women. In the illumination, the composition of which Christine oversaw herself between around 1410 and 1414, the author is depicted with Reason labouring to build the foundations of the city. Reason carries a heavy building stone to Christine, who, with her trowel, applies mortar to set the stone of the foundation in place. This image is positioned alongside a depiction of Christine in her study with the three Virtues, thus visually juxtaposing the two working roles that she performs through her text. She further develops the symbolic parallels between writing and building in the *City*. Reason instructs Christine to build the city in a 'field of letters'; later, Rectitude tells her to 'mix mortar in her ink bottle', thus likening the work of establishing the foundations of the city to the physical and intellectual effort involved in writing.[70]

As Thorington observes in her chapter in this volume, Christine frequently employed images of building tools as metaphors for her intellectual labour and the manual effort of composition. A woman engaged in construction is in itself a compelling image, especially in contrast to the more customary depictions of women in domestic settings. Whilst historical women are recorded as having been employed in aspects of the premodern construction industry,[71] Christine's richly attired women are clearly meant to invite the viewer's identification with the values and gendered expectations assumed to be held by the elite female audience of this manuscript. Representations of women's labour in the *City of Ladies* are not static or passive, but when interpreted in conjunction with the text invite the reader/viewer to imitate and enact the work depicted in a similar process of spiritual, moral, and intellectual endeavour within their selves. Christine's aim is to offer her labour as a model to her reader/viewer, and thus to encourage her audience to exert similar physical and intellectual effort to craft a virtuous self fit to enter the City.[72] More broadly, Christine's use of allegorical parallels to equate writing with construction tools shows her familiarity with a rhetorical tradition in which manual labour was used to describe intellectual endeavours, a tradition which culminated in Erasmus' comparison of his humanist work with the labours of Hercules.[73]

Jeske's analysis of women's letters about love and intimate relationships further illustrates opportunities through which women reshaped classical tradition to assert a distinctly female perspective on the philosophical work involved in moral and ethical self-fashioning. The traditions of friendship and love evinced in these letters were based on classical ideals which articulated a predominantly male rhetoric and practice of friendship. Jeske's analysis shows how women adapted forms of discourse on friendship and intimate relations to offer an alternate ethical model about how to negotiate relationships. Women's epistolary exchanges presented an opportunity for some women to participate in and challenge dominant cultural ideas about women's role in courtly relations, while at the same time enabling these women to articulate and perform literate, courtly identities.

Songs, such as those represented in Old French *chansons de toile*, offered women another opportunity to speak of their experiences. It was through the act of singing that poetic women created sanctioned space in which to voice laments as a challenge to dominant culture. Burns shows how singing is intertwined with sewing in the *chansons de toile*, the labour of sewing producing a creative and representational space in which women voice experience of, and imaginatively enact, the possibility of finding success in love, while negotiating their experiences and hopes for loving relationships. In singing of love, these women created identities as active and desiring subjects, in contrast to the customary portrayal of women in courtly romance as passive objects of desire. Lower-status female cloth workers, elite letter writers, and Christine's elite readers are thus represented or represent themselves as active subjects who adopt and adapt literary and intellectual traditions.

Where to from here?

Women and Work does not claim to be comprehensive in its coverage of the topic across the premodern period; the diversity of women's lives and circumstances is simply too great to cover in a single volume. The volume, however, is intended to stimulate research into aspects of women's activity that are not included, such as medicine and health care, science, and the experiences of work for non-Christian as well as non-Western women in the premodern world. Given the trajectory of the current scholarship and the ongoing interest in exploring expanded notions of historical work, research into women and work will continue to broaden our understanding of women's participation in all domains of endeavour.

One of the goals of this volume is to bring the experiences of individual and collective groups of women to light by giving full credibility to the diversity of premodern women's experiences of work and, where possible, to highlight the nature of these women's working relationships with both men and other women. To this end, the authors explore how these experiences and relationships could be represented through various cultural forms. Moreover, by adopting an inclusive approach, the chapters situate those activities performed by women within a flexible framework that accommodates culturally diverse understandings of work. By considering the intellectual, devotional, domestic, and cultural work performed by women, as well as their economic work, the volume poses new questions of pre-modern sources and historical subjects in connection with ideas about work.

The earlier scholarship on women's work was trailblazing in that it argued for women's presence in the economy and as labourers. Thanks to these studies, and those that followed in a similar vein, we now know much more about the sheer scope of activities in which women engaged. Today this point is assumed; women have been demonstrated to be active across numerous industries and in diverse roles. We continue the spirit of the pre-existing scholarship of Hanawalt, Charles and Duffin, and others by expanding the concept of what work could entail and examining women's roles in working activities from a broader conceptual perspective, using various methodologies from within history and literary studies, and drawing on diverse sources. The questions historians must now turn to challenge different sets of assumptions about the value of cultural and intellectual labour, creating new opportunities to understand women's history more broadly. Indeed, while we no longer need to press home the point that women worked in the economy or for economic gain, we still have much to do to uncover the varied circumstances in which women did so, how they negotiated the circumstances they faced in terms of constraints of gender and class and age. *Women and Work* contributes to this wider picture. Our collective endeavour as historians is now to engage with new ways to identify and interpret women's 'work' in the economy, society, and culture.

Notes

1 Elizabeth Clinton, *The Countesse of Lincolnes Nurserie* (Oxford: John Lichfield and James Short, 1622), B1.

2 Kate McPherson, introduction to *The Countess of Lincolnes Nurserie, An Electronic Edition*, by Elizabeth Knevet Clinton, xvi, Emory Women Writers Resource Project. Accessed August 17, 2017. http://womenwriters.digitalscholarship.emory.edu/essay.php?level=div&id=clinton_000.

3 Dhuoda, *Handbook for her Warrior Son: Liber Manualis*, ed. and trans. Marcelle Thiebaux (Cambridge: Cambridge University Press, 1998); Charity Cannon Willard, 'Christine de Pizan as Teacher', *Romance Languages Annual* 3 (1992); and Ellen Thorington's chapter in this volume.

4 The term premodern has been adopted within economic, religious, and social histories of Europe, usually to explore extensive periods. See for instance Paolo Malanima, *Pre-Modern European Economy: One Thousand Years 10th–19th Centuries* (Leiden: Brill, 2009); Ilinca Tanaseanu-Döbler and Marvin Döbler, eds., *Religious Education in Pre-Modern Europe* (Leiden: Brill, 2012); Patricia Simons, *The Sex of Men in Premodern Europe: A Cultural History* (Cambridge: Cambridge University Press, 2011); Beat Kümin, *The Communal Age in Western Europe, c. 1100–1800: Towns, Villages and Parishes in Pre-Modern*

Society (Basingstoke: Palgrave Macmillan, 2013). Premodern is also used in some literature as an alternative to early modern.

5 Diana Robin examines a broad sweep of women writers in Europe spanning the period 1400–1700 in 'Intellectual Women in Early Modern Europe', in *The Ashgate Research Companion to Women and Gender in Early Modern Europe*, ed. Allyson Poska, Jane Couchman, and Katherine McIver (Farnham: Ashgate, 2013).

6 The concept of the family economy is re-assessed in *Women and Work in Eighteenth-Century France*, ed. Daryl M. Hafter and Nina Kushner (Baton Rouge: Louisiana State University Press, 2015). See also Monica Chojnacka, *Working Women of Early Modern Venice* (Baltimore: Johns Hopkins University Press, 2001), xviii; and Janine M. Lanza, 'Women and Work', in *The Ashgate Research Companion to Women and Gender*, ed. Poska, Couchman, and McIver.

7 Deborah Simonton presents a lucid overview of the categories of 'work', 'women', and how both are gendered by social values in her *A History of European Women's Work: 1700 to the Present* (London: Routledge, 1998), 1–9.

8 Reconceiving and extending concepts of what constitutes 'work' is an explicit aim of the international, multi-disciplinary research network 'Producing Change: Gender and Work in Early Modern Europe' based at the University of Glasgow. Accessed August 7, 2017. http://producingchange.gla.ac.uk. See also *The Cultural History of Work*, ed. Anne Montenach and Deborah Simonton (Bloomsbury, forthcoming) which offers a comprehensive survey of the social and cultural construction of work across six historical periods. The approach to focus on the *cultural* history of work provides an opportunity to explore the dynamics of work and the people and relationships involved in working and the workplace, helping to rethink boundaries and the issues of work.

9 Bonnie G. Smith, 'Afterword', in *Women and Work in Eighteenth-Century France*, ed. Hafter and Kushner, 226.

10 Sheilagh Ogilvie, *A Bitter Living: Women, Markets, and Social Capital in Early Modern Germany* (Oxford: Oxford University Press, 2003). See also Rosemarie Fiebranz, et al., 'Making Verbs Count: The Research Project "Gender and Work" and its Methodology', *Scandinavian Economic History Review* 59 (2011).

11 Fiebranz, et al. 'Making Verbs', 280.

12 Our thanks to Anne Laurence for helpful discussions about this.

13 Daryl M. Hafter and Nina Kushner, 'Introduction', in *Women and Work in Eighteenth-Century France*, ed. Hafter and Kushner, 10.

14 Andromache Karanika, *Voices at Work: Women, Performance, and Labor in Ancient Greece* (Baltimore: Johns Hopkins University Press, 2014).

15 Kimberly A. LoPrete, 'Women, Gender and Lordship in France, *c.* 1050–1250', *History Compass* 5 (2007); and Rafe Blaufarb, 'The Phenomenon of Female Lordship: The Example of the Comtesse de Sade', in *Women and Work in Eighteenth-Century France*, ed. Hafter and Kushner.

16 Josef Ehmer briefly surveys how the concepts of work and labour interact with charity and unemployment in early modern Germany in 'Discourses on Work and Labour in 15th and 16th-Century Germany', in *Work in a Modern Society: The German Historical Experience in Comparative Perspective*, ed. Jürgen Kocka (New York: Berghahn, 2010), 27–30.

17 Jürgen Kocka, 'Work as a Problem in European History', in *Work in a Modern Society*, ed. Kocka, 1.

18 Kocka, 'Work as a Problem', and Josef Ehmer and Catharina Lis, eds., *The Idea of Work in Europe from Antiquity to Modern Times* (Farnham: Ashgate, 2009).
19 Kocka, 'Work as a Problem', 2.
20 Michael Uebel and Kellie Robertson, 'Conceptualizing Labor in the Middle Ages', in *The Middle Ages at Work: Practicing Labor in Late Medieval England*, ed. Kellie Robertson and Michael Uebel (New York: Palgrave, 2004), 4; Kocka, 'Work as a Problem', 2. Using the term 'immaterial' to describe work has been critiqued because it elides the embodied dimension of effort involved in physical labour as mentioned here, as well as emotional or caring labour. However, our use of the term is an effective shorthand for distinguishing between work that produced a tangible object and work that did not.
21 '*work*, n.', in *Oxford English Dictionary* online. Accessed March 1, 2017. www.oed.com.
22 *Cursor Mundi. The Cursur of the World. A Northumbrian Poem of the XIVth Century, In Four Versions*, ed. Richard Morris, EETS OS 57, 59, 62, 66, 68, 99, 101 (London: Kegan Paul, Trench, Trübner, 1874–1893), 1132, l. 19764; and *Gesta Romanorum*, in London, British Library, MS Additional 9066, fol. 341r; each cited in the *Oxford English Dictionary* online entry, '*work*, n.'.
23 Uebel and Robertson, 'Conceptualizing Labor'; Catharina Lis and Josef Ehmer, 'Introduction: Historical Studies in Perceptions of Work', in *The Idea of Work*, ed. Ehmer and Lis.
24 Thomas Aquinas, *Summa Theologica*, II.2, q. 187, art. 3, cited and discussed in Uebel and Robertson, 'Conceptualizing Labor', 4, 14 n. 4; Birgit van den Hoven, *Work in Ancient and Medieval Thought: Ancient Philosophers, Medieval Monks and Theologians and their Concept of Work, Occupations and Theology* (Leiden: Brill, 1996), esp. ch. 3; John Van Engen, 'Medieval Monks on Labor and Leisure', in *Faithful Narratives: Historians, Religion, and the Challenge of Objectivity*, ed. Andrea Sterk and Nina Caputo (Ithaca: Cornell University Press, 2014); Jacques le Goff, *Time, Work, & Culture in the Middle Ages*, trans. Arthur Goldhammer (Chicago: Chicago University Press, 1980), xii.
25 Kocka, 'Work as a Problem', 8; Lis and Ehmer, 'Perceptions of Work', 19–20.
26 On how oeconomics can be a productive way to understand eighteenth-century British domestic patterns, see Karen Harvey, *The Little Republic: Masculinity and Domestic Authority in Eighteenth-Century Britain* (Oxford: Oxford University Press, 2012).
27 Examples of this approach include Barbara A. Hanawalt, ed., *Women and Work in Preindustrial Europe* (Bloomington: Indiana University Press, 1986); and more recently Lanza, 'Women and Work', and her 'Labour, Land, Economy' in *The Oxford Handbook of Women and Gender in Medieval Europe*, ed. Judith M. Bennett and Ruth Mazo Karras (Oxford: Oxford University Press, 2013). These contain useful surveys of women in urban and rural economies which adopt a traditional social economic focus; the latter volume also includes surveys of women and slavery that productively extend concepts and interpretations of work.
28 *Women's Work in Rural England, 1500–1700*. Accessed August 17, 2017. https://earlymodernwomenswork.wordpress.com. Whittle's definition of work is based on the 'third party criterion' developed by the economist Margaret Reid, *The Economics of Household Production* (New York: Wiley, 1934), who sought to account properly for work undertaken within the household.

29 Ruth Mazo Karras, 'Women's Labors: Reproduction and Sex Work in Medieval Europe', *Journal of Women's History* 15 (2004).

30 Selected studies include Martha C. Howell, *Women, Production, and Patriarchy in Late Medieval Cities* (Chicago: University of Chicago Press, 1986); Marjorie K. McIntosh, *Working Women in English Society, 1300–1600* (Cambridge: Cambridge University Press, 2005); *Women at Work in Spain: From the Middle Ages to Early Modern Times*, ed. Marilyn Stone and Caren Benito-Vessels (New York: Peter Lang, 1998); and Ogilvie, *Bitter Living*.

31 Harvey, *Little Republic*, 25.

32 Arlie Hochschild, *The Managed Heart: Commercialization of Human Feeling* (Berkeley: University of California Press, 1983); Joanna Picciotto, 'Devotion and Intellectual Labour', *Journal of Medieval and Early Modern Studies* 44 (2014); and the special issue on 'Intellectual Labor', ed. Keya Ganguly in the *South Atlantic Quarterly* 108 (2009).

33 Patrick Joyce, 'The Historical Meanings of Work: An Introduction', in *The Historical Meanings of Work*, ed. Patrick Joyce (Cambridge: Cambridge University Press, 1987).

34 Karras, 'Women's Labors'.

35 Kocka, 'Work as a Problem'. Karras, 'Women's Labors', 155, adopts a similarly broad concept of work defined as what someone spends her life doing, and what others take to be the main contribution she makes, in relation to women's reproductive work, although the definition has broader application too.

36 Lindsey Charles and Lorna Duffin, eds., *Women and Work in Pre-Industrial England* (London: Croon Helm, 1985); and Hanawalt, ed., *Women and Work in Preindustrial Europe*. David Herlihy's *Opera Muliebria: Women and Work in Medieval Europe* (New York: McGraw-Hill, 1990), was similarly foundational. For historiographical reviews of this field, see Judith M. Bennett, 'Medieval Women, Modern Women: Across the Great Divide', in *Culture and History, 1350–1699: Essays on English Communities, Identities and Writing*, ed. David Aers (London: Harvester Wheatsheaf, 1992), 147–75; Pamela Sharpe, 'Continuity and Change: Women's History and Economic History in Britain', *Economic History Review* 48 (1995): 353–69; and Lanza, 'Women and Work'.

37 Darlene Abreu-Ferreira has published widely on women and work in Portugal, including 'Fishmongers and Shipowners: Women in Maritime Communities of Early Modern Portugal', *Sixteenth Century Journal* 31 (2000); 'From Mere Survival to Near Success: Women's Economic Strategies in Early Modern Portugal', *Journal of Women's History* 13 (2001); and 'Work and Identity in Early Modern Portugal: What Did Gender Have to Do With It?', *Journal of Social History* 35 (2002). For Spain, see Stone and Benito-Vessels, eds., *Women at Work in Spain*; and Ana Rich Abad, '"Able and Available": Jewish Women in Medieval Barcelona and their Economic Activities', *Journal of Medieval Iberian Studies* 6 (2014). For the Mediterranean, see Chojnacka, *Working Women of Early Modern Venice*; Dora Dumont, 'Women and Guilds in Bologna: The Ambiguities of "Marginality"', *Radical History Review* 70 (1998); and Raffaella Sarti, 'Notes on the Feminization of Domestic Service: Bologna as a Case Study', *Acta demographica* 13 (1997). See also Grethe Jacobsen, 'Women's Work and Women's Role: Ideology and Reality in Danish Urban Society, 1300–1550', *The Scandinavian Economic History Review* 30 (1983); Brit Berggren, 'The Female

Peasant and the Male Peasant: Division of Labour in Traditional Norway', *Ethnologia Scandinavica* 14 (1984); and Josef Ehmer, 'Rural Guilds and Urban-Rural Guild Relations in Early Modern Central Europe', in *The Return of the Guilds*, ed. Jan Lucassen, Tine De Moor, and Jan Luiten van Zanden, special issue of *International Review of Social History* 53, suppl. 16 (2008): 143–58.

38 See also chapters by Goldberg, Schmidt, and Thorington in this volume. Schmidt's chapter stems from the Dutch project she led on 'Women's Work in the Early Modern Northern Netherlands, *c.* 1600–1815' funded by the Friends of the IISH, the Stichting Van Winterfonds, and the Netherlands Organisation for Scientific Research (NWO).

39 Judith M. Bennett, *Ale, Beer, and Brewsters in England: Women's Work in a Changing World, 1300–1600* (Oxford: Oxford University Press, 1996); Howell, *Women, Production, and Patriarchy*; and Merry E. Wiesner, *Working Women in Renaissance Germany* (New Brunswick: Rutgers University Press, 1986) and Merry E. Wiesner-Hanks, *Women and Gender in Early Modern Europe*, 3rd edn. (Cambridge: Cambridge University Press, 2008).

40 Allyson M. Poska, Jane Couchman, and Katharine A. McIver, 'Introduction', in *Ashgate Research Companion to Women and Gender*, ed. Poska, Couchman, and McIver, 8.

41 Theresa Earenfight, 'Without the Persona of the Prince: Kings, Queens and the Idea of Monarchy in Late Medieval Europe', *Gender & History* 19 (2007), and *The King's Other Body: María of Castile and the Crown of Aragon* (Philadelphia: University of Pennsylvania Press, 2010); Therese Martin, 'Exceptions and Assumptions: Women in Medieval Art History', in *Reassessing the Roles of Women as 'Makers' of Medieval Art and Architecture*, ed. Therese Martin (Leiden: Brill, 2012), 1:1–33, and 'The Margin to Act: A Framework for Investigation of Women's (and Men's) Medieval Art-Making', *Journal of Medieval History* 42 (2016).

42 Theresa Earenfight, *Queenship in Medieval Europe* (New York: Palgrave Macmillan, 2013); Kimberly A. LoPrete, *Adela of Blois: Countess and Lord (c. 1067–1137)* (Dublin: Four Courts Press, 2007); Fiona J. Griffiths and Julie Hotchin, *Partners in Spirit: Women, Men and Religious Life in Germany, 1100–1500* (Turnhout: Brepols, 2014).

43 Mary C. Erler and Maryanne Kowaleski, eds., *Gendering the Master Narrative: Women and Power in the Middle Ages* (Ithaca, NY: Cornell University Press, 2003) and the articles in the special issue on 'Beyond Women and Power: Looking Backward and Moving Forward', in the *Medieval Feminist Forum* 51 (2015).

44 Lanza, 'Women and Work', 280.

45 Judith M. Bennett, 'Confronting Continuity', *Journal of Women's History* 9 (1997).

46 Merry E. Wiesner-Hanks, 'Do Women Need the Renaissance?', *Gender & History*, 20 (2008).

47 The 'Golden Age' debate about whether women experienced economic improvements following the Black Death followed by their erosion in the sixteenth century is one of the most arresting examples of the desire to track clear trajectories of change. Subsequent debate has questioned whether post-plague conditions materially affected women's opportunities for the better. Some, like Marjorie McIntosh, have found evidence of certain improved conditions but without going so far as to argue for a 'golden age'. See Caroline Barron, 'The

"Golden Age" of Women in Medieval London', *Reading Medieval Studies* 15 (1989); McIntosh, *Working Women.*

48 Bennett, 'Confronting Continuity', 82. Bennett reiterates these arguments in *History Matters: Patriarchy and the Challenges of Feminism* (Philadelphia: University of Pennsylvania Press, 2006), and 'Forgetting the Past', *Gender & History* 20 (2008).

49 Bennett, *Ale, Beer, and Brewsters*; McIntosh, *Working Women.*

50 Howell, *Women, Production, and Patriarchy.*

51 Wiesner, *Working Women in Renaissance Germany.*

52 Janine M. Lanza, *From Wives to Widows in Early Modern Paris: Gender, Economy, and Law* (Burlington: Ashgate, 2007); Micheline White, ed., *English Women, Religion, and Textual Production, 1500–1625* (Burlington: Ashgate, 2011).

53 Hanawalt, ed., *Women and Work.* See also James R. Farr, *Artisans in Europe, 1300–1914* (Cambridge: Cambridge University Press, 2000); Charles and Duffin, eds., *Women and Work in Pre-Industrial England*; L. Shaw-Taylor, 'Occupational Structure and the Escape from Malthusian Constraints in England and Wales, 1381–1911', in *Population Histories in Context*, ed. R.M. Smith and E.A. Wrigley (forthcoming); Jane Humphries and Jacob Weisdorf, 'The Wages of Women in England, 1260–1850', *Journal of Economic History* 75 (2015).

54 Jacques Le Goff, *Must We Divide History into Periods?*, trans. Michael DeBevoise (New York: Columbia University Press, 2015).

55 For surveys of women's economic opportunities that extend beyond geographic scope of this volume, see Kathryn Reyerson, 'Urban Economies', in *Handbook of Women and Gender*, ed. Bennett and Karras, 299–301.

56 Joanna H. Drell, 'Aristocratic Economies: Women and Family', in *Handbook of Women and Gender*, ed. Bennett and Karras.

57 The literature on religious women is vast; studies that address women as monastic leaders and how nuns negotiated their economic, legal, and political interests include Elizabeth A. Lehfeldt, *Religious Women in Golden Age Spain: The Permeable Cloister* (Aldershot: Ashgate, 2005); Amy Leonard, *Nails in the Wall: Catholic Nuns in Reformation Germany* (Chicago: University of Chicago Press, 2005); and Valerie G. Spear, *Leadership in Medieval English Nunneries* (Woodbridge: Boydell, 2005).

58 Lanza, 'Women and Work'; Anne Montenach and Deborah Simonton 'Gender, Agency and Economy: Shaping the Eighteenth-Century European Town', in *Female Agency in the Urban Economy: Gender in European Towns, 1640–1830*, ed. Deborah Simonton and Anne Montenach (New York: Routledge, 2013).

59 Lanza, 'Women and Work', and Schmidt's chapter in this volume.

60 Montenach and Simonton, 'Afterword', in *Female Agency in the Urban Economy*, ed. Simonton and Montenach, 244.

61 Jane Whittle, 'Rural Economies', in *Handbook of Women and Gender*, ed. Bennett and Karras, 321, drawing upon Bennett, *History Matters*, and Sandy Bardsley, 'Women's Work Reconsidered: Gender and Wage Differentiation in Late Medieval England', *Past and Present* 165 (1999).

62 Whittle, 'Rural Economies', 322.

63 Sharon Farmer presents a detailed social and economic study of Parisian silk workers in *The Silk Industries of Medieval Paris: Artisanal Migration, Technological Innovation, and Gendered Experience* (Philadelphia: University of Pennsylvania Press, 2016).

64 Wiesner, *Working Women in Renaissance Germany*.
65 Montenach and Simonton, 'Gender, Agency and Economy', 10.
66 Gerhard Jaritz, 'The Visual Representation of Late Medieval Work: Patterns of Context, People and Action', and Peter Burke, 'Representing Women's Work in Early Modern Italy', both in *The Idea of Work*, ed. Ehmer and Lis; Geraldine Sheridan, *Louder than Words: Ways of Seeing Women Workers in Eighteenth-Century France* (Lubbock: Texas Tech University Press, 2009).
67 Jaritz, 'Visual Representation of Late Medieval Work', 135; italics in original.
68 Catherine Batt, 'The Idioms of Women's Work and Thomas Hoccleve's Travails', in *The Middle Ages at Work*, ed. Uebel and Robertson, 20. For an overview of the range of symbolic, moral, and cultural values associated with the iconography of spinning in early-modern Dutch culture, see Susan Broomhall and Jennifer Spinks, 'Visualizing Women's Work in the Textile Trades at the Dawn of the Dutch Golden Age', in *Early Modern Women in the Low Countries: Feminizing Sources and Interpretations of the Past*, ed. Susan Broomhall and Jennifer Spinks (Farnham: Ashgate, 2011), 49–50; and Randles' chapter in this volume.
69 London, British Library, MS Harley 4431, fol. 292r; Christine de Pizan, *The Book of the City of Ladies*, trans. Earl J. Richards with a foreword by Marina Warner (New York: Persea Books, 1982).
70 Sandra L. Hindman, 'With Ink and Mortar: Christine de Pisan's *Cité des Dames* (an Art Essay)', *Feminist Studies* 10 (1984).
71 Shelley E. Roff, '"Appropriate to her Sex"?: Women's Participation on the Construction Site in Medieval and Early Modern Europe', in *Women and Wealth in Medieval Europe*, ed. Theresa Earenfight (New York: Palgrave Macmillan, 2010).
72 A strikingly similar image of women laboring at building, with similar moral and didactic intent, is the depiction of nuns in British Library, Stowe MS 39, illustrating the spiritual treatise 'Abbey of the Holy Ghost'. Boyda Johnstone, 'Reading Images, Drawing Texts: The Illustrated *Abbey of the Holy Ghost* in British Library MS Stowe 39', in *Editing, Performance, Texts: New Practices in Medieval and Early Modern English Drama*, ed. Jacqueline Jenkins and Julie Sanders (New York: Palgrave Macmillan, 2014).
73 Picciotto, 'Devotion and Intellectual Labor', 7.

Select bibliography

Bardsley, Sandy. 'Women's Work Reconsidered: Gender and Wage Differentiation in Late Medieval England'. *Past and Present* 165 (1999): 3–29.

Barron, Caroline. 'The "Golden Age" of Women in Medieval London'. *Reading Medieval Studies* 15 (1989): 35–58.

Bennett, Judith M. *History Matters: Patriarchy and the Challenges of Feminism*. Philadelphia: University of Pennsylvania Press, 2006.

——— 'Medieval Women, Modern Women: Across the Great Divide'. In *Culture and History, 1350–1699: Essays on English Communities, Identities and Writing*, edited by David Aers, 147–75. London: Harvester Wheatsheaf, 1992.

Bennett, Judith M., and Ruth Mazo Karras, eds. *The Oxford Handbook of Women and Gender in Medieval Europe*. Oxford: Oxford University Press, 2013.

Charles, Lindsey, and Lorna Duffin, eds. *Women and Work in Pre-Industrial England*. London: Croon Helm, 1985.

Fiebranz, Rosemarie, Erik Lindberg, Jonas Lindström, and Maria Ågren. 'Making Verbs Count: The Research Project "Gender and Work" and its Methodology'. *Scandinavian Economic History Review* 59 (2011): 273–93.

Hafter, Daryl M., and Nina Kushner, eds. *Women and Work in Eighteenth-Century France*. Baton Rouge: Louisiana State University Press, 2015.

Hanawalt, Barbara A., ed. *Women and Work in Preindustrial Europe*. Bloomington: Indiana University Press, 1986.

Herlihy, David. *Opera Muliebria: Women and Work in Medieval Europe*. New York: McGraw-Hill, 1990.

Howell, Martha C. *Women, Production, and Patriarchy in Late Medieval Cities*. Chicago: University of Chicago Press, 1986.

Humphries, Jane, and Jacob Weisdorf. 'The Wages of Women in England, 1260–1850'. *Journal of Economic History* 75 (2015): 405–47.

Joyce, Patrick. 'The Historical Meanings of Work: An Introduction'. In *The Historical Meanings of Work*, edited by Patrick Joyce, 1–30. Cambridge: Cambridge University Press, 1987.

Karras, Ruth Mazo. 'Women's Labors: Reproduction and Sex Work in Medieval Europe'. *Journal of Women's History* 15 (2004): 153–58.

Kocka, Jürgen, ed. *Work in a Modern Society: The German Historical Experience in Comparative Perspective*. New York and Oxford: Berghahn, 2010.

Lanza, Janine M. *From Wives to Widows in Early Modern Paris: Gender, Economy, and Law*. Burlington: Ashgate, 2007.

McIntosh, Marjorie K. *Working Women in English Society, 1300–1600*. Cambridge: Cambridge University Press, 2005.

Ogilvie, Sheilagh. *A Bitter Living: Women, Markets, and Social Capital in Early Modern Germany*. Oxford: Oxford University Press, 2003.

Poska, Allyson, Jane Couchman, and Katherine McIver, eds. *The Ashgate Research Companion to Women and Gender in Early Modern Europe*. Farnham: Ashgate, 2013.

Shepard, Alexandra, and Garthine Walker. 'Gender, Change and Periodisation'. *Gender & History* 20 (2008): 453–62.

Simonton, Deborah. *A History of European Women's Work: 1700 to the Present*. London: Routledge, 1998.

Uebel, Michael, and Kellie Robertson, eds. *The Middle Ages at Work: Practicing Labor in Late Medieval England*. New York: Palgrave, 2004.

Whittle, Jane. 'Rural Economies'. In *The Oxford Handbook of Women and Gender in Medieval Europe*, edited by Judith M. Bennett and Ruth Mazo Karras, 311–26. Oxford: Oxford University Press, 2013.

Wiesner, Merry E. *Working Women in Renaissance Germany*. New Brunswick: Rutgers University Press, 1986.

Wiesner-Hanks, Merry E. 'Do Women Need the Renaissance?'. *Gender & History* 20 (2008): 539–57.

———. *Women and Gender in Early Modern Europe*, 3rd edn. Cambridge: Cambridge University Press, 2008.

2 Working through letters

Women's voices and epistolary culture in the *Tegernseer Liebesbriefe*[1]

Diana Jeske

Preserved in a twelfth-century manuscript (Clm 19411) from the Bavarian abbey of Tegernsee are the voices of a number of remarkable medieval women.[2] Scattered among a collection of approximately 300 letters these voices offer insight into the diverse ways in which elite women could use letters to perform and accomplish cultural work of varying kinds in the high medieval period. Beyond providing evidence of women's intercessory activities and their maintenance of familial and social networks, these letters also demonstrate women's engagement with philosophical and literary endeavours. The twelfth century has long been recognised as a period of cultural flourishing in Europe and evidence from the Tegernsee letters helps to situate women's participation in this historical context. Eleven letters from the larger epistolary collection are collectively known as the *Tegernseer Liebesbriefe* (Tegernsee Love Letters). These letters, primarily written by women, are characterised by their engagement with philosophical reflections on the nature of love and friendship and the cultivation of intimate relationships. They form part of a long literary tradition celebrating love and friendship, which, while having its roots in antiquity, flourished in the cultural renewal of the later eleventh and twelfth centuries. An examination of the Tegernsee collection as a whole, and the *Liebesbriefe* specifically, illustrates how these letters offer a rich source of evidence to explore aspects of women's cultural work, including maintaining patronage, familial, and social networks, and female literary artistry in the high medieval period. Letter writing offered these women not only an opportunity to participate in the cultural shaping of attitudes and ideas, but also an opportunity to critique and refashion them.

Letters as evidence of women's work

Letters provide the historian with evidence of medieval women's work, both in their contents as well as their deliberate and careful construction. Much of the research directly addressing women's work in the Middle Ages has tended to focus on economic activity, such as cloth production, or household and estate management.[3] Broadening our purview to consider how women's intellectual and social activities contributed to cultural production significantly expands our conception of the nature of medieval women's work. Scholarly studies have demonstrated the importance, for example, of women's involvement in patronage activities and their maintenance of key political, social, and literary networks.[4] In many cases these networks would have been sustained through frequent correspondence. In examining the women's letters from Clm 19411 cultural work takes on a twofold meaning. Firstly, these women produced material artefacts through the process of writing letters. The act of writing the letter (or dictating to a scribe) produced and participated in culture. Secondly, through their letters these women engaged in, affirmed, and challenged various cultural processes, from patronage and network maintenance through to sophisticated philosophical discussions and talented literary displays. The letter became not only an item of cultural production, but its subject matter too participated in cultural processes. In these ways female letter writers helped shape the cultural norms and expectations for elite women in the twelfth century.

The large volume of letters preserved from the twelfth century offers vital evidence for the cultural flourishing of this period, leading some to claim it as a golden age for medieval epistolary production.[5] A wide variety of work could be accomplished through the production of letters.[6] Letters preserved records of business dealings, legal contracts, and estate management, as well as personal requests for assistance and support. Socially, letters were also extremely important in developing and maintaining relationships, and assisting in negotiations.[7] In all of these uses the medieval letter provided opportunities for the display of education and the performance of identity. Letter writing was a culturally and socially significant act in the Middle Ages, one which declared that the author belonged to an educated, literate elite. For both men *and* women, the composition of elegant letters that were informed by classical models affirmed the writer's place within this elite and offered the opportunity to reinforce or to challenge the cultural norms associated with such a *milieu*.

Using letters as evidence of medieval women's work is a complex task.[8] Women's letters have been preserved with far less frequency than men's, arguably the result of intentional selection as letter collections were compiled.[9] Further complicating interpretation of medieval women's letters is the fact that while letters operated as an important means through which work was done, they were also self-consciously and carefully considered rhetorical compositions in and of themselves.[10] While the content of letters can reveal valuable information, the literary composition of the letters is also a form of work. This complicates ideas of female authorship as questions are frequently raised about whether letters written in the female voice were actually composed by women. Similar critical questions surround the 'reality' of a letter's content, which can be obscured by its deliberate, performative construction, and which, in turn, potentially reduces the letter to a rhetorical exercise, with limited purpose beyond a display of literary artistry. John

Van Engen summarises this interrelated relationship by explaining that 'women authors have suffered, it turns out, from precisely this ambivalence between history and literature [in medieval letters], their work nearly always reduced to rhetoric rather than life, even their rhetoric credited to clerical "handlers" or "impersonators"'.[11] Alison Beach posits that complex theories explaining how men authored texts in the female voice should only be presented if simpler explanations, for example, that a woman actually wrote (or dictated) the text, can be proven wrong.[12] Applying Beach's logic, it can be argued that the compilers of Clm 19411 did not reject the idea that women's letters should be preserved as equally valid examples of rhetorical or compositional style alongside those composed by men, and that they are evidence of the scope of cultural engagement available to women.

The distinction between literary composition and spontaneous expression, or between fact and fiction, can be very difficult to define in medieval letters.[13] The letter in the Middle Ages was a more public and participatory document than its modern counterpart. Scribes were often involved in the composition of letters and once delivered they were often read aloud to the recipient among a group of people.[14] As a result there is often a sense of conscious literary construction in medieval letters, even when they appear to express sincere emotion. Building on Judith Butler's work on gender as an identity that is continually constructed and performed,[15] Elizabeth Freeman has applied similar concepts to medieval letter writing. She argues that 'medieval letters were performances' in which the writer consciously created and presented a subjective identity to a wide audience.[16]

It is not surprising, therefore, that there is an element of performance in the *Tegernseer Liebesbriefe* that belies any notion of purely private communication, despite the intimate topics discussed and language used. Letters thus become performances of philosophical skill, literary talent, and carefully constructed identities. The authors of the *Liebesbriefe* deliberately took advantage of the opportunities the epistolary format presented to them to display their learning and talent by engaging in philosophical debate. They created and staged identities carefully constructed to reflect their status as educated, talented writers proud to participate in a long-standing literary tradition of philosophical and ethical debate. The other letters written by, to, or concerning women throughout the collection testify to similar performances of learning and identity through women's work in maintaining patronage, familial, and other social networks.

The Tegernsee manuscript: The context of a letter collection

The *Tegernseer Liebesbriefe* have received most critical attention from German scholars,[17] and they are also relatively well known in German popular culture because of the short vernacular love-lyric that concludes *Liebesbrief* 10.[18] The *Liebesbriefe* have received little sustained criticism in Anglophone scholarship, and are usually considered in the context of a larger, synthetic study.[19] The publication of a critical edition of the letters in Clm 19411 in 2002 has made these important texts more accessible to scholars in general.[20]

The Tegernsee letter collection, including the *Liebesbriefe*, forms the bulk of the material in Clm 19411. The manuscript was compiled in stages between 1160 and 1186 at the Benedictine abbey of Tegernsee and was likely intended as an educational resource in the monastery's school.[21] While the manuscript is well known for containing a copy of the *Ludus de Antichristo* (a twelfth-century liturgical drama), much of its content is dedicated to the art of letter writing. The manuscript as a whole appears to have had a didactic or referential purpose in teaching students how to compose good letters. Manuscript compilations such as this, which combined theoretical treatises and exemplary letters, are common to the period and represent a standard practice in teaching the art of letter writing.[22] The letters of Clm 19411 include correspondence between popes and German emperors; correspondence of the abbots of Tegernsee; letters to, from, and between various lay nobles; a variety of letters about monks and nuns; and the small collection that comprises the *Liebesbriefe*. The precise date(s) of the *Liebesbriefe* composition is unknown, although Peter Dronke has argued that it likely occurred in the first half of the twelfth century.[23]

As the foliation of Clm 19411 in Appendix 1 demonstrates, it is misleading to refer to the *Liebesbriefe* as a separate, complete set of letters since they are interspersed throughout the collection. Connections between certain letters, however, have been identified. Helmut Plechl has suggested that *Liebesbriefe* 9 and 11, as well as 3 and 4, might be considered 'letter pairs' (*Briefpaar*).[24] Dronke has identified 9, 10, and 11 as a sub-group, with 10 the first letter in the sequence, 11 a reply, and 9 the final letter.[25] The confused order in the manuscript is likely the result of letters copied from loose leaves. Modern editors have traditionally separated the *Liebesbriefe* from the rest of the collection and assigned them a separate numbering system (see Appendix 2), reflecting, for the most part, their shared themes and concerns.[26] Understanding this complexity is important for realising that the *Liebesbriefe* cannot be divorced entirely from the context of the other letters surrounding them.

Assessment of the women's letters in the *Liebesbriefe* must also be accompanied by consideration of women's letters preserved in the rest of the collection. While small in number, other letters written by or to women in the Tegernsee manuscript were also thought worthy of preservation by the compilers as exemplars of good compositional style and rhetoric.[27] In this capacity women's epistolary labour as well as men's served to educate the next generation of letter writers studying at the monastery school.

Unlike other monastic houses, such as Admont in the southern German territories, the abbey of Tegernsee did not have a corresponding women's community attached to it. Recent scholarship into the experience and writing of women in religious communities associated with the Hirsau reform in Germany during the twelfth century demonstrates that many religious women were highly educated.[28] Corresponding study, however, of the religious houses that did not reform and which remained closely allied to the royal court of the Holy Roman Empire (such as Tegernsee itself), and the women connected to such houses, has been noticeably absent from recent scholarship.[29] The anonymous nature of many of the women's letters in Clm 19411 makes it difficult to identify their authors. It is possible that the female authors of the *Liebesbriefe* lived, either as nuns, students, or boarders in ancient female houses associated with royal or noble courts that advocated classical education rather than the educational ideals of religious reform. Examples of such female institutions include the abbeys of Wilton in England, Le Ronceray in Angers, and Argenteuil outside Paris, as well as Obermünster and Niedermünster in Regensburg. The Latinate education such houses advocated is related, at least in part, to training young elite and courtly women for careers as noble wives or high-ranking monastic officers. It is also possible, as some of the letters in the broader collection indicate, that the female authors may have been relatives, either nuns or laywomen, of the monks of Tegernsee.[30] Tegernsee itself was aligned with the imperial court and geographically positioned close to the major route between the imperial heartland and Italy. The letters in the Tegernsee Collection reveal an interest in royal, papal, and other high-level politics, likely partly both a result and a cause of the abbey's secular and classical focus on its educational practices. It is likely, then, that the female authors were part of this elite, educated social context and used elegant Latin composition to display their status and identity. In doing so they navigated the expectations of their social position with such skill that their letters were preserved as models.

The work of networking: Women and the broader letter collection of Clm 19411

Epistolary exchange provided a vital means through which social networks were created and managed. The social work of maintaining patronage systems and family ties fell to noble women as much as to men.[31] The broader collection of letters in Clm 19411 offers evidence highlighting how important women were to the maintenance of such networks. The crucial role of women in processes of intercession and patronage is exemplified by Letter 80, written by a priest to a countess. The substance of the letter involves the priest complaining about the behaviour of the woman's brother towards him. The brother, the priest claims, has not treated him with the dignity and respect he deserves after many years of faithful service to the family and he asks the woman to intercede on his behalf.[32] The priest emphasises the woman's capacity for intercession, implying her presumed ongoing contact with her brother, and the possibility that she could call upon this familial tie in order to offer redress to the priest.

Relying on family connections to help achieve ends is also exemplified in Letter 123. In this letter, dated to the period between 1173 and 1178, the dowager countess of Morit-Greifenstein writes to her relative, the abbot of Tegernsee, confidently asking for his thoughts on, and help in, designing and producing a reliquary.[33] The countess' act of commissioning a reliquary also highlights women's involvement in religious patronage. Such work formed a key part of a royal or noble woman's duty and, in this respect, the countess is acting within contemporary expectations as well as in accordance with her own spiritual inclinations.[34]

Familial support is also expected and requested in Letter 192, in which a nun writes to her brother requesting shelter during a troubling time at her monastery.[35] A woman has been appointed abbess of the community at the insistence of the emperor and without the consent of the sisters. Subsequently, the abbess was excommunicated by agents of the pope, and her attempts to retain her position led to upheaval in the monastery. Nuns thus sought shelter from their male relatives until order could be restored and their autonomy preserved. Though arguably written under more distressing circumstances than Letter 123, Letter 192 displays the same sense of reciprocal obligation owed between family members, and the same expectation that support will be given when requested. Epistolary exchange offered a valuable means for maintaining and exploiting such networks.[36]

Evidence from the letters of Clm 19411 not only helps to illuminate women's activity in maintaining social networks, but also their key involvement in the cultural work of literary patronage and textual production.[37] Just as noblewomen were expected to be directly involved in religious patronage, taking a keen interest in the specifics of a project (as exemplified by the countess in Letter 123), they could also be actively involved in commissioning and overseeing the production of literary works. In Letter 292 a monk writes to a count to inform him of his inability to present a commissioned work on time. He claims that a representative of the count, Lady H (possibly the count's wife), whom the count had sent to review the proposed work, decided that certain portions required amending. Her intervention led to the delay in finalising the project. It is possible that the count entrusted Lady H with the task of assessing the progress of the composition and that he was confident in her ability to critically review and analyse the work. After clarifying for the count that he had in fact met with Lady H, the monk reports that she took with her twenty-three quires from the larger piece. He emphasises that this action was due to the arguments of his enemies, rather than Lady H's own idea.[38] This could indicate his disbelief that she was capable of reviewing the work on her own, but it could also point to his desire to protect her integrity and not offend the count by insulting her behaviour. Her removal of the twenty-three quires suggests she evaluated the work and was not happy with a section; perhaps she wished to examine a portion more closely, confer with others, or keep the section for other purposes. The monk later reveals that it was Lady H's continued possession of these quires which prevented him from presenting the work on time.[39] It is because of this impasse that the monk is calling for the count's intercession as he has the authority to bring an end to the matter.[40] Despite his frustration the monk is keen to reiterate his obedience to Lady H, with the implication that he will continue to abide by the current situation until the count intervenes. Her authority in the matter is still confirmed, despite the dispute, reinforcing her ability to act as an appropriate intermediary.

This letter is significant for a number of reasons. Firstly, we encounter a woman acting as a trusted literary intermediary. Presumably, the count would not have sent H to confer with the monk if he did not trust her ability to properly assess the work and pass judgement on it. Further, her authority, whether derived from her social status and connection to the count and/or her literary ability, is ostensibly respected by the monk even if he disagrees with her actions. We also see a woman acting independently in assessing a literary composition. The monk makes it clear that it was her idea to take with her certain sections of the document and to keep them (though he suggests she may have been influenced in her decision by his 'enemies'). Here we see a woman intervening in literary questions. This implies that H is learned and capable of sophisticated literary analysis. This account reveals how women could be involved in the work of literary composition; in addition to being authors themselves they could also work as collaborative partners and agents.[41]

These letters from the wider collection in Clm 19411 demonstrate the varied forms that medieval women's cultural work could take.[42] From intercession within and the maintenance of social networks, to the patronage of religious objects, and literary analysis and evaluation, these women were active in a broad spectrum of cultural work, evidenced within epistolary exchange. The desire to preserve the letters through which these roles and models were performed is eloquent testimony to the social and cultural significance of women's epistolary labours.

A tradition of intimacy: The literary context of the *Tegernseer Liebesbriefe*

When analysing the *Tegernseer Liebesbriefe* it is important to understand that they form part of a long-standing literary tradition exalting love and friendship in which women's participation is first evidenced during the later eleventh century. This tradition can be traced back to classical antiquity and, in particular, the writings of Ovid and Cicero. Ovid provided a model for understanding and describing love, and Cicero provided a foundation for understanding friendship. During the late Roman Republic Cicero had outlined, most famously in the *De amicitia* (On friendship), a pattern and definition for a system of true friendship between men that was based not on material gain, but on disinterested virtue, love, and devotion.[43] In Cicero's age friendship of this kind was presumed to exist only between patrician male equals.[44] In the early medieval period this tradition was adapted and became the preferred mode of expressing the charismatic loving relationships ideally crafted between male masters and students. Famous writers such as Alcuin adopted its tropes and conventions in their correspondence with friends and colleagues.[45] In the twelfth century the tradition was further adapted to articulate the affective bonds and relationships existing between monastic brethren and communities. Notable monastic writers such as Anselm of Canterbury and Aelred of Rievaulx expertly exploited its forms to express their love for their fellow monastic brothers.[46] Women's participation in this form of discourse is preserved from the later eleventh century. It is within this influential literary tradition of friendship that not only the *Tegernseer Liebesbriefe* but other intimate letter sets from the period should be placed, such as the correspondence of Baudri of Bourgueil and the nuns of Le Ronceray in Angers, the *Epistolae duorum amantium*, and the letters of Peter Abelard (d. 1142) and Heloise (d. 1163).[47]

Of particular relevance to the *Tegernseer Liebesbriefe* are the Regensburg Verses, a collection of letters dating to the eleventh century, written between a group of probably aristocratic women being educated in a convent and a schoolmaster from Liège.[48] While not as sophisticated in their composition as the *Tegernseer Liebesbriefe*, and very likely to have been school exercises, the Regensburg Verses share many of the interests and characteristics of other intimate letters written during this period. The female writers in all of these sets use the opportunity afforded by letter writing to engage in philosophical discourse intended to develop and shape attitudes and to influence ideas about the nature of relationships; in short, to participate in contemporary practices of cultural production. This epistolary activity reveals not only their intimate knowledge of classical scholarship and skill in harnessing it to their intentions, but also, at times, their own unique thoughts on the nature of love and friendship.

The influence of Ovid and the *Heroides*: *Tegernseer Liebesbriefe* 1–8

Ovid's *Heroides*, in particular, offered women a combined example of both female letter writing and female exploration of love. The *Heroides* are a collection of fictional letters written by Ovid in the voice of various heroines from Greek and Roman mythology.[49] Although these were fictional letters written by a man, the *Heroides* provided women with a model for participating in the literary discourse of love and friendship while also offering a way for women to challenge the traditionally exclusively male nature of the discourse. During the medieval period Ovid's works were viewed with ambivalence.[50] While used as school texts from which young students could learn Latin grammar, the erotic content of much of Ovid's work remained a concern for many medieval scholars and teachers who sought to neutralise this problem while preserving his writings as a teaching aid. To that end texts like the *Heroides* were presented as ethical works designed to teach young people about appropriate and inappropriate kinds of love.[51] Despite these concerns the eleventh century witnessed something of an Ovidian revival, particularly in the region of the Loire Valley, where writers were keen to imitate Ovid's style and his exploration of love through poetic composition and exchange.[52] It is within this larger context of Ovidian influence on literary production that the first eight *Tegernseer Liebesbriefe* can be understood.

The first eight *Liebesbriefe*, while intriguing, have not often been considered the stand-out letters from the collection. Dronke's analysis of these letters is hardly encouraging: compared with the sophisticated compositions of Heloise he regards them as 'often clumsy, often repetitive and vary[ing] considerably in manner and quality'.[53] Dronke views the letters, particularly those exchanged between women, as 'too long and aimless' despite containing some 'striking phrases'.[54] However, these women writers, in part, perform a specifically Heroidian type of discourse in their attempts to discuss love and their relationships with the recipients. In each of the *Tegernseer Liebesbriefe* ideal love is characterised as something preferably exclusive, virtuous, true, pure, constant, and honourable. Many of the female letter writers lament the separation between them and their respective recipients (be they kinsmen, teachers, friends, or lovers) and call for their reunion as soon as possible. While longing for the beloved is a general theme characteristic of the *Heroides*, it also recurs among both male and female medieval monastic writings.[55] The *Heroides* may have inspired the effusive display in these letters, but the language and phrasing could be drawn from other sources, including the Bible. In *Liebesbrief* 1, the author writes of her distress since her kinsman has left and longs for his return.[56] In *Liebesbrief* 8 the author writes of her pain, day and night, as she awaits her lover's return and questions her strength in the face of such torment.[57]

Lamenting a separation and pining for the return of the beloved are not the only characteristic Heroidian features within these letters; abandonment of the beloved, and the subsequent anger and pain it inspires in the writer, are found. For example, the author of *Liebesbrief* 2 describes herself as 'abandoned' (*derelicta*) by her male addressee, and she envisages that her soul will be destroyed by grief as a result.[58] After acknowledging that the fault *may* be her own, she concludes that her lover is to blame and renounces both love and relationships with men in the future.[59] While the traditional ideal of true friendships being exclusively male is overtly challenged by the female writers addressing other women in the *Liebesbriefe*, the striking feature in all of these letters is that women writers present exclusive, virtuous love as something that is not only possible for them, but is indeed the desired ideal relationship. Epistolary exchange thus allows these women not only to long for their recipients' return, but also to participate within this literary tradition and demonstrate their own literary skill. These letters are both mirrors of the themes contained in the *Heroides* and also model Heroidian performances themselves.

The influence of Cicero: *Liebesbrief* 10 and the redefinition of literary and courtly traditions

For the vast majority of the female writers in the *Liebesbriefe* the rules and expectations of love are assumed. Through their description of feelings and desires—for example, longing to be with their addressees—the writers implicitly articulate assumptions about the ways in which relationships operate. These assumptions are shared with their recipients by virtue of the education and knowledge of classical texts promoted within an erudite courtly culture. The author of *Liebesbrief* 10, however, is unique in her active discussion of not only what constitutes true friendship, but also how that friendship should operate in her relationship with her recipient, her teacher and a man known only as H. She is keenly aware in her letter of how love and friendship can work in a broader, more abstract sense. This letter is a declaration of love for H, and also a platform for further philosophical and ethical reflection. For this writer, Cicero provides the inspiration for understanding true friendship, and epistolary exchange gives her and the addressee a place to discuss what friendship means, as well as a space in which to grow and strengthen their relationship. Unlike the other female writers in the *Liebesbriefe* this writer is acutely aware of and open about her enjoyment of letter writing and the opportunities it presents. In this letter little of the overtly Heroidian nature of the other letters is present. This author does not write of longing for her beloved to return to her, nor does she feel abandoned and lament the separation between H and herself.

Liebesbrief 10 is arguably the most complex and sophisticated of all the *Tegernseer Liebesbriefe*. It opens with a beautiful, complex salutation, full of classical allusion.[60] H is described as the 'flower of flowers' (*flori florum*), crowned with good behaviour and possessing the beauty and standards of the virtues.[61] The writer sends to him everything that can be valued, and finally sends her whole self. The salutation highlights not only her model epistolary style, but also literary creativity as she demonstrates her affection for H through vivid and effusive imagery. Her salutation is immediately followed by a passage in which she remarks on her inability to reply adequately to her teacher's letters. Again, informed by classical allusion, she observes that even if she had the literary powers of Cicero and Ovid her talents would not be equal to those of her teacher. Despite her doubts and modesty (a standard medieval *topos*), however, she immediately begins the heart of her letter with a complex scholarly discussion of friendship. It is apparent from how the writer introduces her thoughts that it is customary for her and H to discuss this topic in their letters.[62] Cicero provides her intellectual foundation, and from his ideas she uses both prose and verse (demonstrating her literary skill) to build a picture of friendship that is at once both erudite and intimate. Her letter here becomes a performance, demonstrating the author's capacity to articulate an ideal of the truest friendship between a man and woman. She writes:

> True friendship, as attested by Tullius Cicero, 'is the agreement of all divine and human things in charity and benevolence,' which also, as I have learned through you, is more excellent than all other human things and more eminent than all other virtues, it gathers together what is apart, preserves what is together [and] makes larger what has been kept. Nothing is more true than this description or definition.[63]

This passage reveals that friendship becomes the highest virtue that binds everything together. The writer then composes a short poem highlighting the characteristics of friendship: people strive for it and are strengthened through it, it is the hope of the desperate, it restores the fallen and refreshes those who are burdened, it does not allow error and orders things to love, and it rules and commands over all.[64] Her writing begins to sound like a treatise on friendship; however, its epistolary nature allows her to simultaneously discuss these general themes while also reinforcing the intimate relationship she has with H. This woman may have read and studied these definitions before, but she has only experienced and learned them through her relationship with her recipient. Cicero may be her authority but it is the author's intimate relationship with H that has taught her about ideal friendship. By implication, theory is not effective unless practised. The overarching theme of her entire letter is that love and friendship are truly present in a relationship that is exclusive, irreplaceable, and based on faith, trust, truth, strength, honour, and courtesy. As Cicero had advocated, material wealth does not strengthen love. The woman writes that in keeping mind and trust for her lover alone she has the gold and silver of a joyous soul that is more valued by her than if she were to be surrounded by gold and silver piled at her feet.[65]

In reading the whole of this woman's letter one senses that she has spent much time thinking about the wider philosophical questions posed by friendship. She is certain of her convictions and proud of her ability to articulate them in a sophisticated manner, and she fully expects her teacher not only to agree with her, but to follow her precepts.[66] If her teacher breaks faith with her an awful fate awaits him, as he will drown.[67] If he does hold true to her he will have a blessed life, shine like the sun, and conquer the citadel of the virtues.[68] The woman becomes not simply a definer of true friendship, but the arbiter of how a relationship of true friendship is to be achieved between them. She has set the standard and the rule for their continued intimacy.

The author of *Liebesbrief* 10, rather than lamenting the separation that forces her and H to communicate via letter, instead celebrates it. She indicates that their epistolary exchange creates an intimacy between them akin to physical closeness and more important than conversation. She employs a rather unusual metaphor when describing this, writing:

> From the day I saw you I began to love you, you penetrated strongly the inner parts of my heart, and there, wonderful to say, you prepared a seat as a meeting place of pleasant conversation, and so that it would not be broken by any impulse, you established it [the seat] with epistolary discourse most firmly, as a three-legged stool, or rather a four-legged chair.[69]

The metaphor emphasises the importance of epistolary exchange to the relationship. Their love was born of meeting and being physically close at one time; however, epistolary exchange has helped to strengthen their love and provided them with an avenue of continued intimacy. The epistolary format not only gives her the power and opportunity to discuss philosophical and scholarly ideas, and to adapt those ideas to her own intimate relationship, but it also gives both her and H the power and opportunity to continue growing their relationship. According to her literary construct, without epistolary exchange their relationship would wither and die.

In two important respects the author of *Liebesbrief* 10 moves beyond the expressions and feelings of other female letter writers who participated in this literary tradition. The first is in her experimentation with writing in the vernacular in the short, sweet German poem which concludes her letter. It is a tender message of love that compliments, yet in its simplicity contrasts with the preceding complex arguments about love presented by the author:

> Du bist min, ih bin din, des solt du gewis sin;
> du bist beslossen in minem herzen, verlorn ist
> das sluzzellin, du most och immer dar inne sin.[70]
>
> ('You are mine, I am yours, this you should know; you are locked in my heart, the key is lost, you must always remain therein'.)

Having relied on and demonstrated her capacity for classical learning throughout her letter, the author finally, and most powerfully, declares her love in her own language.

The second way in which she deviates from her fellow female letter writers is in her engagement with themes of courtly behaviour and the regulation of relationships beyond the intimate one between her teacher and herself. She writes:

> You are doing well in that you attempt to warn me away from the knights as from certain portents. I know indeed what I should fear, lest I fall into a trap, yet keeping the trust I have in you I do not completely cast them aside, nor do I succumb to that vice of which you accuse them. For they are ones through whom, so to speak, the laws of courtliness are governed. For they are the source and origin of all integrity, about them let these things suffice as long as they do not impede at all our love.[71]

The implication is that she is writing in an environment where the 'laws of courtliness' (*iura curialitatis*) were respected and adhered to. This may be a secular courtly setting, rather than a monastic one; however, it is unclear from the letter. Regardless, *curialitas*, implying a respect for courtly manners, was a relatively rare word in the twelfth century.[72] For this woman, the knights, or *milites*, are neither to be feared nor dismissed *because* they practise *curialitas*. They are the paragons of courtly virtue and integrity, and, despite her teacher's warnings, she is secure enough in her own understanding of the concept, and her judgement of the knights' behaviour, to continue associating with them and dismisses H's concerns. Similarly, in her salutation to H, she declared him as crowned with good behaviour. Her value of correct courtly behaviour extends beyond the knights to include her teacher as well.

H, in his reply to the woman in *Liebesbrief* 11, expresses his happiness in corresponding with her, but criticises her for sending poetry without giving more of herself. He subtly and slyly proposes, through suggestive language, that it is time for her to follow up in action what she has declared in words, otherwise she will have violated the law of friendship.[73] The woman, in *Liebesbrief* 9, responds with a mixture of humour and tenderness, rebuffing his suggestion while protecting his ego.[74] As previously mentioned, the tradition exalting virtuous friendship between men during the earlier Middle Ages was adapted to suit the loving relationships that were encouraged between masters and their male students. C. Stephen Jaeger has described how charismatic, virtuous friendship became an integral part of a German courtly tradition during the Ottonian period that had its roots in the Carolingian age and promoted the virtues associated with correct behaviour and manners.[75] The passionate and articulate author of *Liebesbrief* 10 is clearly positioned as a woman participating in a similar courtly culture where outward behaviour was perceived as a reflection of inward virtue. This woman, moreover, was not only participating in it, but importantly, determining and directing how it should operate.

Conclusion

The letters, and particularly the *Liebesbriefe*, preserved in Clm 19411 offer insights into women's cultural participation in the High Middle Ages, helping to broaden scholarly understanding of what medieval women's work could entail through examination of how women used epistolary practices to promote and achieve their aims. Cultural work in this context involves not only the production of the letter itself, but also the processes, ideas, and negotiations letter exchange allows. For the women of Clm 19411 this involves the maintenance of patronage and familial networks as well as participation in literary and philosophical traditions. The authors of the *Liebesbriefe* utilise the opportunities epistolary exchange provides to present their own thoughts on the nature of love and friendship and how intimate relationships should and could be constructed within a literary tradition customarily engaged with by men. Despite being few in number, women's letters in Clm 19411 were thought worthy of preservation by the manuscript's compilers for their stylistic and rhetorical merit and presumed use in aiding the next generation of letter writers. The composition of these letters along with their contents demonstrate that these women were known and understood to be educated and eager to use the epistolary format to display their learning, perform their identity, and shape cultural processes. The twelfth century is celebrated as a great age of letter writing. Famous female writers from the period, such as Heloise and Hildegard of Bingen (1098–1179), engaged in cultural work by exchanging letters, and the women of Clm 19411, particularly those of the *Liebesbriefe*, help to illustrate the broader context in which these highly talented women operated. The evidence from Clm 19411 broadens our understanding of women's involvement in important cultural production and indicates that women like Heloise were not exceptional anomalies. The *Liebesbriefe* demonstrate that women were actively involved in a literary tradition celebrating love and friendship, ethical debates about intimate relationships and behaviour, as well as the development of courtly ideals. The evidence of *Liebesbrief* 10 indicates that women were part of the process of shaping courtly ideals and behaviour. The women of Clm 19411 were working participants in all these traditions and their contributions will only continue to enhance understanding of women's cultural production in the High Middle Ages.

Appendices

Appendix 1: Foliation of Clm 19411

Table 2.1 Foliation of Clm 19411.

Folio	*Description of Contents*
fols. 1va–2rb	Letters 1–3
fols. 2va–7rb	*Ludus de Antichristo*
fols. 7vb–9vb	Letters 4–12
fols. 10ra–49ra	Extracts from the *Gesta Friderici* by Otto of Freising and Rahewin
fol. 56v	First part of Letter 13, written by Bernard of Clairvaux to Pope Eugenius III
fols. 57ra–64rb	Alberic of Montecassino (d. *c.* 1105), *De dictamine*
fols. 65ra–68rb	Henricus Francigena, Letters (composed 1121–24)
fols. 68rb–68ra	Adalbertus Samaritanus (d. before 1150), *Praecepta dictaminum*
fol. 68vb	Second part of Letter 13, written by Bernard of Clairvaux to Pope Eugenius III
fols. 69ra–70rb	*Liebesbriefe* 1–8
fols. 70rb–72va	Various items including verses on the Virgin Mary, an epitaph for Otto of Freising, and a Greek alphabet
fols. 72va–100rb	Letters 14–139

(*continued*)

Table 2.1 (Cont.)

Folio	*Description of Contents*
fols. 100va–100vb	*Liebesbrief* 9
fols. 100vb–113rb	Letters 140–93
fols. 113va–114vb	*Liebesbriefe* 10–11
fols. 115ra–137vb	Letters 194–306

Note: This table is an overview of the main items contained in Clm 19411. See Plechl for full foliation details.

Source: Plechl, *Die Tegernseer Briefsammlung*, x–xi.

Appendix 2: Tegernseer Liebesbriefe overview

Table 2.2 Tegernseer Liebesbriefe overview.

Liebesbrief	*Sender*	*Recipient*
1	Anonymous Woman	Anonymous Man
2	Anonymous Woman	Anonymous Man
3	Anonymous Woman	Anonymous Man
4	Anonymous Man	Anonymous Woman
5	Anonymous Man	Anonymous Man
6	Anonymous Woman	Anonymous Woman
7	Anonymous Woman	Anonymous Woman
8	Anonymous Woman	Anonymous Woman
9	Anonymous Woman	Anonymous Man
10	Anonymous Woman	Anonymous Man
11	Anonymous Man	Anonymous Woman

Notes

1 I would like to acknowledge and thank Constant Mews, Tomas Zahora, and the participants of the Latin Reading Group at Monash University for their help and support with my translations of certain of the Tegernsee letters. I am also grateful to the editors of this volume, particularly Julie Hotchin, for their invaluable comments on earlier drafts of this essay.

2 Munich, Staatsbibliothek Clm 19411. The manuscript is titled in the library catalogue as *Ludus de aventu et interitu Antichristi. Literae multae et alia excerpta ex Ottonis Frisingensis Gestis Imperatoris Friderici [u.a.] BSB – Clm 19411*. A digital copy of the manuscript exists. Accessed August 28, 2017. http://daten.digitale-sammlungen.de/~db/bsb00008249/images/index.html?id=00008249&fip=xdsydxsewqxdsydeayaewqxdsydeayasdassdas&no=17&seite=1.

3 See, for example: David Herlihy, *Opera Muliebria: Women and Work in Medieval Europe* (Philadelphia: Temple University Press, 1990); Herbert Applebaum, *The Concept of Work: Ancient, Medieval, and Modern* (Albany: State University of New York Press, 1992), 289–307; Barbara Hanawalt, ed., *Women and Work in Preindustrial Europe* (Bloomington: Indiana University Press, 1986). See also the

following essays in *The Oxford Handbook of Women and Gender in Medieval Europe*, ed. Judith M. Bennett and Ruth Mazo Karras (Oxford: Oxford University Press, 2013): Joanna H. Drell, 'Aristocratic Economies: Women and Family', 327–42; Martha C. Howell. 'Gender in the Transition to Merchant Capitalism', 561–76; Kathryn Reyerson, 'Urban Economies', 295–310; and Jane Whittle, 'Rural Economies', 311–26.

4 See, for example, June McCash, ed., *The Cultural Patronage of Medieval Women* (Athens: University of Georgia Press, 1996).

5 Jonathan Lyon, 'The Letters of Princess Sophia of Hungary, a Nun at Admont', in *Writing Medieval Women's Lives*, ed. Charlotte Newman Goldy and Amy Livingstone (New York: Palgrave, 2012), 51.

6 The classic introduction to letter writing in the medieval period is Giles Constable, *Letters and Letter Collections* (Turnhout: Brepols, 1976). This has been supplemented now by *Medieval Letters: Between Fiction and Document*, ed. Christian Høgel and Elisabetta Bartoli (Turnhout: Brepols, 2015). For an overview of medieval women's letter writing specifically, see: Karen Cherewatuk and Ulrike Wiethaus, eds., *Dear Sister: Medieval Women and the Epistolary Genre* (Philadelphia: University of Pennsylvania Press, 1993). For a recent example of scholarship addressing the multiple uses to which the letter could be put in the medieval period, see: Martha Carlin and David Crouch, eds., *Lost Letters of Medieval Life: English Society, 1200–1250* (Philadelphia: University of Pennsylvania Press, 2013).

7 See Kathleen Neal, 'Words as Weapons in the Correspondence of Edward I with Llywelyn ap Gruffydd', *Parergon* 30 (2013); Julian Haseldine, 'Understanding the Language of *amicitia*: The Friendship Circle of Peter of Celle (*c.* 1115–1183)', *Journal of Medieval History* 20 (1994); Julian Haseldine, 'Friendship, Intimacy and Corporate Networking in the Twelfth Century: The Politics of Friendship in the Letters of Peter the Venerable', *English Historical Review* 126 (2011). Joan Ferrante, 'Women's Roles in Latin Letters from the Fourth to the Early Twelfth Century', in *The Cultural Patronage of Medieval Women*, ed. June McCash (Athens: University of Georgia Press, 1996); Joan Ferrante, *To the Glory of Her Sex: Women's Roles in the Composition of Medieval Texts* (Bloomington: Indiana University Press, 1997), 10–35.

8 For an overview of approaching medieval women's correspondence, see: Joan Ferrante, 'What Really Matters in Medieval Women's Correspondence', in *Medieval Letters: Between Fiction and Document*, ed. Høgel and Bartoli.

9 Sally Vaughn, *St Anselm and the Handmaidens of God: A Study of St Anselm's Correspondence with Women* (Turnhout: Brepols, 2002), 254–55.

10 John Van Engen, 'The Voices of Women in Twelfth-Century Europe', in *Voices in Dialogue: Reading Women in the Middle Ages*, ed. Linda Olsen and Kathryn Kerby-Fulton (Notre Dame: University of Notre Dame Press, 2005), 204.

11 Van Engen, 'The Voices of Women', 204.

12 Alison Beach, 'Listening for the Voices of Admont's Twelfth-Century Nuns', in *Voices in Dialogue: Reading Women in the Middle Ages*, ed. Olsen and Kerby-Fulton (Indiana: University of Notre Dame Press, 2005), 195–96.

13 Constable, *Letters and Letter Collections*, 11–14.

14 Elizabeth Freeman, 'Medieval Women, Letter Writing and Performance', *Lilith: A Feminist History Journal* 10 (2001): 62; Walter Fröhlich, trans., *The Letters of Saint Anselm of Canterbury, Volume One* (Kalamazoo: Cistercian Publications, 1990), 25; Constable, *Letters and Letter Collections*, 53–55.

15 Judith Butler, *Gender Trouble: Feminism and the Subversion of Identity* (New York and London: Routledge, 1990).

16 Freeman, 'Medieval Women', 63.

17 For example, see: Sabine Buttinger, *Das Kloster Tegernsee und sein Beziehungsgefüge im 12. Jahrhundert* (Munich: Verein für Diözesangeschiechte von München und Freising e.V., 2004); Josef Breinbauer, 'Kaiser Friedrich Barbarossa und das Kloster Tegernsee', in *Von Sacerdotium und Regnum, Geistliche und weltliche Gewalt im frühen und hohen Mittelalter: Festschrift für Egon Boshof zum 65. Geburtstag*, ed. Franz-Reiner Erkens and Hartmut Wolff (Cologne: Böhlau Verlag, 2002); Jürgen Kühnel, ed., *Du bist min. Ih bin din: Die lateinischen Libes –(und Freundschafts) Briefe des clm 19411. Abbildungen, Text, und Übersetzung* (Göppingen: Alfred Kümmerle, 1977). Certain of the *Tegernseer Liebesbriefe* have also been translated into French. See Étienne Wolff, trans. and ed., *La lettre d'amour au Moyen Âge* (Paris: NiL Éditions, 1996).

18 The love-lyric in question is the famous *Du bist min* (Du bist min, ih bin din, des solt du gewis sin; du bist beslossen in minem herzen, verlorn ist das sluzzellin, du most och immer dar inne sin); see discussion p. 41. See Friedrich Vogt, ed., *Des Minnesangs Frühling: Mit Bezeichnung der Abweichungen von Lachmann und Haupt und unter Beifügung ihrer Anmerkungen*, 2nd edn. (Leipzig: Hirzel, 1914), 262–65. This is a collection of famous traditional love-lyrics.

19 For example, see Peter Dronke, *Medieval Latin and the Rise of the European Love-Lyric: Volume One, Problems and Interpretations* (Oxford: Clarendon Press, 1968), 231–32; Peter Dronke, *Medieval Latin and the Rise of the European Love-Lyric: Volume Two, Medieval Latin Love Poetry* (Oxford: Clarendon Press, 1968), 472–82; W.H. Jackson, *Chivalry in Twelfth-Century Germany* (Cambridge: D.S. Brewer, 1994); Constant Mews, *The Lost Love Letters of Heloise and Abelard: Perceptions of Dialogue in Twelfth-Century France* (New York: Palgrave, 1999), 101–04; Barbara Newman, *Making Love in the Twelfth Century: 'Letters of Two Lovers' in Context* (Philadelphia: University of Pennsylvania Press, 2016), 229–55.

20 Helmut Plechl, ed., *Die Tegernseer Briefsammlung Des 12. Jahrhunderts* (Hanover: Hahnsche Buchhandlung, 2002).

21 Plechl, *Die Tegernseer Briefsammlung*, ix.

22 For more details on these texts and other early letter writing treatises, see William D. Pratt, 'The Early *Ars Dictaminis* as Response to a Changing Society', *Viator* 9 (1978); Martin Camargo, *Ars Dictaminis, Ars Dictandi* (Turnhout: Brepols, 1991); Carol Lanham, 'Freshman Composition in the Early Middle Ages: Epistolography and Rhetoric before the *Ars Dictaminis*', *Viator* 23 (1992).

23 Peter Dronke, 'Women's Love Letters from Tegernsee', in *Medieval Letters: Between Fiction and Document*, ed. Høgel and Bartoli, 216 n. 10.

24 Plechl, *Die Tegernseer Briefsammlung*, xvi.

25 Dronke, 'Women's Love Letters from Tegernsee', 215–45.

26 See, for example, the numbering system employed by Plechl in *Die Tegernseer Briefsammlung*, that used by Peter Dronke in his translation of certain of the letters in the second volume of *Medieval Latin and the Rise of the European Love-Lyric*, as well as the numbering followed by Étienne Wolff in *La lettre d'amour au Moyen Âge* and Barbara Newman in *Making Love in the Twelfth*

Century. For the purposes of this essay I follow the numbering system (1–11) assigned by Plechl.

27 Including the *Liebesbriefe* there are fifteen letters out of over 300 in the total collection written by or to women. These include Epistles (hereafter Ep.) 80, 123, 131, 189, and 192, *Tegernseer Briefsammlung* (hereafter *TB*), ed. Plechl, 106–08, 154–55, 162, 221–22, and 224–25.

28 See: Beach, 'Listening for the Voices'; Alison Beach, *Women as Scribes: Book Production and Monastic Reform in Twelfth-Century Bavaria* (Cambridge: Cambridge University Press, 2004); Alison Beach, 'Voices from a Distant Land: Fragments of a Twelfth-Century Nuns' Letter Collection', *Speculum* 77 (2002); Julie Hotchin, 'Female Religious Life and the *Cura Monialium* in Hirsau Monasticism, 1080–1150', in *Listen Daughter: The Speculum Virginum and the Formation of Religious Women in the Middle Ages*, ed. Constant Mews (New York: Palgrave, 2001). See also the essays by Beach and Hotchin, among others, in Alison Beach, ed., *Manuscripts and Monastic Culture: Reform and Renewal in Twelfth-Century Germany* (Turnhout: Brepols, 2007).

29 Studies of women's connections to male monasteries in the later eleventh and early twelfth century tend to concentrate on the double monasteries associated with reforming movements, such as Admont. For recent work on the relationships between religious men and women in high medieval Germany, see Fiona J. Griffiths and Julie Hotchin, eds., *Partners in Spirit: Women, Men, and Religious Life in Germany, 1100–1500* (Turnhout: Brepols, 2014).

30 See, for example, Ep.123, discussed below.

31 See, for example, Kimberly LoPrete, *Adela of Blois: Countess and Lord (c. 1067–1137)* (Dublin: Four Courts Press, 2007). See also Ferrante's work in both *To the Glory of Her Sex* as well as 'Women's Roles in Latin Letters' for detail on the connection between letter writing and the maintenance of patronage and familial networks.

32 Ep. 80, *TB*, ed. Plechl, 107–08.

33 Ep. 123, *TB*, ed. Plechl, 154–55.

34 For a concise overview of the patronage expectations of a noblewoman, see the example of Queen Matilda, wife of Henry I of England in Lois Huneycutt, *Matilda of Scotland: A Study in Medieval Queenship* (Woodbridge: Boydell, 2003), 158–65.

35 Ep. 192, *TB*, ed. Plechl, 224–25.

36 For further examples and detail on women's involvement in maintaining family ties, see LoPrete, *Adela of Blois*, as well as Amy Livingstone, *Out of Love for My Kin: Aristocratic Family Life in the Lands of the Loire, 1000–1200* (Ithaca: Cornell University Press, 2010).

37 On women's literary patronage in the early high medieval period, see: Ferrante, 'Women's Role in Latin Letters', 73–104.

38 Ep. 292, *TB*, ed. Plechl, 324.

39 Ep. 292, *TB*, ed. Plechl, 324.

40 Ep. 292, *TB*, ed. Plechl, 324–25.

41 For further examples of women working in collaboration on literary projects, see: Ferrante, *To the Glory of Her Sex*, 39–135.

42 For recent reflections on the study of medieval women and cultural patronage, and new directions scholarship can/should take on this point, see: Therese Martin, 'Exceptions and Assumptions: Women in Medieval Art History', in

Reassessing the Role of Women as 'Makers' of Medieval Art and Architecture, ed. Therese Martin (Leiden: Brill, 2012), 8–12.

43 Cicero, *De amicitia*, trans. William Falconer (Cambridge, MA: Harvard University Press, 1923), 139.

44 For *amicitia* in the Roman Republic, see: Neal Wood, *Cicero's Social and Political Thought* (Berkeley: University of California Press, 1988).

45 See Mia Münster-Swendsen, 'The Model of Scholastic Mastery in Northern Europe *c.* 970–1200', in *Teaching and Learning in Northern Europe, 1000–1200*, ed. Sally N. Vaughn and Jay Rubenstein (Turnhout: Brepols, 2006), 307–42. C. Stephen Jaeger has also written extensively on this topic. For a concise overview, see C. Stephen Jaeger, *Ennobling Love: In Search of a Lost Sensibility* (Philadelphia: University of Pennsylvania Press, 1999), 59–81.

46 For more detail on medieval monastic friendship see, for example, Brian McGuire, *Friendship and Community: The Monastic Experience, 350–1250* (Kalamazoo: Cistercian Publishing, 1988).

47 All of these letter sets were produced in French-speaking territories during the late eleventh and early twelfth centuries.

48 The letters are preserved in a twelfth-century manuscript—Munich, Staatsbibliothek Clm 17142—and Dronke suggests that they formed part of an eleventh-century master's papers that were copied haphazardly into Clm 17142 sometime during the early twelfth century. See Dronke, *Medieval Latin: Vol. One*, 221. For Dronke's edition and translation of the letters, see Dronke, *Medieval Latin: Vol. Two*, 422–47. For Barbara Newman's translation, see Newman, *Making Love in the Twelfth Century*, 257–78.

49 Ovid, *Heroides and Amores*, trans. Grant Showerman (Cambridge, MA: Harvard University Press, 1977), 1–311.

50 Ralph Hexter, 'Ovid in the Middle Ages: Exile, Mythographer and Lover', in *Brill's Companion to Ovid*, ed. Barbara Boyd (Leiden: Brill, 2002), 413–42.

51 Personal conversation with Natasha Amendola, Monash University. See also Ralph Hexter, *Ovid and Medieval Schooling: Studies in Medieval School Commentaries on Ovid's* Ars Amatoria, Epistulae ex Ponto, *and* Epistulae Heroidum (Munich: Bei der Arbeo-Gesellschaft, 1986), 137–43.

52 Gerald Bond, '"Iocus Amoris": The Poetry of Baudri of Bourgueil and the Formation of the Ovidian Subculture', *Traditio* 42 (1986).

53 Dronke, *Medieval Latin: Vol. Two*, 482.

54 Dronke, *Medieval Latin: Vol. Two*, 482.

55 E. Ann Matter, 'My Sister, My Spouse: Women-Identified Women in Medieval Christianity', in *The Boswell Thesis: Essays on Christianity, Social Tolerance and Homosexuality*, ed. Matthew Kuefler (Chicago: University of Chicago Press, 2006), 155.

56 *Liebesbrief* 1 (hereafter *Lb.*), *Tegernseer Liebesbriefe* (hereafter *TL*), ed. Plechl, 345. Refer to Table 2.2 above for an overview of the senders and recipients of each of the *Tegernseer Liebesbriefe*.

57 *Lb.* 8, *TL*, ed. Plechl, 356.

58 *Lb.* 2, *TL*, ed. Plechl, 347. 'Derelicta'.

59 *Lb.* 2, *TL*, ed. Plechl, 347.

60 Dronke, 'Women's Love Letters', 217.

61 *Lb.* 10, *TL*, ed. Plechl, 361.

62 *Lb.* 10, *TL*, ed. Plechl, 362.

63 *Lb.* 10, *TL*, ed. Plechl, 362. '*Amicicia* vera attestante Tullio Cicerone *est divinarum humanarumque omnium rerum cum karitate et benivolentia consensio*, que etiam ut per te didici, excellentior est omnibus rebus humanis cunctisque aliis virtutibus eminentior.'
64 *Lb.* 10, *TL*, ed. Plechl, 362.
65 *Lb.* 10, *TL*, ed. Plechl, 363.
66 *Lb.* 10, *TL*, ed. Plechl, 362–63.
67 *Lb.* 10, *TL*, ed. Plechl, 363.
68 *Lb.* 10, *TL*, ed. Plechl, 363.
69 *Lb.* 10, *TL*, ed. Plechl, 362. 'Nam a die, qua te primum vidi, cepi diligere te, tu cordis mei intima fortiter penetrasti tibique inibi, quod dictu mirabile est, sedem affamine iocundissime confabulationis tue preparasti et, ne aliquo deiciatur impulsu, epistolari sermone firmissime quasi / tripodam immo quatripodam collocasti.'
70 *Lb.* 10, *TL*, ed. Plechl, 363.
71 *Lb.*10, *TL*, ed. Plechl, 363. 'Porro quia me a militibus quasi a quibusdam portentis cavere suades, bene facis. Ego quidem scio, quid caveam, ne incidam in caveam, tamen salva fide ad te habita illos omnino non abicio, dum tamen non succumban illi, quod eis infligis, vicio. Ipsi enim sunt, per quos, ut ita dicam, reguntur iura curialitatis; ipsi sunt fons et origo totius honestatis. De istis ista sufficiant, dummodo amori nostro nihil officiant.'
72 The word is rare in the Library of Latin Texts database (published online by Brepols) for the twelfth century.
73 *Lb.* 11, *TL*, ed. Plechl, 365.
74 *Lb.* 9, *TL*, ed. Plechl, 359.
75 C. Stephen Jaeger, *The Origins of Courtliness: Civilizing Trends and the Formation of Courtly Ideals, 939–1210* (Philadelphia: University of Pennsylvania Press, 1985).

Select bibliography

Beach, Alison. 'Listening for the Voices of Admont's Twelfth-Century Nuns'. In *Voices in Dialogue: Reading Women in the Middle Ages*, ed. Linda Olsen and Kathryn Kerby-Fulton, 187–98. Notre Dame: University of Notre Dame Press, 2005.

Butler, Judith. *Gender Trouble: Feminism and the Subversion of Identity*. New York and London: Routledge, 1990.

Constable, Giles. *Letters and Letter Collections*. Turnhout: Brepols, 1976.

Dronke, Peter. *Medieval Latin and the Rise of the European Love-Lyric: Volumes 1 and 2*. Oxford: Clarendon Press, 1968.

Ferrante, Joan. *To the Glory of Her Sex: Women's Roles in the Composition of Medieval Texts*. Bloomington: Indiana University Press, 1997.

———. 'Women's Roles in Latin Letters from the Fourth to the Early Twelfth Century'. In *The Cultural Patronage of Medieval Women*, ed. June McCash, 73–104. Athens: University of Georgia Press, 1996.

Freeman, Elizabeth. 'Medieval Women, Letter Writing and Performance'. *Lilith: A Feminist History Journal* 10 (2001): 58–74.

Jaeger, C. Stephen. *The Origins of Courtliness: Civilizing Trends and the Formation of Courtly Ideals, 939–1210*. Philadelphia: University of Pennsylvania Press, 1985.

McCash, June, ed. *The Cultural Patronage of Medieval Women*. Athens: University of Georgia Press, 1996.
Newman, Barbara. *Making Love in the Twelfth Century: 'Letters of Two Lovers' in Context*. Philadelphia: University of Pennsylvania Press, 2016.
Plechl, Helmut, ed. *Die Tegernseer Briefsammlung Des 12. Jahrhunderts*. Hanover: Hahnsche Buchhandlung, 2002.
Van Engen, John. 'The Voices of Women in Twelfth-Century Europe'. In *Voices in Dialogue: Reading Women in the Middle Ages*, ed. Linda Olsen and Kathryn Kerby–Fulton, 199–212. Notre Dame: University of Notre Dame Press, 2005.

3 Uncourtly cloth workers in the Old French sewing songs

E. Jane Burns

The Old French sewing songs (*chansons de toile*) are generally considered distinctive examples of courtly literature of the thirteenth century because they stage female singers in the role of desiring subjects.[1] Eight songs in the corpus of twenty-two also feature the female singer-lover in the act of sewing. With the exception of the single *bourgeoise*, Euriaus, whose song is found in the narrative of the *Roman de la Violette*, scholars have tended to assume that the women singer-sewers are courtly and aristocratic.[2]

To be sure, the settings for the cloth work are overwhelmingly courtly—a royal chamber, a castle, or tower. And the young women singers are typically described as 'bele', the epithet often forming the first word of the song, followed by the woman's name. Hearing from the outset that the story is about 'Bele Yolanz' or 'Bele Doette', the reader/listener is primed for a tale of courtly love and longing. I have argued elsewhere that the sewing songs actually diverge considerably from the established pattern of the male love song, emphasising, instead of lovelorn distress, the young female singer's hope and often successful arrangement of her own marriage. In fact, the *chansons de toile* can be understood as work songs in two important ways: the women in love are staged as working cloth, and the songs themselves work to bring lovers together.[3]

Equally important, the sewing songs contain other details that are tellingly out of sync with the courtly paradigm. Those details and their implications for providing a fuller understanding of the women workers figured in the *chansons de toile* are the subject of this essay. As we re-read these songs taking full stock of the genre's curiously uncourtly aspects, we will see the extent to which women workers featured in the *chansons de toile* range significantly beyond the strictly courtly 'beles' of their opening lines.

We might begin with the thirteenth-century narrative *Le Roman de la Rose ou de Guillaume de Dole*, which includes three of the eight songs that mention cloth work directly.[4] For the purpose of this essay, I will read these *chansons de toile*, embedded as lyric insertions within the sumptuous world of a courtly romance, in conjunction with the sewing songs that appear in individual manuscripts.[5] Taken together, the eight songs, dated between

1228 and 1250,[6] reveal the extent to which women's work plays a crucial role in the elite world of courtliness.

The romance of *Guillaume de Dole* opens with a springtime love-fest hosted by the emperor Conrad who lavishes expensive gifts on the knights and ladies in attendance. Courtiers sleep in silken tents, countesses wear gowns of heavy silk and cloth of gold, and costly quilts cover the beds (vv. 192–93; 200–01; 230). These luxury items attest to Conrad's excessive wealth, but they are also consonant with his reputation as 'Li bons rois, li frans debonere, / il savoit toz les tors d'amors' (a good king and a very charming man who knew all the tricks of love, vv. 160–61).

The lyric insertions found in this early section of the romance reflect and reinforce the courtly *milieu*. We hear three times of 'Bele Aelis', adorned and prettily dressed, dancing in the meadow and ready for love (vv. 310–15, 318–22, 532–37) along with Robin and Marie cavorting near the spring under the olive tree (vv. 522–27). Two other songs that evoke love in a predictable springtime setting are taken directly from the established *trouvere* corpus.[7] When women's sewing songs first enter the story, we witness the heroine Lienor's mother sing a seemingly conventional song, about a young couple in love: Bele Aude and Doon. The first stanza reads:

> Fille et la mere se sieent a l'orfrois.
> A un fil d'or i font orieuls croiz.
> Parla la mere, qui le cuer ot cortois.
> Tant bon'amor fist [bele] Aude en Doon. (vv. 1–4; p. 158)[8]
>
> (Mother and daughter are seated doing embroidery. With gold thread they make gold crosses. The mother speaks with a courtly heart: 'Such a good love exists between Aude and Doon'.)

Lienor's song: Bele Aye

The tenor of the romance changes abruptly, however, as soon as the heroine Lienor sings. She does so in a private chamber where she and her mother are embroidering. The song is sung at the request of Nicole, a messenger sent by the emperor Conrad, who has fallen helplessly in love with the Fair Lienor based on a minstrel's tale of her incomparable beauty. Although the romance has prepared us to find in Lienor the paragon of courtly perfection, the song she sings reflects instead the dark underbelly of courtliness. Lienor tells of 'Bele Aye' who sews with beautiful stitches but is severely 'beaten morning and night' (el est batue et au main et au vespre, v. 7; p. 159).

Although Lienor's initial invocation of 'Bele Aye' seems to echo previous references to Bele Aelis and Bele Aude in this romance, the heroine of Lienor's song is not 'beautifully dressed' for love or 'sitting and sewing' in the company of her mother. Rather, while working luxury cloth with 'beautiful stitches', Aye sews 'at the feet of a cruel female master/mean mistress'. Her daily beatings cause hot tears to run down her face:

> Siet soit bele as piez sa male maistre.
> Sor ses genouls un paile d'Engleterre,
> [et] a un fil i fet coustures beles.
> ...
> Aval la face li courent chaudes lermes. (vv. 1–3, 6; p. 159)
>
> (Bele Aye is seated at the foot of her cruel mistress. She makes beautiful stitches on the English silk cloth in her lap ... hot tears run down her face.)

It is not uncommon for heroines in the *chansons de toile* to weep over a distant or absent lover, as indeed Bele Aye also does in this song. Belle Doe, the subject of Lienor's second song, similarly 'plaint et regrete' (laments and expresses regret for, v. 3; p. 160) her lover's delayed return, but suffers no dire consequences as a result. She also does not sew.

Bele Aye's case differs perhaps most significantly from Doe's in that she seems to be working for or under an abusive female *maistre*. The term, which also appears in the song about the unhappily married Bele Emmelos, has a range of meanings in Old French. Although a *maistre* can direct and control the actions of another as would a governess, the word is also used to indicate the abuse of power and authority or superior position in a more severe sense, including actions that cause mistreatment, torment, or suffering.

Indeed, Bele Emmelos, who is beaten and disfigured by a *mal mari*, explains, for example, that her husband 'trop me guerroie ... et *maistroie*' (wars against me ... and mistreats/abuses me, vv. 8–9; p. 154, my emphasis). Emmelos complains further that her husband, who insists she has no legal right to take a lover (et dit de vos amer n'ai *loi*, v. 40; p. 155, my emphasis), acts outside the law himself, mistreating her unjustly by going literally 'beyond the law' (*estreloi*, v. 41; p. 155, my emphasis). This song recalls the genre known as the *chansons de mal mariée* in which jealous husbands often enclose and then punish their young wives for having or seeking lovers.[9] Women are also beaten in some of the other *chansons de toile* by fathers or husbands who disapprove of their love choices.[10]

Bele Aye, by contrast, is not married as far as we know and has no father hoping to marry her off to a husband of the appropriate social class. She is beaten for a different reason by an abuser who is curiously not condemned and not even named outright. We know at least that Aye's punishment does not result from the quality of her sewing. Indeed, Aye's stitches are said to be 'beautifully executed' (i fet coustures beles, v. 3; p. 159). Her beating seems rather to stem from her status as a worker.

It is important in this regard not to confuse Aye's accomplished cloth work with the kind of embroidery done by the putatively noble women like Lienor and her mother in *Guillaume de Dole*. To be sure, the expensive silk cloth (*paile d'Engleterre*) that Aye works in her lap would tend to suggest the luxury of a courtly milieu in which noble women sew. Lienor and her mother are said to embroider various kinds of clerical vestments and decorations for the Church: as their pastime and their charity (vv. 1134–37). They give 'what they make to poor churches in need of ornaments' (vv. 1138–39).[11] Their work is designated specifically as 'deduis', a pleasurable undertaking (v. 1137).[12] But they are elite women. Of the eight women depicted as doing cloth work in the *chansons de toile*, only one, Erembours, is described as noble. The social class of Aye and the others, although they are termed 'beles', is tellingly never specified. Aye in particular seems to be 'working' under duress, toiling under the eye of the cryptic 'evil mistress' (*male maistre*) who seems likely to have administered the beating.[13]

Aye's crime is not the more courtly offence of having taken a lover against the wishes of a protective husband or father. This heroine's offence, rather, is to have fallen for a 'soudoier d'autre terre' (soldier from another land, v. 8; p. 159). In stark contrast to Belle Doe, whose lover Doon is evoked repeatedly as a noble vassal, brave and bold, a man whose chivalric excellence has earned the heroine's undying love (vv. 5–8; p. 160), Bele Aye's affections have drawn her beyond the courtly realm. Her heart has been taken unawares, captured, and captivated, we are told, by a foreigner or outsider from another place. As the refrain insists:

> He! He! amors d'autres pais
> mon cuer avez et lie et souspris. (vv. 44–45; p. 159)
>
> (Alas! Alas! My lover from afar / from another place. You have captured and bound my heart.)

A fear of the foreign runs throughout much of Old French literature, but it may have special significance in these songs about women's work, as we shall see.[14]

At this point we might wonder at least whether Bele Aye is to be understood as a French woman who has fallen for a foreign soldier. Or might she herself be a transplanted foreign woman with a prior attachment to a foreign man? And most important for our purposes, how does a heroine like Bele Aye, who is said to be in love with an outsider and also working silk for a seemingly abusive *maistre* fit within the courtly context surrounding her?

Indeed, Lienor's brief song, used to make a first impression on the emissary of the most courtly Conrad, curiously raises a host of uncourtly questions. Most pointedly, it stages women's production of luxury textiles in the *chansons de toile* in relation to physical abuse and foreignness. It suggests at the same time that the women working silk, cloth of gold, and other fabrics in the aristocratic households described in the *chansons de toile* might not be limited to aristocrats alone. Some of those cloth workers, it seems, might function more as professional embroiderers or seamstresses, whether they are skilled in working costly gold and silk threads or in creating and tailoring garments.

More than embroidery

Perhaps the strongest indication of this possibility is the range of cloth work performed by women workers in the *chansons de toile*. If we consider, for example, the second stanza of 'Fille et la mere', we find that Aude, whose social class is unspecified, is instructed to take up, in addition to the kind of highly skilled embroidery that she and her mother were described as doing in the first stanza—that is, working gold thread into golden crosses (vv. 1–3; p. 158)–the broader skills of sewing and spinning. Although Aude's mother spoke earlier with a 'courtly heart', approving of the *bon'amor* between Aude and Doon (vv. 3–4; p. 158), she now turns pointedly away from the courtly register. She instructs Aude to 'forget about loving Doon' (L'amor Doon vos covient oublier, v. 7; p. 158) and concentrate instead on cloth work:

> Aprenez, fille, a coudre et a filer
> Et en l'orfrois les oriex croix lever. (vv. 5–6; p. 158)
>
> (Learn to sew and spin, daughter, and to embroider golden crosses on banded fabric.)

To be sure, the refrain, which remains the same in both stanzas, brings us back to the courtly register. But the deviation from it in the preceding three lines is significant. We are not given a reason for the apparent change of 'heart' on the mother's part. However, it does seem that the range of skills outlined, from luxury embroidery to sewing and spinning, suggest more than a 'pleasurable' pastime practised by aristocratic women like Lienor and her mother.

So too does the song about 'Bele Yolanz', found in an independent *chansonnnier*,[15] begin with a young woman sewing gold and silk thread on luxury cloth that then broadens the parameters of her cloth work to include sewing more generally, cutting or tailoring, and spinning along with embroidering:

> Bele Yolanz en chamber koie
> Sor ses genouz pailes desploie
> Cost un fil d'or, l'autre de soie.
> ...
> Mere, de coi me chastoiez?
> Est ceu de coudre ou de taillier,

Ou de filer, ou de broissier,
Ou se c'est de trop somillier? (vv. 1–3, 11–14; p. 96)

(Lovely Yolanz in a quiet room unfolds silk fabric across her knees. She sews with one golden thread, another of silk. … Mother, why do you reproach me? Is it because of the way I sew or cut or spin or embroider? Or is it because I sleep too much?)

When these skills, listed by the daughter who asks why she is being chastised, are repeated in the mother's answer, we learn that the mother's complaint is not provoked by laziness on the daughter's part (*trop somillier*), nor by insufficient sewing skills:

Ne de coudre ne de taillier
Ou de filer ou de broissier,
Ou se c'est de trop somillier. (vv. 16–18; p. 96)

([It is] not because of the way you sew or cut or spin or embroider. And not because you sleep too much.)

On the contrary, the repetition in these two stanzas drives home the point that this young woman *is* skilled in all the tasks mentioned, from spinning and embroidery to sewing and possibly even dressmaking or tailoring. In stanzas IV and V, the song segues abruptly away from sewing and enters another lyric register altogether, taking up the language of the *chanson de mal mariée*. Bele Yolanz's error, the mother explains here, is in talking too much to her lover, the knight Count Mahi, which will displease her husband:

Mais
…
Trop parlez au conte Mahi,
Si en poise vostre mari. (vv. 19, 21–22; p. 96)

(Because … you speak too much to Count Mahi, and that displeases your husband.)

It is important to note, however, that within this framework, 'Bele Yolanz en chambre koie' describes a woman of unspecified social class who is engaged in types of cloth work that extend beyond purely decorative aristocratic needlework. We can distinguish the singer-sewers like Yolanz and Aude who perform wide-ranging cloth work from the more courtly portraits of elite women who seem engaged in aristocratic embroidery only. Bele Beatris, for example, is seated in a golden chamber, lamenting and weeping as she pulls on the threads of her work (presumably some kind of needlework):

An chambre a or se siet la bele Beatris,
gaiment soi forment, en plorant trais ces fis. (vv. 1–2; p. 130)

(Lovely Beatrice is seated in a golden chamber. She laments loudly and, crying, she pulls the threads of her work.)

She eventually marries Hugh, who is 'courtly and well-mannered' (v. 114, p. 133). Bele Erembours, an emperor's daughter (v. 16, p. 93), sits by the window lamenting her beloved with a coloured silk cloth across her knees (*paile de color*). Precisely what she does with the cloth is not specified, but it is clear that Erembours' cloth work is limited to small scale silk pieces worked in her lap:

Bele Erembors a la fenestre au jor
sor ses genolz tient paile de color. (vv. 7–8; p. 93)

(Lovely Erembours at the window by day holds a coloured silk fabric on her lap.)

By contrast, a second song devoted to Bele Yolanz entitled 'Bele Yolanz en ses chambres seoit', features a predictably lovely woman seated and working luxury cloth—in this case a heavy silk (*samite*), but she seems to sew an entire garment: 'D'un boen samiz une robe cosoit' (v. 2; p. 77). While this 'robe' is destined to be a gift for the singer's beloved, it differs significantly from other love tokens like the *chemise* that the heroine Soredamor sends to her beloved in Chrétien de Troyes' *Cligès*. In that instance, the verb *coudre* (*queudre*) indicates only the stitches Soredamor uses to embellish an existing *chemise* with gold thread mixed at times with strands of her own golden hair:

Tant c'une chemise en a treite
De soie fu, blanche et bien feite,
Molt deliee et molt soutil.
Es costures n'avoit un fil
Ne fust d'or ou d'argent au mains.
Au queudre avoit mises les mains
Soredamors, de leus en leus;
S'avoit antrecosu par leus
Lez l'or de son chief un chevol,
Et as deus manches et au col. (vv. 1145–54)[16]

(She [Guenevere] took out a white silk *chemise*, delicate and soft. The threads in the seams were of gold or at least silver. On several occasions Soredamor's own hands had done the work, stitching next to the gold thread in some places a hair from her head on both sleeves and at the collar.)

Yolanz, on the other hand, is actually fashioning an outfit from high-quality silk fabric (*samite*), exhibiting the skills a seamstress might have.

Bele Aiglentine too sews and tailors/cuts a garment, in this case a *chemise*, presumably from whole cloth. We hear first that she 'cousoit une chemise' (sewed a chemise) and later that she 'cousoit et si tailloit' (sewed and cut, the 'cutting' presumably referring to the fabric from which she makes the chemise, vv. 2, 6; p. 161). Although placed in an aristocratic setting, this heroine does not embroider at all. We find her seated in a royal chamber working 'in front of her dame' (devant sa dame, v. 2; p. 161), a formulation that resonates tellingly with the Bele Aye sitting at the feet of her 'evil mistress' (*male maistre*). In fact, we hear twice that Aiglentine does her cloth work 'devant sa dame' (vv. 2, 6). Is it possible that the skilled Bele Aiglentine could be working for this lady within the royal household? The refrain asks us to acknowledge at the end of every stanza the extent to which this beauty *works*:

> Or/ orrez ja
> Conment la bele Aiglentine esploita. (vv. 4–5)[17]
>
> (Now you will hear how Bele Aiglentine worked/did her work.)

Working for others

The romance of *Guillaume Dole* contains any number of passing references to servants working for the elite classes, most often without indication of payment or gain. We are told specifically that Conrad employs many competent and experienced servers trained in courtly manners (vv. 463–64). During the hunt, well-schooled servants arrange quilts, beds, carpets, comfortable tents, and table settings for the guests (vv. 339–46). Later they care for items of clothing and ply needle and thread to help sew up courtly sleeves (v. 2590). We witness Guillaume de Dole himself travelling with servants on his visit to Conrad, and we hear that Guillaume's mother instructs her servants to prepare the bed upstairs for the seneschal's arrival (vv. 3274–75). Might Conrad, Guillaume, and his mother all be considered in some sense 'maistres' presiding over and governing these servants from whose skilled work the aristocracy benefits?

Guillaume is said, at one point, to use monies generously bestowed by Conrad to pay 'his servants and bourgeois creditors' (por paier la menue gent / et as borjois cui il devoit, vv. 1934–35). Presumably the reference is to household servants, but whether they are women or men, French or foreign is not indicated. Neither are such details available for Conrad's servants, including those we have noted who are involved with clothing or cloth work. Their stories are obscured by the sumptuous courtly *milieu* surrounding the emperor, in particular the lavish silks and brocades that bedeck the attendees of Conrad's festivities. If ornate cloth work is critical to the success of courtliness and to the very identities of emperors, kings, and counts, the story of that textile production is only faintly suggested.

We hear, for example, that Guillaume de Dole, while housed one evening at one of the emperor Conrad's palaces before the tournament at St.-Trond, 'has his doublet covered with cloth of gold' (Il fist d'un drap d'or et de soie / au soir covrir son beau pourpoint, vv. 2038–39). Whether the doublet is re-covered or re-done in cloth of gold or made anew from that highly costly and extravagant fabric is unclear. Even more hidden in this account, however, is who might have undertaken the work that Guillaume 'had done'.

Sewing as women's professional *mestier*?

An interesting passage in the twelfth-century *Roman d'Enéas* categorises the acts of 'filer', 'coldre', and 'taillier', all the types of non-decorative cloth work mentioned in the *chansons de toile*, specifically as the profession (*mestier*) of women. When the heroine Camille, in this early romance text, takes up the garb and profession of knighthood, she pointedly rejects the 'women's work' of spinning and sewing:

> Onc d'ovre a feme ne ot cure
> Ne de filer ne de costure. (vv. 3971–72)[18]
>
> (I have never had any interest in women's work, whether spinning or sewing.)

When others chastise Camille for this choice, they contrast the paid profession of soldier/knights specifically with what would seem to be the paid profession of women workers (*mestier*), now expanded to include cutting along with sewing and spinning:

> Ce ne est pas vostre *mestier*
> mes filer, coldre et taillier
> en bele chanbre soz cortine
> fet bon esbatre o tel meschine. (vv. 85–88, my emphasis)
>
> (That is not the *mestier* for you, but rather spinning, sewing, and cutting. It is nice to please oneself in a chamber behind a bed curtain with such a girl.)

The sexual innuendo of men 'enjoying themselves' with women who sew is a significant detail to which we will return.

Meanwhile, the definition of women's cloth work as a *mestier* rather than a pastime might help explain the curious change of heart expressed by Bele Aude's mother in 'Fille et la mere', which we discussed above. Could the mother's insistence in the second stanza that Aude abandon her love for

Doon and concentrate instead on sewing and spinning (and in this case also embroidery) suggest that Aude, as someone highly skilled at cloth work, is not of a sufficiently high social class to pursue the more courtly Doon? Could her pointed advice that Aude stick to sewing be equivalent to saying she should stick to her *mestier* as a professional woman, and to the social rank that accompanies it?

Although we have tended to assume that the mother and daughter in this song are noble ladies, following the model of Lienor and her mother, mention of their social class is tellingly absent, along with the location of their work and any indication of the scale of their enterprise. Might they in fact both be professional embroiderers working in the employ of aristocrats? These women are said to produce highly skilled embroidery with gold thread including *orfrois*, which tends to indicate a level of expertise surpassing that of most elite women historically.[19] And in fact, even Lienor's own mother in the *Roman de la Rose ou de Guillaume de Dole* is introduced by Guillaume as an *ouvriere* of incomparable skill who knows everything about the *mestier* of sewing (vv. 1131–33). But how has she acquired this knowledge? Has she at some point perhaps also worked professionally?[20]

There is, of course, evidence of professional embroidery as early as the mid-thirteenth century, especially in royal workshops in London and Paris. Other embroidery workshops probably existed early in the Middle Ages to produce the luxurious decorated garments that were an integral part of medieval international diplomacy as gifts and attire for kings, popes, princes, and prelates.[21] Sharon Farmer has examined Parisian embroidery statutes at the close of the thirteenth century, which indicate that seventy-nine of the ninety-four embroiderers registered with the guild were women. By the fourteenth century, she explains, royal households and ecclesiastical institutions were commissioning embroiderers to produce luxury garments for their use.[22] There is also documentation in the fourteenth century of in-house *cousturieres* at royal households.[23]

Perhaps the most telling literary evidence of professional embroidery by women does not take place in a courtly household at all but in an urban embroidery business in Montpellier, as Sahar Amer has shown.[24] In Jean Renard's *L'Escoufle*, the lesbian couple Aleis and Ysabel escape their elite existence and travel to Montpellier where they set up a highly successful embroidery business, building on the skills of working silk and gold thread that Aleis had acquired as an aristocrat. As Aelis explains to her business partner and lover, Ysabel: 'Bien sachies que jou / referoie / Joiaus de fil d'or et / de soie; / K'il n'est feme ki tant en sache; / D'orfrois, de cainture, d'atache, / De ce faire ai je tot le pris' (Please know that I will embroider luxury accessories with gold and silk thread, no woman knows as much as I do about gold embroidery for belts and fasteners. I am renowned for this work, vv. 5457–61). The business flourishes and the women are said to be well paid for their cloth work.[25]

In the *chansons de toile*, possible indications of employed or professional women are necessarily subtler than the descriptions provided in *L'Escoufle*. We might think of Bele Amelot, who appears at first, like so many of the other women singer-lovers featured in the *chansons de toile*, alone in her chambers singing to a beloved. And yet in this case the heroine's only work is spinning: 'Bele Amelot soule an chambre feloit' (Lovely Amelot, was spinning alone in a chamber, v. 1; p. 102). She would likely be spinning flax (used to make linen), perhaps participating in the kind of economy that surrounds Guillaume and Lienor's mother in *Guillaume de Dole* who uses some of the money her son sends home 'to have her flax sown' (por fere semer ses linieres, v. 1938). Whether the mother also pays to have her flax spun is not specified, although we are told that she uses another portion of money received from Guillaume to defer household expenses (maintenir un bon hostel, v. 1939). We should at least wonder whether Amelot, and perhaps her own mother, might both be employees of the household where they work.[26]

Cloth workers as 'foreigners'

If indications of social class and status are most often lacking in the *chansons de toile*, so too are references to ethnicity. This makes the assertion that Bele Aye is beaten because she loves a 'foreign soldier' (soudoier d'autre terre) all the more intriguing. To be sure, foreign lands and their inhabitants are often cast as dangerous and threatening within the larger corpus of the *chansons de toile*. A knight travelling to Outremer can be the cause of the lovers' painful separation, as in 'Bele Ysabiauz' (vv. 43–48; p. 109). Knights can be killed jousting 'en autres terres' (in far-off lands) as is the lover of Bele Doette (vv. 1–5; p. 90). Or ladies like Bele Yzabel can be delivered into the hands of 'une estrainge gent' (foreigners) without hope of rescue: 'de mes amins nus secors nen atant' (I could hope for no rescue from my friends, vv. 8–9; p. 98). The logic of the *chansons de toile* suggests that a 'soudoier d'autre terre', whether from a distant land or neighbouring region, would exist in that unknown realm beyond the pale of courtliness. By contrast, Yzabel seeks a 'cortois chivelier' (courtly knight) who is 'loeiz and prisiez' (praised and esteemed, vv. 22–23; p. 98), much as bele Amelot chooses Garin who is 'vaillans et prous' (valiant and capable, v. 64; p. 104) over a higher ranking duke or count, and Bele Doe waits for Doon because he is such an accomplished warrior, the flower of knighthood:

> Dex quel vassal. Dex, quel baron!
> Ja n'amerai se Doon non.
> —Com ez chargiez, com ez floriz. (vv. 6–8; p. 160)

> (God, what a warrior, what a knight! I will love no one but Doon. You are so competent, so prized as a knight.)

Similarly, Bele Erembours waits for Reynaud who returns from the king's court among the prestigious Franks of France:

> Que Franc de France repairent de roi cort,
> Reynauz repaire devant, el premier front. (vv. 2–3; p. 93)
>
> (When the Franks of France return from the king's court, Renaud is in the first row.)

The very job of many of these knights, metaphorically at least, is to fight foreigners in the threatening lands of 'outremer', presumably confronting the kind of 'soudoier d'autre pais' that Bele Aye has taken as a lover. Indeed, in stark contrast to Aye's problematic foreign soldier lover, Bele Aiglentine's beloved is termed specifically 'a *courtly* soldier, valiant Henri who is so highly esteemed' (un cortois soudoier, le preu Henri qui tant fet a proisier, vv. 20–21; p. 162). When this knight carries Aiglentine off to 'son pais', she becomes not a captive but a countess: 'si enporta la bele en son pais / et espousa: riche contesse en fist' (he took her to his country and married her, making her a rich countess, vv. 47–48; p. 162). Bele Emmelos succeeds similarly in escaping a violent and abusive husband by fleeing to the 'pais' of her lover Gui (v. 49; p. 155). Bele Ydoine takes refuge from her abusive father's beating by fleeing with Count Garsile, one of many contestants from 'mainte terre estrange' (many foreign lands, v. 140; p. 119), to 'sa terre' (his land) where he is said to treat her honourably (v. 169; p. 120).

These 'courtly' men from 'd'autre pais' do not pose the kind of threat that Bele Aye's foreign *soudoier* does because they are foreigners made over in a courtly mould. They are praised and sought after, not unlike Conrad, who emerges in this narrative as a German emperor in name only. His generosity is said to be boundless (vv. 88–91, 130–31, 150–51) in terms often applied to King Arthur and the legendary Alexander the Great before him, and Conrad is further compared to the French courtly heroes Tristan and Lanval (vv. 5507, 5511). Although Conrad is known for protecting merchants and travellers and for facilitating the economic prosperity of townspeople and peasants (vv. 593–604), he does so while living in a courtly dream world composed only of nobles:

> This emperor, an honorable man, reserved positions of authority for God-loving noblemen who cherished his honor and authority as much as their own eyes.
>
> (Cist empereres, cist prodom / lor fu toz tens adés eschis / De vavassors fesoit baillis / qui aiment Deu et criement honte, / qui s'onor et quanqu'a lui monte / li gardoient come lor oils, vv. 587–92.)

Conrad, the 'noble prince who lives well, maintains and rules his lands so wisely' (Bien vit li hauz princes et regne / qui si sagement tient sa terre, vv. 619–20), is especially blind to the uncourtly and foreign-influenced economics of cloth work that Lienor's song about Bele Aye lays bare.

Indeed, in an important sense, many of the women working costly fabrics in the *chansons de toile*—especially those who sew threads of silk and gold—participate in bringing a telling element of foreignness into the very centre of the courtly world. The *pailes*, *orfrois*, and *samit* they work are marked specifically in the narrative portions of *Guillaume de Dole*, as they are typically in Old French romance texts, as 'imported' or 'foreign'.[27] The guests attending Emperor Conrad's festivities wear tunics and cloaks 'of samite, cloth from overseas, or rich gold silk from Baghdad embroidered with birds' (de samiz, de dras d'outremer / de baudequins d'or a oiseaus, vv. 233–36). When the Fair Lienor arrives in Mainz, she marvels at the entire city bedecked with 'fine cloth' while 'the gables of the houses were draped in expensive *cendal* and Baghdadi silks, ermine, and gold brocade' (vv. 4181–86). When Lienor and Conrad wed, guests at the wedding wear no end of foreign-derived fabrics:

> Tant baudequin, tant ciglaton
> Tant bon diaspre, tant samit
> Onques nuls emsemble ne vit. (vv. 3564–66)
>
> (No one had ever seen so much Baghdad-style brocaded silk, so much light silk cloth with patterned roundels, so much brocaded silk, and so much heavy silk cloth.)

In these examples the foreign is understood to be enthralling and magical rather than threatening.

I have argued elsewhere that women and women's cloth work in courtly texts often create rich sites of cultural crossing between the Christian West, Byzantium, and the Muslim world. It is often through fictional depictions of women and women's silk work in particular that the threat of the 'eastern', 'Saracen', or 'foreign' is transformed in Old French romance texts into a highly valued mark of Frenchness itself.[28] Women's cloth work in the *chansons de toile* can perform a similar function.

Indeed, from the point of view of the women singers in the *chansons de toile*, the greatest threat to court life is posed, not by attack from a foreign enemy, but by domestic abuse within the castle walls. Emmelos' mean and evil husband beats and disfigures her (la bat et laidoie, v. 3; p. 154) until her flesh turns blue (v. 25; p. 154) because she has a lover, much as the *malz mariz* in 'En Un Vergier' mistreats and disfigures the unnamed 'bele' in that song until she becomes blue and discoloured: 'Tant la bati q'ele en fu perse et tainte' (He beat her so long that she became blue and discoloured, v. 15; p. 86).

In 'Bele Ydoine' it is the father himself who beats his daughter until he has stained all her white flesh red: 'que toute sa char blanche li fait en vermeil taindre' (v. 72; p. 116). She, like Bele Aye, loves a foreign soldier (vv. 15–16, p. 114). And yet, this heroine describes her foreign lover at length as utterly without baseness (ainc n'ot vilenie, v. 31; p. 115). In fact he exhibits in her account every sign of courtliness that any 'king's son' preferred by her father might display. Garsile, she claims is 'douz et franz, courtois et debonaire' (kind and noble, courtly and charming, v. 36; p. 115), and later 'le bel, le preu, le sage' (handsome, valiant, and wise, v. 123; p. 118). The father's beating of Ydoine appears then an unwarranted punishment for his courtly daughter: 'Ydoine la courtoise' (v. 101; p. 117).

In Bele Aye's case, by contrast, the 'love from another land' is not described by Bele Aye herself. An unnamed voice details the foreign lover without mention of a single courtly attribute, much as Bele Aye herself is not characterised as noble in any way. She appears rather to be an outsider in terms of both class and amorous behaviour, a foreigner in the sense of not belonging to the dominant court culture, and perhaps even a foreigner in the sense of being someone 'from elsewhere'.

Physical abuse

We might compare her to the 300 exploited and abused silkworkers in Chrétien de Troyes' *Yvain,* women who work the same luxury fabrics that we find in the *chansons de toile*: various kinds of silk, cloth of gold, and *orfrois*, but on a much larger scale of commercial production.[29] The 300 captives, who actually differ less from courtly ladies than one might expect—they could be 'beles et gentes' (v. 5228), we are told, if only they were not mistreated—are also said specifically to be beaten to excess (tant sont acorees, v. 5205). But why?

We know that thirty new workers are sent every year, through no fault of their own, as a tribute payment to the lord of a far-off land (*Yvain*, vv. 5275–79). They are pooled together in what appears to be a kind of great hall-turned-workhouse (v. 5184), occupying what seems to be part of a larger castle in King Arthur's realm (v. 5264). In this case there is no question that the silkworkers are paid—if vastly underpaid—employees (vv. 5298–313). Most important for our purposes, they toil under the control of an overseer who abuses them physically, economically, and sexually, as the women explain:

> Et nos somes ci an poverte,
> s'est riches de nostre desserte,
> cil por qui nos traveillons.
> Des nuiz grant partie veillons
> et toz les jorz por gaaignier,
> qu'il nos menace a mahaignier
> des manbres, quant nos reposons
> et por ce reposer n'osons. (vv. 5311–18)

> (The man we work for has become rich from our service while we live in poverty. We stay awake a good part of the night and all day long to prevent him from threatening to maim our members while we are at rest. For this reason we dare not rest.)

Their liberator Yvain is described tellingly, in stark contrast to the evil master, as a 'biax mestre' (good master, v. 5211). But until the women are freed, they live 'a honte, … et a dolor et a meseise' (in shame, pain, and discomfort, vv. 5286–87) because, although they produce one of the most valuable commodities in the Western medieval economy, these women workers are vulnerable to physical abuse and sexual predation. That is the story they tell the 'biax mestre' Yvain: that whereas their work is highly valued, their lives are not. Imported into the Arthurian world from a cryptic 'elsewhere' (vv. 5251, 5801), they are abused and beaten, it seems, simply because they are workers.[30]

I have argued in *Sea of Silk* that this highly anomalous scene tucked into the courtly world of King Arthur's knights might in fact be a kind of narrative keyhole revealing working conditions not in France but in the neighbouring silkworks in Palermo, taken over from their Muslim founders by the Norman kings in the twelfth century.[31] The song 'Bele Aye' may also give us an unexpected glimpse into the plight of foreign women cloth workers, abused and mistreated in this instance by a different sort of evil master in a less commercial setting. Aye is clearly working expensive silk. But where? And for whom? We should remember in this regard that the silkworkers depicted in *Yvain* only fall victim to exploitation and physical harm once they enter the world of courtliness. They are fictive versions of foreign workers who have been transposed into the Arthurian landscape.

Lienor's song about Bele Aye allows us to see yet another aspect of this deeper and darker world of cloth work that subtends courtly extravagance. Reading the *chansons de toile* in relation to Bele Aye's story helps us grasp the wide variations among the singer-sewers figured in these songs. Whereas some of the highly skilled working women embroider as a pastime, others, whether paid or not, can cut and sew whole garments. Still others spin. Some may be foreign, others are abused, but all are part of the production of textiles that define the French elite classes in the world of courtly romance.

If this is the story that Lienor's song about Bele Aye opens up for us, it is important to situate it in relation to the story of Lienor's own assault later in the tale. At first this courtly heroine seems to hold little in common with Bele Aye, resembling instead the lovely Aelis who is 'beautifully dressed' (vv. 310–15, 318–22, 532–37).[32] Yet as the tale unfolds, Lienor becomes a young woman alone, helpless, and overcome with weeping, a woman whose plight reminds us increasingly of the beleaguered Bele Aye. Lienor's plight results initially from the false accusation levelled by Conrad's jealous seneschal that Lienor is not a virgin. It is worsened, however, by a relentless string of verbal attacks, first from her brother Guillaume and then from his nephew, accusations that create the rhythmic effect of a prolonged verbal beating. After Guillaume asserts that Lienor has been a faithless whore, vile and rotten, calling her 'that slut' who has disgraced us (la jaianz, la jaieus, v. 3807; la bordeliere, v. 3809), his nephew continues the assault, claiming 'she must be destroyed … I'll kill her with my own two hands' (vv. 3833;

3835). He repeats the violent threat subsequently to Lienor's mother, calling Lienor a 'whore' of 'vile conduct' (vv. 3921–23) whom he hopes to kill with his own two hands (vv. 3942–43). And the attack continues as he calls her a 'faithless woman who dishonoured' Guillaume (v. 3959) and who should die 'a most horrible death' (v. 3958), a seductress whose beautiful long hair has so ruined the family's standing that he, Guillaume's nephew, 'would like to have taken his sword and chopped it all off' (vv. 3962–64). Finally, Lienor, known up to this point as 'the most capable of young women' (v. 4072), is forced to prove her virginity in a public trial where she resembles a beaten woman. She bows her head, sighs from time to time (vv. 4638–39), and assumes a pose strikingly similar to that of Bele Aye as hot tears (de chaudes lermes, v. 4637) run down her face.[33]

Everything changes, however, when Lienor begins to speak, rebutting the seneschal's claims by brashly accusing him of sexual assault. Although the charge is part of a fiction that Lienor invents to prove her innocence, its terms are significant. She asserts that the seneschal assaulted her and took her virginity in a place where women, like Bele Aye, are vulnerable to various kinds of abuse, that is, in the sewing room:

> vint un un lieu, par aventure,
> ou ge fesoie ma cousture.
> Si me fist mout let et outrage,
> qu'il me toli mon pucelage. (vv. 4781–84)
>
> (He came, as it happened, to the place where I was sewing. He badly mistreated and dishonoured me by taking my virginity.)

We have already encountered the assumption that women who are sewing provide potential sexual prey for knights seeking 'pleasure', in the passage we considered earlier from the *Roman d'Enéas*.

In terms of the *Guillaume de Dole*, more specifically, mention of the 'place' where Lienor was sewing carries us back, not only to the room where Aye was sewing before being beaten, but also to the site where Lienor herself sat embroidering with her mother when Guillaume brought Conrad's messenger to hear her sing the *chanson de toile* about Bele Aye. Guillaume, we are told, 'took him [the messenger, Nicole] to see his mother and Lienor … *in her private rooms*' (Sa mere et bele Lienor / le maine *en la chambre* veoir; my emphasis, vv. 1116–17). And in that encounter too, Lienor was subjected to force, although in a different and more subtle way. Whereas Lienor's mother 'loved to sing and did so willingly' (vv. 1146–47) at her son's request, Lienor did not respond when Guillaume suggested that she sing in turn (vv. 1170–72). She remained utterly silent until her mother explained that Lienor had no choice in the matter: 'Il vos estuet feste et honor fere / au vallet l'empereor' (You cannot refuse to do honour to the emperor's messenger and entertain him, vv. 1178–80).

Conclusion

Lienor *cannot refuse* to please the emperor, but she can sing of Bele Aye and thus bring to his attention and to ours the untold story of women cloth workers in aristocratic households who, while easily confused with courtly ladies, can also suffer at the hand of an evil *maistre* and be beaten without cause. Lienor's song about Bele Aye reveals the extent to which the decorative embroidery work done by elite women in the *chansons de toile* is shadowed at every turn by the less visible work of an exploited population of unpaid or underpaid women who create the luxurious and putatively 'foreign' garments that noble men and women wear.

Notes

1 I would like to thank Sahar Amer for her insightful comments on an earlier version of this essay.
For a detailed analysis of the range of songs included under the rubric of *chansons de toile* and the many challenges they pose for medievalists, see E. Jane Burns, *Courtly Love Undressed: Reading Through Clothes in Medieval French Culture* (Philadelphia: University of Pennsylvania Press, 2002), 88–118; and on female subjectivity in particular, 262–63 nn. 10–12.

2 For a detailed account of scholarship on this complex genre of women's songs, see Burns, *Courtly Love Undressed*, 92–94. Key studies include Pierre Bec, *La lyrique française au Moyen Age (XIIe*–XIIIe *siècles)*, 2 vols. (Poitiers: Picard, 1977), 1:47–136; and his 'Trobairitz et *chansons de femme*: contribution à la connaissance du lyrisme féminin au Moyen Âge', *Cahiers de civilisation médiévale* 22 (1979): 235–62; Pierre Jonin, 'Les types féminins dans les chansons de toile', *Romania* 91 (1970): 433–66; Edmond Faral, 'Les chansons de toile ou chansons d'histoire', *Romania* 69 (1946–47): 433–62; Michel Zink, ed., *Les chansons de toile* (Paris: Champion, 1977), 3–71; Maureen Barry McCann Boulton, *The Song in the Story: Lyric Insertions in French Narrative Fiction, 1200–1400* (Philadelphia: University of Pennsylvania Press, 1993).

3 Burns, *Courtly Love Undressed*, 100–18. From this perspective, only three songs of the twenty-two-song corpus generally designated as *chansons de toile* do not exhibit the otherwise prevalent feature of women's work: *Bele Ysabiauz*, a lament staged wholly from the male lover's point of view, although it contains a scenario of the *mal mariée*; *Or vienent Pasques les beles en avril*, actually a *reverdie* classed as a *chanson de toile* because its refrain cites Aigline and Guis as mutually satisfied lovers; and *Lou Samedi a soir fat la semaine* (Gaiete et Oriour), marked similarly by a refrain that records sweet sleep between lovers.

4 Quotations of the romance text are from Jean Renart, *Le Roman de la Rose ou de Guillaume de Dole*, ed. Félix Lecoy (Paris: Champion, 1962). Translations are mine. For the complete text in English, see Patricia Terry and Nancy Vine Durling, trans., *The Romance of the Rose or Guillaume de Dole* (Philadelphia: University of Pennsylvania Press, 1993). The inserted songs include: *Fille et la mere se sieent a l'orfrois*, *Siet soit bele Aye as piez sa male maistre*, and *Bele Aiglentine en roial chamberine*. For details about the surviving manuscript in which Renart's

romance is located (Vatican City, Biblioteca Apostolica Vaticana, MS Reg. lat. 1725, fols. 68va–98va), see Lecoy, cited above.

5 *Bele Beatris* is found in a collection attributed to Audefroi le Batard; *Bele Yolanz en chambre koie* and *Bele Yolanz en ses chambres seoit*, *Quant Vient en mai (Erembors)*, and *Bele Amelot soule an chambre feloit*, are in the anonymous *Chansonnier de Saint-Germain-des-prés*. For details about manuscripts containing these *chansons*, see Zink, ed., *Les chansons de toile*, 76–102, 107–53.

6 Zink, ed., *Les chansons de toile*, 23.

7 Gace Brulé, vv. 844–852; Le Chastelain de Couci, vv. 923–30; along with a selection from the troubadour known for 'love from afar', Jaufré Rudel, vv. 1301–07. For other songs by known male poets that appear later in the romance, see Terry and Durling, trans., *Guillaume de Dole*, 111–14.

8 Texts of the sewing songs are from Zink, ed., *Les chansons de toile*. Translations are mine.

9 For examples, see Eglal Doss-Quinby et al., eds., *Songs of the Women Trouveres* (New Haven: Yale University Press, 2001), 33, 47.

10 Women are beaten in 'Bele Ydoine', 'En Un Vergier', 'Bele Emmelos', and 'Bele Aye'.

11 The description is in keeping with the heroine Fresne's assertion that embroidery is the most traditional occupation for noble women in medieval romance. See Renaut, *Galeran de Bretagne*, ed. Lucien Foulet (Paris: Champion, 1925), v. 3881.

12 In fact, as the tale develops we see that Lienor also crucially uses decorative embroidery to exculpate herself from false legal charges. See E. Jane Burns, *Sea of Silk: A Textile Geography of Women's Work in Medieval French Literature* (Philadelphia: University of Pennsylvania Press, 2009), 83–94.

13 Although I suggested in *Courtly Love Undressed* that there was only a remote possibility that the 'male maistre' might have delivered the beating (267 n. 53), I think now, in light of evidence presented in this essay, that we should reconsider that possibility.

14 See, for example, Sharon Kinoshita, *Medieval Boundaries: Rethinking Difference in Old French Literature* (Philadelphia: University of Pennsylvania Press, 2006), who explains the simultaneous familiarity and fear of 'foreignness' characteristic of many Old French literary texts.

15 See note 5 above.

16 Chrétien de Troyes, *Cligès*, ed. Alexandre Micha (Paris: Champion, 1957).

17 For an extended discussion of how this singer-heroine works at sewing and at loving simultaneously, see Burns, *Courtly Love Undressed*, 90–91.

18 *Enéas: roman du XIIe siècle*, ed. J.J. Salverda de Grave (Paris: Champion, 1925).

19 See Kay Staniland, *Embroiderers* (Toronto: University of Toronto Press, 1991), 8. Staniland cites exceptional noble women embroiderers in England.

20 Categorisations of the social class of Guillaume de Dole's family fluctuate throughout the narrative. Although Guillaume has creditors, he and Lienor are described generally as noble and wealthy. Both are said to be 'highborn' (v. 749; vv. 1371, 3025) and Gui 'lives very well, like a great lord' (vv. 1434–36). Nonetheless, Lienor's marriage to Emperor Conrad would constitute a move up the social ladder for all members of her family (vv. 5282–83, 5313). Conrad asserts, for example, that he can rightfully marry Lienor because, based on her beauty alone, she 'could be a queen or an empress' (vv. 812–13), although she

is not from a royal family. The absence of a father, making Lienor an 'orphan', complicates the family's social standing further (v. 4068).

21 Staniland, *Embroiderers*, 5.

22 Sharon Farmer, '*Biffes*, *Tiretaines* et *Aumonieres*: The Role of Paris in the International Textile Markets of the Thirteenth and Fourteenth Centuries', in *Medieval Clothing and Textiles*, 2, ed. Robin Netherton and Gale R. Owen-Crocker (Woodbridge: Boydell, 2006), 85.

23 Francois Maillard, ed., *Comptes royaux, 1314–1328*, 2 vols. (Paris: Imprimerie nationale, 1961), 2:161 (Comptes de l'argenterie 1317) notes Jehanne la Cousturière (no. 14098), Flourie la Cousturière (no. 14097), and Erembour de Monstereal (no. 14096). L. Douet-d'Arcq, ed., *Nouveau recueil de comptes de l'argenterie des roys de France* (Paris: Librairie Renouard, 1874), 158 notes Margot Bourcière, cousturière du Roy, and Robinette Brisemiche, cousturière de la Royne. My thanks to Sharon Farmer for bringing these references to my attention.

24 Sahar Amer, *Crossing Borders: Love Between Women in Medieval French and Arabic Literatures* (Philadelphia: University of Pennsylvania Press, 2008), 121–37.

25 Amer, *Crossing Borders*, 126. Interestingly, the romance of *Guillaume de Dole*, while offering no indication of the possible remuneration of women cloth workers, does provide two examples of payment for women singers. Guillaume gives Aelis, the innkeeper's daughter, 'a silver-trimmed belt to reward her for her singing' (vv. 1841–45), much as he pays minstrels at other moments in the tale with luxury garments. Later, Lienor encounters a group of 'minstrels from many lands who are trying to earn a living in Mainz', one of whom is a woman from Troyes named Doete (vv. 4564–66).

26 If so, they would seem to be well remunerated since Amelot's mother gives gold and silver to Amelot's lover, Garin, at the end of the song to enable the couple to wed (vv. 67–69).

27 Burns, *Sea of Silk*, 184–94.

28 Burns, *Sea of Silk*, 2–4.

29 For a fuller analysis of this important scene, see Burns, *Sea of Silk*, 37–69 and esp. 44–48.

30 It is never made clear exactly who is responsible for holding the women silkworkers captive. See Burns, *Sea of Silk*, 55.

31 Burns, *Sea of Silk*, 41–59.

32 Lienor, whose splendid attire is described at length before her trial (vv. 4350–8478), is also said to have an astonishing number of clothes for an orphan maiden (vv. 4068–69). Even more specifically, Aelis stands in as an obvious cipher for Lienor in the song Conrad sings about the 'Fair Aelis' in whom he has found his 'heart's desire' (j'ai amors a ma volente; I have the love I desire, v. 5441).

33 The image of Lienor overcome by tears is prolonged for several pages. See vv. 4709 and 4765.

Select bibliography

Amer, Sahar. *Crossing Borders: Love Between Women in Medieval French and Arabic Literatures*. Philadelphia: University of Pennsylvania Press, 2008.

Bec, Pierre. *La lyrique française au Moyen Âge (XIIe–XIIIe siècles)*. 2 vols. Poitiers: Picard, 1977.

——— 'Trobairitz et chansons de femme: contribution à la connaissance du lyrisme féminin au Moyen Âge'. *Cahiers de civilisation médiévale* 22 (1979): 235–62.

Boulton, Maureen, and Barry McCann. *The Song in the Story: Lyric Insertions in French Narrative Fiction, 1200–1400*. Philadelphia: University of Pennsylvania Press, 1993.

Burns, E. Jane. *Courtly Love Undressed: Reading Through Clothes in Medieval French Culture*. Philadelphia: University of Pennsylvania Press, 2002.

——— *Sea of Silk: A Textile Geography of Women's Work in Medieval French Literature*. Philadelphia: University of Pennsylvania Press, 2009.

Doss-Quinby, Eglal, Joan Tasker Grimbert, Wendy Pfeffer, and Elizabeth Aubrey, eds. *Songs of the Women Trouveres*. New Haven: Yale University Press, 2001.

Faral, Edmond. 'Les chansons de toile ou chansons d'histoire'. *Romania* 69 (1946–47): 433–62.

Farmer, Sharon. '*Biffes*, *Tiretaines* et *Aumonieres*: The Role of Paris in the International Textile Markets of the Thirteenth and Fourteenth Centuries'. In *Medieval Clothing and Textiles*, 2, ed. Robin Netherton and Gale R. Owen-Crocker, 73–89. Woodbridge: Boydell, 2006.

Jonin, Pierre. 'Les types féminins dans les chansons de toile'. *Romania* 91 (1970): 433–66.

Kinoshita, Sharon. *Medieval Boundaries: Rethinking Difference in Old French Literature*. Philadelphia: University of Pennsylvania Press, 2006.

Maillard, Francois, ed. *Comptes royaux, 1314–1328*. 2 vols. Paris: Imprimerie nationale, 1961.

Renart, Jean. *Le Roman de la Rose ou de Guillaume de Dole*. Ed. Félix Lecoy. Paris: Champion, 1962.

Renaut. *Galeran de Bretagne*. Ed. Lucien Foulet. Paris: Champion, 1925.

Staniland, Kay. *Embroiderers*. Toronto: University of Toronto Press, 1991.

Terry, Patricia, and Nancy Vine Durling, trans. *The Romance of the Rose or Guillaume de Dole*. Philadelphia: University of Pennsylvania Press, 1993.

Zink, Michel, ed. *Les chansons de toile*. Paris: Champion, 1977.

4 'When Adam delved and Eve span'

Gender and textile production in the Middle Ages

Sarah Randles

During the Peasants' Revolt of 1381, the Lollard preacher John Ball rhetorically asked:

> When Adam delved and Eve span
> Who was then the gentleman?[1]

In Ball's context, this text primarily references social rank rather than gender, but it also represents medieval ideas on the division of work based on gender, a division, moreover, understood as biblically sanctioned and representing the natural order of the things since the Fall of Man. Common medieval iconography of the post-lapsarian Adam and Eve shows them labouring, as in the illumination from the twelfth-century Hunterian Psalter in Figure 4.1.[2] Adam is shown tilling the soil while Eve works with a distaff and spindle to produce thread. However, the issue of gender and textile production in the Middle Ages is a complex one and the dichotomy suggested by Ball's lines does not accurately represent the realities of medieval textile work. Certainly, medieval women engaged in spinning and other forms of textile production, but there is also abundant evidence that men too engaged in many forms of textile work and that the gendering of medieval textile production is both multi-faceted and dynamic.

This chapter aims to raise two broad questions: how was medieval textile production gendered, in specific times and places, and what are the factors which govern this gendering? It will consider how different sorts of evidence might provide information about the ways in which medieval textile production was practised and viewed in the Middle Ages, while acknowledging that the answers to these questions can be difficult to determine. Such questions include: were different sorts of textiles made by men and by women, or were different aspects of textile-making processes gendered differently? Were there gender differences between domestic and commercial textile production? How did position in the social order intersect with gender in the field of textile work? What factors governed the ways that textile production was gendered? What ideological bases were there for the divisions of labour in textile production?

Figure 4.1 Eve spinning and Adam delving. Hunterian Psalter, *c.* 1170. Glasgow, University of Glasgow Library, MS Hunter U.3.2 229, fol. 8r. By permission of the University of Glasgow Library, Special Collections.

This chapter will not attempt to provide definitive answers to these questions. It is important to acknowledge that there will always be differences in the circumstances governing how textile production was gendered in particular instances, but this chapter aims to highlight a range of approaches to this complex field, including some new avenues for further research. It will also make a case for the importance of interdisciplinarity in textile history. Clearly, the task of considering the evidence for gender and textile production across the whole of Europe for the length of the Middle Ages is far beyond the scope of this chapter, so this study is limited to presenting some cross-disciplinary case studies from England and France, from the mid- to late Middle Ages, which might serve as examples to illuminate the field. The term 'work' is used here expansively to encompass all aspects of textile production, from the processing of raw materials to the embellishment of luxury textiles, regardless of whether the worker was paid for their labour, or whether they made textiles as part of a domestic or gift economy. This approach acknowledges that all textile production required time, effort, skill and resources, and that, whatever their purpose or status, textiles and their making were an integral part of medieval society and culture.

Historiography and methodology

A considerable literature on gender and textile production exists, most of it primarily focused on women rather than men, produced by scholars from a range of disciplinary fields.[3] Analysis of women's involvement in textile production has focused variously on their participation in professional guilds, their role as artists in producing decorative work, and their contribution to households or the Church. This literature largely reflects disciplinary concerns. Research by economic historians has focused on the documentary records of particular towns and guilds, and the differences between rural and urban economies, as well as providing broader overviews of the roles of women in the textile industry;[4] literary scholars have discussed the representations of women's textile work in romantic, didactic, and other literary texts;[5] archaeologists have focused on textile tools in the context of burials and gendered spaces;[6] art historians have considered women's part in producing decorative textiles,[7] particularly embroidery, and, to a lesser extent, the depictions of women and men making textiles.[8] A smaller body of work has considered the metaphysical and ideological aspects of textile production.[9] Many of these studies are narrowly focused, looking at a particular set of records or texts and, more rarely, individual textile works or workers, whereas more wide-ranging discussions of medieval textile production often occur only within the context of broader histories of textiles or considerations of the status of women in the Middle Ages.

This body of research on medieval textiles provides a basis for asking broader questions about the ways in which medieval textile work was gendered. While there remains a great deal of fine-grained work on this topic to be done within disciplines, there is also a need to synthesise findings across disciplinary boundaries in order to develop a more comprehensive picture of women's and men's textile work and the role that gender played in influencing medieval attitudes and practice. It is also necessary to examine critically the different forms of evidence for the types and circumstances of medieval textile production, and to consider how various media of representation—and the disciplinary traditions of interpreting them—affect our understanding of the medieval ideas of gender they present.

There are, of course, significant difficulties in attempting to synthesise a large body of research across not only disciplinary boundaries, but also across the vast geographical and temporal stretches of medieval Europe. There are enormous differences between, for example, the circumstances of an eighth-century domestic weaver using a warp-weighted loom in Scandinavia, and a fifteenth-century professional dyer in a workshop in Italy, and little that can be gained from making direct comparisons between them. However, looking at a long and geographically broad sweep of medieval European textile history has the potential to identify patterns of how textile production and the factors which influenced it were gendered, and so facilitate the development of theoretical approaches. Such patterns might include whether particular crafts are consistently gendered in different places or times, whether technological change affected the gendering of aspects of production, or whether the relative legal and economic status of men and women affected the types of textiles they produced.

It must also be stated that there is a great deal that we simply do not know about textile history, where we are limited by the paucity of the record, whether documentary, literary, archaeological, or visual. We know, for example, relatively little about the gendered production of textiles outside of the towns and in domestic settings, compared to the records of urban commercial production, and much less about unpaid than paid textile work; these absences can skew the picture. We have, as it were, a series of dots left by records from particular towns, discrete archaeological finds, and the depiction of particular social groups and certain kinds of textile workers in art made for the elite. All of this evidence provides valuable information, which needs to be interpreted by appropriate specialists, but it is also the role of the textile historian to attempt to join these dots, while acknowledging that some of the dots are not present.

In addition to the usual problems encountered when dealing with medieval sources, particularly their uneven survival and the under-representation of women in documentary records, there is also a need to sift through the historical layers of assumption that have accreted to the field of gender and textile production, and to separate modern and medieval ideologies about gender and work from the lived experience of medieval textile makers. That certain ideologies have had an ongoing impact on ideas of gender and textile production in the Middle Ages, sometimes on the basis of very little evidence, has been illustrated by Rozsika Parker in her influential book *The Subversive Stitch*.[10] Parker charts the Victorian process of myth making, in which the history of medieval embroidery was heavily influenced by Victorian ideals of femininity, which cast it as either professional work which was gendered male, or as a female pastime which was both domestic and elite. In countering this ideology, Parker sought to frame medieval women's embroidery as both professional work and a site of female creativity to be celebrated alongside men's art and scholarship. But 'reclaiming' embroidery as women's work can also distort the picture. Parker's argument that some of the women listed in accounts as suppliers of embroidery were embroiderers rather than merchants sits uneasily against her assertion that men similarly listed were merchants rather than embroiderers, and her claims that some women were professional embroiderers are in some cases overstated.[11]

There is often little or no evidence to support prevalent assumptions that the makers of textiles were female. Brigitte Kurmann-Schwarz has pointed out, for example, that despite the long-held belief that the Bayeux Tapestry was embroidered by women, the gender of its makers remains unknown.[12] Documentary sources identify male professional embroiderers in medieval London and Paris, indicating that men as well as women practised this craft professionally.[13] Similarly, spinning has been framed as an 'exclusively female' pursuit, an assertion which has frequently been repeated, but which does not always hold true.[14] Archaeologists have traditionally interpreted finds of textile tools in burials and other spaces as conclusive evidence of a female presence, to the extent that there is a risk of producing a circular argument which reinforces the idea that only women used textile tools.[15] In order to understand the nature of gendered textile production in the Middle Ages, it is necessary to pay attention to the work of men as well as women, and to consider the ways in which male and female textile work interacted.

Sources for textile history and problems of interpretation

An interdisciplinary approach to textile history allows us to consider a broad range of evidence for the experiences of medieval men and women in textile production. However, an understanding of how diverse forms of evidence shape the information they convey is crucial to their analysis. In particular, when dealing with sources in which the communication of information about gender is not their primary aim, a critical siting of each source in its historical and cultural context is fundamental to understanding both the limitations and the value of the evidence it presents. The following sections provide examples of the possibilities and constraints of evidence in different media, and the way that using multiple, diverse sources can build a complex and nuanced picture.

Civic records

A collection of thirteenth-century Parisian guild statutes, published as the *Livre des métiers* (Book of Crafts),[16] together with the tax rolls from late thirteenth- and early fourteenth-century Paris provide detailed sources of information about gender and occupation in the medieval textile and other industries. The *Livre des métiers* was compiled by the Royal Provost of France, Etienne Boileau, between 1266 and 1272. The tax assessments in the rolls cover the years from 1292 to 1313, with the exception of the period from 1293 to 1295.[17] Both sets of records have been used extensively by scholars. Janet Archer, in her doctoral thesis, used the *Livre des métiers* and the tax rolls to examine the role of women in the Parisian economy in the late thirteenth century, across all of the trades in which they worked.[18] Sharon Farmer has used the same records to assess the various Parisian silk industries, including considerations of gender.[19]

Archer has presented in detail the problems and limitations of these documents as sources of information about gender in textile production.[20] Principal among them is that these records do not include the work of married women, who remain invisible to the record, or the work of artisans not organised in *métiers*.[21] Similarly, the tax rolls are limited to lists of the heads of taxpaying households, who were predominantly male, and Farmer has estimated that around 75 per cent of artisans were not taxed.[22] The tax rolls too, therefore, significantly underestimate the contribution of women. This under-representation means that the absence or low numbers of women textile workers in records for particular *métiers* does not necessarily indicate that women did not perform these crafts, but rather that their work has not been documented. Conversely, however, in those cases where women dominated a particular *métier*, or it is listed as exclusively female, we can be more confident that the men in that craft are not under-represented. Of the forty-one textile crafts that Archer identifies from the records, sixteen list solely women members, while a further five show more female than male members.[23] Women dominated the various kinds of spinning in particular, and crafts involving silk.[24] Of the textile crafts in which only men are listed, many list only a small number of members, and given that women are under-represented in the records, it is possible that men did not actually outnumber women in these crafts at all, or in those crafts where the numbers of men and women were more evenly balanced. Only in a few of the textile crafts, notably the cloth weavers, the tapestry weavers, the fullers, and the dyers, are the differences in numbers so large as to be indicative of genuine male dominance.[25]

Visual evidence

The limitations of documentary evidence for the role of women in textile production in the Middle Ages, much of which derives from the financial and legal record, can be mitigated by comparing and correlating this data with the representations of textile production in visual, literary, and other sources. Visual depictions of textile production can offer valuable contemporary, albeit frequently idealised, representations of women and men undertaking textile work, such as the sculptures of women preparing fibre on the north portal of Chartres Cathedral,[26] or the images illustrating the fifteenth-century *Trattato dell'Arte della Seta*, a handbook for silk manufacturers.[27] However, as historical sources, these visual sources need to be examined critically, particularly with regard to the context in which they were produced and used, and the extent to which they portray the conditions of actual, contemporary textile production. As Ilja Veldman has noted in her discussion of postmedieval art, 'just as in literature, a great many themes are rooted in tradition or based on topoi, which often reduces the usefulness of the arts as historical source material'.[28] Gerhard Jaritz has similarly pointed out that medieval depictions of work are frequently idealised.[29]

Medieval images of textile work are often reproduced in studies of medieval women and of textile history as generic examples, without due regard for context. The illumination on folio 263 of the twelfth-century English

Eadwine Psalter, reproduced as the cover of David Herlihy's book *Opera Muliebria: Women and Work in Medieval Europe*, provides an example.[30] It depicts four women grouped within and around an open-walled structure. To the right are several sheep, and a shepherd sitting on a hill nearby blows a horn. One of the women to the left of the structure holds out long hanks of warp threads on a stick; another standing next to her grasps a large pair of shears. Under the structure, one woman is kneeling beside a vertical loom, while another stands next to it, also holding a large pair of shears. Herlihy captions this image 'Women shearing sheep, spinning and weaving' and interprets it, and the image in the ninth-century Carolingian Utrecht Psalter from which it is copied, as evidence that such medieval textile work was both gendered female and that the women carrying it out worked outside under specially constructed structures.[31] Despite the caption, it is clear that the women depicted are neither spinning nor shearing sheep, but rather are concerned with the weaving of cloth on a vertical loom.[32] The rationale underlying the composition of the image becomes clearer when we recognise that it was not intended to be primarily a depiction of contemporary textile practice, but rather of the Old Testament passage dealing with the lamentation of Hezekiah: 'Like a shepherd's tent my house has been pulled down and taken from me. Like a weaver I have rolled up my life, and he has cut me off from the loom.'[33] While the image of the weavers must have been one familiar enough to the medieval audience to be recognisable, it cannot automatically be interpreted as an accurate depiction of textile practices in either twelfth-century England or the ninth-century Carolingian Empire. Nonetheless, the depictions of weaving in both the Eadwine and Utrecht Psalters provide useful indications that the audiences for these works would have understood that weaving was gendered female, and that women could be expected to use a vertical, probably warp-weighted loom to produce it.

Visual evidence may also be useful tracking shifts in technology and medieval understanding of the gendering of textile work. The *Reiner Musterbuch*, an artist's model book made between around 1200 and 1220, probably in the Cistercian monastery of Rein, near Graz, shows both a man and a woman weaving (Figure 4.2). A second male figure, holding a shuttle and reed, appears in the upper spandrel, perhaps representing God, in a role as a creator or weaver of the world.[34] It is significant that the woman on the left uses the vertical warp-weighted loom, but the man on the right weaves using what appears to be a treadle-operated floor loom. This image suggests that men as well as women could be weavers, and that there might have been differences in the equipment that they used.[35] It is around this time that the horizontal loom began to replace vertical looms, but there is debate as to whether this explains why men apparently began to replace women as weavers in a commercial context at this time.[36] While there are numerous images of women using horizontal looms in medieval iconography, the majority of these are depictions of biblical and mythological figures, such as Naamah, Penelope, and Minerva. In contrast, those images

Figure 4.2 Weavers using vertical and horizontal looms. *Reiner Musterbuch*, *c.* 1200–20. Vienna, Österreichische Nationalbibliothek, MS 507, fol. 2r. By permission of the Österreichische Nationalbibliothek.

which show contemporary weavers using horizontal looms, such as those in the *Nürnberger Hausbuch* of Karl Mendel, which portrays members of the craft guilds in Nuremberg, depict these weavers as men.[37] The images of women weaving on horizontal looms, therefore, cannot be considered as evidence that medieval women actually used such looms.

Literary sources

Literary texts similarly provide valuable information about the nature of gendered textile production in the Middle Ages, but also require critical reading. E. Jane Burns notes in the introduction to her book on women's silk work in medieval Europe that there are significant differences between the picture of women's work provided by documentary evidence and that depicted in French literature.[38] While documentary sources such as the *Livre des métiers* provide evidence of ordinary women earning or supplementing their livings from textile production, often alongside men in domestic or commercial settings, literary documents tend to depict mostly elite women's textile production. In one respect this reflects the work that such elite women are described as having produced in inventories, hagiographies, and chronicles, particularly in the many examples of gifts for the Church, especially of needlework, 'made by her own hand'.[39] The range of textile production portrayed in romance literature is similarly limited, offering a narrower view of the extent of women's activities when compared to evidence of historical female textile producers of the lower orders. In literature, elite women frequently embroider and spin, almost always using silk, but do little else. They are not generally portrayed carding wool, hackling flax, weaving cloth or dyeing, or any of the more strenuous aspects of textile production. The imprisoned noble women in Chrétien de Troyes' *Yvain* and its English version *Ywain and Gawain*, as described by Stephanie Trigg, produce decorative work rather than large-scale utilitarian textiles.[40] E. Jane Burns' chapter in this volume explores the differences between literary depictions of textile work as a pastime and as a professional craft, challenging traditional readings of women textile workers in the French *chansons de toile* as solely elite. She argues that the broader range of work these women are depicted as undertaking, including sewing, spinning, cutting, and tailoring, marks them as being lower-class, professional textile workers.

Medieval art and literature cannot be understood as transparent representations of the realities of textile production, and they require careful interpretation, particularly regarding the way they use iconographical forms or literary tropes. Perhaps more importantly, they may represent and reproduce contemporary gendered assumptions about textile work and its social status, providing valuable insights into the attitudes which themselves shaped medieval practice.

Lexical evidence

As well as documentary, visual, and literary sources, lexical evidence can also provide an insight into the changing relationships between gender and textile production. Focusing on Middle English, for instance, the suffix -ster, deriving from Old English -estre, was used to indicate a female version of a descriptive noun for an occupation.[41] There are many occupations that record both female and male variants, for example, *baker* and *baxter*, *webbe* and *webster*; many of these survive as modern surnames. Examining the relationship between the terms for male and female variants of textile occupations can provide insight into how the gendered nature of the crafts themselves changed over time.[42] The most obvious example of a female occupational term is *spinster*, attested from 1362 and simply denoting a female spinner in Middle English. The term *spinner* was also used, from *c.* 1450, but in this instance denoted women rather than men, suggesting that men as professional spinners were so rare that they did not need a specific term. The late date of the first attestation of *spinner*, compared to a date of 725 for the verb *to spin*, is perhaps an indicator that while the work of spinning was certainly common, the idea that someone should use the term to identify their occupation was relatively unusual. Similarly, the term *throwster*, attested from 1455, denoting a woman who twists silk fibres into thread, and *kempster*, one who combs fibres for spinning, have no male equivalent.[43]

In a number of cases, the female variant of a textile occupation came to be used over time for male practitioners of the trade as well. The word *webster*, recorded from 1100 to denote a female weaver and still current in 1300,[44] was used by William Langland in 1362 to denote a male weaver, despite the fact that *webbe* had been used for male weavers from *c.* 1100, and continued to be used in this way into the fifteenth century. The term *dyer* is recorded from 1369, in an instance clearly denoting a male, but *dyester* appears from 1350 in a context which does not specify a gender. From 1497, however, *dyester* is clearly used for male dyers. Such examples suggest that a type of textile production, which may have started out as exclusively or predominantly female, became mixed or male-dominated over time.

Other occupational terms are not recorded in the feminine form. The term *fuller* appears from *c.* 1000, but there is no *fullster*, which might suggest that it was rare for English women to practise the craft of fulling. In contrast, *carder*, appearing only from *c.* 1450 and meaning someone who cards wool, is glossed with the Latin feminine term *carpetrix*, suggesting that it remained a female profession, perhaps overtaking the earlier term *kempster*. The Anglo-Norman-derived *tailor*, first attested in 1297, has no direct female equivalent, but may have been borrowed to fill a lexical need to differentiate this male occupation from that of the *seamster*, recorded from *c.* 995 but which by *c.* 1000 could also apply to a man, suggesting that by the thirteenth century there was a perceived difference in the nature of women's and men's work of this type.

The lexical evidence for gender in textile production is, at present, too sparse to be conclusive, but textile terminology is an area of lexicography in which there is room for further research. It is likely that as more Middle English texts, especially those of a legal or commercial nature, are published, that earlier dates of first recorded usage and variant citations will be found for some of these terms for textile workers, thus further refining the picture they project of medieval gender relationships in this field. Nonetheless, a broad pattern emerges in which some terms for textile workers originally denoting women were gradually expanded to encompass both men and women, while others remained exclusively female, most notably terms for carders and combers, spinners and silk workers. Even when the lexical forms do not signal female gender, it seems that some crafts were understood to be gendered female. The English Parliament Rolls for 1450 record a petition to King Henry VI on the part of aggrieved textile workers which records precisely this gender division: 'As yet no redress has been made, to the most intolerable harm of all the commons of this realm ... many cloth makers, that is to say male weavers, fullers and dyers. And female combers, carders and spinners'.[45] There is room for further research to assess whether there might be correlations between lexical changes and the social changes which saw shifts over time in the way that certain textile crafts were gendered.

Material and social influences shaping gender and textile work

The variety of documentary, visual, literary, and lexical records allows for an analysis of the material, social, and cultural conditions which shaped the gendering of textile work, and for comparison across areas traditionally considered from different disciplinary traditions. It is significant that the division of labour in textile production indicated by the English lexical evidence echoes broadly that indicated by the French *Livre des métiers*. Spinning and the associated fibre preparation were predominantly undertaken by women, while the work of producing and finishing cloth, including weaving, fulling, and dyeing, was mostly performed by men. It is important to note, however, that the divisions are not entirely clear cut, and there are women and men who worked in industries where their gender was a minority.[46] Nonetheless, this is a significant pattern in the gendering of medieval textile production which requires explanation.

Earlier scholars suggested that physical strength may have precluded women from the more strenuous crafts, but more recently scholars have been reluctant to accept this as the only reason.[47] The *Livre des métiers* shows that some women worked as butchers, metal workers, and carpenters, occupations which might have been considered physically arduous, and that men worked as embroiderers and the makers of various dress accessories, tasks which required finer manual skills.[48] Visual images also depict medieval women undertaking flax breaking, crop harvesting, and laundry, tasks which required considerable strength.[49] Archer comments that if women are spinning on larger spindles than men, it 'goes against the common wisdom that women were usually involved in small fine work, presumably because of the size of their hands'.[50]

Other explanations have been provided for the tendency for specific textile professions to be gendered as either male or female. Drawing on Judith Brown's observations about the historical need for women's work to be compatible with breastfeeding and childcare, Elizabeth Barber theorises that this is the reason why most textile production has been performed by women since prehistoric times. Work which is compatible with childcare must be able to be easily interrupted and easily resumed and must not pose a hazard to the child. Ideally it should be carried out in the home.[51] Barber's theory does not necessarily apply to every instance of later medieval textile production, when, from the twelfth century onwards, the rise of urbanisation meant that many textiles were produced commercially and in larger quantities, but it does provide an explanation for the traditional gendering of certain aspects of textile production as male or female. Moreover, it must be remembered that a large proportion of medieval textiles, including those produced professionally, were still made in whole or in part in a domestic environment.[52]

Certain types of textile work do admirably satisfy Barber's criteria. Highest on the list is spinning. This, when done with a spindle as opposed to a wheel, was highly portable, and in the hands of a skilled practitioner required very little concentration. It is likely that up to five hours of carding, combing, and spinning were needed for each hour of weaving. Therefore, in order to keep weavers operating productively, women, whose days consisted of other tasks, could profitably use spare moments in the day to spin, either to supply their household needs or to sell the products.[53] The image of Eve in Figure 4.1 combining spinning and childcare illustrates the potential for multi-tasking possible with spinning, as do many other medieval images such as the woman feeding chickens with her distaff tucked under her arm in the Luttrell Psalter.[54] Other textile work which similarly satisfied the criteria of being intermittent and safe included carding or combing wool for spinning, some kinds of weaving (although setting up the warp threads for a piece of cloth is a task which requires a reasonable degree of concentration and is best not interrupted), embroidery and, once it was introduced to Europe in the thirteenth or fourteenth century, hand knitting. Knitting is one of the few medieval textile techniques where raw fibre can be processed into finished garment using entirely portable, simple equipment, making it ideal for a home-based industry.

Some aspects of textile processing are, however, much less suitable for intermittent, home-based activity of the sort compatible with childcare. Commercial cloth dyeing, for instance, used poisonous dyes and mordants, and large vats of boiling dye-stuffs. An illustration from a fifteenth-century Flemish manuscript of the *Liber de natura rerum* depicts male dyers working in a dedicated workshop space, using a large, purpose-built dyebath and manipulating the heavy bolts of cloths with poles (Figure 4.3).[55] While medieval women did undertake dyeing in the home, it is likely that their domestic work was limited to dyeing yarn rather than cloth, or to smaller yardages of cloth for domestic use, allowing for a process which could be much more easily contained and controlled.[56] Other aspects of textile production which follow the same pattern include the fulling of wool; that is, partly felting the finished cloth by trampling it in hot water with urine or fuller's earth to produce a denser cloth. While this can also be undertaken in small quantities in the home, the *Livre des métiers* does not record any women working in this industry. Fulling was also mechanised from the twelfth century, with

Figure 4.3 Men dyeing, from a Flemish manuscript of the *Liber de natura rerum*, *c.* 1482. London, British Library, MS Royal 15 E III, fol. 269r. © The British Library Board.

water-powered mills replacing the heavy labour, but requiring capital investment and dedicated space and equipment.[57]

The pattern of work whereby women engaged in 'by-industries' is a common one in the Middle Ages across different fields of endeavour. Judith Bennett defined a by-industry as 'productive work carried out in the home as one of many employments, not a sole occupation'.[58] However, not all women's textile work was necessarily a by-industry. The records of the *Livre des métiers* show that women worked formally in many of the same textile crafts as men, earning a living, paying taxes, and taking apprentices, and that men also engaged in some of the crafts which might have been performed as by-industries, even if they apparently did so in smaller numbers. The *Livre des métiers* also lists a large number of male *ouvriers* and female *ouvrières* belonging to various crafts. Archer interprets these as pieceworkers, working in their homes, using raw materials supplied by others.[59] In the textile crafts, there are far more women than men in these categories, and it is likely that many of them were spinners or throwsters.[60] Using the tax rolls, Farmer calculates that there were 159 female silk throwsters, including sixty-six *ouvrières*, active in late thirteenth-century Paris, but no men. In addition, she identified eight female gold spinners but no male equivalents.[61] The lower numbers of men recorded working as *ouvriers* in the textile industries may mean that this form of work was exceptional, perhaps performed only by men who had particular reasons for working in less demanding jobs, such as age or infirmity.

A broad pattern can be discerned in which women's textile production in the Middle Ages appears more likely to have been based within the household than that of men, notwithstanding the invisibility of women in male-dominated workshops. However, we should look beyond the needs of childcare to explain the gendered division of textile labour, particularly in later medieval cities. Jane Whittle observes that throughout the Middle Ages the vast majority of people lived in rural rather than urban areas.[62] The available documentary evidence, however, indicates that it was in the cities and towns that men increasingly became involved in textile production, and that the majority of their work was of a commercial rather than domestic nature.[63] That the majority of surviving medieval documents concerning textile production derive from urban environments necessarily skews the evidence towards this conclusion, but since the cities also concentrated the markets for professional textile production, it is likely that this pattern did indeed apply. The economics of textile production, particularly in the medieval cities, might therefore have had a significant effect on how textile labour was gendered.

Economic influences shaping gender and textile work

Archer suggests that the more lucrative textile trades were performed more by men than women. She notes that in the Parisian records, it appears that spinning with a large spindle was done only by women, while both men and women used the small spindle. In attempting to explain the spinning that men did undertake, she speculates that: 'If the small spindle produced a tighter thread, cloth made from this thread was more valuable. Thus it may be that artisans in this speciality could expect to be paid more than those who used the large spindle.'[64] John Munro states, however, that the larger, heavier drop spindles were used for spinning linen and worsted yarns, while the lighter and smaller ones were used for cheaper woollen and cotton yarns. If this is the distinction meant in the *Livre des métiers*, it would suggest that spinning on larger spindles was the better-paid occupation.[65] It is true, however, that women in the Middle Ages were generally poorer than men, especially if they were single or widowed, and that their work was less financially rewarding.[66] It is likely, then, that Archer is correct in concluding that the textile work undertaken by women was probably more poorly remunerated, although the levels of pay for different tasks do not themselves explain why such tasks were gendered male or female.

Another factor in the gendering of textile production is that women were less likely than men to own the materials with which they worked. The regulations of the large-spindle silk spinners specifically prevent spinners from pawning the silk with which they had been entrusted, something that Archer claims is 'common with many métiers in which women are prominent'.[67] This suggests that women were more likely to have worked on commission, presumably paid by the weight of thread they produced, making them effectively outworkers rather than business owners, and less able to make a profit by marking up the cost of the materials. It also suggests that they may have found this a financially precarious way to make a living, requiring them to pawn the raw fibre as a way of making ends meet until they were paid for their work. If women's ability to undertake textile work was dependent on their capacity to afford raw materials, particularly more expensive ones like silk, then this was likely to have been a limiting factor in the kinds of work they were able to choose.

Archer notes an anomaly in the regulations of silk weavers with regard to gender in medieval Paris: the *mestier des tissuz de soie* (craft of silk textiles) has exclusively female membership apart from the inspectors, whereas the *ouvriers de draps de soie* (craft of silk cloth) are all masculine. Archer notes that the right to practise the latter craft had to be purchased from the king.[68] The difference between *tissuz* and *draps* suggests that the distinction may well have been on the size of the cloth produced. *Drap* is generally used to indicate a length of cloth,[69] whereas *tissu* may refer to smaller types of woven cloth, including those later described as 'narrow wares'. Chrétien de Troyes uses the term *tissu* to describe such a belt or girdle:

> Cains fu d'un tissu bien ovré
> Dont le bocle et trestuit li membre.
>
> (At the waist a finely woven belt
> Whose buckle and trimmings were of gold.)[70]

The term 'narrow wares', as the name suggests, encompassed decorative weaving for trims and cords. Narrow wares represented a different kind of weaving to the large lengths of cloth woven on floor or upright looms, since they were produced on small, rigid-heddle or box looms, or by tablet weaving or finger-loop braiding.[71] In medieval England, too, the makers of such narrow wares were predominantly female. Women petitioned parliament to protect them from imported goods under the title of the 'sylkewymmen and Throwestres' in 1455, although they did not form an organised guild until much later than the Parisian makers of *tissuz de soie*.[72] The predominance of women in the narrow wares silk industry may have reflected their lower economic power as the amount of silk required to make a girdle or braid is far less than that required to make a length of cloth. Further, the amount of time required to make these smaller objects would have resulted in faster turnaround and required lower capital investment, regardless of whether the makers paid for the materials themselves, or were provided with them by third parties commissioning the work. It is likely, however, that this would also have resulted in lower income.

The cost of the equipment was likely to have been as significant a factor as the cost of the raw materials in shaping how that particular aspect of textile production was gendered. While a small rigid-heddle or box loom, or a set of weaving tablets, on the one hand might be made or purchased cheaply and allow for the production of small, luxury textiles as a by-industry, a large floor loom represented an enormous outlay, which would have required more sustained dedicated labour in order to recoup its costs. As well as making large-scale cloth production unsuitable for a domestically-based by-industry, particularly in the case of the broadloom, the consistently lower socio-economic status of women in the Middle Ages is likely to have limited their access to this means of production. This is not to say that women did not work as weavers using larger looms, either domestically or commercially, but that the type of weaving they did might have been dependent on the kinds of loom they could afford, or that they were employed to work on looms owned by others rather than being in business for themselves.[73]

Issues of space and place of work also had an impact on gender and the textile worker's relationship to their means of employment. Given that women's textile production was more likely to be domestic and undertaken as a by-industry, the equipment used for it tended to be portable and take up less dedicated space in comparison to men's commercial production. Such limitations may explain the gender divisions in weaving depicted in the *Reiner Musterbuch* image, discussed above (Figure 4.2). The upright warp-weighted loom traditionally associated with women's domestic weaving was a much less sophisticated and expensive piece of equipment than the horizontal floor loom. It would also have required much less space to operate, and could easily be moved and stored against a wall. However, producing cloth on the warp-weighted loom, or the other vertical, two-beam loom was slower, more labour intensive, and the length of the cloth was limited in comparison to the horizontal loom. The cloth produced on an upright loom was therefore more likely to be suitable for domestic than commercial purposes, although it is likely that women also sold or traded some of the finished cloth and so engaged in a transactional economy in this way.

Another significant technological advance in textile production in the Middle Ages was the spinning wheel, believed to have been introduced to western Europe in the later twelfth or early thirteenth centuries for cotton, and in the later thirteenth and fourteenth century in the form of the great wheel for wool.[74] The spinning wheel allowed thread to be spun at twice the rate of the drop spindle, but, like the horizontal loom, it required capital expenditure and more dedicated space than its predecessor. This might suggest that spinning on a wheel was likely to have been the preserve of men rather than women, but there is little direct evidence to support this, and only very few medieval images of men using a spinning wheel.[75] This might be explained by the fact that the spinning wheel was initially only partially successful. The thread produced on it was weaker than thread produced on a drop spindle, and was therefore only suitable for weft threads. As a result, a division occurred between those who used the drop spindle and the wheel, with the former commanding a higher price. It was not until the late fifteenth century that the more efficient Saxony wheel, which overcame these problems, began to be more widely used.[76]

Since making narrow wares and spinning, as well as other crafts such as embroidery, allowed women to work in the home and produce luxury or high-quality goods without having to rely on establishment capital to purchase materials or equipment, the cost of setting up either a formal or informal business could be much less than that required for a dedicated workshop or larger-scale business. Whether a particular textile craft was gendered male or female, therefore, was likely to have depended more on the ability of women to pay for raw materials and equipment and to command dedicated space and time, than on their small hands and 'longe fyngres'.[77]

Researchers investigating the status of women's work in late medieval towns have generally agreed that women were for the most part systematically disadvantaged by the guild systems which excluded them or limited their involvement, and by the patriarchal nature of the household as the base for production.[78] This disadvantage was not absolute, however, and there are examples of exclusively female guilds, such as the linen drapers in Rouen, which managed to wield considerable wealth and power,[79] as well as the widespread practice of allowing widows of masters in various crafts to continue to run their husbands' workshops and practise their trades. Even when women could not be guild members, and were therefore less visible in the records, this does not mean that they did not practise textile crafts commercially, although their economic power was almost certainly less than that of their husbands or families. As Kathryn Reyerson has noted, women's experiences around work have varied greatly, according to time and place, and there remains considerable scholarly debate about the extent of the disadvantage they suffered.[80] There is also a need for further research comparing the status of women in different textile industries to those in other crafts. In general, however, and notwithstanding some important exceptions, the lower socio-economic situation of medieval women in comparison to men is likely to have limited their access to space, equipment, and raw materials. Lack of guild membership, and the access to more profitable markets that such membership allowed, also would have cemented the lower-status of female textile workers, restricted their choices, and thereby shaped the gendered nature of medieval textile production.

Ideology and iconography

While pragmatic and material conditions significantly shaped the ways in which medieval textile production was gendered, ideological factors also contributed to how medieval ideas of gender influenced women's and men's involvement in this industry. If we return to the medieval iconography of the post-lapsarian Eve, it is important to note that there is no biblical source for her spinning. In the account of the Fall in Genesis God condemns Adam to work the ground and Eve to bear children in sorrow, but there is no mention of Eve's work beyond the implicit childrearing. Both Adam and Eve are depicted as making their clothes from fig leaves once they comprehend their nakedness, and it is God who fashions clothing from skins for them to wear after their expulsion from Eden.[81] Eve spins in medieval iconography, not because God has ordained that she should, but because she has been fashioned in the image of the ideal medieval woman.

It is the description of the ideal wife in Proverbs 31 which reinforces the idea of textile production as appropriate for women in both medieval Jewish and Christian tradition.

> [The] wife of noble character, worth far more than rubies ... selects wool and flax and works with eager hands ... In her hand she holds the distaff and grasps the spindle with her fingers ... When it snows, she has no fear for her household; for all of them are clothed in scarlet. She makes coverings for her bed; she is clothed in fine linen and purple. ... She makes linen garments and sells them, and supplies the merchants with sashes.[82]

Significantly, the woman in Proverbs 31 produces textiles both for domestic and commercial use. However, the ideal of femininity in medieval Christendom was not Eve, but the Virgin Mary, and in medieval iconography she takes on both the virtues and the textile work of the woman in Proverbs. Like Eve, Mary is frequently depicted spinning, including at the Annunciation.[83] While there is no canonical biblical description of her doing so, much of the iconography is based on description in the apocryphal Protoevangelium of James, in which Mary spins thread for the temple veil. The Virgin is also frequently depicted undertaking other forms of textile work such as embroidering, weaving, and knitting, although again there is no biblical text on which such imagery is based.[84] In these images, the Virgin's textile work generally takes place within a domestic interior, and on a small scale. While there are numerous images of the Virgin weaving, in these she is most frequently depicted producing narrow

Figure 4.4 Virgin Mary tablet weaving in a domestic setting. Book of Hours, Paris, France, *c.* 1425–30. New York, The Pierpont Morgan Library, MS M.453, fol. 24r. By permission of The Morgan Library & Museum, New York. Purchased by J. Pierpont Morgan (1837–1913) in 1911. Photographic credit: The Pierpont Morgan Library, New York.

wares, using tablets or a small box loom (Figure 4.4). In the much rarer examples where she is depicted weaving cloth, she is shown using a vertical loom.[85] The textile work of the ideal woman, therefore, was presented as being exactly along the lines of medieval women's production: principally small-scale and domestic. While these images undoubtedly reflect the realities of the societies in which they were made, they also served to reinforce the prevailing gender distribution of textile work, and invest the demarcation between men's and women's textile production with the highest moral authority.

This ideal of womanhood expressed through textile production was, however, one which could be subverted. There are numerous medieval images which depict women beating men with distaffs, as a trope of the destructive power of women, or of the world turned upside down, wherein the distaff, a symbol of morally appropriate femininity, becomes a weapon.[86] These images reverse an order widely understood as an ideal, even if it is an ideal which exists in tension with the realities of medieval textile production. The presence of many of such images in manuscript marginalia might suggest that they were intended to be humorous, although they might also be read as commentary or warning.[87] The fifteenth-century woodcut by Israhel van Meckenem, known as 'The Quarrelsome Couple' (*c.* 1465–1500) shows not only a woman threatening a man with her distaff, but the male figure meekly winding spun yarn on to a niddy-noddy (Figure 4.5).[88] To reinforce that this composition contravenes the natural order, the woman is depicted putting on a pair of underpants, an exclusively male garment. The message is clear that spinning and the associated task of winding yarn are proper activities for women, whereas men who undertake them are emasculated.

A series of images in the lower margin of folios 138 to 148 of the Smithfield Decretals, illuminated in fourteenth-century London, depict men and women engaged in textile production and other work. These images ostensibly form a narrative sequence with folio 139 (Figure 4.6) showing a man apparently leading a woman away from her work at the spinning wheel; folio 147 (Figure 4.7) showing the same woman spinning at the wheel, while the man cards wool; and the following image, folio 147 verso (Figure 4.8) showing the man using the wheel to spin.[89] The marginal context for this image suggests that it was not intended to represent a straightforward depiction of male spinning. Andrew Taylor has described the illuminations of the Smithfield Decretals as depicting scenes of 'carnivalesque revelry', which function 'as a site of resistance' to the authority of the text which they accompany.[90] Yet we know from the *Livre des métiers* that men did spin professionally. Clearly, the context in which the textile work is represented was as important for the way it was gendered as the nature of the work itself.

Even when spinning was appropriately undertaken by women, it could have negative connotations. Chaucer's Wife of Bath states in her prologue that 'Deceite, wepyng, spynnyng, God have yive / to wommen kyndely', suggesting that spinning is considered a natural property of women, but that like weeping and deceitfulness, it is an indication of weakness.[91] Christine

Figure 4.5 Israhel van Meckenhem, 'The Quarrelsome Couple', *c.* 1465–1500. London, British Museum, No. 1873, 0809.651. © The Trustees of the British Museum.

de Pizan in the *Book of the City of Ladies* presents a view of spinning as the societal norm for girls, even as she decries it:

> It was because your mother, as a woman, held the view that you should spend your time spinning like the other girls, that you did not receive a more advanced or detailed initiation into the sciences.[92]

While textile work and learning are each endowed with moral value, here they are juxtaposed as inimical to one another. However, Christine also attributes the invention of cloth making to the goddesses Minerva and

Figure 4.6 Woman spinning. Smithfield Decretals, *bas-de-page*, *c.* 1300–40. London, British Library, MS Royal 10 E IV, fol. 139r. © The British Library Board.

Figure 4.7 Man carding. Smithfield Decretals, *bas-de-page*, *c.* 1300–40. London, British Library, MS Royal 10 E IV, fol. 147r. © The British Library Board.

Figure 4.8 Man spinning. Smithfield Decretals, *bas-de-page*, *c.* 1300–40. London, British Library, MS Royal 10 E IV, fol. 147v. © The British Library Board.

Arachne, placing textile work securely in the female domain. She defends this 'woman's work' against criticism: 'These techniques have all benefited humankind enormously, despite the fact that some men scorn women for performing such activities.'[93] Noah's wife in the Wakefield Cycle enacts a type of female disobedience when she refuses to board the Ark because she is busy with her spinning. Catherine Batt has outlined a range of negative representations of spinning in medieval literature, particularly in what she terms 'regulatory fiction' and the inherent misogyny in many of these treatments.[94] Advising women to limit themselves to their spinning rather than engage in debate was a trope for silencing women who were vocal or unorthodox, and it is worth remembering the predominance of male voices in medieval didactic literature and the written record more generally. Even in a religious context, women's textile production could be morally ambiguous. While making textiles, particularly embroidery, fulfilled the requirement for nuns to work, it was also a subject of concern that they did not become overly attentive to their needlework at the expense of their prayer.[95] Textile production therefore sat in an uneasy morally gendered space, approved of as a practice because it was necessary and because it was the proper work for women, but conversely disapproved of because it could be a cause for disobedience, lack of learning and a distraction from prayer. As Laura F. Hodges points out, there is a difference between the Virgin's exemplary textile production, and that of Eve, which carries with it the taint of her original sin.[96]

Conclusion

The gendering of medieval textile production was complex. It is not just a story of women's work, and nor is it a simple narrative in which women's textile production was progressively taken over by men and relegated to the domestic sphere. It was dependent on ideological as well as economic and social factors, and there were enormous variations across time and place, and across and within different crafts. Whether men or women undertook particular aspects of textile production in specific times and places was governed by factors including their relative economic and social influence, their access to the technology and equipment of their craft, their purchasing power or other means of acquiring the raw materials that they needed. The types of textile work they could undertake were influenced by whether they lived in the country or the town, their access to suitable space, and how well their craft fitted around the other demands on their time. The nature of their work might be limited by their physical ability and health. Their relationship to the means of production, whether as an owner of a business, an employee or a dependent or independent pieceworker, determined whether their work had the potential to be profitable, while their social status affected whether they needed to make a living from their textile work, or whether they worked to clothe their families. For women, their ability to carry on a particular trade could depend on their marital status, and the regulations of the relevant guild. Women and men understood their textile work within the framework of social and religious ideology. The act of making thread or cloth or narrow wares might be considered either as normative or subversive, morally worthy, or tainted with the sin of Eve.

In examining and suggesting explanations for how medieval textile production was gendered, I acknowledge that there will be exceptions which do not fit the patterns, cases where women engaged in forms of textile production which might be expected to have been men's work, and men whose textile making might be considered women's work, despite the prevailing notions of gender within particular crafts. There were certainly individuals who had more or less power as a result of their textile production than overarching theories of gender might suggest, but such theories nevertheless provide a frame within which these anomalies might be understood. The medieval realities of gender and textile production must be disentangled from the assumptions made about women's work by subsequent eras, and careful distinctions need to be made between the actuality of how textile production was gendered and the ideals which governed the ways that it was represented and understood in the Middle Ages. Documentary records need to be treated with caution, and supplemented by evidence from archaeological, lexical, visual, and literary sources, themselves also appropriately and carefully interpreted in the light of prevailing tropes and traditions. Medieval ideals of gender, and the representations they informed, doubtless had an impact on how practice was gendered, as women and men sought to work in ways that they considered appropriate for their gender. Medieval gender, ultimately, both constructed and was constructed by the work of producing textiles.

Notes

1 Richard B. Dobson, *The Peasants' Revolt of 1381* (Bath: Pitman, 1970), 373–75. Ball was probably adapting a text earlier used by Richard Rolle: 'When Adam dalfe and Eve spane / So spire if thou may spede / Where was then the pride of man / That nowe merres his mede?'. George G. Perry, ed., *Religious Pieces in Prose and Verse*, EETS O.S. 26, 2nd edn. (London: Kegan-Paul, Trench, Trübner, 1914), 79.

2 Glasgow, University of Glasgow, Special Collections, MS Hunter U.3.2 (229), fol. 8r, *c.* 1170.

3 Influential examples include Marian K. Dale, 'The London Silkwomen of the Fifteenth Century', *Economic History Review* 1st ser., 4 (1933): 324–35, whose conclusions were reviewed by Maryanne Kowaleski and Judith M. Bennett in 'Crafts, Gilds, and Women in the Middle Ages: Fifty Years After Marian K. Dale', *Signs: A Journal of Women in Culture and Society* 14 (1989); David Herlihy, *Opera Muliebria: Women and Work in Medieval Europe* (New York: McGraw-Hill, 1990), especially 75–102; Elizabeth Wayland Barber, *Women's Work: The First 20,000 Years: Women, Cloth and Society in Early Times* (New York: Norton, 1994); Martha C. Howell, *Women, Production, and Patriarchy in Late Medieval Cities* (Chicago: University of Chicago Press, 1988); P.J.P. Goldberg, *Women, Work and Life Cycle in a Medieval Economy: Women in York and Yorkshire c. 1300–1520* (Oxford: Clarendon Press, 1992). Recent overviews of the field of medieval women's textile production are included in Kathryn Reyerson, 'Urban Economies', and Jane Whittle, 'Rural Economies', in *The Oxford Handbook of Women and Gender in Medieval Europe*, ed. Judith M. Bennett and Ruth Mazo Karras (Oxford: Oxford University Press, 2013).

4 For examples, see the body of work by John H. Munro, especially 'Medieval Woollens: Textiles, Textile Technology and Industrial Organisation, *c.* 800–1500', in *The Cambridge History of Western Textiles, Volume 1*, ed. D.T. Jenkins (Cambridge: Cambridge University Press, 2003); and Angela Ling Huang and Carsten Jahnke, eds., *Textiles and the Medieval Economy: Production, Trade and the Consumption of Textiles, 8th–16th Centuries* (Oxford: Oxbow Books, 2015).

5 Examples include Stephanie Trigg, '"Ye Louely Ladyes with Youre Longe Fyngres": The Silkwomen of Medieval London', *Studia Anglica Posnaniensia* 38 (2002): 469–84; Monica L. Wright, '"De Fil d'Or et de Soie": Making Textiles in Twelfth-Century French Romance', *Medieval Textiles and Clothing* 2 (2006): 61–72; and E. Jane Burns, *Sea of Silk: A Textile Geography of Women's Work in Medieval French Literature* (Philadelphia: University of Pennsylvania Press, 2009).

6 Examples include Sue Harrington, *Aspects of Gender Identity and Craft Production in the European Migration Periods: Iron Weaving Beaters and Associated Textile Making Tools from England, Norway and Alamannia*, British Archaeological Reports, S1797 (Oxford: John and Erica Hedges, 2008); Ingvild Øye, 'Production, Quality and Social Status in Viking Age Dress', *Medieval Clothing and Textiles* 11 (2015): 2–7.

7 See, for example, Rozsika Parker, *The Subversive Stitch: Embroidery and the Making of the Feminine* (London: The Women's Press, 1982); and Alexandra Gajewski and Stefanie Seeberg, 'Having her Hand in it? Elite Women as "Makers" of Textile Art in the Middle Ages', *Journal of Medieval History* 42 (2016).

8 For a rare example, see R.L. Wyss, 'Die Handarbeiten der Maria', in *Artes Minores: Dank an Werner Abegg*, ed. Michael Stettler and Mechthild Lemberg (Bern: Stamfili, 1973).

9 See Kathryn M. Rudy and Barbara Baert, eds., *Weaving, Veiling, Dressing: Textiles and their Metaphors in the Late Middle Ages* (Turnhout: Brepols, 2007).

10 Parker, *Subversive Stitch*.

11 Parker, *Subversive Stitch*, 43–47.

12 Brigitte Kurmann-Schwarz, 'Gender and Medieval Art', in *A Companion to Medieval Art: Romanesque and Gothic in Northern Europe*, ed. Conrad Rudolph (Malden, MA: Blackwell, 2006).

13 Marc Fitch, 'The London Makers of *Opus Anglicanum*', *Transactions of the London and Middlesex Archaeological Society* 27 (1976): 288–96; Sharon Farmer, 'Medieval Paris and the Mediterranean: The Evidence from the Silk Industry', *French Historical Studies* 37 (2014): 395. Farmer notes that the list of members of the Paris Embroiderers' Guild compiled around 1300 includes seventy-nine female members and fifteen male members.

14 Michael Camille, 'At the Sign of the "Spinning Sow": The "Other" Chartres and Images of Everyday Life of the Medieval Street', in *History and Images: Towards a New Iconology*, ed. A. Bolvig and P. Lindley (Turnhout: Brepols, 2003). Frances Biscoglio, writing in 1995, stated 'since its origins spinning has always been gender-determined: it is exclusively feminine work'; see 'The Iconography of the Spinning Woman in the Middle Ages', *Journal of Medieval and Renaissance Studies* 5 (1995): 163. Eileen Power's highly influential book *Medieval Women*, first published in 1975, but based on lectures given decades earlier, states that spinning was practised 'almost exclusively by women'. *Medieval Women*, ed. M.M. Postan (Cambridge: Cambridge University Press, 1975), 65. Subsequent writers hardened this view to a certainty. Evidence for men spinning will be discussed further, below.

15 Roberta Gilchrist, discussing finds of spindle whorls, needles, thimbles, scissors, shears, and a wool comb at a priests' community in York, argues that 'in medieval culture these objects and activities are associated exclusively with women, and their presence strongly suggests that female domestic servants were living in Vicar's Choral'. *Medieval Life: Archaeology and the Life Course* (Woodbridge: Boydell, 2012), 131. An alternative possibility is that when living in an all-male environment, men undertook textile work to supply their own needs. Shane McLeod has recently shown that swords do not always denote male burials in the Viking period. 'Warriors and Women: The Sex Ratio of Norse Migrants to Eastern England up to 900 CE', *Early Medieval Europe* 19 (2011).

16 René de Lespinasse and François Bonnardot, *Les métiers et corporations de la ville de Paris: XIIIe siècle. Le livre des métiers d'Etienne Boileau* (Paris: Imprimerie nationale, 1879).

17 Only some of these rolls have been published. For a discussion of the data the rolls contain, see J.M. Archer, 'Working Women in Thirteenth-Century Paris' (PhD diss., University of Arizona, 1995), 77–79.

18 Archer, 'Working Women'.
19 Sharon Farmer, 'Medieval Paris and the Mediterranean'; and *The Silk Industries of Medieval Paris: Artisanal Migration, Technological Innovation, and Gendered Experience* (Philadelphia: University of Pennsylvania Press, 2016).
20 Archer, 'Working Women', 17–22.
21 Archer, 'Working Women', 106.
22 Farmer, *Silk Industries*, 9.
23 Archer, 'Working Women', 252–53.
24 Farmer estimates, by extrapolating from the records, that 'there were somewhere around 1,418 Parisian women who contributed to the production of silk cloth and narrow ware and that they constituted at least 80 per cent of the artisans who participated in the activities that were necessarily for the production of those textiles'. *Silk Industries*, 107. Archer also discusses crafts which she classifies as 'needlework', including some of the making of clothing and accessories and household goods, for which the gender distinctions are less clear. 'Working Women', 257–59.
25 Archer, 'Working Women', 252–53.
26 Images of the fibre-working women, believed to depict the active life, can be seen at https://throughjillseyes.wordpress.com/2014/10/29/the-active-life-six-sculptures-at-the-chartres-cathedral/. Accessed March 12, 2018. Although these images have often been described as 'women working wool', they actually depict both wool and linen preparation. The first sculpture, working upwards from the bottom of the left side of the archivolt, shows a woman washing wool, the second combing (rather than carding) wool, the third scutching flax, and the fourth hackling flax. The fifth and sixth images, which show women spinning and winding yarn, could depict either wool or linen.
27 Florence, Biblioteca Medicea Laurenziana, MS Plut. 89 sup. 117.
28 Ilja M. Veldman, 'Representations of Labour in Late Sixteenth-Century Netherlandish Prints: The Secularization of the Work Ethic', in *The Idea of Work in Europe from Antiquity to Modern Times*, ed. Josef Ehmer and Catharina Lis (Farnham: Ashgate, 2009), 149.
29 See Gerhard Jaritz, 'The Visual Representation of Late Medieval Work: Patterns of Context, People and Action', in *The Idea of Work*, ed. Ehmer and Lis.
30 Cambridge, Trinity College, MS R.17.1, fol. 263. Accessed August 20, 2017. http://trin-sites-pub.trin.cam.ac.uk/james/viewpage.php?index=1229.
31 Herlihy, *Opera Muliebria*, cover image, 81–83. The corresponding image is in the Utrecht Psalter (Utrecht, Universiteitsbibliotheek, MS Bibl. Rhenotraiectinae I Nr 32, fol. 83). Accessed August 20, 2017. http://psalter.library.uu.nl/page?p=174&res=3&x=0&y=0.
32 The looms most commonly used in Europe in the early Middle Ages were variations on the vertical loom, in which the cloth was woven in an upwards direction, and the warps were held in place either with a lower beam or by being tied in bundles to weights.
33 Isaiah 38:12 (NIV). The large shears held by two of the women in the image reference the cutting of the cloth from the loom.
34 Österreichische Nationalbibliothek, MS 507, fol. 2r.
35 On the technical and gender differences between these types of loom, see Agnes Geijer, *A History of Textile Art: A Selective Account* (Stockholm: Pasold Research Fund, 1979), 30–35, 77–80.

36 Constance H. Berman, 'Women's Work in Family, Village and Town after 1000 CE: Contribution to Economic Growth?', *Journal of Women's History* 19 (2007): 15–16.
37 Examples of women weaving using a horizontal floor loom include a frequently reproduced image of the biblical character Naamah from the Egerton Gospels (London, British Library, MS Egerton 1894, fol. 2v); and images of Penelope, Minerva, and Tanaquil, especially in illustrations of Boccaccio's *De mulieribus claris* (e.g., Paris, Bibliothèque nationale de France, MS fr. 598) and Ovid's *Metamorphoses* (e.g., London, British Library, MS Royal 17 E IV, fol. 87v). Men are depicted using horizontal floor looms in the donor images in the thirteenth-century windows of SS Savinien, Potentien, and Modesta, and of SS Theodore and Vincent in Chartres cathedral, and in fifteenth-century portraits of named guild members in the Mendel Hausbuch (Amb. 317.2°, fol. 38 (Mendel I)).
38 Burns, *Sea of Silk*, 1.
39 For a discussion of these textiles, usually embroideries, see Jane Tibbetts Schulenburg, 'Holy Women and the Needle Arts: Piety, Devotion, and Stitching the Sacred ca. 500–1150', in *Negotiating Community and Difference* in *Medieval Europe: Gender, Power, Patronage, and the Authority of Religion in Latin Christendom*, ed. Katherine Allen Smith and Scott Wells (Leiden: Brill, 2009). However, Gajewski and Seeberg argue that while numerous medieval records specified that elite women made textiles 'with their own hands', it is impossible to know the extent to which they really were personally responsible, rather than acting in a supervisory capacity, noting that the term 'fecit' can denote a broader range of meaning than simply 'made', also encompassing commissioning and patronage, 'Having her Hand in it?', 26–50.
40 Trigg, 'Ye Louely Ladyes', 476–80. In *Yvain*, the imprisoned women undertake silk weaving, but it is likely that they are weaving narrow wares rather than cloth, as discussed below.
41 See *Oxford English Dictionary* entry for -ster, *suffix*.
42 The dates quoted in the following discussion are those given for earliest attestation in the *Oxford English Dictionary*.
43 The *Oxford English Dictionary* equates the term *throwster* with *silkwoman*, attested from 1440, but it is clear from the 1455 petition to parliament from both the silkwomen and throwsters that *silkwoman* was a broader term, encompassing working silk thread into finished articles. See also Dale, 'London Silkwomen'.
44 While the term was used in the Northumbrian poem *Cursor Mundi* to describe the biblical Naamah, its use is testament to its currency. The southern version of the poem describes her as a *webbe*.
45 *The Parliament Rolls of Medieval England, 1275–1504*, vol. 12 (Woodbridge: Boydell and Brewer, 2012), 60.
46 See Archer, 'Working Women', 252–58.
47 Howell presents a discussion of previous scholars espousing this view, as well as discussing other factors influencing the gender divisions in late medieval textile productions, *Women, Production, and Patriarchy*, 176. Berman notes that the argument that women did not have sufficient strength for weaving was one made in late medieval Norwich, 'Women's Work', 498 n. 49. John Munro also rehearses, and questions, the argument that the shift in the gendering of weaving from feminine to masculine was due to the strength required to operate the horizontal loom, 'Medieval Woollens', 221.

48 Archer, 'Working Women', 258, 266–68.
49 For examples, see manuscript illuminations in the Da Costa Hours, New York, Morgan Library and Museum, MS M. 399, fol. 12v; the Très Riches Heures of the Duc de Berry, Chantilly, Bibliothèque du Château (formerly Musée Condé), MS 65, fol. 6v; and an illuminated copy of *The Decameron*, in Paris, Bibliothèque de l'Arsenal, MS 5070, fol. 51v.
50 Archer, 'Working Women', 115.
51 Barber, *Women's Work*, 29–30. Judith Brown, 'A Note on the Division of Labour by Sex', *American Anthropologist*, 72 (1970).
52 While in urban and commercial contexts, there was room for specialisation in textile production, with workers undertaking discrete aspects of the textile processes, in rural and domestic contexts, end to end processing from raw fibre to finished cloth could be performed in the home. See Whittle, 'Rural Economies', 312.
53 John H. Munro, 'Gold, Guilds and Government: The Impact of Monetary and Labour Policies on the Flemish Cloth Industry, 1390–1435', *Jaarboek Voor Middeleeuwse Geschiedenis* 5 (2002): 174.
54 Luttrell Psalter, London, British Library, MS Additional 42130, fol. 166v, lower margin illustration.
55 London, British Library, MS Royal 15 E III, fol. 269.
56 The *Livre des métiers* records a small number of women working as cloth dyers, presumably in workshops, and the separate craft of silk dyers, who presumably dyed yarn rather than cloth, is exclusively female. Archer, 'Working Women', 153.
57 Munro, 'Medieval Woollens', 204–05.
58 Judith M. Bennett, *Ale, Beer and Brewsters in England: Women's Work in a Changing World, 1300–1600* (New York: Oxford University Press, 1996), 58.
59 Archer, 'Working Women', 56.
60 Archer argues that the *ouvrières de soie*, of which there are seventy-seven listed compared to four *ouvriers*, are weavers since many of them are listed with the weavers' guild, but it is far more likely that the majority of them are throwsters, with the large number needed to twist reeled silk thread into yarn for the silk weavers. 'Working Women', 58.
61 Farmer, *Silk Industries*, 108.
62 Whittle, 'Rural Economies', 312.
63 Herlihy argues that while women made most cloth in domestic settings before 1000, men gradually became more involved in clothmaking during the central Middle Ages, and had taken over all but the low-status aspects of cloth production by the end of the fifteenth century. *Opera Muliebria*, ix.
64 Archer, 'Working Women', 115. Archer appears to be making a distinction between the occupations of *filandrière* and *filaresse* which are listed separately in the *Livre des métiers*, but it is not clear that the source intended a distinction between the sizes of the spindles. Farmer suggests that the large spindles might be spinning wheels but wheel spinners are listed separately as *filaresses a touret.* Farmer, 'Medieval Paris', 388; Archer, 'Working Women', 252.
65 Munro, 'Medieval Woollens', 200.
66 Reyerson, 'Urban Economies', 296.
67 Archer, 'Working Women', 116.
68 Archer, 'Working Women', 116.
69 Louise M. Sylvester, Marc C. Chambers, and Gale R. Owen-Crocker, eds., *Medieval Dress and Textiles in Britain: A Multilingual Sourcebook* (Woodbridge: Boydell,

2014), 370. Although this work focuses on medieval textiles in England, the term is used in French language contexts.

70 Chrétien de Troyes, 'Perceval', ll. 2804–05, trans. D.D.R. Owen, *Arthurian Romances* (London: Dent, 1987), 411.

71 Elisabeth Crowfoot, Frances Pritchard, and Kay Staniland, *Textiles and Clothing c. 1150–1450* (London: H.M.S.O., 1992), 6.

72 Dale, 'London Silkwomen', 324. A subsequent petition to Parliament in 1482 was presented by a much broader group, 'menne and women on the hole craft of Silkewerk of the Cite of London and all other Citeis, Townes, Boroghes, and Vilages of this Realme of Englond'. *Rotoli Parliamentorum* (Rec. Comm., 1832), V, 325a, VI, 222b.

73 Munro argues on the basis of iconography that the earliest versions of the horizontal loom were operated by women but that when the more complicated broadloom evolved, they were exclusively operated by men. John H. Munro, 'Textile Production for the Market', in *Women and Gender in Medieval Europe: An Encyclopaedia*, ed. Margaret Schaus (New York: Routledge, 2006), 792. However, as discussed earlier, the interpretation of this iconography needs to be undertaken with care.

74 Munro, 'Medieval Woollens', 201.

75 The donor image depicting the weavers in the window of SS Savinien and Potentien in Chartres Cathedral, *c.* 1210–1225, shows a man using a spinning wheel, but he is using it to wind shuttle bobbins from a swift, rather than to spin. Accessed May 19, 2017.
www.medievalart.org.uk/chartres/17_pages/Chartres_Bay17_Panel18.htm. See also the discussion of the images of spinning from the Smithfield Decretals, p. 90.

76 Munro, 'Medieval Woollens', 201–03.

77 'What sholde we wommen werche the while?'
'Somme shul sowe the sak' quod Piers, 'for shedyng of the whete;
And ye lovely ladies with youre longe fyngres,
That ye have silk and sandel to sowe whan tyme is
Chesibles for chapeleyns chirches to honoure.
Wyves and widewes, wolle and flex spynneth:
Maketh cloth, I counseille yow, and kenneth so youre doughtres.
The nedy and the naked, nymeth hede how thei liggeth,
And casteth hem clothes, for so commaundeth Truthe'.

William Langland, *Piers Plowman*, B text, Passus VI, ll. 8–16. In this passage Langland sets out divisions of textile labour for women based on their social standing.

78 See, for example, Kowaleski and Bennett, 'Craft, Gilds and Women', 21; and Howell, *Women, Production, and Patriarchy*, 9–11. See also chapters in this volume by Anne Montenach and Jeremy Goldberg for the ways that late medieval and early modern women worked to mitigate this disadvantage.

79 Susan Broomhall, 'Women, Work and Power in the Female Guilds of Rouen', in *Practices of Gender in Late Medieval and Early Modern Europe*, ed. Megan Cassidy-Welch and Peter Sherlock (Turnhout: Brepols, 2008).

80 Reyerson, 'Urban Economies', 298–99.

81 Genesis 3:7, 16–21 (NIV).

82 Proverbs 31:10–24 (NIV).

83 Wyss, 'Die *Handarbeiten der Maria*'. These images often associate the act of spinning with the Virgin's state of pregnancy.
84 Wyss, 'Die *Handarbeiten der Maria*'. The images of the Virgin knitting may be based on the tradition that she made Christ's 'seamless garment' for which the soldiers drew lots at the Crucifixion (John 19:23).
85 The only two images of the Virgin weaving cloth of which I am aware are a depiction in stained glass from the Cathedral of Ulm, *c.* 1395–1400 (accessed August 20, 2017; http://id.corpusvitrearum.de/images/2084.html), and a woodcut image from Johann Grashove's *Boek Van Der Bedroffenisse Marien*, 1486. In these instances, the first depicting the Virgin's education in the Temple, and the second in the context of the Holy Family, she is weaving at a vertical loom. I am grateful to Mark Calderwood, Vicki Bismire, and Dr Katrina Hunt for directing my attention to these images. I have not found any depiction of the Virgin using a horizontal loom.
86 Examples include Luttrell Psalter, London, British Library, MS Additional 42130, fol. 60 and a Netherlandish metal plate, *c.* 1480, in the Metropolitan Museum of Art, New York, Acquisition Number 64.101.1499.
87 For ways of reading marginal images as subversive, see Michael Camille, *Image on the Edge: The Margins of Medieval Art* (London: Reaktion, 1992), especially 9–10.
88 London, British Museum, No. 1873, 0809.651.
89 London, British Library, MS Royal 10 E IV, fol. 147v, *c.* 1300–1340. The British Library website suggests that they might represent a housewife setting tasks for her husband or lover, but many of the tasks in this sequence do not obviously represent such a narrative. Accessed August 20, 2017. www.bl.uk/manuscripts/FullDisplay.aspx?ref=Royal_MS_10_e_iv.
90 Andrew Taylor, 'Playing on the Margins: Bakhtin and the Smithfield Decretals', in *Bakhtin and Medieval Voices*, ed. Thomas J. Farrell (Gainesville: University Press of Florida, 1995), 17.
91 Chaucer, *Canterbury Tales*, The Wife of Bath's Prologue, ll. 401–02.
92 Christine de Pizan, *The Book of the City of Ladies*, intro. and trans. Rosalind Brown-Grant (London: Penguin, 1999), 141.
93 Pizan, *City of Ladies*, 215. On this and the dialectic between women weaving and writing, see Natasha Amendola, 'Weaving Virtue: Laura Cereta as a New Penelope', in *Virtue Ethics for Women, 1250–1500*, ed. Karen Green and Constant Mews (Dordrecht: Springer, 2011).
94 Catherine Batt, 'The Idioms of Women's Work and Thomas Hoccleve's Travails', in *The Middle Ages at Work: Practicing Labor in late Medieval England*, ed. Kellie Robertson and Michael Uebel (New York: Palgrave-Macmillan, 2004).
95 Jeffrey Hamburger, *Nuns as Artists: The Visual Culture of a Medieval Convent* (Berkeley: University of California Press, 1997), 182.
96 Laura F. Hodges, 'Noe's Wife: Type of Eve and Wakefield Spinner', in *Equally in God's Image: Women in the Middle Ages*, ed. Julia Boston Holloway, Joan Bechtold, and Constance S. Wright (New York: Peter Lang, 1990), 31–32.

Select bibliography

Archer, J.M. 'Working Women in Thirteenth-Century Paris'. PhD diss., University of Arizona, 1995.

Bennett, Judith M., and Ruth Mazo Karras, eds. *The Oxford Handbook of Women and Gender in Medieval Europe*. Oxford: Oxford University Press, 2013.

Burns, E. Jane. *Sea of Silk: A Textile Geography of Women's Work in Medieval French Literature*. Philadelphia: University of Philadelphia Press, 2009.

Dale, Marian K. 'The London Silkwomen of the Fifteenth Century'. *Economic History Review*, 1st ser., 4 (1933): 324–35.

Farmer, Sharon. *The Silk Industries of Medieval Paris: Artisanal Migration, Technological Innovation, and Gendered Experience*. Philadelphia: University of Pennsylvania Press, 2016.

Gajewski, Alexandra, and Stefanie Seeberg. 'Having her Hand in it? Elite Women as "Makers" of Textile Art in the Middle Ages'. *Journal of Medieval History* 42 (2016): 26–50.

Munro, John H. 'Medieval Woollens: Textiles, Textile Technology and Industrial Organisation, *c.* 800–1500'. In *The Cambridge History of Western Textiles, Volume 1*, ed. D.T. Jenkins, 181–227. Cambridge: Cambridge University Press, 2003.

Parker, Rozsika. *The Subversive Stitch: Embroidery and the Making of the Feminine*. London: The Women's Press, 1982.

5 'Fortune ce mestier m'aprist'[1]

Christine de Pizan as writer, teacher, and Voice of Wisdom

Ellen Thorington

Christine de Pizan (*c.* 1365–*c.* 1431), considered to be Europe's first professional woman of letters, became a writer largely out of necessity. Widowed in 1390 with three children, her mother, and a niece to support, Christine needed to find a way to make ends meet since amounts owed to her late husband remained unpaid, debts had piled up, and she was involved in a number of lawsuits.[2] In becoming a writer and publisher, Christine made an unusual choice for a woman. She became a writer, a *métier* most often associated with men; she wrote that Fortune had transformed her into a man and taught her the craft so that she and her dependents could survive.[3] Both she and her contemporaries remarked on the novelty of a woman writer; Christine suggested that a number of princes may have accepted her works for this reason rather than for the worth of their contents.[4] Yet it is precisely the unique perspective of a woman who writes that makes Christine such an important figure for a discussion of women and work.

Christine has left us a number of autobiographical and semi-autobiographical details that reveal her experience as a working woman. For example, her works relate her ideas on what it meant to be a writer, the circumstances that brought her to take up her pen, and what she hoped to accomplish through the work of writing. She was a mindful writer, concerned that her works show by example the very matter she intended to portray. Christine saw herself as a teacher, and much of her work concerned the education of the young, the instruction of princes, and the ways to good government.[5] This reflects the concerns of the period in which she was writing, for France was in real crisis: King Charles VI suffered from mental illness, the dauphin Louis of Guyenne was too young to govern in his stead, and the ensuing power struggle led the country into civil war. Christine's work was intricately connected to the fate of her adopted country and derived from her combined responsibilities to her family, community, and France as a whole. In the face of political crisis, Christine presented herself as a Voice of Wisdom, a writer whose qualities as a humble woman and mother allowed her to call on the authority of the Virgin Mary and to forge an affinity with the queen of France, in order to offer her own wisdom, in text and image, for the betterment of France.[6]

On becoming a writer

Christine's entry into the professional world beyond the home began around 1390, following the tragic death of her young husband, Etienne de Castel, from an epidemic. However, little trace remains of the earliest years of Christine's career, the period from her husband's death to 1399, which marks the date she viewed as the start of her literary career.[7] Much of what we know comes from a few references in her more autobiographical works; the rest must be extrapolated from these writings and from what we know of her and of her society. To further complicate matters, the very notion of work and most particularly of women's work at the time when Christine lived is problematic, for expectations about what work could entail for women varied widely according to a woman's social, economic, and marital status, as well as her stage in life.[8] Christine was no exception to this rule: as a young married woman, her work was primarily based in the home, where she described herself as occupied with childbearing and the 'affaires que ont communement les mariees' (tasks common to married women).[9]

Christine had been encouraged in learning and probably educated in large part by her father, Thomas de Pizan, although her mother seems not to have approved.[10] Until she became a widow, Christine did not have time for serious study and a program of self-education; it was only when she was alone and confronted by financial disaster that she made the decision to become a writer to support herself and her family.[11] Like many women in her circumstances, Christine's options were limited. Widows could remarry, invest in real estate if they had the funds, take over the husband's business (particularly in the artisan and merchant classes), or take religious vows and enter a convent.[12] Yet Christine, whose marriage appears to have been very happy, stated that she had no desire to remarry.[13] Given that her finances left her no possibility of investing—in fact she was obliged to sell some property to pay debts—Christine had even fewer options.[14] Entering a convent would have required her to find an alternative solution for her dependants. Instead, she chose to follow in the footsteps of both her father and her husband, taking up the life of the scholar.[15] This was a remarkable choice: at higher levels of the social hierarchy, women were excluded from many positions, such as the posts of notary and royal secretary held by her husband Etienne, and from earning the credentials required for them.[16] With no business, as it were, for Christine to continue, she had to find her way through a different route. It seems most likely, as Charity Cannon Willard has suggested, that Christine's first steps were to use her husband's contacts to earn some money through copy work.[17] This would have been essential to her success as it gave her a network within clerical and bureaucratic circles and afforded her continued access to the nobility and to potential patrons.

Circumstantial evidence found in both Christine's handwriting and her rhetorical style suggests a strong association with the chancellery, her husband's workplace. The handwriting of scribe 'X', identified as that of

Christine by Gilbert Ouy and Christine Reno, is characterised by 'une exubérance' and a love of 'jeux de plume', flourishes of the pen that were often practised by chancellery clerks.[18] It is quite possible that Etienne de Castel taught her the form of calligraphy he used as a notary, perhaps so she could help him with his work.[19] Her rhetorical style also demonstrates this influence, for it contains 'echoes of the style *clergial* and *curial* ... Latin styles ... that were especially influential in the juridical language used in the Chancellery where Christine's husband and many of her friends worked'.[20] The fact that both Christine's style and handwriting appear to have been influenced by her husband and his workplace—and that she may have helped him with his work—corresponds to contemporary practice, particularly in the crafts. It was quite common for women to work along with their husbands or parents in artisanal production and for women to learn a craft within the family.[21] The suggestion that Christine began first as a copyist at the chancellery thus seems a natural progression, the outgrowth of skills and relationships dating from her marriage.[22] Willard also proposes that Christine may 'have been a sort of editor for an *atelier* which copied literary manuscripts', perhaps through her connection with the workshop responsible for the dissemination of the first Boccaccio manuscripts.[23] This type of position would have given her access to a number of texts and sources that she later cites in her works.[24]

Although it is uncertain how Christine managed financially during the early years of her career, her survival and subsequent success may be due in part to the influence of the queen, Ysabel of Bavaria (1370–1435).[25] There is some suggestion that she served as *chamberiere* (an honorary position that could encompass a number of different functions) to the queen beginning in the early 1390s; she herself employed this term in a letter to Ysabel but did not mention the position elsewhere in her works.[26] Certainly she seems to have worked in close association with the queen: Ysabel's accounts show a number of gifts given to a certain Christine; Christine also figures among the list of those receiving New Year gifts in 1402 and 1405, suggesting that she was a member of the queen's entourage at that time.[27] Such a position would have placed her within the queen's sphere of influence, eventually given her access to works owned by the queen, and left her well situated to encounter potential patrons among the men and women frequenting the queen and her ladies. Ouy, Reno, and their colleagues Olivier Delsaux and Inès Villela-Petit, hypothesise that Ysabel may have had a hand in the composition of Christine's own *atelier*. They suggest that Christine presented the first copy of her collected works, Chantilly, Bibliothèque du Château (formerly Musée Condé) MS 492, begun in 1399, to the queen. Wishing to reward the author, Ysabel likely exerted her influence to help Christine enlist a brother or cousin of a scribe in her service. It was this new recruit, Pierre de la Croix, who probably helped initiate Christine in the art of book making, and Pierre likely trained another scribe, whose name is still not known. These two scribes became Christine's principal collaborators; the resulting *atelier* would have worked from its outset under the protection of the queen.[28] Not insignificantly, Christine dedicated a number of works to Ysabel throughout her career, including London, British Library, Harley MS 4431. This exquisitely decorated manuscript also contains Christine's collected works, and is one of only five such surviving collections to have been produced in her own workshop.[29] Both its dedication and clear connection to Ysabel testify to a continuing—and long-standing—relationship between patron and author.

When she completed the *Livre de l'advision Cristine* in 1405, Christine was clearly an accomplished scribe, writer, and publisher. In this work, she dates the beginning of her literary career to 1399 and describes her development as a writer.[30] She likens it to that of a workman (*ouvrier*), who refines his work as he spends more and more time on it.[31] From 'forging' 'pretty things' that were 'lighter' (*legiere*) in subject, she has moved on, employing a more subtle style that reflects her study of 'diverses matieres' (diverse subjects).[32] In addition to developing her subject matter and style, Christine also demonstrates her knowledge as a bookmaker; her easy use of technical vocabulary reveals a familiarity with the techniques employed by copyists and illuminators.[33] For example, when referring to the 'XV volumes principaux' (15 principal volumes) that she has composed and the 'LXX quayers de grand volume' (70 large quires) in which they are contained, Christine writes as someone experienced in manuscript composition.[34] By 1405, then, Christine has plainly moved beyond the status of amateur connoisseur to become a master of her craft.[35]

The testimony of the *Livre de la cité des dames*, also completed in 1405, further details Christine's experience as a master-editor, one who hires illuminators and executes manuscripts. She speaks in particular of Anastaise, a female manuscript illuminator specialising in ornamental borders whose skill as an artist is so great (*tant est expert*) that Christine claims it could not be surpassed by any other artisan in Paris: 'qu'il n'est mencion d'ouvrier en la ville de Paris ... qui point l'en passe ne qui aussi doulcement face fleureteure et menu ouvrage qu'elle fait ne de qui on ait plus chier la besongne' (one cannot find an artisan in all the city of Paris ... who can surpass her, nor who can paint flowers and details as delicately as she does, nor whose work is more highly esteemed).[36] Christine was very familiar with Anastaise's work, for the illuminator had completed several projects for her.[37] From this we can see that Christine hired illuminators for her work, she was familiar with the illuminators available in the Paris area, and she was not the only woman working in the book trade at the time.

Indeed, her work as a master-editor placed her within the flourishing book trade in Paris, a space within which women could and did take on a professional role. *Taille* rolls indicate that, like many trades, book making was often a family affair, where women worked alongside husbands, fathers, or sons.[38] Nevertheless, women's participation in the book trade was 'probably pervasive, but for the most part invisible'; they trained primarily within the family rather than through formal apprenticeships and their names rarely appear on official documents.[39] Only in the case of widows like Jeanne de Montbaston, a mid-fourteenth-century illuminator who took over her husband's business, are women's names recorded as members of the book trade.[40] Christine thus fits into the latter model: although she did not take over a business from her husband, as a widow working as copyist and master-editor, she would not have been that unusual a figure. It was her work as author and scholar that took her beyond more conventional roles for women and enabled her to develop an international reputation. As Christine remarks in the *Advision*, it is her way of life (*maniere de vivre*) in scholarship (*l'estude*) that causes princes to take notice and to spread her works to different realms (*pars et pays divers*).[41]

The fact that Christine viewed herself as a scholar is essential, for it underlies both the philosophy of her work and her uniqueness as a woman writer. For Christine, the scholar has an obligation to share wisdom with others. Like her father, who was an advisor to King Charles V and whom she describes as counselling princes about everything from peace and war to the weather, she too needed to share her wisdom.[42] She, however, adapted the work of the scholar to her own situation and her own gender, becoming a female Voice of Wisdom. In taking up her pen and working her way into the life of the scholar, Christine gained for herself a position where she too could be the advisor of princes, and where she was able to make her own contribution to the betterment of society.

Christine's vision of the writer's role

In her works, Christine expresses a clear notion of what it means to be a woman writer in the fifteenth century and the types of responsibilities she attaches to this. The experience was not always positive: she remarks rather wryly on contemporaries, specifically the 'princes benignes' (gentle princes), who sought out her works because it was seen as unusual (*non usagee*) for a woman to write.[43] While being a novelty spread her renown and helped disseminate her works throughout Europe, Christine was not always taken seriously as a writer because of her gender. Her critics seem to have had difficulty believing that a woman could have composed her 'compillacions et volumes' (collections and volumes), arguing instead that they must have been written for her by 'clercs ou religieux' (scholars or religious men).[44] Christine, with characteristic spirit, has Dame Opinion in the *Advision* dismiss such naysayers as 'ignorans' (ignorant) and unfamiliar with works that speak of the valiant wise women (*vaillans femmes sages*) of the past who were learned (*lettrees*) and who even served as prophets (*profetes*).[45]

Even with such determination, it was not easy for a woman to become a writer in the fourteenth and early fifteenth centuries. As Jacqueline

Cerquiglini-Toulet argues, Christine found two different solutions to the problem: on the one hand, she transformed herself, figuratively speaking, into a man, as we see in the *Livre de la mutacion de fortune* (1403); on the other, she made herself into a woman of unparalleled excellence (*se faire femme superlativement*), which was the solution she employed from the *Cité des dames* (1405) onwards.[46] Ilse Paakkinen contends that as a woman transformed into a man, Christine could take up where contemporary men had failed in their duty to become womankind's defender.[47] Her ability to engage in a different mode of feminine exegesis, re-reading older anti-feminine narratives in new and more positive ways, formed a large part of the *Cité des dames* and is particularly evident in the learning process she underwent to become became a female scholar under the tutelage of Ladies Reason, Rectitude, and Justice.[48] I would argue that Christine in fact adapted the role of writer to suit her own ideals and personal experience: she fashioned her own concept of what it meant for a woman to take on an authorial role as well as the responsibilities entailed by that that role.

Christine's notion of the scholar was largely inspired by her father's example. In the *Mutacion de fortune* she praises his learning, likening it to a treasure of precious gems (*pierres precieuses*) collected at the fountain of Wisdom.[49] Yet even as she admires his learning, she notes that her gender was an obstacle preventing her from following his example. Because she was born a girl (*pour ce que fille fu nee*) she could not inherit the riches of this fountain, even though this was due more to custom than for any other reason (*plus par coustume que par droit*).[50] Indeed, until her husband's death and despite what she called a natural inclination to scholarship, various impediments kept her from fully profiting from learning. Christine's mother preferred that she stick with spinning (*fillasses*); 'folle jeunesce' (foolish youth) kept her more interested in play than in study; and upon her marriage she was occupied with childbearing and caring for a household.[51] It was therefore not so incidental that after her husband's death Christine should describe her changed circumstances as a transformation where Fortune caused her to become a man and taught her the trade. Cerquiglini-Toulet suggests that in this way she becomes the son her father wished for.[52] As a man, Christine could truly begin to profit from her father's riches and follow his example, taking up his work but in her own way.

Yet, as we have noted, Christine was undeniably conscious of her unusual position as a woman writer. Catherine Attwood and Mary Anne Case, among others, have shown that Christine used this position in strategic ways, highlighting the fact that she alone could write as she chose and about her experiences.[53] The numerous references in her poetry and other works to her solitude both as a widow and as a female writer and scholar underline her originality (*singularité*), presenting her as the only person who could express certain ideas and certain experiences.[54] The first lines of the *Mutacion de fortune* are a case in point, for Christine explains that no man (and likely no woman), no matter how learned, could possibly write what she wishes to:[55]

> Comment sera ce possible
> A moy simple et pou sensible
> De proprement exprimer
> Ce qu'on ne peut extimer
> Bonnement, ne bien comprendre,
> Non, *tant ait homs sceu apprendre,*
> *Qu'entierement peust descrire*
> *Ce que bien voulsisse escripre.*
>
> (How will it be possible for me, simple and of small understanding, to express adequately that which cannot be well expressed or well understood? No, *no matter how much learning a man might have, he could not fully describe what I would wish to write.*)[56]

Although she describes herself unassumingly as simple and 'peu sensible', only Christine is able to write what she herself has experienced as a result of the vagaries of Fortune. In fact, by virtue of her experience, she views herself as extremely well qualified to speak of Fortune, and even as having a privileged relationship with this figure.[57] Christine thus plays with the humility topos: although she is 'just a simple woman', she too has something useful to offer through her life experience, something that no one else can write.[58]

Even when describing the act of writing, Christine draws attention to those experiences in her life that are unique to women. Although she associates the work of the scholar and writer with men, Christine, like her contemporaries, sees the work of writing as one that generates or gives birth to ideas.[59] This is particularly evident in the *Advision* where Christine juxtaposes masculine and feminine metaphors for writing.[60] In this text, Nature first exhorts Christine to use the forge, 'Prens les outilz et fier sur l'enclume' (Take the tools and strike the anvil) in order to create pleasing things (*delictables*) out of the durable material Nature provides. She then urges Christine to envisage the pains of writing as that of childbirth: Christine will bring forth volumes from her memory, birthing them in spite of the 'labour et traveil' (pain and labour); then, again like a mother, she will forget the pains as she hears the voice of her volumes for the first time.[61] Although both metaphors are employed by earlier authors, Christine's description of writing as being like the pains of childbirth extends the generative metaphor and carries the weight of experience behind it.[62] This serves to make the work of writing Christine's own, to translate the act into terms that are specific to Christine as a female writer while at the same time highlighting the value and worth of women's experience.

Through writing her own and other women's experience into her books, Christine transforms the role of the writer, making it conform to her own existence while at the same time legitimising the expression of that existence. Female experience, Christine's in particular, is important and needs to be articulated, in part because it has much to teach. Christine is quite clear on this point in the prologue to the *Livre du chemin de lonc estude* (1402–03). She describes herself as an unworthy woman (*indigne*) and sets herself, as Walters notes, below her noble patron.[63] Nonetheless, she insists that from 'simple personne / peut bien venir vraye raison et bonne' (a simple person, true and good reason may well come).[64] Christine's juxtaposition of the humility topos with the worth of her words again justifies her work as a writer. Similarly, as Hult suggests, her use of the humility topos in the *Epistres du debat sus le Rommant de la Rose* enabled Christine to 'establish a dialogue with her interlocutors from a feminine perspective', in some sense pitting her experience as a woman against the formal clerkly training received by her learned adversaries.[65]

Yet this defence of her work and of her worth as a woman writer, is grounded in sound theology. The use of the humility topos is intended to recall the Virgin Mary, the humble handmaiden who bore the Word in the form of the incarnated Christ. Not surprisingly, it appears in the work of other medieval women writers. As Newman argues in her discussion of Hildegard of Bingen, it 'typified ... a central paradox of Christianity: all who humble themselves will be exalted'.[66] Christine's extensive use of this theme helps link her work to the Virgin, thereby evoking a female figure who is associated with Wisdom and with literacy.[67] In creating this association, Christine safeguards her work against critics who would reject it solely on the basis of her gender. Like the Virgin herself, Christine is a humble handmaid who—as courtly writer—can also be inspired by Holy Wisdom to serve as messenger to the French court through the words she writes.[68]

Christine considers it her duty to transmit her wisdom to others. Yet, her work encompasses the responsibilities incumbent upon her dual roles as scholar and as woman. For Christine, women had an obligation to teach by moral and by example and to inspire others through their virtue. This is perhaps most clearly expressed in the *Livre des trois vertus* (1405) composed for Marguerite of Nevers, the bride of the dauphin, Louis of Guyenne. Christine details the responsibilities of the high-born lady, saying that such a lady should surpass all others in 'bonté, sagece, meurs, condicions et manieres' (good prudence, moral standards, conduct, and manners) and serve as a model (*exemplaire*) for other women.[69] While this passage refers specifically to the high-born lady, Christine is careful to note at the beginning of both Books II and III that much of the advice she provides is applicable to all women, regardless of their rank.[70] Moreover, through virtuous conduct and goodness, women may serve as examples and inspiration to men: the example Christine provides in the *Cité des dames* of Blanche of Castile is a case in point. Blanche's 'tres grant savoir, prudence, vertus et bonté' (great learning, prudence, virtue, and goodness) as well as her 'sages paroles' (wise words) inspire Thibault of Champagne to cease his attacks against Saint Louis and even to fall in love with Blanche herself.[71]

Through the act of writing, Christine set herself up as a model for others. Her works—in which she herself is often the example or the messenger—exhort others to a right life of honour and virtue and are themselves 'good works' that are both example and execution of that example. This was clearly a conscious choice, one which she articulates in the prayer at the end of the *Livre des trois vertus*. This prayer, which Christine hopes women will say in her memory, emphasises her role in the transmission of wisdom. She asks them to pray that she may be granted knowledge (*sapience*) and true wisdom (*vraye sapience*) such that she may use it in the noble labour of study (*noble labour d'estude*) for the 'exaltation of virtue in good examples to every human being' (*l'exaulcement et eslevacion de vertus en bons exemples a toute humaine creature*).[72] In this way, she portrays herself as practising the very virtues she promotes in an effort to bring wisdom to all humanity. Yet it is the very nature of Christine's experience in the world and her knowledge of the bottom side of Fortune's wheel that form and shape her notion of what it means to be a writer and enable her to mould the work of the writer to fit her own situation. In this way, while she claims to have been transformed by Fortune into a man, Christine's notion of her duty as a female writer results in large part from her understanding of women's obligations to the world they inhabit. It is only as a writing woman that she may become a Voice of Wisdom, serving as divinely inspired intermediary between her adopted country and Holy Wisdom.

The wisdom of Christine

As a scholar, Christine models her work on her father's example, regarding it as a calling to offer wise counsel in an effort to better the world around her. As she notes in the *Livre des trois vertus*, she perceives wisdom as a means to salvation and a closer relationship with God.[73] She views it as her duty to share this gift through her writings and accomplished this on a number of different levels.[74] She provides spiritual and practical advice to teach young people in works such as the *Enseignemens* (*c.* 1398) (commonly known as the *Enseignemens moraulx*), the *Proverbes moraulx* (1405), the *Epistre Othea* (*c.* 1400), and the *Livre des trois vertus*.[75] Similarly, the *Livre du corps de policie* takes the form of a mirror of princes. Still other works, such as the *Livre du chemin de lonc estude* and the *Advision Cristine*, contain her political advice and commentary on France's problems. Throughout, Christine offers her wise words and her experience to others.

As we have seen, the notion of a woman as a bearer of Wisdom is an important trope. In examining Christine's role as a Voice of Wisdom who offers her experience and knowledge in the service of her adopted country, it is essential to consider both Christine's name, and her relationship with her patron, Ysabel of Bavaria. The name Christine is the feminine form of Christ. Christine herself brings attention to this in the *Mutacion de fortune*:

> Mais, quant pour ester a droit nommé
> Le nom du plus parfait homme,
> Qui oncques fu, le mien nomme,
> I. N. E. faut avec mettre,
> Plus n'y affiert autre lettre.
>
> (In order for me to be correctly named, just add the letters I, N, E, to the name of the most perfect man who ever lived; no other letter is necessary.)[76]

The emphasis on writing is critical, for the representation of her name in the manuscripts is often created with the Chi and the Rho plus 'ine': 'xpine'.[77] While orally and aurally, her name represents a feminisation of Christ, the use of the Chi and the Rho forges symbolic connotations. The figure of Wisdom appears both as female (Old Testament Wisdom) or occasionally as male (Christ-as-Logos).[78] Hence the conjunction of male and female here, of Christ and Christine, through the Word, brings out the Wisdom trope and authorises Christine's construction of herself as a Voice of Holy Wisdom.

Yet to function well in such a role, Christine could not act alone. To transmit her advice and counsel, Christine worked through female agency, focusing on women as intercessors who were capable of influencing men and their actions for the greater good.[79] One of the best examples of this is her work for her patron Ysabel of Bavaria, queen of France. Ysabel had the difficult task of being queen during the civil unrest and political strife occasioned by the periodic madness of her husband, Charles VI.[80] His frequent inability to rule required her to act in the capacity of regent, serve as peacemaker between rival factions, and look out for the interests and education of the royal children, most importantly the young dauphin.

The parallels between Christine and Ysabel are fascinating for a consideration of women and work. As Walters observes, they shared a number of similar life experiences. They were born outside France to Italian mothers. Their daughters, both named Marie, entered the abbey of Saint-Louis-de Poissy in 1398. Each lost a husband, one to death, the other to mental illness. They also both embraced a common goal in furthering the well-being of France.[81] Moreover, in order for Christine to achieve her purpose as a writer, and serve as a vehicle and a Voice for the Holy Wisdom that could help the kingdom of France, she needed not just a patron, but an association or partnership with a temporal authority, a figure who could aid the dissemination of that wisdom and serve as intercessor.[82] The queen was ideally situated to take on such a role: as the 'feminine face of power' she provided the perfect counterpart to Christine's construction of herself as the Voice of Wisdom.[83]

Ysabel was important not just as Christine's benefactress, but also as the recipient of many of her works and as a subject depicted within them. For example, Christine's depiction of the 'Wise Princess' in the first book of the *Livre des trois vertus* 'closely echoes [Ysabel's] situation and illuminates the difficulties the queen faced'.[84] In this text and elsewhere, Christine appeared to consider it her duty to use her writing as a means to support the queen for the betterment of France.[85] The picture that emerges is of a working relationship, of patronage on the part of the queen and a kind of advisory and supportive role on Christine's part.[86] In her work with and for the queen, Christine assumes her father's vocation, but in a feminine reflection of his role: where he was an advisor to King Charles V, she became an advisor to Ysabel of Bavaria.[87]

The suggestion of this supportive role can be seen quite early on in Christine's career with her composition of MS Chantilly 492–493.[88] Christine probably presented the major part of it to Ysabel in 1399 or shortly thereafter.[89] The presentation of a manuscript to the queen carried significance beyond that of a personal gift: manuscripts were often read aloud in the houses of the aristocracy and their contents were heard and discussed by the entourage surrounding such figures as the queen and other nobles.[90] Consequently the gift of a manuscript reached a much larger public than the recipient alone. The contents of MS Chantilly 492 offer a strong message about female authority and female teachings. This was particularly relevant, for at this time it was becoming increasingly clear that the king was never going to overcome his madness. Hence the problem of regency—and particularly the queen's ability to act as regent—was a chief concern.[91]

MS Chantilly 492 contains a number of works which develop the idea of female authority and sanction the transmission of wisdom from a female figure. For example, the *Epistre Othea* (*c.* 1400) is specifically oriented towards the education of a young prince (Hector) by a female figure (the goddess Othéa) and appears 'designed to exemplify the wisdom of women'.[92] Accordingly, it furnishes an excellent argument on the one hand for Ysabel's suitability as guide, counsellor, and teacher to the dauphin, and on the other for the wisdom transmitted by a female writer. Another work included in the manuscript is the first set of letters from the Debate over the *Roman de la Rose*. These are accompanied by a letter of dedication and explanation addressed to the queen (1402).[93] This letter introduces the Debate and submits it to the queen as an arbiter of higher authority. Christine asks Ysabel to approve her arguments in support of women and to provide 'saige et benigne correction' (wise and gentle correction).[94] Accordingly Christine attributes both authority and wisdom to Ysabel. Both as woman and as ruling queen, Ysabel has the experience and authority to judge the Debate and Christine's role within it as women's defender. In a last example, this manuscript also contains the *Enseignemens*, moral teachings that Christine composed for her son. By offering these to the queen, Christine emphasises Ysabel's role as Mother Queen of France, providing her with material and wisdom for the education of her own children, the future kings of France.[95] At the same time, she also reinforces her own authority as a writer and Voice of Wisdom.

Yet nowhere is Christine's support of the queen as a source of wisdom more evident than in the ways she links Ysabel's symbolic role to that of the Virgin Mary. In many of her works, Christine pairs Ysabel and Mary, developing the parallels between Heavenly Queen and her earthly counterpart.[96] This relationship is of particular consequence for the queen's suitability as regent: Christine uses references to the Virgin Mary as the 'ultimate coregent' in support of the queen's authority.[97] Adams, who rereads the *Cité des dames* as an argument for coregency, suggests that Christine's use of the Virgin in this work allows her to marry both terrestrial and spiritual authority through female agency. The *Cité des dames* both 'begins and ends with the Virgin Mary, a regent, a woman who ruled on behalf of her son'.[98] The fact that Christine then places Ysabel at the 'head of the good and generous princesses of France' is significant for it situates Ysabel in the leading position, 'first among female partners of the realm'.[99] She becomes Mary's counterpart on earth, a temporal authority, first among women in the contemporary terrestrial sphere.[100]

The *Epistre a la Royne*, also composed in 1405, develops further parallels between the wisdom of Ysabel and Mary. Where Mary is the Mother of all Christianity (*mere de toute christienté*), Ysabel, as a wise and good queen (*saige et bonne royne*), is her worldly equivalent, serving as the mother and comforter (*mere et conffortarresse*) of her subjects.[101] It is she who can mediate better than any other on their behalf.[102] Motherhood also plays an essential role here, for while Mary is the mother of Christ and hence of all Christianity, Ysabel is mother of the future rulers of France and by extension mother of all France. By drawing these parallels between Ysabel and Mary, Christine gives prominence to Ysabel's symbolic role, delineating and describing it for her audience. While the *Epistre a la Royne* is usually interpreted as Christine's urgent call to a reticent queen to act and mediate for peace, Adams argues that it can be read as a reminder directed to Christine's readers 'of the precedent for queenly intervention'.[103] The letter is thus intended to educate this public and enable them to push the warring factions, in this case the dukes of Orleans and Burgundy, to accept Ysabel as mediator and peacemaker.[104] It teaches them about the queen's role and 'bolster[s] support' for female regency.[105] Yet it also serves as a way to join both spiritual and temporal authority, constructing Ysabel herself as an allegorical figure, the Mother Queen of France.

Christine brings out this alliance between the female figure and Wisdom in her manuscripts both visually and textually. One of the best examples of this is in MS Harley 4431. This manuscript, the last compilation of Christine's collected works to be published under her direction, was also presented to the queen, most likely as a New Year gift in 1414.[106] Famous for its magnificent opening miniature which shows Christine's presentation of her book to the queen (fol. 3r), the manuscript takes on the theme of the book as a gift of wisdom.[107] Through textual and iconographic associations, many of the works contained within it show women, including Christine herself, as the bearers of Holy Wisdom. Of particular interest is the miniature heading the *Oroison de Nostre Dame* (*c.* 1402), a prayer to the Virgin that implores Mary's aid both for the royal family and for France and invokes the Virgin as a source of wisdom.[108]

The miniature, seen in Figure 5.1, shows the Virgin sitting with the Christ-child on her lap in a red-upholstered chair with lion's paw feet; Christine kneels to the Virgin's left, holding a written page in her hands as the visible representation of the prayer she offers. The image emphasises Mary's association with Holy Wisdom through colour symbolism and iconography. Wisdom was seen as part of a 'liturgical and exegetical tradition poised uneasily between Christ and Mary, affiliating Wisdom now with one and now with the other', and hence providing for a 'feminization of Christ and the divinization of Mary'.[109] Accordingly, the combination of the colours blue, which was associated with the Virgin from the twelfth century, and red, which recalled the 'blood spilled by and for Christ, and hence the passion, martyrdom, sacrifice and divine love', reflect the dual nature of Holy Wisdom and remind the viewer of the Virgin's connection to this figure.[110] The connection to Wisdom is also reinforced by the lion's paw feet on the chair, which are an allusion to the Throne of Solomon. This image creates a series of parallels, developing a metaphor that connects Christine's gift to the Virgin and Child. Just as Mary, in giving birth to Christ (the Word), gives the gift of salvation to the world, Christine gives birth to her work (her prayer and the manuscript in which it is contained) for the salvation of France.[111] In this, we come full circle: Christine, in her role as courtly poet—or now as *poète curiale*—serves as a unique intermediary between her patron, Ysabel, and the Holy Wisdom of the Virgin.[112] As Wisdom's Voice, her gift of her words and her book to the queen mirrors that given by the Virgin herself.[113] At the same time, as can be seen in the majesty of the book presentation scene at the beginning of the manuscript, Christine's gift also highlights Ysabel's role as model in her own right of female authority in whom Wisdom must reside.

Thus Christine, whose notion of what it means to work as a woman-scholar requires her to offer her knowledge to others and for the betterment of France, constructs a network of associations through her writing as well as partnerships to accomplish these goals. On the one hand, she calls attention to her name, linking herself to Christ-as-Wisdom as a way of authorising her own role in wisdom's transmission. Similarly, in her association with Ysabel of Bavaria, she also draws attention to symbolic aspects, linking Ysabel to Mary. The figure of the Virgin Mary serves to link temporal and spiritual realms, making possible the birth of Christ-as-Logos and thus the transmission of Holy Wisdom through Christine. The theme of motherhood also ties all three together: Mary incarnates the Word; Ysabel brings into the world the future leaders of France. Christine, who equates writing

Figure 5.1 Christine de Pizan kneels and offers her prayer to the Virgin seated with the Christ-child. *Oroison de Nostre Dame* in the 'Book of the Queen', *c.* 1410–14. London, British Library, MS Harley 4431, fol. 265r. © The British Library Board.

with giving birth, engenders wisdom in her writing and even a Wisdom text in the *Enseignemens* she composes for her son. Her construction of these associations allows her to deflect contemporary ambivalence about women as rulers and as writers, anchoring her work in the most orthodox of doctrines.

Conclusion

Christine de Pizan's decision to make a living as a writer was extraordinary for a woman in the late fourteenth and early fifteenth centuries and her work provides a fascinating window into her experiences. As a woman working in what was primarily a man's field, Christine suggests that Fortune transformed her into a man. Nevertheless, she reworks the male authorial role to suit herself and her abilities, making her female gender a fundamental part of her uniqueness as a writer. Christine herself becomes an essential component of her writing, both as author and as written example for others to follow. Even within the context of the *Epistres du debat sus le Rommant de la Rose* Christine stands as the lone female voice against the almost universal condemnation of women found in the *Rose* and condoned by her clerkly adversaries.

In the unusual circumstances of the power vacuum created by the madness of Charles VI, Christine plays a particularly important role. She follows her scholar father's model, becoming an advisor to princes; yet she expands this model to incorporate both genders, a necessity in a time when the normal power structure was not functional.[114] In becoming an advisor to the queen, she underlines the importance of the role Ysabel needed to play and educates her audience about female authority. She does this in part by emphasising the common experience of women and by depicting women—particularly Mary, Ysabel, and herself—as figures of Wisdom. Through visual and textual associations, she presents all three allegorically: Mary as Heavenly paradigm for female authority, Ysabel as Mother Queen and earthly representative of that authority, and Christine herself as the Voice of Wisdom who serves as intermediary between the courtly and heavenly realms. Christine, as writer and as Voice of Wisdom, manifests her love for her adopted country and demonstrates the value both of women's work and women's wisdom.

Notes

1 Christine de Pizan, *Le livre de la mutacion de fortune*, ed. Suzanne Solente, 4 vols. (Paris: Picard, 1959–66), 1:53 (v. 1393).

2 Christine de Pizan, *Le livre de l'advision Cristine*, ed. Christine Reno and Liliane Dulac (Paris: Champion, 2001), 100–01 (III.6); Charity Cannon Willard, *Christine de Pizan: Her Life and Works* (New York: Persea Books, 1984), 39–40.

3 Pizan, *Mutacion de fortune*, 1: 12 (vv. 141–43). Pizan, *Mutacion de fortune*, 1:53 (vv. 1388–94).

4 Pizan, *Advision*, 111 (III.11). She also notes the effect of novelty in her letter to Pierre Col during the Debate of the *Roman de la Rose* on those who wanted her works: they were 'esmerveillés de mon labour, non pour grandeur qui y fait mais pour le cas nouvel qui n'est accoustumé' (astonished by my labour, not for any greatness to be found there, but because of its novelty, which is out of the ordinary). 'A maistre Pierre Col, secretaire du roy nostre sire', in Christine de Pisan, Jean Gerson,

Jean de Montreuil, Gontier et Pierre Col, *Le Débat sur le Roman de la Rose*, ed. Eric Hicks (Genève: Slatkine Reprints, 1996), 148. English translation from Christine de Pizan, *Debate of the 'Romance of the Rose'*, trans. and ed. David F. Hult (Chicago: University of Chicago Press, 2010), 191.

5 See Charity Cannon Willard, 'Christine de Pizan as Teacher', *Romance Languages Annual* 3 (1992). See also Roberta Krueger, 'Christine's Anxious Lessons: Gender, Morality and the Social Order from the *Enseignements* to the *Avision*', in *Christine de Pizan and the Categories of Difference*, ed. Marilynn Desmond (Minneapolis: University of Minnesota Press, 1998); as well as Astrik L. Gabriel, 'The Educational Ideas of Christine De Pisan', *Journal of the History of Ideas* 16 (1955).

6 Cf. Jacqueline Cerquiglini-Toulet, 'Fondements et fondations de l'écriture chez Christine de Pizan. Scènes de lecture et scènes d'incarnation', in *The City of Scholars. New Approaches to Christine de Pizan*, ed. Margarete Zimmermann and Dina De Rentiis (Berlin: Walter de Gruyter, 1994), 80–82, 84.

7 Pizan, *Advision*, 111 (III.10); Charity C. Willard, 'A Fifteenth-Century View of Women's Role in Medieval Society: Christine de Pizan's *Livre des Trois Vertus*', in *The Role of Woman in the Middle Ages*, ed. Rosmarie T. Morewedge (Albany: State University of New York, 1975), 94.

8 Barbara Hanawalt, 'Introduction', in *Women and Work in Preindustrial Europe*, ed. Barbara Hanawalt (Bloomington: Indiana University Press, 1986), x.

9 Pizan, *Advision*, 108 (III.8); Christine's Vision, trans. Glenda McLeod (New York: Garland Pub., 1993), 117.

10 Willard, *Life and Works*, 203–05. Christine de Pizan, *La città delle dame*, ed. Earl Jeffrey Richards, trans. Patrizia Caraffi (Milan: Luni, 1998), 316 (II.36).

11 Pizan, *Advision*, 107–08 (III.8).

12 Hanawalt, 'Introduction', xi. Simone Roux, *Christine de Pizan: Femme de tête, dame de cœur* (Paris: Payot, 2006), 65.

13 Pizan, *Advision*, 98 (III.4), 100 (III.6).

14 Willard, *Life and Works*, 39–40; Nicolae Iorga, *Philippe de Mézières, 1327–1405* (London: Variorum Reprints, 1973), 510 n. 5.

15 Roux, *Christine de Pizan*, 67.

16 Roux, *Christine de Pizan*, 67.

17 Willard, 'A Fifteenth-Century View', 94.

18 Gilbert Ouy and Christine Reno, 'Identification des autographes de Christine de Pizan', *Scriptorium* 34 (1980): 226.

19 Ouy and Reno, 'Autographes', 222. See also Gilbert Ouy, Christine Reno, and Inès Villela-Petit, *Album Christine de Pizan* (Turnhout: Brepols, 2012), 25.

20 Glenda McLeod, 'Introduction', Pizan, *Christine's Vision*, xlv.

21 Bronislaw Geremek, *Le salariat dans l'artisanat parisien aux XIIIe–XVe siècles: étude sur le marché de la main-d'œuvre au Moyen Âge* (Paris: Mouton & Co, 1968); Richard H. Rouse and Mary A. Rouse, *Manuscripts and their Makers: Commercial Book Producers in Medieval Paris, 1200–1500*, 2 vols. (Turnhout: Harvey Miller, 2000), 1:237.

22 Willard, 'A Fifteenth-Century View', 95.

23 Willard, 'A Fifteenth-Century View', 94–95.

24 Willard, 'A Fifteenth-Century View', 94.

25 On the spelling of the queen's name, see Lori Walters, 'The Book as a Gift of Wisdom: The *Chemin de lonc estude* in the Queen's Manuscript, London, British

Library, Harley 4431', *Digital Philology* 5 (2016): 229 n. 7. I am very grateful for the author's generosity in sharing an early version of this article with me.

26 'La Premiere epistre, a la royne de France' in *Débat*, 5. Martha Breckenridge, 'Christine de Pizan's "Livre d'epitre d'Othea a Hector" at the Intersection of Image and Text' (Ph.D. diss., University of Kansas, 2008), 29. Cf. also Roux, *Christine de Pizan*, 92; Andrea Tarnowski, 'Introduction', in Christine de Pizan, *Le chemin de longue étude*, trans. and ed. Andrea Tarnowski (Paris: Librairie générale française, 2000), 12; Eric Hicks and Thérèse Moreau, 'L'*Epistre à la Reine* de Christine de Pizan (1405)', *Clio. Histoire, femmes et sociétés* 5 (1997): n. 1. On the role of the *chamberiere*, see Walters, 'Book', 229 n. 12. See also Patrick M. de Winter, *La bibliothèque de Philippe le Hardi, duc de Bourgogne: 1364–1404. Étude sur les manuscrits à peintures d'une collection princière à l'époque du style gothique international* (Paris: Centre national de la recherche scientifique, 1985), 14, 19.

27 Olivier Delsaux, et al., 'Le premier recueil de la Reine', in *Christine de Pizan et son époque*, ed. Danielle Buschinger (Amiens: Centre d'études médiévales, Université de Picardie-Jules Verne, 2012), 49–50.

28 Gilbert Ouy, Letter to Olivier Delsaux, quoted in Delsaux, et al., 'Le premier recueil', 51–52; Ouy, Reno, and Villela-Petit, *Album*, 22–38, 739–40.

29 Ouy, Reno, and Villela-Petit, *Album*, 173, 173–85.

30 Pizan, *Advision*, 111 (III.10).

31 Pizan, *Advision*, 111 (III.10). English translations are mine unless otherwise noted.

32 Pizan, *Advision*, 111 (III.10).

33 Ouy and Reno, 'Autographes', 222.

34 Pizan, *Advision*, 111 (III.10). Cf. James Laidlaw, 'Christine de Pizan: A Publisher's Progress', *Modern Language Review* 82 (1987): 37.

35 Ouy and Reno, 'Autographes', 222.

36 Pizan, *La città delle dame*, 192 (I.41). English translation from Christine de Pizan, *The Book of the City of Ladies*, trans. Earl Jeffrey Richards, rev. edn. (New York: Persea Books, 1998), 85. Anastaise is known to us only through Christine's references to her in the *Cité des dames*.

37 *La città delle dame*, 192 (I.41).

38 See for example, the family of Nicolas d'Etampes. Rouse and Rouse, *Manuscripts and their Makers*, 1:116–19.

39 Rouse and Rouse, *Manuscripts and their Makers*, 1:236–37.

40 Rouse and Rouse, *Manuscripts and their Makers*, 1:237.

41 Pizan, *Advision*, 111 (III.11).

42 Pizan, *Mutacion de fortune*, 1:16 (vv. 260–84).

43 'lesquelz de leur grace comme princes benignes et tres humains les virent voulentiers et receurent a joie—et plus, comme je tiens, pour la chose non usagee que femme escripse, comme pieça n'avenist, que pour la digneté que y ssoit'. (These they willingly saw and by their grace joyfully received like kind and gentle princes, and more I think for the novelty of a woman who could write (since that had not occurred for quite some time) than for any worth there might be in them.) Pizan, *Advision*, 111 (III.11). English translation from Pizan, *Christine's Vision*, 120.

44 Christine does not name these critics directly, choosing instead to designate them as 'aucuns' (certain people). Pizan, *Advision*, 88 (II.22).

45 Pizan, *Advision*, 88 (II.22).

46 Cerquiglini-Toulet, 'Fondements', 82–83.
47 Ilse Paakkinen, 'The Metaphysics of Gender in Christine de Pizan's Thought', in *Gender in Late Medieval and Early Modern Europe*, ed. Marianna G. Muravyeva and Raisa Maria Toivo (New York: Routledge, 2013), 45.
48 Susan Schibanoff, 'Taking the Gold out of Egypt: The Art of Reading as a Woman', in *Gender and Reading: Essays on Readers, Texts, and Contexts*, ed. Elizabeth A. Flynn and Patrocinio P. Schweickart (Baltimore: Johns Hopkins University Press, 1986), 99.
49 Pizan, *Mutacion de fortune*, 1:14 (vv. 211–20).
50 Pizan, *Mutacion de Fortune*, 1:21 (vv. 413–19).
51 Pizan, *La città delle dame*, 316 (II.36). Pizan, *Advision*, 108 (III.8). Pizan, *Mutacion de fortune*, 1:46 (vv. 1165–66).
52 Jacqueline Cerquiglini, 'The Stranger', in *The Selected Writings of Christine de Pizan: New Translations, Criticism*, ed. Renate Blumenfeld-Kosinski, trans. Renate Blumenfeld-Kosinski and Kevin Brownlee (New York: W.W. Norton & Co., 1997), 270.
53 Catherine Attwood, 'Fortune et le "moi" écrivant à la fin du Moyen Âge: autour de la *Mutacion de fortune* de Christine de Pizan', *Nottingham French Studies* 38 (1999): 26; Mary Anne Case, 'Christine de Pizan and the Authority of Experience', in *Christine de Pizan and the Categories of Difference*, ed. Marilynn Desmond (Minneapolis: University of Minnesota Press, 1998), 71, 84.
54 Attwood, 'Fortune et le "moi" ', 26.
55 Attwood, 'Fortune et le "moi" ', 30.
56 Pizan, *Mutacion de fortune*, 1:7 (vv. 1–8). English translation from *The Selected Writings of Christine de Pizan*, ed. Blumenfeld-Kosinski, 89. Emphasis mine.
57 See Attwood, 'Fortune et le "moi" ', 26.
58 Cf. Cerquiglini-Toulet, 'Fondements', 80–82, 84.
59 Jacqueline Cerquiglini, 'Introduction', in *Christine de Pizan: Cent ballades d'amant et de dame*, ed. Jacqueline Cerquiglini (Paris: Union générale d'éditions, 1982), 14.
60 Cerquiglini, 'Introduction', 14.
61 Pizan, *Advision*, 110 (III.10).
62 Cerquiglini, 'Introduction', 14.
63 Walters, 'Book', 231.
64 Christine de Pizan, *Le chemin de longue étude*, trans. and ed. Tarnowski, 88–90 (vv. 28, 53–54). English translation mine.
65 Marilynn Desmond, 'The *Querelle de la Rose* and the Ethics of Reading', in *Christine de Pizan: A Casebook*, ed. Barbara K. Altman and Deborah L. McGrady (New York: Routledge, 2003), 168; David F. Hult, 'Introduction', in *Debate of the 'Romance of the Rose'*, trans. and ed. Hult, 2–3.
66 Barbara Newman, *Sister of Wisdom: St. Hildegard's Theology of the Feminine* (Berkeley: University of California Press, 1997), 2–3.
67 Cf. Georgiana Donavin, *Scribit Mater: Mary and the Language Arts in the Literature of Medieval England* (Washington, DC: Catholic University of America Press, 2012), 4–5; Laura Saetveit Miles, 'The Origins and Development of the Virgin Mary's Book at the Annunciation', *Speculum* 89 (2014): 668.
68 Cf. Gérard Gros, '"Mon oroison entens…". Étude sur les trois opuscules pieux de Christine de Pizan', *Bien dire et bien aprandre* 8 (1990): 101.

69 Christine de Pizan, *Le livre des trois vertus. Édition critique*, ed. Charity Cannon Willard and Eric Hicks, (Paris: H. Champion, 1989), 111 (I.27); Christine de Pizan, *The Treasure of the City of Ladies or the Book of the Three Virtues*, trans. Sarah Lawson (London: Penguin, 1985), 99.
70 Pizan, *Livre des trois vertus*, 171 (III.1).
71 Pizan, *La città delle dame*, 412–14 (II.65); Pizan, *City of Ladies*, 207–08.
72 Pizan, *Livre des trois vertus*, 225–26 (Fin); Pizan, *Treasure of the City of Ladies*, 180. Emphasis mine.
73 Pizan, *Livre des trois vertus*, 11 (I.2).
74 Walters argues that Christine offers Harley 4431 as a gift of wisdom to the queen. Walters, 'Book', 229.
75 Christine never calls the *Enseignemens* the 'Enseignemens moraulx', but names it the 'notables moraulx' or the 'enseignemens'. I follow her final appellation of it, found in Harley 4431, fol. 261v. Ellen Thorington, 'Figures de la Sagesse et de l'autorité féminine. L'exemple des Enseignemens de Christine de Pizan', *Le Moyen Français* 78–79 (2016): 223 n. 2.
76 Pizan, *Mutacion de fortune*, 1:20 (vv. 374–78); Christine de Pizan, 'The Book of Fortune's Transformation', in *The Selected Writings of Christine de Pizan*, ed. Blumenfeld-Kosinski, trans. Blumenfeld-Kosinski and Brownlee, 94.
77 Lori Walters, 'Signatures and Anagrams in the Queen's Manuscript (London, British Library, Harley MS 4431)', (2012). Accessed August 17, 2017. www.pizan.lib.ed.ac.uk/waltersanagrams.html. See also Cerquiglini, 'The Stranger', 274.
78 Joan M. Ferrante, *Woman as Image in Medieval Literature from the Twelfth Century to Dante* (Durham, NC: Labyrinth Press, 1985), 4.
79 Christine herself often plays a dual role of both author and character within works such as the *Chemin de longue étude*. As writer she is responsible for the transmission of the words that contain the message borne by Christine-the-character to the French court. See Walters, 'Book', 231.
80 Cf. R.C. Famiglietti, *Royal Intrigue: Crisis at the Court of Charles VI, 1392–1420* (New York: AMS Press, 1986), 7.
81 Walters, 'Book', 232.
82 On the idea of female-female partnership, see Walters, 'Book', 233–35, 237.
83 Tracy Adams, 'Christine de Pizan, Isabeau of Bavaria, and Female Regency', *French Historical Studies* 32 (2009): 26.
84 Adams, 'Regency', 4, 27; Tracy Adams, *The Life and Afterlife of Isabeau of Bavaria* (Baltimore: Johns Hopkins University Press, 2010), 80–83. Cf. Pizan, *Livre des trois vertus*, 7–120 (I).
85 Adams, 'Regency', 3.
86 Walters, 'Book', 237.
87 Walters, 'Book', 237.
88 The first volume of the manuscript dates to 1399–1402; the second volume, MS 493, to between 1403 and *c.* 1405. Ouy, Reno, and Villela-Petit, *Album*, 190, 205.
89 Delsaux, et al., 'Le premier recueil', 51–52.
90 Adams, 'Regency', 25. See also Joyce Coleman, *Public Reading and the Reading Public in Late Medieval England and France* (Cambridge: Cambridge University Press, 1996), 95–97; Pizan, *Livre des trois vertus*, 50 (I.12).
91 Adams, 'Regency', 9–17. See also Adams, *Life.*

92 Bonnie A. Birk, *Christine de Pizan and Biblical Wisdom: A Feminist-Theological Point of View* (Milwaukee, WI: Marquette University Press, 2005), 65.
93 Pizan, *Debate of the 'Romance of the Rose'*, 99 n. 129.
94 *Débat*, 6, l. 42.
95 Cf. Ellen M. Thorington, 'Le "lait de sagesse": les *Enseignemens moraux* de Christine de Pizan comme legs civique', in *Le legs des pères et le lait des mères ou comment se raconte le genre dans la parenté du Moyen-Âge au XXIème siècle*, ed. Isabelle Ortega and Marc-Jean Filaire-Ramos (Turnhout: Brepols, 2014).
96 Walters, 'Book', 232.
97 Adams, 'Regency', 3.
98 Adams, 'Regency', 26.
99 Adams, 'Regency', 26.
100 Cf. Adams' discussion of the *Goldenes Rössl*. Adams, *Life*, 110–11; see also 104–12.
101 Christine de Pizan, *The 'Epistle of the Prison of Human Life', with 'An Epistle to the Queen of France' and 'Lament on the Evils of the Civil War'*, trans. and ed. Josette Wisman (New York: Garland, 1984), 78.
102 Adams, 'Regency', 30.
103 Adams, *Life*, 189; Adams, 'Regency'.
104 Adams, *Life*, 189; Adams, 'Regency'.
105 Adams, 'Regency', 24–25.
106 Ouy, Reno, and Villela-Petit, *Album*, 319; James Laidlaw, 'The Date of the Queen's MS (London, British Library, Harley MS 4431)', (2005): 7. Accessed August 17, 2017. www.pizan.lib.ed.ac.uk/harley4431date.pdf. On the gift of books and manuscripts for *étrennes*, see Brigitte Buettner, 'Past Presents: New Year's Gifts at the Valois Courts, ca. 1400', *The Art Bulletin* 83 (2001): 604.
107 London, British Library, Harley MS 4431. Images of the manuscript are available online: James Laidlaw, 'Christine de Pizan: The Making of the Queen's Manuscript (London, British Library, Harley MS 4431)', Edinburgh University Library. Accessed August 17, 2017. www.pizan.lib.ed.ac.uk/. For the manuscript as a gift of wisdom, see Walters, 'Book', 229.
108 Cf. Thorington, 'Le "lait de sagesse"', 56–60.
109 Barbara Newman, *God and the Goddesses: Vision, Poetry, and Belief in the Middle Ages* (Philadelphia: University of Pennsylvania Press, 2002), 193.
110 Michel Pastoureau, *Blue: The History of a Color*, trans. Markus I. Cruse (Princeton: Princeton University Press, 2001), 37, 50. See the representations of Wisdom in New York, Morgan Library and Museum, MS M. 791, fol. 288r, and New York, Morgan Library and Museum, MS M. 392, fol. 239r.
111 Thorington, 'Lait', 60. Walters, 'Book', 234–35.
112 Gros, 'Oroison', 101.
113 Walters, 'Book', 232.
114 Walters, 'Book', 233.

Select bibliography

Adams, Tracy. 'Christine de Pizan, Isabeau of Bavaria, and Female Regency'. *French Historical Studies* 32 (2009): 1–32.

——— *The Life and Afterlife of Isabeau of Bavaria*. Baltimore: Johns Hopkins University Press, 2010.

Attwood, Catherine. 'Fortune et le "moi" écrivant à la fin du Moyen Âge: autour de la *Mutacion de fortune* de Christine de Pizan'. *Nottingham French Studies* 38 (1999): 25–43.

Case, Mary Anne C. 'Christine de Pizan and the Authority of Experience'. In *Christine de Pizan and the Categories of Difference*, ed. Marilynn Desmond, 71–87. Minneapolis: University of Minnesota Press, 1998.

Cerquiglini, Jacqueline. 'Introduction'. In *Christine de Pizan: Cent ballades d'amant et de dame*, ed. Jacqueline Cerquiglini, xi–xlvi. Paris: Union générale d'éditions, 1982.

Cerquiglini-Toulet, Jacqueline. 'Fondements et fondations de l'écriture chez Christine de Pizan. Scènes de lecture et scènes d'incarnation'. In *The City of Scholars. New Approaches to Christine de Pizan*, ed. Margarete Zimmermann and Dina De Rentiis, 79–96. Berlin: Walter de Gruyter, 1994.

Gros, Gérard. '"Mon oroison entens ...": Étude sur les trois opuscules pieux de Christine de Pizan'. *Bien dire et bien aprandre* 8 (1990): 99–112.

Hanawalt, Barbara. 'Introduction'. In *Women and Work in Preindustrial Europe*, ed. Barbara Hanawalt, vii–xviii. Bloomington: Indiana University Press, 1986.

Hult, David F. 'Introduction'. In *Debate of the Romance of the Rose*, trans. and ed. David F. Hult, 1–25. Chicago: University of Chicago Press, 2010.

Newman, Barbara. *Sister of Wisdom: St. Hildegard's Theology of the Feminine*. Berkeley: University of California Press, 1997.

Ouy, Gilbert, and Christine Reno. 'Identification des autographes de Christine de Pizan'. *Scriptorium* 34 (1980): 221–38.

Ouy, Gilbert, Christine Reno, and Inès Villela-Petit. *Album Christine de Pizan*. Turnhout: Brepols, 2012.

Paakkinen, Ilse. 'The Metaphysics of Gender in Christine de Pizan's Thought'. In *Gender in Late Medieval and Early Modern Europe*, ed. Marianna G. Muravyeva and Raisa Maria Toivo, 37–52. New York: Routledge, 2013.

Rouse, Richard H., and Mary A. Rouse. *Manuscripts and their Makers: Commercial Book Producers in Medieval Paris, 1200–1500*. 2 vols. Turnhout: Harvey Miller, 2000.

Roux, Simone. *Christine de Pizan: Femme de tête, dame de cœur*. Paris: Payot, 2006.

Thorington, Ellen M. 'Figures de la Sagesse et de l'autorité féminine. L'exemple des *Enseignemens* de Christine de Pizan'. *Le Moyen Français* 78–79 (2016): 223–39.

———'Le "lait de sagesse": les *Enseignemens moraux* de Christine de Pizan comme legs civique'. In *Le legs des pères et le lait des mères ou comment se raconte le genre dans la parenté du Moyen Âge au XXIème siècle*, ed. Isabelle Ortega and Marc-Jean Filaire-Ramos, 45–63. Turnhout: Brepols, 2014.

Walters, Lori. 'The Book as a Gift of Wisdom: The *Chemin de lonc estude* in the Queen's Manuscript, London, British Library, Harley 4431'. *Digital Philology* 5 (2016): 228–46.

Willard, Charity C. 'A Fifteenth-Century View of Women's Role in Medieval Society: Christine de Pizan's *Livre des Trois Vertus*'. In *The Role of Woman in the Middle Ages*, ed. Rosmarie T. Morewedge, 90–120. Albany: State University of New York, 1975.

6 Home work

The bourgeois wife in later medieval England

Jeremy Goldberg

This chapter will consider the bourgeois wife, that is the wife of the urban craftsman or merchant running his own business and employing labour, in rather general terms, but I will begin with one specific wife about whom we know somewhat more than most. In the last years of the fourteenth and early years of the fifteenth century, Agnes, wife to the York mason Hugh Grantham, managed a relatively substantial and well-furnished house, supervised live-in servants, raised a son, attended diligently to her devotions, and ran a substantial brewing business. In some ways Agnes is not entirely typical of the wives of late medieval urban artisans. First, her husband, by reason of his craft, would regularly have worked away from home; for most artisans and their wives the workshop and the home were essentially one and the same and husbands would not have 'gone out' to work. Much the same is true of numbers of mercantile households. Second, Agnes is unusually well documented. A detailed probate inventory in respect of her husband, who predeceased her, survives, as do the comparatively full records of a matrimonial action in the ecclesiastical Court of York from only months after her husband's death. This last tells how she fled the family home to avoid the attention of one John Dale, who had abducted and probably raped her in an attempt to secure her agreement to marry him.[1] In many ways, however, Agnes reflects wider experience: the bourgeois wife was a home maker, a domestic manager, an economic partner, a sexual partner, and a mother. To understand 'work' in relation to the lives of such women by privileging the economic partnership alone and interrogating what craft or trade activity a woman might participate in seems both to undervalue the full range of activities that the bourgeois wife had to juggle and to disregard the value of their labour as home makers, as mothers, and as spouses. This present chapter is an attempt to view this range of activities holistically.

Documenting the bourgeois wife

Craft or, as I will tend to refer to them, artisanal households and mercantile households were at the very heart of the urban economy. They also played a key role in governance since householders were expected to exercise control over dependent members of the household.[2] Trade, manufacture, and commerce were largely dependent upon these households and, indeed, very often physically located within them. Within a pre-industrial economy, craft workshops, which might double as retail spaces, were often physically part of the house.[3] Even activities such as metal working, tanning, and dyeing were undertaken in relatively close proximity of the main dwelling. Mercantile traders often used the upper rooms of their houses as secure storage space and customers were invited into the house to view stock or negotiate terms.[4] Only a privileged minority—in essence men who headed artisanal and mercantile households—enjoyed the status of citizens or burgesses; they alone had automatic rights to run retail premises and to take on and train apprentices.[5] In larger towns and cities some third of households can be identified as artisanal or mercantile, often characterised by the presence of live-in servants.[6] Many of the remaining two thirds of households would have been dependent on these privileged households for employment and even some meals. Many artisanal and mercantile households engaged journeymen, who did not live with their employers and might be married with families of their own. These workers would be provided with meals during the working day.[7] Numbers of others, particularly women pieceworkers, such as carders, spinsters, and seamstresses, were employed by mercantile households following a proto-industrial model.[8] We should also notice numbers of petty retailers such as hucksters of bread and tapsters or barmaids, who likewise owed their livelihoods to mercantile and artisanal employers.

From a documentary perspective the artisanal and mercantile households just described were primarily associated with male householders, who were themselves identified by a craft or trade. Thus the Grantham household in Petergate, York, would have been identified as the household headed by Hugh Grantham, mason. It is Hugh's name, not Agnes', that is listed in the city's franchise register, even though Agnes ran a substantial brewing business in her own right.[9] It is Hugh, likewise, who would have been expected to exercise order and discipline over his *mesnie*—that is, his household dependents—and Hugh who would have taken responsibility for household debts. This comparative documentary invisibility of wives is, however, but one facet of a larger and more nuanced story. The documentary record is often concerned primarily with the public identity of the householder, with whom rested formal responsibility for the ways in which the activities of the household impinged upon the public sphere. The actual internal dynamics of the household are both more complex, but also more difficult to recover.

The problem of documentation is graphically illustrated in respect of evidence for the wives of artisans assisting their husbands in his craft. There exists little substantive evidence to show that wives normally worked as craft helpers. A witness in a matrimonial cause within the ecclesiastical Court of York explained, by way of upholding the reputation of another key witness, that Juliana del Grene made her livelihood as a carder of wool and by following 'the craft of the saddler with her husband' and that she and another key witness had 'goods to the value of ten pounds' in the form of 'silver and household utensils'.[10] The implication was that she was an honest, hard-working woman of some means and thus unlikely to have been bribed, but it also provides a rare statement that this particular wife assisted her husband in his craft. The statement is all the more valuable because other indicators are that the leather trades, including saddlery, tended to favour male labour in contrast to the textile or victualling trades.[11] A second example is slightly more oblique. In the last years of the fourteenth century, the founders' craft of York registered ordinances before the mayor and these were duly entered into the city's *A/Y Memorandum Book*. One clause concerned apprentices. In order to ensure that apprentices were adequately trained, to protect against an oversupply of prospective craft masters, and to prevent masters using apprentices as a source of cheap labour to undercut their fellow craft members, provisions to limit the number of apprentices a master was allowed at any one moment were commonplace at this date. Entirely atypically, however, the founders added a rider. Giles de Bonoyne was permitted a second apprentice 'because he has no wife'.[12] Why should Giles be permitted an extra apprentice merely because he lacked a wife? Implicitly because he had lost his wife—he would not have set up in trade in the first place without a spouse to help him, so it is hardly likely that he had simply never married; without a wife to assist him, he was short of help in the workshop and taking on an additional apprentice offered a form of compensation for this. Clearly he could simply have hired additional labour from a skilled journeyman, but in the high-wage economy at the end of the fourteenth century, an additional apprentice represented an inexpensive and—because resident with the employer—highly dependable extra pair of hands. The third example reinforces the second. The Coventry cappers' ordinances of 1496 provided that 'no persone of the Craft teche no point of his Craft to no persone save to his prentes [apprentice] and his wife'.[13] We may also note that both the York curriers' ordinances of 1424 and the undated tapiters' ordinances made explicit reference to wives working in the craft.[14]

These few documentary examples can be set alongside the literary evidence of the conduct text 'How the Goodwife Taught her Daughter'. Although in origin this poem predated the plague, it seems to have circulated in urban and particularly metropolitan contexts for the next couple of centuries. The text appears in household compilations where it is likely to have been used to socialise adolescent girls for marriage and becoming householders in their own right. In so doing, it offers guidance on how a bourgeois wife and mistress of a household should behave—indeed Felicity Riddy has argued that the text may first have been used as much to socialise wives and mothers as adolescent servant girls living away from home.[15] The extant versions of the text are not only found in what appear to have been urban manuscripts, but the variant versions of the text imagine an artisanal household where the mistress has some oversight of servants, and where there is a workshop and some sense of an urban identity. There is, however, nothing that would make the text incongruous in a rural artisanal household. The important point here is that the imaginary wife is told that she must assist in the workshop when the need arises. She is also advised that, in her husband's absence, she should lock up the workshop at the end of the day, in addition to directing the servants—a generic term for all employees which does not necessarily imply live-in servants alone—and ensuring that all are properly and promptly paid their wages.[16] We should be wary of reading conduct literature as a simple mirror of social practice, but in the light of the York and Coventry evidence it suggests at least a cultural expectation that the bourgeois wife was to be present in the workshop at least some of the time and that this was understood as very much part of such a wife's identity.

'How the Goodwife', as a text directed at adolescents likely in service, provides another clue as to how and why wives of artisans were in a position to make a useful contribution in the workshop. Whereas young men who aspired to becoming craft masters with workshops of their own often found positions as apprentices, relatively few women were apprenticed formally and then only in a very restricted range of occupations around embroidery and working in silk. It is likely that outside of London the female apprentice was a rarity.[17] Going into service—that is, living in an artisanal or mercantile household on contracts that normally ran for a year at a time, though sometimes longer—was a common experience for girls growing up within urban communities. This was also true for many girls born in the countryside who were sent to town as adolescents.[18] Employers provided food, clothing and a place to sleep.[19] They also provided informal training in a whole range of household and craft skills, moral guidance and advice, which could be reinforced by discipline. Occasionally they physically or sexually abused their charges, but also, we suspect, in some instances provided genuine affection.[20] Servants provided general labour. The particular boon to their employers in the labour-starved decades of the later fourteenth and early fifteenth centuries was that their labour was both cheap and dependable. Although servants had time off—the slight evidence points particularly to evenings and holidays (holy days)—they were in principle always at their employers' beck and call. Contracts could be renewed when both servant and employer were satisfied with one another, but the servant girl was normally free to leave after a year in the hope of finding better terms and conditions. Equally, the employer who took on a girl barely in her teens to help mind the children and run errands may not have found her so useful once she had grown into a young adult.

Learning to become a bourgeois wife

The informality of the training provided to adolescent and young adult women by the institution of life-cycle service makes it much less visible in the records. We have, however, a few clues. Depositions from the Court of York show female servants assisting in a mercantile shop and helping to carry goods to a customer's home. A tanner's male employee remembered having to fetch water from the river—necessary for both domestic and industrial use—while a female servant was temporarily absent. From yet another case we glimpse a female servant lighting candles and tucking a woman up in bed at night.[21] An erotically charged poem, 'The Serving Maid's Holiday', which appears rural and agricultural in context, ostensibly tells us of all the tasks the female servant is able to leave aside—and the few she still has to complete—because she has the day off. These include both domestic tasks, such as sweeping floors, preparing rushes, and kneading, and economic activities, including weaving, spinning, and milking the cow.[22] The important point is that the female servant was expected to learn and to perform a wide range of tasks. Whereas the male apprentice might, and did, complain vociferously if he were diverted from craft activity to menial tasks, the female servant was expected to juggle tasks without complaint and as directed.[23] That some of the time these tasks made her an integral part of the workshop is indirectly, but tellingly, suggested by the propensity of many workshops to employ some female servants in the later fourteenth century when labour was scarce. This was an era of labour shortage consequent upon the ravages of the Black Death and subsequent epidemics which consequently particularly advantaged women in the labour force. Textile, victualling, and mercantile households seem particularly to have preferred female over male servants (including apprentices). This pattern was, however, eroded during the course of the fifteenth century as the economy contracted and the resultant growth in competition for work tended to marginalise women workers. By the later fifteenth century artisanal households tended no longer to employ female servants, who came to be largely concentrated in mercantile households. These last may have employed numbers of servants as a mark of wealth and status, but perhaps primarily as domestic help or shop assistants.[24] As the female employee moved between households during the course of her adolescence, she probably also worked in more than one type of workshop. It follows that women were effectively trained as teenagers and young adults to assist in a range of domestic and craft activities, but also to be versatile and adaptable so as to fit within whatever workshop she subsequently married into.

The corollary of this period of socialisation in the years prior to marriage was that women who had had experience as servants, at least in the century following the Black Death, would have been well grounded both in the skills needed to run a home, but also in those transferable skills—and the capacity to learn—that would be of value in the workshop regardless of their eventual husband's occupation. Scholars who doubt the extent to which women were involved in craft production or trade may point to the exiguous nature of the evidence for female apprentices, the like paucity of evidence for women admitted as burgesses or citizens—and hence able to set up shop and train apprentices—in their own right, and the lack of reference to women in guild ordinances. But this is an optical illusion. Young bourgeois women were neither socialised nor expected to set up workshops and businesses in their own right, but they were socialised and expected to marry men who did. Moreover the young woman who had spent time in service was likely seen as an asset by a young man seeking to find a wife to help him run a business. Certainly there is plenty of evidence that former servants, including male apprentices, tended to marry other former servants, having sometimes conducted courtships while in service.[25] The evidence showing that the widows of artisans regularly continued to manage the workshop following their husbands' deaths strengthens this argument, though once again this seems to have become less common by the later fifteenth century. Indeed numbers of later fourteenth-century craft ordinances recorded in the *A/Y Memorandum Book* kept by the civic government in York were attested by female craft members, all presumably widows.[26]

Contributing to the familial economy

As the example of Juliana del Grene immediately demonstrates, the direct economic contribution of wives to the household economy was not confined to assisting husbands in their trade. We are told that Juliana worked in 'kempstercraft' or the carding of wool. Carding and spinning were primary processes necessary to support textile production. They were seen as quintessentially women's work that girls probably learned from an early age. Indeed most women would have engaged in one or the other since the product of a single weaver demanded the production of many spinsters and carders. In practice, however, we tend to know more about women whose livelihood was dependent on spinning than about married women who spun to supplement the familial economy. The 1395 inventory of Robert de Crakall, another York mason, itemises eight stones of wool, two pairs of cards (for carding), and three wheels—implicitly spinning wheels in the chamber—alongside various beds, bedding, clothing, and a cradle, a pattern that suggests that women socialised together while engaged in spinning and perhaps keeping an eye on the baby.[27] In several other inventories, spinning wheels and cards are located in the hall, which could indicate that carding and spinning were activities carried on, *inter alia*, alongside recreational activity of an evening.[28] Spinning, however, was probably primarily a daytime activity. Depositions from a later fourteenth-century disputed marriage case from York tell us how from the doorway of the hall, Mariota de Walde, her friend Margaret, and her husband's apprentice John listened in on Mariota's husband and his mistress, his servant Joan, in the adjacent garden. When her husband made to come in, Mariota rushed to her spinning wheel in the hall. John was not so lucky. His master chased him into the garden and struck him hard on the foot with a staff.[29]

Brewing was another activity that numbers of young women would have gained knowledge of as servants, but with which again some girls migrating from the countryside might well have been familiar from childhood. Agnes Grantham, for example, employed female servants in her brewing business and brewing seems to have been very much a female activity in better-off peasant households.[30] Once again York probate inventories demonstrate that a number of well-to-do artisanal households engaged in brewing alongside the craft activity of the household head, though some of the largest enterprises were, like the Grantham household, associated with masons whose work necessarily regularly took them outside the home and whose wives would probably not have been particularly active in the trade. This is true of the households of Robert de Crakall and the Beverley mason, John Cadeby, but separate brewhouses are also found in the homes of a barber, a baker, a girdler, a merchant, and a skinner.[31]

Other commercial activities on the part of wives undertaken independently of their husbands are still harder to notice. Margery Kempe, who had turned her hand to brewing supposedly without success, briefly managed a horse-mill in the earlier fifteenth century, but we would not know this from Lynn's extant administrative or probate records.[32] At much the same date Robert Schylbotyll of Scarborough appears to have managed a hostelry, and owned a horse and a horse-mill, but there is nothing to indicate whether his wife managed this part of the business, brewed in the brewhouse, or helped by seeing to guests and ensuring that clean bedding and tablecloths were provided.[33] Butchers' wives seem to have specialised in making use of offal and fat. As is apparent from Norwich market, they might prepare and also sell black puddings and they are also found manufacturing Paris or tallow candles.[34] The York saucemakers' ordinances from 1417 noted that not only did butchers' wives make tallow candles, but also the wives of skinners and others 'in great number'.[35] Margaret Harman, who was married to a York weaver, likewise was the manufacturer of candles on some scale since she is observed in a case dated 1430 purchasing 23*s* 10*d* worth of candlewick, a quantity so large that it required two people to carry.[36]

The value of wives as assistants in the workshop and as providers of additional sources of income made marriage for the young man intending to set up in trade an imperative. This is implicit in the apprentice John Waryngton's plea to his master when made to marry the fellow female servant he had seduced: 'You are able to be so good and so generous towards me and can show me favour such that you can make me more willing to betroth and have her to my wife.' Though unspecified, the implication is that he wanted his master to help him towards obtaining his own workshop, which would give him both the need for a wife and the means to support her.[37] Completion of an apprenticeship, establishing a workshop, and marrying a wife were crucial life-stages that ideally coincided. For Waryngton, marrying a wife without having obtained the first two objectives was almost unimaginable. But the wife was more than a valued assistant in business, though it was probably often she who served customers at the shop window and it might be she who kept the accounts.[38] A wife also shared her husband's bed, gave birth to and suckled the children they had together, saw that meals were prepared and the house kept clean and orderly, oversaw at least the women servants, took charge in her husband's absence, helped to entertain guests and, to borrow a cliché, made the house a home.

Household manager

The role of the wife as household manager is symbolised by her control of the keys that provided access to locked chests and cupboards in which vessels, napery, and drink were secured. A wife received the keys from her husband and was charged 'with kepyng of all at evur þai had'.[39] The eponymous Goodwife advised her daughter that when she was mistress of her own house, she should 'take the keies into thi warde'.[40] The thirteenth-century legal treatise known as 'Bracton' explains that a young woman came of age to inherit when 'she knows how to order her house and do the things that belong to the arrangement and management of a house, provided she understands what pertains to "cove and keye"', that is, closet and key. The text goes on to explain that 'such things require discretion and understanding' and hence a young woman must be at least thirteen or fourteen.[41] In the sixth joy of the fifteenth-century French misogynistic satire *Les quinze joyes de mariage*, the wife pretends to have lost her keys when her husband brings four important guests to dinner and so ensures they have no napkins for the table, no towels with which to wash, no clean sheets or pillows for the beds, and no clean nightcaps.[42] When Margery Kempe recovered from a bout of mental illness she asked her husband that she be given back the keys to the buttery, which he did despite the opposition of the women servants who said she would simply give away all the food and drink locked up there.[43]

As mistress of the household, wives had charge of the possessions in their care. A good wife would know the whereabouts and condition of every sheet and every utensil. This is clearly demonstrated in the 1450 will of Joan Buckland in respect of her country house at Edgcote (Northants). As the daughter of a London fishmonger who had married another London fishmonger, Joan was very much a bourgeoise, though her husband's eventual success as a merchant and royal servant had made her a country landowner at his death. In the course of the will, Joan moves mentally from room to room remembering every item of furniture, every utensil, the colour and material of every bed hanging, the width of every sheet, and the numbers of silver spoons before finally moving out of the house to remember her carthorses, her cattle, and her tenants.[44] Wives were responsible for ensuring that the household was supplied with fuel and kept warm. This is reflected in the prominence of provision of fuel to the poor on the part of female testators. Joan Johnson, for example, left at her death in 1474 'all the faggots to be distributed amongst Christ's poor together with firewood ("Astilwod") and turves'.[45] That this was an extension of lifetime provision is indicated by the example of Agnes Grantham, with whom this chapter began, who was accustomed 'to give alms to the poor by bringing them wood, fuel, and other necessaries'.[46] A wife's responsibility for feeding her household is similarly mirrored in an expectation that wives would help to feed the needy.[47] A story in the *Alphabet of Tales* tells of a wife who failed to perform this duty. When she died it was suggested that alms be distributed for the benefit of her soul, but her husband refused, saying that she had not done this in her lifetime for the benefit of his soul and so he would not do it now for the benefit of her soul.[48]

We may presume that wives took responsibility for preparing meals, a point regularly asserted in the scholarly literature, but not something that appears to be especially well documented. In contemporary writings it is understood and so not specifically discussed. The French cookery manual *Le viandier* observes of a variety of everyday dishes and vegetables that 'women and their mistresses and everyone knows how to cook them'.[49] When the husband in *Les quinze joyes* sends word that he is bringing guests home, it is plainly understood that his wife is expected to organise their entertainment by her own efforts and by directing the servants, but instead she deliberately sends the servants out on pointless errands and retires to her room claiming illness.[50] The York cooks' ordinances dated 1425 refer specifically to the wives of various other craftsmen who sold foodstuffs that they have cooked.[51] Visual sources, albeit not necessarily English, are more telling. In manuscripts of the *Tacuinum sanitatis* it is regularly women who are depicted as engaged in cooking, for example roasting meats, cooking the legs and feet of young animals, cooking tripe, or preparing wheaten soup. Often more than one woman is engaged and it is not entirely clear which, if any, is the mistress and which the female servants, but in some instances it would appear to be the mistress aided by a servant.[52] There is a well-known image from an early fourteenth-century Flemish manuscript of a woman holding a baby on her knee while she stirs a cooking pot with her left hand. A small boy applies bellows to the fire beneath.[53] This is not an image suggestive of a bourgeois context, but helps to reinforce a cultural understanding that cooking, like childcare, was seen as women's work.

As probate inventories show, the bourgeois house was often moderately well equipped for cooking. More substantial houses might have detached kitchens, but some would have allowed for cooking to take place over a hearth associated with the hall. Hugh Grantham's inventory lists, *inter alia*, brass pots, frying pans, pewter vessels, and mortars. Also itemised under the same heading of 'coquina' were a cow and calf, a cockerel, four hens, four capons, and a couple of ducks.[54] Grantham was not alone in keeping a cow. Two other earlier fifteenth-century York inventories show that Thomas Overdo, a baker, and William Garton also kept cows in outbuildings.[55] John Cadeby, a mason of Beverley, likewise kept ducks and chickens, but also pigs in his garden.[56] The Grantham, Overdo, and Garton households were thus supplied with fresh milk, and fresh eggs were available to the Cadeby and Grantham households. Cadeby's household also had access to fresh pork. Wives would again have supervised the care and regular milking of the cow and the feeding of the chickens since these tasks were seen as women's work.[57] Garton's inventory further lists 'fruits and herbs in the garden' as extensions of the woodshed entry, a reminder that even small garden areas were often exploited to produce vegetables and herbs for both culinary and medicinal purposes. Once again the cultivation of gardens and the provision of primary health care takes us firmly into the wife's domain.[58]

Childcare

The much put-upon peasant wife in a later fifteenth-century poem dubbed by its nineteenth-century editors 'The Ballad of the Tyrannical Husband' tells how she is kept awake at night by their child and how in the morning the children will wake up and start crying and so she had to attend them.[59] The wife of this poem is especially burdened because she has no servant to assist her, but in mentioning the demands of childrearing the text unusually draws attention to something that is otherwise uncommented on. The rather earlier, though popular over many years, 'How the Goodwife Taught her Daughter' advises that children should be sharply disciplined and a mother should start to collect against a daughter's marriage from the time she is born, but otherwise has nothing to say about the rearing of children.[60] Again the point is about significant silences. A bourgeois wife would likely have given birth every two to three years or so until she reached her forties. Maternal breastfeeding was likely the norm except for some mercantile wives, and infants were not fully weaned until aged three.[61] The fourteen children that Margery Kempe, mayor's daughter and merchant's wife, had with her husband fits an elite pattern of fertility unmoderated by the contraceptive effect of nursing, though for all mothers infant mortality, especially high in the post-plague decades, would have much reduced the actual numbers of children alive at any given moment. What we may extrapolate is that most bourgeois wives would have spent many years suckling young children, a number being pregnant, and many more actually caring for children. This was crucial work. Younger children might contribute little to labour requirements of the household and older children may often have been sent into service in other households, but most men would probably have liked a son to succeed them. Younger sons could enter the Church and so offer spiritual succour. Both daughters and sons might enter into marriages that reinforced existing social and trade networks or helped to forge new ones. Children could also be expected to offer some comfort in old age.

Beyond the commonplace claim that it was mothers and womenfolk who cared for children, there is almost no scholarship on medieval childcare and bourgeois childcare in particular. Barbara Hanawalt's classic and highly influential article on peasant childrearing is predicated on refuting the view attributed to Ariès that parents were not emotionally attached to their children. It offers a number of suggestions pertaining to age and gender based on a statistical analysis of coroners' rolls, but the underlying evidential basis is profoundly flawed. In fact the coroners' evidence points to a degree of benign neglect, irrespective of sex, at least of younger children. Whereas younger children and boys generally may often have been left to their own devices, older girls may have been more constrained.[62] For bourgeois society the picture differs again. Whereas in peasant society much work and even socialising took place outdoors, place of work and place of residence coincided in the artisanal household. Manuscript representations of the Holy Family show Joseph carpentering and Mary sewing, weaving, or spinning, while the young Jesus plays within sight of both parents.[63] It is in this bourgeois context of more substantial houses with comparatively level floors that the baby-walker, ubiquitous as a symbol of infancy in art—and which the baby Jesus is using in a Holy Family miniature from the Morgan Library's Hours of Catherine of Cleves—could have been afforded and would have been practical. It is, moreover, in this urban and implicitly bourgeois context that we find evidence for purchased toys, such as pewter miniature utensils and knights.[64] This then is a level of society with the interest and resources to spend time with their children, to take an interest in their development, and to encourage their play. It may well be that little girls were encouraged to play with miniature cooking utensils and little boys with miniature knights. It may also be that they were discouraged from wandering into the street, both because the busier streets of the town were dangerous for small children and because bourgeois parents may not have wanted their youngsters mixing with the children of parents who were regularly out at work during the day.

How much childcare was hands-on for mothers and how much was delegated to female servants we cannot know. The evidence of the later fourteenth-century poll taxes and the mention of servants in wills suggests that artisanal households regularly employed at least one servant, and often two or more.[65] Although the propensity to hire female servants varied considerably according to the occupation of the male head, in the century after the plague it was common that, where more than one servant was employed, at least one would have been female. We may suppose, therefore, that wives often had direct oversight of at least one female servant even if that servant, like the wife herself, was employed in the workshop alongside domestic duties. Wives would have had to instruct their charges in how to perform various tasks, be they how to cook certain dishes, to brew ale, to set the table, or to receive guests, although the servant could have been expected to bring some knowledge of cleaning, spinning, fetching water, and childcare from their natal homes. Servant girls from rural backgrounds would probably have known how to milk a cow or to care for poultry. It is likely that the moral supervision of such adolescent girls and young women fell specifically to wives, something that is reflected in the circulation of a text like 'How the Goodwife'. This last itself advises careful supervision of all 'þi meyne' and charges the wife to ensure that servants are paid promptly and generously.[66] It is likely that wives passed on some of their clothing to their female servants; servants leaving to get married often received cooking utensils and bedding, but probably also advice about married life.

'Kinship work': Forging social networks

It is possible, but so far as I am aware yet to be explored, that employment of servants might sometimes serve to help reinforce ties between households. Certainly it is apparent that servants were sometimes kin, but there is also evidence that they were sometimes connected by ties of trade, and that these may in fact represent business associations and even friendships. Joan Kyrkby was the daughter of John Kyrkby, a dyer, and craft associate of John Usburn who was employing Joan as one of his servants at his death in 1428.[67] Of course it would have been Usburn's wife Elena who would have had most immediate supervision of Joan, and we may speculate that she had played a role in engaging Joan in the first place. Wives' kin and friendship networks are sometimes apparent from the carefully itemised bequests of clothing, household goods, and devotional items such as beads, to other women, so characteristic of the wills of wives and of widows. Such women's networks would have reinforced male networks and also extended their husbands' range of personal contacts. These contacts may in turn have impacted positively on the business of the household.[68] The long-established business partnership between the drapers William Pountfret and John Thornton can, for example, only have been strengthened by the obviously close friendship between Avice Pountfret and Katherine Thornton, their respective wives: Avice described Katherine as 'my faithful friend' in her will and named her as executor alongside her husband.[69] In a cash-starved economy networks of credit were essential, but personal contacts could also have translated into custom or recommendations for custom, in other words, a wife's work helping to build and maintain kin and friendship ties may have impacted directly upon the success of the household economy. Women also used networks to promote the careers of family members. When Agnes Grantham received an invitation to dine with the Master of St Leonard's hospital, whose household she supplied with ale, she saw it as an opportunity to try to secure a preferment for her son, who was pursuing a clerical career.

As we saw obliquely earlier in *Les quinze joyes*, dining and entertaining guests was a key activity for bourgeois wives. In more prosperous and mercantile households especially, such entertaining was necessary in order to test and reinforce trust or to build new business relationships. For example, the York merchant Robert Lascelles and his wife Isabel entertained Margaret Harman and her husband for dinner, using their summer hall for the purpose.

Margaret, a chandler, seems to have traded with Robert, who may well have stocked her candles. We know this because at the dinner Margaret allegedly acknowledged before her husband that she had purchased on credit the very large quantity of candlewick noted earlier from Robert. This was used as evidence in a breach of promise action in the ecclesiastical court when Margaret failed to repay Robert, presumably because the business relationship went sour.[70] Wives probably had some influence, moreover, in organising the furnishing of the hall to create a comfortable and welcoming space for entertaining. We see this in the presence of cushions, coloured textile hangings and coverings, ample sitting places and furniture, such as a cupboard.[71] It was likely also the wife's role simply to make the living areas comfortable and attractive for her husband.

Chamber work: Sex and intimacy

The wife's work extended to the more intimate space of the chamber. Again the comfortably furnished chambers with their colourful coverlets and bed curtains, their feather pillows and linen sheets, and their secure chests as found, for example, in the 1415 inventory of the York vintner Robert Talkan, may owe something to wives' influence on household budgeting underpinned by their own contribution to the household economy.[72] It was in this space that wives were permitted to question or even challenge their husband's conduct, whereas earlier in the day they would have dutifully kept silent before others, to urge moderation and promote harmony. The Knight of the Tower, for example, advises 'when she shall fynd hym alone and tyme but that she may reprehende hym in shewyng curtoysly that he had wrong and unright with hym'. He goes on to suggest that a reasonable husband would be duly grateful to his wife.[73] When John Bown's apprentice, John Waryngton, was so sure that his irate master had done wrong by him it was to his mistress, Margaret Bown, that he complained, presumably in the hope that she would quietly win his master round.[74] Whereas the paterfamilias had to keep firm and strict discipline, wives, like queens, were permitted to intercede and to urge clemency in the governance of the household.

The most intimate duty of the wife—that is, to have sex with her husband—may not immediately be understood as work or as an activity having an economic value, but neither interpretation is in fact straightforward. Indeed, the eponymous young wife in a text tentatively attributed to Lydgate describes sex as 'chambre werk'.[75] Chaucer, in his 'The Shipman's Tale' about a merchant and his wife, makes puns on tale, tail (= pudenda), and tally so as to create or play on cultural resonances between sex, commerce, and the marital debt.[76] Perhaps more telling, however, is the case of Margery Kempe, daughter of a merchant and married to a merchant. Margery's pursuit of celibacy was resisted by her husband since, in his words, 'now may I usyn you with-owtyn dedly synne', but he came to agree in return for her paying his debts.[77] These are not easy texts to read as evidence of social practice or ideology, but there is an implication to be drawn that husbands expected to have regular sexual intercourse with their wives and that bourgeois and mercantile wives understood providing sexual services as a form of work.[78] I do not suppose that—*pace* Kempe—wives also imagined that this work had an economic value, but it was nevertheless a real contribution to the success of the household that so depended on the partnership of the master and the mistress. There is, however, a more immediate economic value to the wife's work in bed.

Husbands who did not find their wives willing or able to satisfy them in bed might stray and, by purchasing sexual services elsewhere—whether with a sex-worker or a mistress—haemorrhage household resources. More importantly, any failure of the orderly dynamics of the conjugal relationship that was central to the success of the household impacted on the effective authority and reputation of the head, and thus on his ability to exercise discipline. This is dramatically illustrated by the fortunes of the household of the York goldsmith William Snawschill. In 1442 one of his male servants was presented for fornication with two different women, one of whom was his fellow servant. The following year another female servant in the Snawschill household was similarly presented for fornication with one of the Minster's vicars choral. Two years later Snawschill's wife Alice was presented for adultery.[79] At much the same time another York household presided over by Thomas Peny saw disorder as a consequence of Peny's unmarried state. He seems to have had a long-running affair with Joan Smyth, but by the mid-1450s also had a simultaneous relationship with Marion, the wife of John Bosse. In the absence of a vigilant wife to set an example, these affairs no doubt distracted Peny from keeping proper surveillance of his servant Joan, who in time became pregnant by a cordwainer.[80]

Conclusion

This chapter has argued that work too narrowly defined offers only a rather myopic picture of the past. In a culture that liked to imagine households to be headed by men who enjoyed a clear and singular craft identity, wives and their activities at first appear marginal and comparatively invisible. Such a magisterial perspective, however, is readily undercut even by the very sources generated by urban governors and the courts they administered: not all households were headed by men and the household was often associated with a range of commercial activities sometimes recognised even in guild ordinances registered before the mayor. When the governors of Beverley issued an ordinance in 1493 'that ther shall no man occupy none occupacyon ... bott allonely that att he is brother withal, and in clothyng', they added the clarification 'And att evere man be in clothynge with the crafte that he moste gets hys lyffyng by'.[81] Such an acknowledgement that livelihoods were rarely made solely from a single trade is atypical, but no less valid for that. It is often wives who were active in other enterprises that, like brewing or spinning, grew out of production for domestic consumption. We have to look with care to notice these activities, but they are documented precisely because they impacted the marketplace beyond the home. The same is less true of activities that are more completely contained within the house, but by drawing upon a range of sources, and particularly narrative sources, the dynamics of the household become a little clearer.[82] Husbands appear as household heads, but so much of the day-to-day management of the household and quite possibly aspects of the household budget were in the hands of wives. Here we may recover a bourgeois femininity, marked by a concern to demonstrate good household management, a concern to ensure that the home was a place of comfort and cleanliness, that servants worked diligently and brought no shame on their employers, that guests were received hospitably, that husbands were served according to the marriage vows at board and in bed, and that children grew up dutiful to their parents and their God. To see this range of activities as essentially discrete and unrelated or to deny them the label 'work' is to misconstrue what it was to be a bourgeois wife.

Notes

1 The case is York, Borthwick Institute for Archives (hereafter BI), CP.F.36. I have translated some of the depositions in *Women in England, c. 1275–1525: Documentary Sources*, ed. and trans. P.J.P. Goldberg (Manchester: Manchester University Press, 1995), 152–55. The case is discussed as 'Brewing Trouble: The Devout Widow's Tale', in Jeremy Goldberg, *Communal Discord, Child Abduction, and Rape in the Later Middle Ages* (New York: Palgrave, 2008), 129–45.

2 Sarah Rees Jones, 'Household, Work and the Problem of Mobile Labour: The Regulation of Labour in Medieval English Towns', in *The Problem of Labour in Fourteenth-Century England*, ed. James Bothwell, P.J.P. Goldberg, and W.M. Ormrod (Woodbridge: York Medieval Press, 2000).

3 David Clark, 'The Shop Within? An Analysis of the Architectural Evidence for Medieval Shops', *Architectural History* 43 (2000).

4 Clark, 'The Shop Within?', 72–74; P.J.P. Goldberg, 'Gender and Space in the Later Medieval House', *Viator* 42 (2011).

5 In fact numbers of towns such as Nottingham and Canterbury seem to have operated a second tier of annual licences to trade.

6 P.J.P. Goldberg, *Women, Work, and Life Cycle: Women in York and Yorkshire, c. 1300–1520* (Oxford: Clarendon Press, 1992), 161, table 4.1.

7 Charles Phythian-Adams, *Desolation of a City: Coventry and the Urban Crisis of the Late Middle Ages* (Cambridge: Cambridge University Press, 1979), 75, 133.

8 Goldberg, *Women, Work, and Life Cycle*, 118–22.

9 See n. 1 above.

10 Deposition of John Wyrsdall in BI, CP.E.159 in Goldberg, ed. and trans., *Women in England*, 107.

11 Goldberg, *Women, Work, and Life Cycle*, chapter 3.

12 'a cause qil nad nulle femme': Maud Sellers, ed., *York Memorandum Book*, 2 vols., Surtees Society 120, 125 (Durham: Andrews and Co.,1912–15), 1:106.

13 Mary Dormer Harris, ed., *Coventry Leet Book*, EETS O.S. 134, 135, 138, 146 (London: Kegan Paul, 1907–13), 574.
14 Sellers, ed., *York Memorandum Book*, 2:169, 190.
15 Felicity Riddy, 'Mother Knows Best: Reading Social Change in a Courtesy Text', *Speculum* 71 (1996).
16 'How the Good Wijf tauȝt Hir Douȝtir', in *The Babees Book*, ed. Frederick J. Furnivall, EETS O.S. 32 (London: N. Trübner and Co., 1868), 36–47.
17 Caroline M. Barron, 'The Education and Training of Girls in Fifteenth-Century London', in *Courts, Counties and the Capital in the Later Middle Ages*, ed. Diana Dunn (Stroud: Alan Sutton, 1996); Richard Goddard, 'Female Apprenticeship in the West Midlands in the Later Middle Ages', *Midland History* 27 (2002); Barbara A. Hanawalt, *Growing Up in Medieval London: The Experience of Childhood in History* (New York: Oxford University Press, 1993), 142–44.
18 Goldberg, *Women, Work, and Life Cycle*, 290–91.
19 Goldberg, *Women, Work, and Life Cycle*, 168–86; Stephanie Hovland, 'Apprenticeship in the Records of the Goldsmiths' Company of London, 1444–1500', *Medieval Prosopography* 22 (2001); Stephanie Ruth Hovland, 'Apprenticeship in Later Medieval London, *c.* 1300–*c.* 1530' (PhD diss., University of London, 2006); Hanawalt, *Growing Up*, 135, 180–81.
20 Goldberg, *Women, Work, and Life Cycle*, 183–84; P.J.P. Goldberg, 'What was a Servant?', in *Concepts and Patterns of Service in the Later Middle Ages*, ed. Anne Curry and Elizabeth Matthew (Woodbridge: Boydell and Brewer, 2000); Hanawalt, *Growing Up*, 160–61, 170–71, 185–88, 190–91.
21 Goldberg, ed., *Women in England*, 105 (deposition of Walter de Mellerby), 153–54 (deposition of Agnes Kyrkeby).
22 Of course the distinction is somewhat arbitrary and artificial since in this implicitly rural context both the woven cloth and the milk were likely used, at least in part, for household consumption. 'The Serving Maid's Holiday', in *Secular Lyrics of the XIVth and XVth Centuries*, ed. Rossell Hope Robbins (Oxford: Clarendon Press, 1955), 24–25.
23 Hanawalt, *Growing Up*, 156, 160.
24 Goldberg, *Women, Work, and Life Cycle*, 194–202.
25 Goldberg, *Women, Work, and Life Cycle*, 232, 257, 259–61.
26 E.g., the glovers and parchment makers, and the dyers: Sellers, ed., *York Memorandum Book*, 1:50, 82, 112.
27 Philip M. Stell, trans., *Probate Inventories of the York Diocese, 1300–1500*, Historical Sources for York Archaeology 2, 3 (York: York Archaeological Trust, 2006), 494.
28 Stell, trans., *Probate Inventories*, 517, 521, 534, 610.
29 BI, CP.E.111 (1372).
30 Goldberg, 'Brewing Trouble', 132–33; Goldberg, *Women, Work, and Life Cycle*, 111–14, 141–44; Judith M. Bennett, *Ale, Beer, and Brewsters in England: Women's Work in a Changing World, 1300–1600* (New York: Oxford University Press, 1996).
31 Stell, trans., *Probate Inventories*, 494, 524, 535, 551, 559–60, 566, 581. John Stubbes, the barber, likely ran a hostelry in addition to his York barber's business and so brewing may have been an aspect of this other business.
32 Sanford Brown Meech and Hope Emily Allen, eds., *The Book of Margery Kempe*, EETS O.S. 212 (London: Oxford University Press, 1940), 9–11.

33 Stell, trans., *Probate Inventories*, 525–27; Goldberg, *Women, Work, and Life Cycle*, 136.
34 Goldberg, *Women, Work, and Life Cycle*, 109, 133.
35 Sellers, ed., *York Memorandum Book*, 1:155–56.
36 Goldberg, *Women, Work, and Life Cycle*, 134.
37 BI, CP.F.127; deposition of John Gamesby in Goldberg, ed. and trans., *Women in England*, 111.
38 The English evidence for essentially ephemeral small business accounts is exiguous. Regulations of the Leiden fullers' craft from the late fifteenth century forbade wives from keeping their husbands' accounts alongside their own, a sure indication that hitherto wives there had kept business accounts without censure: Martha C. Howell, *Women, Production, and Patriarchy in Late Medieval Cities* (Chicago: University of Chicago Press, 1986), 91.
39 Mary Macleod Banks, ed., *Alphabet of Tales: An English 15th Century Translation of the Alphabetum Narrationum of Etienne de Besançon*, EETS O.S. 126–27 (London: Kegan Paul, 1904–05), 1:66, no. LXXXIV.
40 'Take the keys into your care': 'How the Good Wijf', 42, l. 133.
41 Bracton, *On the Laws and Customs of England*, trans. Samuel E. Thorne, 2 vols. (Cambridge, MA: University of Harvard Press, 1968) 2:250–51.
42 Richard Aldington, trans., *The Fifteen Joys of Marriage* (London: George Routledge and Sons, n.d.), 135–37.
43 Meech and Allen, eds., *The Book of Margery Kempe*, 8.
44 Andrew Clark, ed., *Lincoln Diocese Documents, 1450–1544*, EETS O.S. 149 (London, Kegan Paul, 1914), 37–45; Jenny Stratford, 'Joan Buckland (d. 1462)', in *Medieval London Widows*, ed. Caroline M. Barron and Anne F. Sutton (London: Hambledon Press, 1994), 113–28. Joan made a later will which was similarly detailed.
45 P.H. Cullum, '"And Hir Name was Charite": Charitable Giving by and for Women in Late Medieval Yorkshire', in *Woman is a Worthy Wight: Women in English Society, c. 1200–1500*, ed. P.J.P. Goldberg (Stroud: Alan Sutton, 1992), 196–97, 208 n. 87.
46 Goldberg, ed. and trans., *Women in England*, 153.
47 Cullum, '"And Hir Name was Charite"', 191.
48 Banks, ed., *An Alphabet of Tales*, 1:66, no. LXXXIV.
49 Barbara Ketcham Wheaton, *Savoring the Past: The French Kitchen and Table from 1300 to 1789* (London: Chatto and Windus, 1983), 22.
50 Aldington, trans., *The Fifteen Joys*, 133–37.
51 Such potential rivals to the cooks were only to cook commercially if they were 'capable' (*habiles*). Presumably even the cooks realised that they could hardly prevent wives who regularly cooked using these skills to supplement household incomes: Sellers, ed., *York Memorandum Book*, 2:160.
52 Two of the most frequently reproduced manuscripts are Paris, Bibliothèque nationale de France, MS NAL 1673, and Vienna, Österreichische Nationalbibliothek, MS series nova 2644.
53 Oxford, Bodleian Library, MS Douce 6, fol. 22. This is used in Barbara A. Hanawalt, *The Ties that Bound: Peasant Families in Medieval England* (New York: Oxford University Press, 1986), 176.
54 James Raine, ed., *Testamenta Eboracensia*, vol. 3, Surtees Society 45 (Durham: Andrews and Co., 1865), 48–49; Stell, trans., *Probate Inventories*, 518. Grantham

also possessed oxen outside of York, presumably as a source of income rather than primarily for domestic consumption.

55 Stell, trans., *Probate Inventories*, 563, 567.

56 Stell, trans., *Probate Inventories*, 560.

57 Goldberg, *Women, Work, and Life Cycle*, 139–40.

58 Howell, *Women, Production, and Patriarchy*, 11; Hanawalt, *Ties that Bound*, 147.

59 Thomas Wright and James Orchard Halliwell, eds., *Reliquiae antiquae: Scraps from Ancient Manuscripts*, 2 vols. (London: John Russell Smith, 1845), 2:197.

60 'How the Good Wijf', 46, ll. 188–201.

61 The frequency of births suggested here follows the patterns described by Dorothy McLaren from early modern English sources for sections of the population practising extended maternal breastfeeding. Whereas there is evidence that the medieval English aristocracy regularly employed live-in wet-nurses, there is little to suggest that this practice was used elsewhere save perhaps in some mercantile households: Dorothy McLaren, 'Marital Fertility and Lactation, 1570–1720', in *Women in English Society, 1500–1800*, ed. Mary Prior (London: Methuen, 1985), 38–46; P.J.P. Goldberg, *Medieval England: A Social History, 1250–1550* (London: Arnold, 2004), 28, 80–81.

62 Hanawalt is relatively uncritical of her source material and by grouping a large number of verdicts from different dates and counties she fails to notice very significant variations in the propensity to report child fatalities that cast serious doubts over the value of her findings: Barbara A. Hanawalt, 'Childrearing Among the Lower Classes of Later Medieval England', *Journal of Interdisciplinary History* 8 (1977); P.J.P. Goldberg, 'The Public and the Private: Women in the Pre-Plague Economy', in *Thirteenth Century England III*, ed. P.R. Coss and S.D. Lloyd (Woodbridge: Boydell and Brewer, 1991); P.J.P. Goldberg, 'Childhood and Gender in Later Medieval England', *Viator* 39 (2008).

63 E.g., Hours of Catherine of Cleves, New York, Morgan Library and Museum, MS M. 917, p. 149.

64 Geoff Egan, 'Children's Pastimes in Past Time: Medieval Toys Found in the British Isles', in *Material Culture in Medieval Europe: Papers of the Medieval Brugge 1997 Conference*, 7, ed. Guy de Boe and Frans Verhaeghe (Zellik: Insituut voor het Archeologisch Patrimonium, 1997).

65 Goldberg, *Women, Work, and Life Cycle*, 161, table 4.1; 181, table 4.4.

66 'How the Good Wijf', 42–43, ll. 125–30, 139–42.

67 Goldberg, ed. and trans., *Women, Work, and Life Cycle*, 177–78.

68 Cf. Katherine J. Lewis, 'Women, Testamentary Discourse and Life-Writing in Later Medieval England', in *Medieval Women and the Law*, ed. Noël James Menuge (Woodbridge: Boydell, 2000). It has been observed by scholars of later eras that 'kinship work', the active cultivation of kinship ties, was often understood as the work of wives. See, for example, Micaela Di Leonardo, 'The Female World of Cards and Holidays: Women, Families and the Work of Kinship', *Signs* 12 (1987).

69 'fidel' socie mee': BI, Prob. Reg. 3, fols. 111–12. I discuss Pountfret and Thornton at length in 'Brewing Trouble' (see n. 1 above): Pountfret gave shelter to Agnes Grantham and Thornton entered into a contract of marriage with her.

70 Goldberg, ed. and trans., *Women in England*, 239–43.

71 Cf. the York inventories of Robert Talkan, vintner and mayor, or of John Carter, tailor: Raine, ed., *Testamenta Eboracensia*, 3:87–89, 300–04.

72 P.J.P. Goldberg, 'The Fashioning of Bourgeois Domesticity in Later Medieval England: A Material Culture Perspective', in *Medieval Domesticity: Home, Housing and Household in Medieval England*, ed. Maryanne Kowaleski and P.J.P. Goldberg (Cambridge: Cambridge University Press, 2008), 137–38; Raine, ed., *Testamenta Eboracensia*, 3:88.

73 William Caxton, trans., *The Book of the Knight of the Tower*, ed. M.Y. Offord, EETS SS 2 (London: Oxford University Press, 1971), 35. The author offers this advice after recounting the story of the bourgeois wife who challenged her husband publicly before witnesses and refused to hold her tongue. He, moved to anger, struck his wife, knocking her to the ground and breaking her nose. The wife's consequent disfigurement is held up as her punishment for her improper public challenge to her husband's authority.

74 BI, CP.F.127; Goldberg, ed. and trans., *Women in England*, 110–14; P.J.P. Goldberg, 'Masters and Men in Later Medieval England', in *Masculinity in Medieval Europe*, ed. Dawn Hadley (London: Longman, 1999). The Knight of the Tower gave with approval the example of one of King David's wives who persuaded her husband not to put Absalon to death for the murder of his half-brother Amnon even though she was not his mother: Caxton, trans., *Knight of the Tower*, 124–25.

75 John Lydgate (?), *Prohemy of a Mariage Betwixt an Olde Man and a Yonge Wife, and the Counsail*, in *The Trials and Joys of Marriage*, ed. Mary Ellzey and Douglass Moffatt, rev. Eve Salisbury (Kalamazoo, MI: Medieval Institute, 2002), l. 432. I owe this reference to Hollie Morgan.

76 Geoffrey Chaucer, 'The Shipman's Tale', in *The Riverside Chaucer*, ed. Larry D. Benson, 3rd edn. (Oxford: Oxford University Press, 1987), 203–08, esp. ll. 413–17, 453–54; Ardis Butterfield, 'France', in *Chaucer: Contemporary Approaches*, ed. Susanna Fein and David Raybin (University Park: Pennsylvania State University Press, 2010), 40–41. As Davis shows, this is not the only moment where the Canterbury Tales offers 'a critique of the commodification of human relations': James Davis, *Medieval Market Morality: Life, Law and Ethics in the English Marketplace, 1200–1500* (Cambridge: Cambridge University Press, 2012), 88–90.

77 Meech and Allen, eds., *The Book of Margery Kempe*, 24. He also required that the couple continued to share a bed and that Margery cease her custom of fasting on Fridays.

78 Cf. Ruth Mazo Karras, *Sexuality in Medieval Europe: Doing Unto Others*, 2nd edn. (London: Routledge, 2012), 108–09. A fifteenth-century verse 'Arise Early' concludes its brief instructions for how properly to organise the day by informing its male reader to 'Goo to thy bed myrely / And lye therin jocundly / And plesse and loffe thy wyffe dewly / And basse hyr onys or tewyis myrely': Nicola McDonald, 'Fragments of *(Have Your) Desire*: Brome Women at Play', in *Medieval Domesticity*, ed. Kowaleski and Goldberg, 255.

79 Goldberg, 'Masters and Men', 64.

80 Peny was also presented for fornication with a third woman: Goldberg, 'Masters and Men', 63–64.

81 Arthur F. Leach, ed., *Beverley Town Documents*, Selden Society 14 (London: Bernard Quaritch, 1900), 59. The very last clause seems subsequently to have been crossed through.

82 For a discussion of the value of narrative sources, be they court records or conduct literature, see Jeremy Goldberg, 'Some Reflections on Women, Work, and the Family in the Later Medieval English Town', in *Ser Mujer en la Ciudad Medieval Europea*, ed. Jesús Á. Solórzano Telechea, Beatriz Arízaga Bolumburu, and Amélia Aguiar Andrande (Longroño: Instituto de Estudios Riojanos, 2013), especially 209ff.

Select bibliography

Barron, Caroline M. 'The Education and Training of Girls in Fifteenth-Century London'. In *Courts, Counties and the Capital in the Later Middle Ages*, ed. Diana Dunn, 139–53. Stroud: Alan Sutton, 1996.

Bennett, Judith M. *Ale, Beer, and Brewsters in England: Women's Work in a Changing World, 1300–1600*. New York: Oxford University Press, 1996.

Cullum, P.H. '"And Hir Name was Charite": Charitable Giving by and for Women in Late Medieval Yorkshire'. In *Woman is a Worthy Wight: Women in English Society c. 1200–1500*, ed. P.J.P. Goldberg, 182–211. Stroud: Alan Sutton, 1992.

Goldberg, P.J.P. 'Masters and Men in Later Medieval England'. In *Masculinity in Medieval Europe*, ed. Dawn Hadley, 56–70. London: Longman, 1999.

——— 'Some Reflections on Women, Work, and the Family in the Later Medieval English Town'. In *Ser Mujer en la Ciudad Medieval Europea*, ed. Jesús Á. Solórzano Telechea, Beatriz Arízaga Bolumburu, and Amélia Aguiar Andrande, 191–214. Longroño: Instituto de Estudios Riojanos, 2013.

——— 'What was a Servant?'. In *Concepts and Patterns of Service in the Later Middle Ages*, ed. Anne Curry and Elizabeth Matthew, 1–20. Woodbridge: Boydell and Brewer, 2000.

——— *Women, Work and Life Cycle: Women in York and Yorkshire c. 1300–1520*. Oxford: Clarendon Press, 1992.

Hanawalt, Barbara A. *Growing Up in Medieval London: The Experience of Childhood in History*. New York: Oxford University Press, 1993.

——— *The Ties that Bound: Peasant Families in Medieval England*. New York: Oxford University Press, 1986.

Howell, Martha C. *Women, Production, and Patriarchy in Late Medieval Cities*. Chicago: University of Chicago Press, 1986.

Karras, Ruth Mazo. *Sexuality in Medieval Europe: Doing Unto Others*, 2nd edn. London: Routledge, 2012.

Riddy, Felicity. 'Mother Knows Best: Reading Social Change in a Courtesy Text'. *Speculum* 71 (1996): 66–86.

7 Gender, authority, and monastic work

Holy Cross in Brunswick, *c.* 1500

Julie Hotchin

In July 1491 Mechthild von Vechelde, abbess of the Cistercian monastery of Holy Cross (1490–1507), near Brunswick in Lower Saxony, announced that all the inhabitants of the monastery would come together to beat flax for linen.[1] This was a labour-intensive activity that the nuns customarily performed as a festive occasion. The anonymous sister who recounted this event describes how on the 'happy day' (*dies oportunus*) the flax was brought into the monastery precinct where the nuns joined 'our family' (*nostrum familiam)*—the laysisters, their provost, priests, young scholars in training, male and female boarders and servants—in the strenuous activity. The nuns sang devotional songs, including some they had composed for the occasion, while the boarders and others, including some of the sisters, sang secular songs. The provost, George Knochenhauer (1491–1503), also sang songs he had composed specially for the occasion. He, together with Mechthild and her monastic officials, also awarded small gifts as prizes. The occasion enabled the entire community to share the physical exertion and also to perform important social work, contributing to cohesion and the collective identity of the different groups that comprised the monastery's *familia*.[2]

Although the nuns of Holy Cross reportedly delighted in an event that provided a welcome interruption to their routine work of liturgical prayer, others were not so pleased. We learn from the sister who described this incident in her 'convent diary' (*Konventstagebuch*) that certain people from outside the convent, most likely members of the city council, were 'scandalised' at the event.[3] The ramifications of this for the convent were lasting. Their confessor and provost, both of whom had participated without criticism, responded to external pressure to amend the nuns' behaviour. George Knochenhauer ensured that this practice did not reoccur by refusing to allow the nuns to sow flax in their fields.[4] Rather than risking open confrontation with the abbess and convent, he employed an indirect approach, yet one still underlining the scope of his authority.

This incident and its fallout illustrate the dynamic tension that characterises the relations between the abbess and provost in the shared work of governing a monastery. Women's religious communities relied upon priests to provide various material and spiritual services. The institutional arrangements to support this took diverse forms depending upon religious order, location, and patronage.[5] Reflecting medieval ideas about governance as a primarily masculine preserve, many monastic women in German regions shared the direction and management of their monastery with a senior cleric, the provost.[6] The abbess and provost were each responsible for managing different but interrelated aspects of the monastery's *spiritualia*, primarily the nuns' spiritual work of prayer and the clerics' intercessory masses for donors, and the *temporalia*, the administration of monastic properties and incomes, and the maintenance and well-being of the convent and other people who worked to provide for the nuns' material needs. Joint governance functioned as a partnership and the nature of the relationships between the two key officials had material implications for how women exercised their office and conducted their work.[7]

Drawing on the account of daily life within Holy Cross recorded in the anonymous nun's convent diary, this chapter examines the interplay of gender and authority in jointly governing the spiritual and temporal affairs of a monastery. Focusing on the dynamic tension between nuns and their clerical officials, I explore how women perceived their role and performed their duties as abbess in relationship with their provost. Recent research into women's activities as rulers has shifted critical attention from how women exercised royal or lordly office as individuals to how they performed the duties of their office relationally.[8] As Elena Woodacre has recently observed, 'one of the situational factors that could prove crucial for a woman's ability to access or exercise power was her relationships with those around her', in this instance the provost with whom she shared governance.[9] The interdependent nature of joint monastic governance invites examination of how the scope of women's activities, the limits to her authority, and how she undertook her duties as abbess were influenced by her relations with the monastery's provost.

The convent diary provides evidence for how abbesses of Holy Cross and successive provosts worked together or in tension to direct the monastery. The entries cover the latter decades of the fifteenth century, documenting a period of political turmoil in Brunswick and the region and how it impacted upon the monastery. Written from the perspective of a first-person observer, if not necessarily a participant in all the events she records, this narrative is an unusually rich source for the inner workings of convent life, how the relations between abbesses and provosts were perceived, and the attitudes of the author and her community towards how their spiritual and material affairs were directed. The text presents valuable evidence for how the abbess managed the convent, what activities she undertook, what she was responsible for, who she directed, and how she sought to extend the scope of her authority. Attention to what and how the abbess is described as managing and how she worked with—or against—the monastery's provost shows how personal and working relationships were vital to shaping the scope and experience of an abbess' work.

Holy Cross and the convent diary

Holy Cross was the most important monastery for women in Brunswick. It was founded around 1230 on a site outside the north-west gates of the city as an act of atonement to conclude a local war between *ministeriales* of the duke of Brunswick-Lüneburg and the city.[10] An abbess and provost are first mentioned by name at Holy Cross in 1266, indicating that the nuns managed the monastery's business with a provost from an early date after its foundation.[11] The abbess and provost were jointly responsible for the spiritual and material well-being of perhaps sixty to seventy souls, including the convent of around thirty to forty sisters, the chaplains who served in the monastery's church and altars, boarders, and the various male and female workers in the *familia* who managed or laboured on the estates, or worked as artisans or servants.[12] The abbess directed the spiritual work of the convent, principally the regular sung prayer of the divine office. The provost supervised the work of the priests who celebrated intercessory masses for donors in the monastery's church and altars, and performed sacramental functions. He directed the nuns' confessor and as the example of the flax beating shows, he also was responsible for the spiritual tenor of the monastery.

These spiritual duties were made possible by the economic endowments of families and donors who invested in the spiritual work of the nuns' prayer and commemorative masses for their salvation. In the late fifteenth century the monastery held extensive landed properties concentrated in the vicinity of the city and maintained close financial ties to Brunswick through investments in the city's annuities markets.[13] The abbess and provost were jointly responsible for managing these economic interests and the multitude of legal, administrative, and representational duties they required. Both roles demanded considerable leadership, organisational ability, and financial competence.

The institutional arrangements to govern the work of the inhabitants of Holy Cross reflect the monastery's place within intersecting social, political, and religious networks. The nuns of Holy Cross were first mentioned as following Cistercian customs in 1256. The monastery was not formally recognised by the General Chapter as incorporated into the order, although throughout the medieval period the convent perceived itself to be and was recognised locally as Cistercian.[14] This juridical status had implications for how its spiritual and economic affairs were directed. In female monasteries that remained unincorporated the provost as senior cleric was responsible for the monastery's spiritual and temporal affairs. In incorporated monasteries, however, the Chapter sought to minimise the risks presented by this consolidation of power by assigning responsibility for spiritual and material administration to different officials.[15] The office of provost (*praepositus*) originated within male religious houses, where the incumbent was responsible for the administration of the institution's temporal affairs.[16]

Membership of the convent of Holy Cross attracted the daughters, aunts, and cousins from the lesser nobility and patrician families in and around Brunswick.[17] Elisabeth Pawel (1484–90) and Mecththild von Vechelde, the two abbesses whose rule is described in the convent diary, were members of important mercantile families in the city.[18] By the fifteenth century Holy Cross was closely integrated into the administrative control of the city of Brunswick. The city's governing body, the Council (*Rat*) comprised members of patrician families, many of whom had female relatives within the convent of Holy Cross. Economic and administrative oversight of Holy Cross was part of the Council's broader control over religious institutions within the city. The Council appointed influential citizens as procurators (*procuratores*) to assist the nuns and their provost and to provide administrative oversight, thus serving as a mechanism through which the monastery was integrated into the city's social politics and administration. These officials were often related to the nuns of Holy Cross.[19] The priests who acted as the monastery's provost were drawn from the city's churches and religious foundations, further reinforcing the institution's close civic ties. The provost of Holy Cross was also a member of the *unio clerici*, the group of leading prelates who determined ecclesiastic affairs in Brunswick. The choice of candidate to this office thus held significance beyond the governance of the monastery because the incumbent also participated in administering the spiritual affairs of the city.[20]

The Council also exercised significant influence in the monastery's spiritual affairs. Most notably, Holy Cross was the only female monastic house in the region not to adopt the stricter interpretation of monastic life advocated by religious reformers in the later fifteenth century.[21] In Brunswick, the Council's resistance to reform at Holy Cross preserved its interests in the monastery and limited the potential for external interference from neighbouring territorial powers, primarily the bishops of Hildesheim and the dukes of Brunswick-Lüneburg. Nevertheless, the author of the convent diary reveals how shifting expectations of what was considered to be appropriate religious conduct for women influenced aspects of the nuns' daily lives. The convent adopted certain practices that point to the influence of reforming ideals, such as maintaining enclosure, sharing a common table, and the nuns' desire to conform to Cistercian liturgical customs.[22] The negative reactions to the festive activities that accompanied the flax beating, however, draw attention to differing spiritual attitudes. The measures taken by provost George Knochenhauer to prevent the event from reoccurring shows how external expectations of religious women's behaviour could affect nuns' scope to directly manage their affairs within the cloister.

The convent diary from Holy Cross is a unique witness into daily life within a female monastic community that did not adopt reform in the latter fifteenth century, providing valuable testimony into how the abbesses directed aspects of the nuns' spiritual work and material affairs.[23] The author offers no clues to her identity in the text. She probably came from one of Brunswick's patrician families, although she does not appear to have been one of the senior nuns or to have held office.[24] The author wrote in Latin, the language in which the nuns' spiritual duties were performed.[25] It commences sometime before late 1484 and the text finishes abruptly in June 1507, very likely because the author died of an outbreak of the plague that killed around thirty members of her convent. The work has some characteristics of a chronicle, in its chronological ordering of events, although it is not an institutional history and rarely extends beyond the walls of the cloister except where events impact on the narrator's life. It also shares some features of a personal diary or 'ego-document' in which subjective accounts of experience are recorded, although the standpoint is clearly that of the community, the 'we' rather than a personal perspective.[26] Her focus is her present and future generations of sisters, and she frames events and anecdotes as edifying lessons for future readers with clear instructive and didactic commentary. For example, she wants her readers to understand why new practices were introduced, such as new prayers to be recited for the monastery's donors, so that later generations of sisters grasped the purpose of their spiritual work and why they performed certain duties: 'I have written this so that those who follow will know why we have this form of prayer.'[27]

As a record of daily life the author's account reveals insights into how the abbess and provost worked together and the difficulties the convent could encounter when these relations broke down. She stresses the importance of stability and collaboration in the key relations for the monastery's material security, and comments on occasions of tension or conflict as a warning about the adversity that could ensue from dissension.[28] Her insider perspective on how these officials worked together or in conflict affords a closer examination of how the work of joint governance was negotiated in practice.

Gender and governance arrangements at Holy Cross

The abbess and provost each held separate and distinct, as well as interdependent, responsibilities to direct the monastery's spiritual obligations and the economic activities that enabled them. The abbess ensured the convent fulfilled its spiritual duties. The primary obligation of religious women was the correct performance of the divine office or 'work of God' (*opus Dei*), the regular sung prayer of the canonical hours. In addition, the author of the convent diary refers to 'all of our works' (*omnia nostra opera*) as encompassing, in addition to the divine office, a range of other collective monastic practices such as collation, readings at mealtimes, reciting commemorative prayers in chapter, and the nuns' spiritual discipline.[29] 'Work' (*opus*) is used by the author to refer to the nuns' spiritual obligations as distinct from *labor*, which she uses to refer to activities that involved physical exertion, such as the manual activity that punctuated their rounds of prayer.[30] No details of what this *labor* involved are given in the text, although the description of beating flax and a reference to teaching the nuns at Wienhausen how to spin and weave fabric for monastic garments indicates that the sisters at Holy Cross performed or supervised cloth work of various kinds.[31] The obligation to perform a substantial programme of sung prayer of up to eight hours each day could be physically exacting, leading these duties to be recognised as the 'burdens of the choir'.[32] Moreover, in some communities nuns may have used certain foodstuffs, in particular saffron, as a stimulant to assist them to overcome fatigue due to the long hours of singing this work involved.[33]

Although the abbess' ability to directly manage the monastery's temporal affairs was restricted by the requirement that she work with the provost, nevertheless she managed extensive financial responsibilities such as those pertaining directly to the convent, including the annual payments by relatives for the nuns' maintenance. The abbess was assisted in her administrative duties by several female monastic officials. The most important of these were two senior nuns, or *capellana*, one of whom assisted the abbess to direct the *spiritualia* of the convent, the other of whom supported the abbess to manage the convent's finances or *temporalia*, such as the incomes and expenses and business matters.[34] Prior to taking on the abbacy, Mechthild had herself acquired considerable administrative experience in managing the convent's *temporalia* as *prima capellana*. Her entries in the surviving account book indicate her careful attention to maintaining these records.[35] The author refers to the prospect of the abbess and her officials undertaking financial and administrative responsibilities as 'laborious' and a 'burden', emphasising the effort this work involved.[36]

Abbesses Elisabeth Pawel and Mechthild von Vechelde also demonstrated a keen interest in how the convent's farm and the monastery's estates were managed. They were responsible for the convent's material well-being and sought to minimise the economic damage when a provost incurred heavy debts. On occasion, an abbess also personally intervened to assess the economic state of affairs. In 1488, after the convent returned to the cloister buildings following an eighteen-month exile in the city to avoid the danger of a local war, Abbess Elisabeth and Mechthild, who then managed the convent's estates, travelled to the village of Wetlenstedt to assess the extent of the damage for themselves.[37] The provost was obliged to provide accounts of income and expenses to the abbess and her senior officials. He also took an oath not to sell, mortgage, transfer or otherwise dispose of any property without the knowledge and consent of the abbess and the Council of Brunswick.[38] These provisions underlined the provost's obligation to act in the interests of the convent as well as to seek the approval of the abbess when important financial decisions were made. Further, they express the presupposition that the abbess and her officials were capable administrators with the knowledge and ability to make decisions and discuss proposals about property transactions, and to know when to seek financial or legal counsel and how to oversee the provost's actions.

The provost as the senior cleric held the superior authority over the abbess, convent, and all those who worked in the monastery. He was responsible for the provision of sacramental services to the nuns and for public religious services in the monastery's church and chapels. In practice he only performed these functions himself on special occasions. He also supervised the nuns' confessor, and the chaplains and priests who performed the commemorative masses for donors.[39] The provost directed the administration of the monastery's estates and properties, which comprised the farms held by the convent, the *Propstei* (*praepositura*), which included the properties that he maintained himself, the priests and *scholares* (priests in training), as well as the properties that supported the monastery in general.[40] Together with the abbess he represented the convent in external legal, financial, or ecclesiastical proceedings.

An individual who served as provost could also be powerful in his own right.[41] As an influential position with authority over a religious institution's property and affairs, the office of provost of a female monastery could be appealing to career-minded clerics seeking influence and lucrative benefices. The office could thus attract candidates who were more interested in the possibilities for advancement than in genuine concern or commitment to perform the duties of office in the nuns' interests, a failing the nuns were well aware of and sought to avoid. This could be exacerbated by the requirement that nuns observe enclosure, which limited their ability to directly manage their temporal affairs. Women's ability, therefore, to secure someone of their preference to perform the office was a crucial means through which they could limit the inherent asymmetries of power in this structure. It was critical for them to have male officials whom they could trust to manage the day-to-day activities of the monastic economy and to represent the convent's interests.[42]

The convent diary offers a fascinating glimpse into what motivated the nuns when they were selecting a provost and how they sought to have their interests met. In October 1505, when the convent was looking for suitable candidates to serve as provost after the death of Henning Duve (1503–05), the author of the convent diary eloquently expresses the nuns' frustration in finding a suitable successor: 'We did not want to have wealthy or distinguished priests, but humble men who were not rich so that they would be [our] servants (*famuli*) and providers and not provosts.'[43]

The nuns at Holy Cross drew on their familial networks and the monastery's procurators to identify potential candidates from among the secular clerics serving in the city's religious institutions.[44] The nuns could be forthright in setting out what they expected a provost to undertake and how they wanted him to work with them. The author describes how the extent of the convent's requirements outlined by Elisabeth Pawel to a prospective candidate to replace Heinrich Karstens (1483–88) in 1488 'did not please everyone who was there', suggesting that the scope of the nuns' expectations may have contributed to their difficulty in finding suitable candidates.[45]

Three years later, the author observed that Mechthild von Vechelde sought to avoid conflict with the Council about the nuns' choice of a provost, stating that she did not want to accept anyone into the office whom the Council would not confirm.[46] The comment underlines Mechthild's strategic approach in seeking to avoid any tensions with the Council that could lead to external interference in how the monastery was managed.

A provost could be appointed for life, although in effect they served varied lengths of tenure in office, some departing for other appointments, others removed for negligent administration, and still others, such as George Knochenhauer, serving until death.[47] In the latter decades of the fifteenth century Holy Cross had nine different provosts over a period of thirty-seven years, of which the longest serving was George, for twelve years, and the others between two to five years. The frequent change in incumbents could create instability in the monastery's administration, which was balanced by the continuity of the sixteen-year abbacy of Mechthild von Vechelde. Despite the provost's main responsibility to fulfil the representative and economic functions of the monastery, in practice the abbess, supported by convent officials and the lay estate managers, was crucial in managing these transitions and providing stability to the monastery's governance.

Managing spiritual work

Monastic life was fulfilled through spiritual work. The duty to perform the divine office was the central aspect of nuns' lives; it represented their spiritual effort for the world.[48] The abbess bore a weighty responsibility for her complex work as the convent's spiritual leader and example: she had the obligation to answer for her own conduct and that of the nuns in her charge on Judgement Day.[49] She exercised ultimate authority for the correct performance of the convent's spiritual work of liturgical prayer and for observing the customs of their rule. The convent diary offers glimpses into how Elisabeth and Mechthild's actions shaped the spiritual environment of the convent, and their efforts to extend these actions to the wider monastery. Analysis of occasions where the abbess and provost worked together to manage the monastery's spiritual obligations brings into focus the respective scope of their responsibilities and how the limits placed upon the extension of women's actions into wider spiritual affairs were enacted.

The manner in which the abbess led the nuns to fulfil their spiritual duties could have material consequences. The way in which the nuns followed the requirements of their rule and correctly maintained their regular rounds of sung prayer were examined by monastic visitors at intermittent intervals. If an abbess or her nuns were found to require correction in how their spiritual work was undertaken this could result in unwanted external intervention into the affairs of the convent. It is not surprising, then, that the author of the convent diary describes the nuns' delight when in September 1502 the papal legate Johannes von Palz visited Holy Cross, where after an examination of the cloister he pronounced that he had discovered no fault. His presence, the author declared, 'honours the monastery', but more importantly for Mechthild his affirmation of the manner of her leadership lent her and her monastery greater spiritual prestige, and with it potential appeal to donors. Performing the spiritual work of prayer generated worldly benefits in ongoing financial terms.[50]

The abbess had the scope to shape the spiritual environment of the convent by introducing new practices, within the requirements of the rule. One of Mechthild von Vechelde's first acts as abbess in August 1490 was to establish her spiritual leadership through a clever strategy to promote the value of the nuns' spiritual work to their kin and the monastery's patrons. Her decision to introduce a new commemorative practice to recognise the convent's patrons and benefactors underlines the central importance of nuns' spiritual duties and how they expressed the convent's role within a broader spiritual economy. Cistercian customs stipulated that memorial masses or celebration for donors and benefactors would be celebrated once a year to restrict the expansion of commemorative practices for individual donors from becoming too onerous.[51] Mechthild's solution shows her concern to observe Cistercian statutes in daily practice while also enhancing the appeal of the monastery through introducing special commemorative prayers for the nuns' kin and benefactors. She determined that the convent would recite special prayers in chapter each Monday for specific groups—former sisters, their priests, and 'for those who give annual incomes to the monastery or make other gifts', thus singling out the nuns' kin, who paid regular annuities for their maintenance—for regular special commemoration.[52] By working to establish new practices Mechthild sought to enhance the appeal of the nuns' intercessory prayer to the monastery's donors and the nuns' families. Mechthild's actions underline how she asserted her direction of the convent's spiritual business to shape the work her nuns' prayer entailed. Her decisions demonstrate her keen awareness of the interrelationship between the nuns' spiritual labour and its economic benefits. Through her actions Mechthild sought to encourage continuing financial investment in the work of women's intercessory prayer.[53]

The abbesses of Holy Cross also took steps to promote the interests of the convent when external events impacted upon their ability to perform their spiritual duties in their customary manner. The convent diary records how, during two periods of interdict, the nuns were not permitted to celebrate divine office with the full solemnity of singing or ringing bells, but to recite the words only; nor were they permitted to receive communion.[54] The way in which the nuns received news about the interdict, and how its practical implications for the monastery's spiritual obligations were worked out, illustrates how the abbess and provost managed their respective areas of responsibility. In 1487, for example, Heinrich Karstens announced that the monastery was required to observe an interdict that had been placed on the diocese of Hildesheim. After consulting with other prelates in the city to confirm what it entailed, he informed Elisabeth of the changes required to ensure that the monastery observed the ecclesiastic requirements correctly. The author makes clear that all communication about the interdict and what it involved was conducted through the provost; Elisabeth and her senior officials were limited to discussing the changes required with the provost and implementing them within the convent. When she received news that the interdict had been lifted, Elisabeth rejoiced, and in a striking display of her spiritual agency, she ordered a celebratory mass, accompanied by the organ, to be sung for the dedication of a new chapel to mark the end of the long period of musical absence.[55]

Although abbesses Elisabeth and Mechthild were bound by obedience to perform the convent's liturgy to conform with the interdict, they nevertheless saw their responsibility as being to mitigate its most serious effects. They drew upon their networks in efforts to release their monastery from its restrictions. At first glance the respective roles or fields of action could imply that the spiritual authority of abbess and provost were aligned with the categories of external/public/male and internal/private/female. Although Heinrich managed the external and official formalities relating to the interdict's requirements, Elizabeth was not passive or restricted from exerting external influence in ecclesiastic politics. In November 1487 she sought assistance from Wulbrand von Oberg, a cathedral canon from Hildesheim with influence in Rome.[56] She informed him about the impact of the interdict upon the convent, how it prevented the nuns from fulfilling their spiritual duties through 'the neglect of our divine office', and implored him to act on their behalf to lift the ban. Wulbrand promised to petition Rome, and to assist the convent in various, unspecified, ways.[57] Elizabeth drew upon her office and her social and political networks to petition for the monastery's interests. Her actions offer an instructive example of how enclosed monastic women utilised their broader networks of social relations beyond the cloister to promote the interests of their institution.[58]

The spiritual leadership of the abbesses at Holy Cross also extended to obtaining privileges, such as indulgences, through which they shaped the monastery's spiritual environment. These privileges provided a further means to promote the monastery's spiritual prestige to donors and benefactors, to maintain its appeal within a competitive spiritual economy, and to shape the devotional experience of the nuns and *familia* through participation in popular devotional events. The account of how Mechthild secured the jubilee indulgence for Holy Cross in 1500 draws attention to the relational quality of her authority to determine the monastery's spiritual affairs. Her actions illustrate how she perceived the scope of her spiritual responsibilities and how her claims were subtly contested.

The convent's longing to share in the spiritual benefits of the papal jubilee in 1500 accounts for the urgency and excitement with which abbess Mechthild seized an opportunity to obtain the indulgence towards the end of the jubilee year.[59] On the evening of November 2, 1500 a monk claiming to be from the Cistercian monastery of Walkenried (in Saxony) arrived at Holy Cross. When the jubilee was announced in Rome, the Cistercian General Chapter acquired the privilege to obtain the indulgence for members of the order—such as nuns—who could not make the pilgrimage to Rome. The monk informed Mechthild that he was authorised by the order to communicate the jubilee to Cistercian communities. The presence of a monk in these unusual circumstances could have raised doubts; nevertheless, in the absence of provost George, Mechthild assumed authority to acquire the privilege for all inhabitants of the monastery.

Mechthild directed the nuns and the *familia* to be gathered into the nuns' church that evening to participate in the reading of the privilege before the monk departed the next day. He received a solemn reception in the church, where he read the bull aloud to the assembled congregation from the altar. The spiritual significance of the occasion was lost on many members of the *familia* as in the haste to gather everyone together there had been little time to communicate what was happening or its purpose. Moreover, the bull was read in Latin, which contributed to the confusion of those in the *familia* who could not understand what the monk said or why they were there. In contrast to the confusion the circumstances generated among the *familia*, the author describes how the nuns listened to the bull being read aloud with rejoicing, crying 'tears as if they were married to their spouse', whereas others wondered why the sisters reacted in this manner. Even those who did grasp the potential significance of the event, the clerics, did not trust the credentials of the Walkrenreid monk, criticising him as a 'vagrant and seducer'. Moreover, the author adds that the clerics laughed at the sisters 'as if we were more simple than usual people and therefore more easily fooled', underlining the subtle tensions that shaped relations between the nuns and priests. On the following day Mechthild obtained a copy of the bull for the large sum of one gold florin.

When provost George returned the next day and heard about the incident, he also queried the monk's credibility, although after making enquiries he confirmed that the monk's claims were legitimate. The author notes that he reassured the nuns that they had not been deceived and the indulgence was valid, although Mechthild was admonished for paying too much for a copy of the bull. George's actions, and the reassurance they generated, underline how ultimate authority to act in this matter rested with him as the senior cleric of the monastery.[60]

Mechthild's actions and the reactions of the clerics and others within the monastery's *familia* highlight how her authority for spiritual matters that extended beyond the convent relied upon a consensus between the provost, other clerics, and members of the *familia*.[61] Mechthild's hasty action and the lack of communication with the groups within the *familia*—clerics, laysisters, labourers, and boarders—about the purpose of the event led to confusion. The divergent attitudes of these various groups highlight how they influenced the limits of her authority. Although Mechthild accepted the legitimacy of the monk's claims to represent the order, the nun records that many people remained suspicious about his veracity, suggesting a lingering doubt about Mechthild's judgement and whether the scope of her spiritual work extended into affairs beyond the convent. Customarily she would be expected to consult with the provost to determine whether to proceed with the monk's offer. We see here how Mechthild understood her responsibility as extending to procuring spiritual benefits for the monastery. Her behaviour on this occasion, however, appears to have led to doubts in some quarters about her capability as a leader. The relational quality of Mechthild's authority is also evident in George's response. By confirming the legitimacy of the monk, and thereby the indulgence, he simultaneously affirmed her decisions and reinforced his ultimate authority to determine spiritual matters pertaining to the monastery.

Managing temporal affairs

Sound economic management of the monastery's temporal affairs was of paramount concern for the author of the convent diary. Nuns' spiritual labours were made possible by the endowments of properties and incomes from pious benefactors, and the convent relied upon co-operative relations between the abbess and provost to provide for their material welfare. The author makes sharp observations about the impact on the convent's financial security and well-being that disagreement and conflict could create, and she attributes the monastery's impoverished state to dissension between the abbess and provost.[62] Poor economic management also aroused anxieties for ecclesiastic and civic officials, because they wanted to avoid the prospect of religious women leaving their cloister to manage their own affairs.[63] Despite the restrictions of enclosure, in certain circumstances nuns nevertheless did leave the cloister to conduct monastic business. The convent diary is a witness to Elisabeth and Mechthild's active engagement in the convent's financial concerns and their desire to ensure that their provost managed the monastery's estates to reflect their interests. The author documents the growing tension from the late 1480s between these officials, reflecting different attitudes about who rightly directed certain aspects of the monastery's estates, and how the provost's rule was undertaken. The nuns' anxieties were fuelled by their deteriorating relations with Provost George and mounting debt. The nun's account is particularly striking for the evidence it provides for how economic necessity also led to circumstances in which women's economic management could be recognised as legitimate, granting a capable female administrator enhanced authority to direct her monastery's affairs.

The tensions arising from differing opinions about how the monastery's farms were to be managed in the interests of the nuns are illustrated by a dispute about maintaining cows. As the example of beating flax showed, the provost could control what was produced on the estates, with far-reaching ramifications for the customary social, spiritual, and economic activities of the convent. In August 1486 the convent asked Provost Heinrich Karstens to acquire cows to provide the nuns with a regular supply of dairy produce, so that they could avoid paying high prices for fresh produce. He refused, the author claiming that he 'impeded us' from obtaining the cows many times because it had not been 'our custom' to manage cows. Heinrich may have been reluctant to outlay the expenditure or to take on additional responsibility. Eventually he succumbed to pressure from the convent's supporters, and he grudgingly agreed to manage the livestock.[64] Around the same time the nuns received gifts of cows which they arranged to be tended on the convent's farm. Elizabeth Pawel hired a female servant to tend to them. In this she acted independently from the provost, securing a servant who laboured under her direction and not that of the provost. On the day of her election as abbess, August 1, 1490, Mechthild von Vechelde used the occasion as an opportunity to test her new authority over the question of the dairy cows. She asked provost Heinrich Biwende (1488–91) to maintain the cows for the convent, but he too refused and the author laments that Mechthild's efforts 'came to nothing, and the constant quarrels and anger remained between provost and the abbess just as it had before'.[65] In this move, Mechthild may have hoped to gain the backing of the abbot of the nearby Cistercian monastery of Riddagshausen, who officiated at her election. The dispute over whether the provost would maintain a dairy herd to provide the nuns with fresh produce underlines the limits to the abbess' authority to direct what was produced on the monastery's estates and also how the nuns were restricted in their ability to control how they sourced food supplies and managed their expenditure.[66]

The author's mention that Abbess Elizabeth employed a female servant to tend the cows alludes to one of the underlying causes of deeper differences in attitudes that shaped relations between the nuns and their provosts, namely the respective authority to direct how the monastery's estates and female servants were managed. The abbess had authority to direct the convent and certain laypeople to perform activities on lands belonging to the convent whereas the provost exercised authority over all remaining members of the *familia*. These tensions come into clearer view in the divergent attitudes of the abbess and provost to the presence of *donatas*, laywomen who worked on the convent's farm and the lands held by the *Propstei*, and who owed obedience directly to the abbess.[67] The presence of the *donatas* at Holy Cross was contested and a source of disruption in some parts of the *familia*. These female servants did not follow the same customs as the convent's laysisters but instead those devised by Elizabeth Pawel. Their black tunics further set them apart from the monastery's laysisters, alongside whom they worked. The author of the convent diary expresses her own doubts about the suitability of their form of life, observing that the women 'did not live according to the statutes of [our order] but according to those of our abbess [Elizabeth] who located them [on the convent's farm] and proposed their manner of living'. The nun also comments on the friction that the different customs for the *donatas* and other members of the *familia* aroused. The *donatas* at times refused to share in the heavy work with the rest of the *familia*, claiming that they were not required to perform this labour as a privilege of the rule they followed.[68]

Two *donatas* joined the monastery in 1488, and although they gave obedience to the abbess she directed them to work on the farm which was managed by the *Propstei*, where their activities supported the provost and clerics, as well as the rest of the monastery's community. Control over who had authority to manage this farm had been at issue between the abbess and provost for some years, with the provost seeking to shift responsibility for the farm from the convent to the *Propstei*. George Knochenhauer was unhappy with the presence of the *donatas* working on the farm alongside other lay servants. At Easter in 1493 he terminated the arrangement and removed the *donatas* from the farm, replacing them with laywomen who worked under his authority. He acted without consulting Mechthild and refused to permit the *donatas* to remain there.[69]

The disputes about estate management and direction of the monastery's servants demonstrate that by the 1490s George Knochenhauer was gradually asserting increased control over the direction of laypeople working at the monastery and the activities that were to be performed on the estates. George's precipitate action indicates the increasing levels of tension arising on both sides at the inability to negotiate a compromise to resolve their differences. It is likely that he considered the presence of these women in the lands of the *Propstei* as an interference in his domain. A lasting resolution was eventually reached when the women themselves approached Mechthild with a request to make their vows as laysisters, and so adopt the same status as other women who laboured for the monastery. The narrator implies that the women may have been pressured into making this request, as they reportedly expressed concern about the dangers of living according to the wish (*voluntatem*) or rule of the abbess rather than 'according to the institutes prescribed for them, and claimed that they weighed this decision as a matter of conscience'. Mechthild eventually agreed to accept this change in status and invested the women as laysisters in 1495.[70] In doing so she relinquished the abbess' former custom of having female servants directly under her authority, a further acknowledgement of the provost's claims to direct all of the monastery's *familia*. Moreover, the transition of the *donatas* into laysisters resulted in Mechthild losing aspects of direct control over agricultural production for the convent.

One of the inherent risks in arrangements for joint governance was how to make decisions effectively and exercise authority when one party was ill or incapacitated. The strain that this situation could place on all of the *familia* is evident in the nun's description of the effects of George Knochenhauer's failing health upon his capacity to perform his duties. In April 1503 tensions flared between Mechthild and George over the construction of a new bakehouse. The narrator describes how George was afflicted by memory loss and difficulty in reasoning, which resulted in him refusing to listen to advice or to relinquish his duties.[71] George organised timber to be prepared for the construction of the bakehouse, even though he knew that the *Propstei* did not have the funds to pay for it. When asked about the money he retorted that if he ran out of money the 'lady abbess would make it up from the treasury of the monastery'. He was also reportedly heard to say: 'I will borrow, auntie Mette [Mechthild] ought to pay.'[72] George's actions suggest that his growing incapacity influenced his attitude towards the authority of the women. His public comments also point to an underlying attitude that, as provost, he was not ultimately responsible for the expenses he incurred on behalf of the monastery, and his expectation and knowledge that ultimately the nuns would have to address them. This situation provided nuns with powerful motivation to maintain close oversight over the state of the monastery's finances. The convent eventually secured financial support from the Council, and with the assistance of their procurators the bakehouse was completed.[73] Although George had served the convent faithfully during his early years in office, his incapacity now severely disadvantaged the nuns.

George's reportedly flippant attitude towards his financial accountability is the most colourful example of the poor state of relations that divided all who lived in the monastery at the time. The author describes how the co-operation and negotiation of authority so critical to sharing governance effectively had now hardened into delineated spheres of authority that allowed little possibility of overlap. The provost and abbess controlled the management of their respective farms, refusing to permit the laypeople subject to the authority of the other party to labour on their domains.[74] The provost's refusal to accept counsel exacerbated the ongoing debt issues, and Mechthild lacked authority to prevent him from authorising expenditure. The convent diary's account exhibits remarkable balance in depicting this fragmented scenario. The author also recognises how Mechthild's traits contributed to the conflict. She observes that although Mechthild firmly resisted any efforts by George to involve himself in convent affairs, when she sought to intervene in the *Propstei* she claimed divine authority, 'thinking that she herself worked in submission to God'.[75] Of greater potential damage was the impact of these divisive relations upon the rest of the *familia*. The loyalties of the monastery's inhabitants were divided; those who sympathised with the provost 'despised the abbess', arousing her anger towards them in return. These circumstances show how the breakdown in consensus across the different groups threatened to undermine Mechthild's personal authority.

The monastery's debts weighed heavily on the sister who composed the convent diary.[76] This is a common theme in nuns' accounts of their relations with their provost.[77] A monastery could acquire debt through mismanagement, self-interest, or lack of ability, but for the nuns affected the result was the same, as a *Propstei* burdened with debt impacted upon the economic security of the convent. A heavily indebted *Propstei* also deterred potential candidates for the position of provost from taking the office, as they did not want the work involved. The desire to alleviate the debts of a monastery could be a strong motivator for women to seek greater control over their own economic management, although the requirement to observe enclosure limited their scope to directly manage temporal affairs.

The level of debt that encumbered the monastery at George's death in 1503 also aroused considerable anxiety among the councillors in Brunswick. When Mechthild approached the Council to search for a new provost they made her a counter-offer: the procurators suggested to Mechthild and her senior nuns that they undertake the rule (*regimen*) of the *Propstei* and all the *familia* themselves.[78] The benefits, the procurators continued, would be to release Holy Cross from debt and 'preserve it for the future'. The council's willingness to adapt the long-standing governance arrangements that restricted Mechthild's authority demonstrates how economic pragmatism could outweigh gendered assumptions about female capacity to rule. The Council presumably recognised Mechthild as a competent administrator and apparently trusted her ability to manage the estates of the *Propstei* effectively. The Council's proposal also indicates an acknowledgement of shared interests; Holy Cross was closely intertwined with the Council through shared social relations so it was in all interests to ensure the monastery's financial survival.

Before accepting the offer to extend her authority, Mechthild expressed the reservation that she could not perform the full duties of economic management without breaching enclosure. The narrator presents this dilemma as evidence of Mechthild's commitment to 'regular observance', implying that she would only take the unusual step of breaking enclosure out of necessity. Mechthild did not accept the proposal until she had consulted with every member of the monastery's *familia*. She received the governance of the temporal affairs of the *Propstei* and the abbacy in September 1503.[79] The procurators appointed the priest Henning Duve as provost, to supervise the monastery's *spiritualia* and to assist Mechthild; he remained subject to her in temporal matters. The author records that after twelve months of this arrangement the nuns had made some small progress in reducing the burden of debt.[80] Mechthild's cautious and consultative approach was strategic, especially in view of the deteriorating relationships between the *familia* and the convent in recent years. In talking to all members of the *familia* she could counter potential criticism from within the *familia* about how she proposed to conduct herself; these negotiations also enabled her to establish authority over people who had previously owed obedience to the provost. Given the emotional climate engendered by the divisions within the monastery, Mechthild needed to gain confidence that the *familia* would work with her.

In accepting authority to govern the *Propstei*, Mechthild and her officials implemented a fundamental shift in how female authority was exercised at

Holy Cross. The convent diary presents Mechthild as obedient to the will of the Council and as acting out of necessity. The author reports her as saying to the procurators that 'although it seems a burden to us and each and every member of our convent to undertake such a laborious task' (*laboriosum opus tale*), nevertheless, the nuns assented because 'your authority has advised this' and out of the 'necessity of our poverty and penury'.[81] Mechthild is depicted in terms that assert her humility and obedience, these monastic virtues emphasise her claims to authority. The nun's depiction seeks to redress the unusual practice of a female leader extending her authority into what was customarily the provost's domain. Moreover, Mechthild is presented as taking on this additional work not for her own sake, but because she has been asked to and in the context of dire need. Mechthild acted with the full knowledge that her ability to direct all of the monastery's economic affairs depended upon building consensus for her authority with all members of the *familia*. She was only able to extend female abbatial authority within a broad network of consensual relations involving the support of the Council and of the people whom she directed. Further, this portrayal echoes the language used to describe Mechthild's self-understanding in her conflict with George, in which she claimed to be 'acting in submission to God'. The question arises, then, whether Mechthild proposed herself to the procurators to direct the *Propstei*, presenting herself as humble and obedient, and above all as the most experienced candidate, to govern the monastery out of its economic difficulties.

Conclusion

This examination of how the abbess and provost directed the spiritual and temporal affairs at Holy Cross highlights the inherently relational character of the work involved in monastic governance. The 'insider perspective' of the convent diary provides evidence not available from other sources such as charters or financial records about how monastic women understood the nature and scope of their responsibilities, as well as those of their provost. This author's descriptions of how the monastery was managed in practice shed light on the personal and working relationships between the abbess and her provosts; they illustrate how vital these relationships were to the abbesses' effective spiritual leadership and temporal administration.

The abbesses of Holy Cross expressed a strong self-understanding as leaders responsible for the spiritual and material well-being of their monastery. The responsibilities of abbess and provost for managing the spiritual work of the monastery imply a spatial delineation of their roles, the abbess directing the convent's spiritual work within the monastery and the provost as the senior cleric supervising the monastery's public religious services and ecclesiastic matters. Abbesses, however, promoted the interests of their monastery by drawing on their social and political networks and through their actions to shape its spiritual environment. Whereas the abbess directed the liturgical work of the convent independently of the provost, her ability to direct spiritual matters for the monastery could be contingent upon her relations with the provost. Mechthild's decisions—for example, acting in the absence of Provost George to secure the spiritual benefits of the jubilee indulgence—shows how she perceived the full extent of her spiritual work for the monastery, but also illustrates how her claims were contested by some within the monastery's *familia*. Her decisions were eventually confirmed by the provost, demonstrating how the scope and nature of her actions were both affirmed by and contingent upon the provost's validation.

It has been argued that the provost's responsibility for a monastery's temporal affairs acquired greater importance in the later Middle Ages as the result of the increasing emphasis on the enclosure of religious women.[82] In the provost's absence, the spiritual responsibilities of the office could be performed by other priests, but as George's deterioration shows, the loss of a capable administrator to govern the monastery's estates could contribute to financial difficulties. Although religious women were required to rely upon a provost to conduct the monastery's temporal affairs, nuns were not precluded by enclosure from maintaining close involvement in, if not direct control over, the management of their monastery's economic affairs. The abbesses of Holy Cross undertook extensive financial work for the convent and exercised keen oversight of their provosts' administration. Religious women's limits on their ability to directly manage the economic work of their monastery made their relations with their male officials all the more vital. It was crucial for nuns to influence the selection of a provost, in order to secure a person whom they could trust and with whom they could work. The vagaries of personality, capability, and experience meant that problems still arose; however, it is worth noting that the support nuns could muster from kin, patrons, and officials outside the monastery demonstrates how sound working relationships were widely recognised as key to managing the monastery's business effectively.

The relational character of monastic governance comes to the fore in Mechthild's response to the offer to take on the 'laborious' task of administering the estates of the *Propstei*. The obligation to maintain enclosure meant that her relations with the diverse groups of the monastery's *familia* were all the more important to enable her to direct the work, usually the responsibility of a provost, effectively. Whereas her actions to secure the indulgence had been hasty, arousing confusion and disaffection about her leadership within the *familia*, on this occasion she acted with greater strategic caution, working to build consensus across 'every member' of the monastery before consenting to undertake the task. The author presents her actions as a model of monastic virtue, but lying behind this is the practical reality that Mechthild needed to gain the support of a community divided by conflicting loyalties between abbess and provost for her rule to be possible. Her actions crystallise the inherently relational character of monastic governance, and how, even in overcoming the perceived limitations of her gender to assume authority for all the monastery's temporal affairs, the manner in which she fulfilled the role was contingent upon her working relations within and outside the monastery.

Notes

1 A note on terminology: I use 'convent' in its broadest meaning to refer to the community of nuns (*conventus*) who lived and worked at Holy Cross, and 'monastery' to refer to the institution and its inhabitants.
2 Eva Schlotheuber, *Klostereintritt und Bildung. Die Lebenswelt der Nonnen im späten Mittelalter. Mit einer Edition des 'Konventstagebuchs' einer Zisterzienserin von Heilig–Kreuz bei Braunschweig (1484–1507)* (Tübingen: Mohr Siebeck, 2004), 101–03 and the text in the edition at fols. 64v–67r, 383–85. I cite the edition hereafter as *TB*. This anecdote is a valuable witness to the nature and importance of musical culture for religious women's devotional life; Linda Maria Koldau, *Frauen-Musik-Kultur. Ein Handbuch zum deutschen Sprachgebiet der frühen Neuzeit* (Vienna: Böhlau, 2005), 643–48.
3 *TB*, fol. 66r, 384: 'aliqui de extraneis scandalizabant'.
4 *TB*, fol. 67r, 385: 'Et hoc provenit, quod prepositus, cui forte hoc displicuerat, tam callide impedivit, ut postmodum numquam permisit nobis linum in nostro orto seminare, sed causam noluit dicere, ne videretur nos reprehendere.'
5 For an overview see Fiona J. Griffiths and Julie Hotchin, eds., *Partners in Spirit: Women, Men and Religious Life in Germany, 1100–1500* (Turnhout: Brepols, 2014), and Klaus Schreiner, 'Pastoral Care in Female Monasteries: Sacramental Services, Spiritual Edification, Ethical Discipline', in *Crown and Veil: Female Monasticism from the Fifth to Fifteenth Centuries*, ed. Jeffrey F. Hamburger and Susan Marti, trans. Dietlinde Hamburger (New York: Columbia University Press, 2008).
6 Julie Hotchin, 'Female Religious Life and the *cura monialium* in Hirsau Monasticism, *c*. 1080–1150', in *Listen Daughter: The Speculum Virginum and the Formation of Religious Women in the Middle Ages*, ed. Constant Mews (New York: Palgrave, 2001), and Eva Schlotheuber, 'The "Freedom of their Own Rule" and the Role of the Provost in Women's Monasteries of the Twelfth and Thirteenth Centuries', in *Partners in Spirit*, ed. Griffiths and Hotchin.
7 Theresa Earenfight, 'Without the Persona of the Prince: Kings, Queens and the Idea of Monarchy in Late Medieval Europe', *Gender & History* 19 (2007): 1–21, and Elena Woodacre, 'Contemplating Royal Women's Access to Power and the Transition between the Middle Ages and the "Monstrous Regiment" of the Early Modern Era', *Medieval Feminist Forum* 51 (2015): 61–68.
8 In addition to the works cited in n. 6 above, see also Theresa Earenfight, 'Medieval Queenship', *History Compass* 15 (March 2017): 1–9 and Amalie Fößel, 'Gender and Rulership in the Medieval German Empire', *History Compass* 7 (2009): 55–65.
9 Woodacre, 'Royal Women's Access to Power', 64.
10 Schlotheuber, *Klostereintritt*, 31–36.
11 Ute Römer-Johannsen, 'Braunschweig, Hl. Kreuz', in *Germania Benedictina, Band XI Norddeutschland. Die Frauenklöster in Niedersachsen, Schleswig-Holstein und Bremen*, ed. Ulrich Faust (St Ottilien: Eos, 1984), 70.

12 Römer-Johannsen, 'Heilig Kreuz', 87.

13 Römer-Johanssen, 'Heilig Kreuz', 81–85, outlines the scope of the monastery's landed holdings and their geographic relation to the monastery. For individual nuns' financial dealings in northern Germany, see: June Mecham, *Sacred Communities, Shared Devotions: Gender, Material Culture, and Monasticism in Late Medieval Germany* (Turnhout: Brepols, 2014), 90–126.

14 Schlotheuber, *Klostereintritt*, 48–58, discusses the Cistercian links and self-identity of Holy Cross. For the broader debate about the relationships of Cistercian nuns to the order, see: Eva Schlotheuber, 'Die Zisterzienserinnengemeinschaften im Spätmittelalter', in *Norm und Realität. Kontinuität und Wandel der Zisterzienser im Mittelalter*, ed. Franz J. Felten and Werner Rösener (Berlin: LIT, 2009), 265–84, Emilia Jamroziak, *The Cistercian Order in Medieval Europe: 1090–1500* (London: Routledge, 2013), 124–55, and Elizabeth Freeman, who examines the debate about Cistercian nuns and adduces new evidence to identify them in England: '"Houses of a Peculiar Order": Cistercian Nunneries in Medieval England, with Special Attention to the Fifteenth and Sixteenth Centuries', *Cîteaux: Commentarii Cistercienses* 55 (2004), 245–87.

15 Margit Mersch, *Das ehemalige Zisterzienserinnenkloster Vallis Dei in Brenkhausen im 13. und 14. Jahrhundert* (Mainz: Philipp von Zabern: 2007), 89–93, 106; and Schlotheuber, 'Zisterzienserinnengemeinschaften'.

16 Albert de Vogüé, 'Propst (*praepositus*)', in *Lexikon des Mittelalters* (Munich: Artemis, 1995), 7:264.

17 Schlotheuber, *Klostereintritt*, 36–44. See also the prosopographical details about the identified members of the convent mentioned in the *Konventstagebuch* in Appendix 6.2, 'Konventsmitglieder und Kandidatinnen', 481–526.

18 Elisabeth Pawel was from a family of money changers and goldsmiths and Mechthild von Vechelde was from a family of drapers, one of the leading families in the city. Her cousin, Albert II von Vechelde, was mayor of the Brunswick *Altstadt* between 1481 and 1501. For brief prosopographical details, see Schlotheuber, *Klostereintritt*, Appendix 6.2, no. 51, 510–11 and no. 64, 519–20.

19 *Ordinarius der Stadt Braunschweig*, cap. 51 'Van vormunderen uppe dem Rennelberghe', in *Urkundenbuch der Stadt Braunschweig*, ed. Ludwig Hänselmann and Heinrich Mack (Berlin: C.A. Schwetschke and Son, 1862), 1:162, no. 63; and Schlotheuber, *Klostereintritt*, 19–20. Mechthild's cousin Albert II von Vechelde served as procurator between 1464 and 1488 (Schlotheuber, *Klostereintritt*, 346, n. 53). This practice was not uncommon in the century after the monastery was founded; Schlotheuber, *Klostereintritt*, 38.

20 Römer Johannsen, 'Heilig Kreuz', 88. For a list of provosts of Holy Cross, see Romer-Johannsen, 'Heilig Kreuz', 94, updated for the fifteenth century by Schlotheuber, *Klostereintritt*, 480.

21 Schlotheuber, *Klostereintritt*, 58–103. For an orientation to the vast literature on late medieval monastic reform and its implications for religious women, see Mecham, *Sacred Communities*; Heike Uffmann, *'Wie in einem Rosengarten'. Monastische Reformen des späten Mittelalters in den Vorstellungen von Klosterfrauen* (Bielefeld: Verlag für Regionalgescichte, 2008); and Anne Winston-Allen, *Convent Chronicles: Women Writing About Women and Reform in the Late Middle Ages* (University Park: Pennsylvania State University Press, 2004).

22 Schlotheuber, *Klostereintritt*, 99–103.

23 Wolfenbüttel, Herzog August Bibliothek, Cod. Guelf. 1159 Novi. The manuscript is described by Schlotheuber, *Klostereintritt*, 335–36. Numerous convent histories and narratives were written by women in the later fifteenth century to justify the changes that reform entailed or to provide moral and edifying exemplars for their community; Uffmann, '*Wie in einem Rosengarten*'; Winston-Allen, *Convent Chronicles*.

24 Schlotheuber, *Klostereintritt*, 313. The original opening of the work, in which the author may have referred to herself and her purpose in writing, has not survived. The details she provides in the account indicate that she did not have access to sources of information about the city's politics in the same way as nuns from the leading Brunswick families and that she was not part of the circle of noble nuns within the convent; *Klostereintritt*, 315.

25 On Latin instruction and proficiency in northern German convents, see Schlotheuber, *Klostereintritt*, 268–96; and Eva Schlotheuber, 'Intellectual Horizons: Letters from a Northern German Convent', in *A Companion to Mysticism and Devotion in Northern Germany in the Late Middle Ages*, ed. Elizabeth Anderson, Henrike Lähnemann, and Anne Simon (Leiden: Brill, 2013), 343–72.

26 Schlotheuber, *Klostereintritt*, 321–27.

27 Schlotheuber, *Klostereintritt*, 317 and *TB*, fol. 56r, 378: 'Hec scripsi, ut sciant postere, unde talis oracio institutionem habuerit.'

28 *TB*, fol. 222r, 467: 'Et hoc ideo scripci, ut posteri precaverant sibi, ne discencionem parant inter prepositum et abbatissam, quia hoc fuit origo omnis mali et penurie, que nobis evenit.'

29 *TB*, fol. 87v, 398.

30 *TB*, fols. 127v–128r, 421. In her description of how nuns spent their days during an interdict in 1498 the author records that the nuns performed manual labour, or work, before vespers: 'tempore laboris ad domum operis, tempore congruo in capitolio vesperas'.

31 Subprioress Elze Broitzem and a laysister spent two months at the nearby Cistercian monastery of Wienhausen in September–November 1487 where they instructed the nuns there how to spin and weave *culcullas*, a long cowl or robe that formed the nun's habit, and to sew the cloth band crowns nuns wore atop their veil; *TB*, fols. 21r–22v, 352–53.

32 Bishop Gray to the nuns of Elstow in England in 1432: 'et talem que onera chori [illegible word] ceteris religionem concernentibus poterit supportare', cited in Anne Bagnall Yardley, *Performing Piety: Musical Culture in Medieval English Nunneries* (New York: Palgrave Macmillan, 2006), 76.

33 Volker Schier argues this point from evidence for the Birgittine monastery of Maria Maihingen in Franconia: 'The *Cantus sororum*: Nuns Singing for their Supper, Singing for Saffron, Singing for Salvation', in *Cantus planus: Papers Read at the 12th Meeting of the IMS Study Group, Lillafured/Hungary, 23–28 August 2004*, ed. László Dobszay (Budapest: Institute for Musicology of the Hungarian Academy of Sciences, 2006), 858.

34 The *capellanae* were an administrative office that appear to have been unique to northern German convents. They were senior officials appointed by the abbess, in addition to the customary monastic officials such as the subprioress, *cantrix*, *sacrista*, and cellaress. For a list of convent officials for the period covered by the convent diary, see Schlotheuber, *Klostereintritt*, Appendix 6.1, 'Ämter', 478.

35 The surviving account book (Wolfenbüttel, Staatsarchiv, L Alt Abt. 11 S. Crucis Fb III 1) was initiated by Mechthild in July 1490; Schlotheuber, *Klostereintritt*, 329–32, 375 n. 364.
36 *TB*, fol. 218v, 464–65.
37 *TB*, fol. 39v, 368.
38 *Ordinarius*, cap. 50: 'Van dem proueste vp dem Rennelberghe', in *Urkundenbuch der Stadt Braunschweig*, ed. Hänselmann and Mack, 162.
39 Ulrike Hascher-Burger and Henrike Lähnemann, *Liturgie und Reform in Kloster Medingen. Edition und Untersuchungen des Propst-Handbuchs Oxford, Bodleian Library, MS. Lat. lit. e. 18* (Tübingen: Mohr Siebeck, 2013), 51–56; Ida-Christine Riggert, *Die Lüneburger Frauenklöster* (Hanover: Hahnsche Buchhandlung, 1996), 105–39; Schlotheuber, 'Zisterzienserinnengemeinschaften'.
40 The *Propstei* (*praepositura*) designated the properties that maintained the provost and clerical members of the monastery and also referred to the building in which they were accommodated, usually located just outside the monastic enclosure.
41 For the backgrounds and careers of men who served as provosts at the Benedictine monasteries of Ebstorf, Lüne, Walsrode, and the Cistercian monasteries of Medingen, Wienhausen, and Isenhagen, all to the north of Brunswick, see Riggert, *Lüneburger Frauenklöster*, 115–21. For the office of provost as the highpoint of a career for clerics in male religious institutions see Brigide Schwarz, 'Hannoveraner in Braunschweig. Die Karrieren von Johann Ember (d. 1423) und Hermann Pentel (d. nach 1463)', *Braunschweigisches Jahrbuch für Landesgeschichte* 80 (1999): 9–54.
42 On religious women's efforts to obtain and exercise the privilege to elect a provost of their choice, see Riggert, *Lüneburger Frauenklöster*, 112–27; and Uffmann, *'Wie in einem Rosengarten'*, 232–40. In Britain religious women also sought to obtain men they could trust to serve as lay estate officials; Kimm Perkins-Curran, '"Quhat say ye now, my lady priores? How have ye usit your office, can ye ges?" Politics, Power and Realities of the Office of a Prioress in her Community in Late Medieval Scotland', in *Monasteries and Society in the British Isles in the Later Middle Ages*, ed. Janet Burton and Karen Stöber (Woodbridge: Boydell, 2008), 130.
43 *TB*, fol. 230r, 472: 'Noluimus habere sacerdotes divites et honoratos, sed humilies et non potes, ut essent famul{i} et provisores et non prepositi.'
44 For example, prior to assuming office as provost in 1488, George Knochenhauer was vicar at the church of St Michael in Brunswick. A member of the family, Grete Knochenhauer is recorded as a nun at Holy Cross in 1399. His successor, Henning Duve, was treasurer of the confraternity of St Matthew in Brunswick and later deacon there prior to his appointment as provost. Schlotheuber, *Klostereintritt*, 383 n. 426 and 460 n. 902. By the fifteenth century, the Council of Brunswick retained the right to confirm the nuns' choice and the new provost received full authority to exercise the *spiritualia* and *temporalia* of the monastery from the bishop of Hildesheim.
45 *TB*, fols. 30v–31v, 359.
46 *TB*, fol. 63r, 383.
47 Römer-Johannsen, 'Heilig-Kreuz', 87–88.
48 For the liturgy and how it shaped religious women's practice and outlook, see Jürgen Bärsch, 'Liturgy and Reform: Northern German Convents in the

late Middle Ages', in *Companion to Mysticism and Devotion*, ed. Anderson, Lähnemann, and Simon, 21–46; Gisela Muschiol, 'Liturgy and Rite in Female Monasteries of the Middle Ages', in Hamburger and Marti, *Crown and Veil*, 191–206; and Yardley, *Performing Piety.*

49 *The Rule of St Benedict*, trans. with an introduction and notes by Anthony C. Meisel and M. L. del Mastro (New York: Doubleday, 1975), chapter 2, 48.

50 *TB*, fols. 153v–155v, 434–35.

51 For the Cistercian practice of cumulative commemoration of groups of donors over individual commemorative prayers, see Jamroziak, *The Cistercian Order*, 33–38.

52 *TB*, fols. 55v–56r, 378.

53 On the continued value of nuns' intercessory prayer in the late medieval period, see Elizabeth Lehfeldt, *Religious Women in Golden Age Spain: The Permeable Cloister* (Aldershot: Ashgate, 2005), 39–46.

54 *TB*, fols. 15r–18r, 349–51. The monastery observed the spiritual restrictions of interdict from June 8, 1487 to July 1, 1488, and January 14, 1498 to December 25, 1498.

55 *TB*, fol. 38r, 366–67.

56 Wulbrand von Oberg was a notary at the Roman Rota or appeals court, and from 1508 procurator; Schlotheuber, *Klostereintritt*, 354 n. 150.

57 *TB*, fols. 24v–25r, 354.

58 Nuns' ability to harness familial and patronal networks to assert their authority and pursue their monastery's interests has been a hallmark of recent research into women's monasticism, for example: Jennifer C. Edwards, '"Man Can be Subject to Woman": Female Monastic Authority in Fifteenth-Century Poitiers', *Gender & History* 25 (April 2013); Sigrid Hirbodian, 'Reformschwestern und Reformverliererinnen. Strategien und Handlungmöglichkeiten geistlicher Frauen in den Reformen des 15. Jahrhunderts', in *Reformverlierer 1000–1800: Zum Umgang mit Niederlagen in der europäische Vormoderne*, ed. Andreas Bihrer and Dietmar Schiersner (Berlin: Duncker and Humblot, 2016); Sherri Franks Johnson, *Monastic Women and Religious Orders in Late Medieval Bologna* (Cambridge: Cambridge University Press, 2014); and Lehfeldt, *Religious Women in Golden Age Spain.*

59 Schlotheuber, *Klostereintritt*, 52–54; the events are documented in *TB*, fols. 135v–140v, 425–28.

60 Schlotheuber, 'Zisterzienserinnengemeinschaften', 11.

61 For broader analysis of the power of female rulers as contingent on a consensus of their subjects, see Fößel, 'Gender and Rulership', 58.

62 For example her observations about the financial damage to the monastery that could arise when there was dissension between the abbess and provost; see n. 28 above and discussion below.

63 Lehfeldt, *Religious Women in Golden Age Spain*, 105–36, and Nancy Bradley Warren, *Spiritual Economies: Female Monasticism in Later Medieval England* (Philadelphia: University of Pennsylvania Press, 2001), 55–72.

64 *TB*, fols. 9v–10r, 346–47.

65 *TB*, fol. 53v, 377: 'sed nichil profecit, sed semper lis et indignacio inter prepositum et abbatissam perseveravit, sicut ante fuerat'.

66 Schlotheuber, *Klostereintritt*, 78. The convent maintained the monastic custom of the common table, reflecting their sympathies with the ideals of a shared life

promoted by religious reformers. This practice may have made the convent more reliant upon their provost to supply the stipulated foodstuffs, such as dairy produce, so the nuns did not have to purchase it themselves.

67 Riggert, *Lüneburger Frauenklöster*, 209–12, discusses the general role and duties of *donatas*.

68 *TB*, fol. 53v, 377: 'Erant tunc in allodio due converse vestite nigris tunicis viventes non secundum statuta conversarum ordinis, sed secundum statuta abbatisse. Que eas ibi locaverat et modum vivendi eis posuerat.'

69 *TB*, fols. 100r–101r, 404.

70 *TB*, fols. 116v–117r, 413: 'Et dicebant, quod periculosum esset eis sit vivere solum secundum voluntatem abbatisse et non secundum instituta eis prescripta, et fecerunt eis scrupulosas et perplexas in conciencia sua.'

71 *TB*, fol. 202v, 457.

72 *TB*, fol. 202r, 457: 'hoc domina abbatissa de reposito claustra thesauro faciliter supplevet ... *Eck wil borghen, Mette mome scal betalen*'. In August 1503, the convent's accounts record that Rose Osterlo, the mother of a certain M. Osterlo (unknown whether she was a nun or a laysister) donated money for the completion of the bakehouse; Schlotheuber, *Klostereintritt*, 510.

73 *TB*, fol. 212r, 461.

74 *TB*, fols. 203v–204v, 457–58.

75 *TB*, fol. 204r, 457: 'Abbatissa vero, cum de rebus preposature aliquid valuit abbacie attrahere, estimabat se obsequium deo operare.'

76 The author laments the monastery's financial position and when George Knochenhauer was elected provost in 1491 she expresses the hope of the convent that 'we would be liberated from debt through his efforts' (*per industriam*), although this did not eventuate; *TB*, fol. 64r, 383.

77 Mecham, *Sacred Communities*, 96–101; Riggert, *Lüneburger Frauenklöster*, 132–34; and Winston-Allen, *Convent Chronicles*, 41–43.

78 *TB*, fol. 218r, 464; 'Missi ergo rogaverunt dominam nostrum, ut concilio habito cum senioribus ascensum preberent ad suscipiendum regimen preposture et tocius familie sicut et ceterorum cenobiorum prelate pene omnes fecissent.'

79 *TB*, fols. 218v–220v, 464–66.

80 *TB*, fol. 222r, 467: 'In festo Michaelis [September 29, 1504] {fin}itus est primus annus, quod habuimus regimen utriusque, prepositure et abbacie, et modicum profecimus, quia debita prepositure gravabant claustrum, quod vix erat nobis spes reparationis, nisi deus nos specialiter adiuvaret.'

81 *TB*, fols. 218v–219r, 464–65: 'Licet nobis et omnibus et singulis personis conventus nostri videatur grave et laboriosum opus tale aggredi et tantis curis nos implicari, tamen, quia vestra hoc consuluit auctoritas et penurie seu paupertatis nostre exigit necessitas ascentire.'

82 Hascher-Burger and Lähnemann, *Liturgie und Reform*, 54; and Riggert, *Lüneburger Frauenklöster*, 111.

Select bibliography

Anderson, Elizabeth, Henrike Lähnemann, and Anne Simon, eds. *A Companion to Mysticism and Devotion in Northern Germany in the Late Middle Ages*. Leiden: Brill, 2013.

Fößel, Amalie F. 'Gender and Rulership in the Medieval German Empire'. *History Compass* 7 (2009): 55–65.

Griffiths, Fiona J., and Julie Hotchin, eds. *Partners in Spirit: Women, Men and Religious Life in Germany, 1100–1500*. Turnhout: Brepols, 2014.

Hascher-Burger, Ulrike, and Henrike Lähnemann. *Liturgie und Reform in Kloster Medingen. Edition und Untersuchungen des Propst-Handbuchs Oxford, Bodleian Library, MS. Lat. lit. e. 18*. Tübingen: Mohr Siebeck, 2013.

Lehfeldt, Elizabeth. *Religious Women in Golden Age Spain: The Permeable Cloister*. Aldershot: Ashgate, 2005.

Mecham, June. *Sacred Communities, Shared Devotions: Gender, Material Culture, and Monasticism in Late Medieval Germany*. Turnhout: Brepols, 2014.

Riggert, Ida-Christine. *Die Lüneburger Frauenklöster*. Hanover: Hahnsche Buchhandlung, 1996.

Römer-Johannsen, Ute. 'Braunschweig, Hl. Kreuz'. In *Germania Benedictina, Band XI Norddeutschland. Die Frauenklöster in Niedersachsen, Schleswig-Holstein und Bremen*, ed. Ulrich Faust, 67–99. St Ottilien: Eos, 1984.

Schlotheuber, Eva, *Klostereintritt und Bildung. Die Lebenswelt der Nonnen im späten Mittelalter. Mit einer Edition des 'Konventstagebuchs' einer Zisterzienserin von Heilig-Kreuz bei Braunschweig (1484–1507)*. Tübingen: Mohr Siebeck, 2004.

——— 'Die Zisterzienserinnengemeinschaften im Spätmittelalter'. In *Norm und Realität. Kontinuität und Wandel der Zisterzienser im Mittelalter*, ed. Franz J. Felten and Werner Rösener, 265–84. Berlin: LIT, 2009.

Uffmann, Heike. *'Wie in einem Rosengarten'. Monastische Reformen des späten Mittelalters in den Vorstellungen von Klosterfrauen*. Bielefeld: Verlag für Regionalgescichte, 2008.

Winston-Allen, Anne. *Convent Chronicles: Women Writing About Women and Reform in the Late Middle Ages*. University Park: Pennsylvania State University Press, 2004.

Yardley, Anne Bagnall. *Performing Piety: Musical Culture in Medieval English Nunneries*. New York: Palgrave Macmillan, 2006.

8 'Any *Man or Woman* beyng hole & mighty in body'

Women's work under Tudor vagrancy law

Nicholas Dean Brodie

In 1548, under the heading 'Vacabund', a scribe in Norwich noted the following in the Mayoral Court records:

> The satrday the xvij day of mrche a ijde R.E. vi [in the second year of the reign of King Edward VI] Isabell Sudderon born in newarsall is assigned to new oulstell wher she was born.[1]

If the letter of the law was being followed, and if Isabell had been caught only a month later, she could have been made a slave. The 1547 *Act for the Punishment of Vagabonds and for the Relief of the Poor* (*1 Edw.VI.c.3*) authorised the expulsion of vagabonds from the place of their punishment to their place of origin, and it was very careful to record that such punishment was for any 'man *or woman* being not Lame Impotent or so aged or diseased wth sicknes that he *or she* can not worke, [etc.]'.[2] As it was, Isabell's expulsion from Norwich to Newcastle was authorised under *12 Hen.VIII.c.12* (1531), which similarly provided for removing vagabonds to their home localities, but also for putting them to work, a fact often overlooked by scholars of this subject.[3] The later 1547 act, *1 Edw.VI.c.3*, really only expanded on this earlier principle.

Historians have mostly approached the Tudor vagrancy laws from the perspective of social welfare, and looked at the legislation's features primarily through two presumptive lenses. Firstly, there has been a notion that legislative poor relief slowly developed during the sixteenth century in response to a worsening problem. Secondly, there are persistent assumptions that the legislation was directed at the labouring classes and that it was mostly about employment. Early writers like S. Webb and B. Webb, and R.H. Tawney, saw in early vagrancy statutes a repressive response to growing unemployment, where people were compelled to work by the stick.[4] In their view people such as Isabell had to be punished for not working. Subsequent historians have focused mostly on the later mid-sixteenth-century statutes, seeing legislative poor relief mechanisms as attempts to grapple with unemployment, informed largely by local practices, humanist theorising, and a growing recognition that not everybody could find sufficient work.[5] In this alternative view people like Isabell had to be supported if they were unable to labour, or be put to work if they could. The consensus has been that there was a hardening of attitudes towards the unemployed, followed by a growing recognition that many people were not unemployed by choice, ultimately expressed in the workhouses of later sixteenth-century England. But this model is too simplistic, and the causal elements more often assumed than proved. When examined closely, most legislative action is best explained by administrative legislative processes and particular political causes, meaning that social and economic concerns are not necessarily the principal drivers of 'new' statutes. Scholarly understandings of the social and economic context of the statutes have been informed in part by the statutes themselves, which means that subsequent analysis has often been based upon arguments which are self-referential in nature and are characterised by circularity. The differences between statutes have been misunderstood and overstated. In short, there was more consistency and less 'development' than has generally been assumed.

Throughout the late medieval and early modern period, English statute law maintained three core principles: begging was regulated, vagrancy was forbidden, and localities were responsible for their own poor.[6] Recognising this fundamental conceptual continuity allows for a more nuanced appreciation of shifting conceptions of work over this period, because complementing these three principles was an assumption that a person should work for their living if they could. And work, it needs to be noted, did not necessarily mean waged employment. If a beggar had a licence to beg, for instance, then as far as the law was concerned they were doing legitimate work. Thus work, normally understood, was what one did to earn a living. This is why vagrancy, which is basically wandering and apparently maintaining oneself without work, was subject to such suspicion. Through examining this idea of not working, and exploring what constituted sufficiently legitimate work to avoid running afoul of the authorities, this chapter contributes to an understanding of women's work, through studying both governmental attitudes and everyday experiences. By unpicking notional and applied punishments for breaches of law, social expectations are brought into relief. Examining the regulation of beggary complicates notions of what constituted ready occupation. And highlighting the roles that women played on both sides of poor relief exchanges further clarifies their position in local economies. The whole builds up a sense of a strong and lasting perception by legislators that women should work, even across a period of significant social and political change, and that they were active participants in late medieval and early modern economies. To the medieval and early modern mind, Paul's injunction to the Thessalonians that 'anyone unwilling to work should not eat' clearly included women.[7]

Moreover, a specific focus on the way that women's work was represented and experienced under the vagrancy laws is welcome precisely because it is an area of study that has adopted some gendered perceptions of poverty and vagrancy that are at odds with the language of the statutes and the experiences of poor women in the period. These scholarly views seem to have accrued over time, rather than having been deliberately examined and formulated. Therefore this chapter serves as part corrective, as well as part exploration, of the role of women's work under the vagrancy statutes, even if much of the evidence is of prescribed and performed punishments of women for being vagrant or unemployed.

Historiographical trends

The gendering of research into vagrancy and poverty has arisen from a complex mix of historical evidence, historiographical baggage, and the habits of research. Legal and administrative terms and concepts have become seen as gendered in ways that contemporaries may not have recognised. Within most relevant documentary sources, terms like 'beggar', 'vagrant', and 'poor' were administrative denotations. Their application may have been classed and/or gendered, but the terms themselves were not. Begging derived from an act, vagrancy from either an act or a state, and poverty from a relational positioning to another person or a certain norm like social status. Kings could beg, knights could be vagrant, and cardinals could be poor. So too could women be vagrants, but they tend to be studied only when simultaneously poor.

The historiographical trend to combine these categories is perhaps most easily illustrated by reference to the simplistic ways that the term 'mighty beggar' has been readily conflated with 'vagabond', and both with 'masterless man', as even the title of A.L. Beier's still-influential study *Masterless Men* suggests.[8] But this linguistic slippage reflects deeper research tendencies.

In the first instance, there is apparently established evidence that vagrancy predominately related to men. Peter Clarke's analysis of Kentish migrants from the 1580s to the 1640s focuses on male vagrants, as does Paul Slack's analysis of the origins of vagrants in several major English towns. Yet while these studies remain useful, they are not necessarily indicative of wider trends, especially in the preceding decades.[9] Perhaps with a hint of some frustration, Jodi Mikalachki noted that 'to read the social histories of vagrancy uncritically' is to be confronted with '"historical evidence" that female vagrants were not statistically important, [and] that little can be known about those who do figure in extant records'.[10] Mikalachki's reference to the 'dominant statistical profile of the single, young adult male labourer or servant, within fifty miles of his parish of origin, and travelling alone' highlights the extent to which regional case studies have borne a disproportionate contextual burden and have been used to fill in blanks across wide periods and geographies. The evidence of the sixteenth-century male vagrant is actually much slimmer than often assumed.

As poor women came to the fore as research subjects in the later twentieth century, these contrasted with the tendency to focus on vagrant men. However, the development of deliberately gendered social histories reaffirmed earlier frames of reference about masculine vagrancy and likely exacerbated notions of feminine poverty. These assumptions certainly have some merit. As my own research into 1560s and 1570s Exeter helps show, more poor women received parish relief than men, something recognised as fairly common.[11] Furthermore, as Susan Broomhall's research into the poor of Tours illustrates, because of the over-representation of women among the early modern poor, a greater proportion of poor women's circumstances were documented and are therefore available for study.[12] Historians are now fairly well versed in the lives of the poor women of sixteenth-century England, particularly in the latter half of that century, and even more particularly in the city of Norwich where the 'Census of the Poor' of 1570 has facilitated a remarkable degree of research into how poor women made shift.[13]

Nevertheless, this tendency to see poverty and vagabondage as having gendered profiles in opposition to one another has effectively become entrenched, and has fed into the spheres of social policy and law. Take for example the following assertion by Marjorie K. McIntosh:

> Gender was also an issue. Descriptions of the poor throughout the second half of the sixteenth century were marked by increasingly gendered language. The deserving poor of both sexes were represented as weak and dependent. Like women, they needed support but were not respected. The idle poor, by contrast, were associated with uncontrolled, potentially violent, and threatening masculinity.[14]

McIntosh's argument is as much a product of the increasing historiographical focus on women in the past as it is on the documentary records of the sixteenth century. How language associated with need and dependence (criteria for relief) was feminine, and that of idleness and wandering (criteria for punishment) deemed masculine, is not fully explained. Legal sources such as canon law, statute, and proclamation mostly created these characteristics, while administrative areas such as towns, parishes, and courts applied them. Other commentary in literature and letters often reflects these contexts as well as other social agendas. I would suggest that assertions about the gendered nature of these terms are, as yet, unproven, and rather reflect the historical ascendency of the poor woman as a research subject.[15]

It is clear that there is a historiographical tendency to gender the archive. A timely review of legislative gendering, therefore, offers a pointed means of cutting through a historiographical tradition that sees this subject in the binary terms of masculine vagrancy and feminine poverty.

A lack of women's work: Mighty men and women

I opened this chapter by pointing out that Isabell Sudderon was deemed a vagabond, and noting how the law of 1547 specifically allowed for her punishment as such. A longer historical sweep shows that Isabell was not a peculiar episode in the statutory history of vagrancy, but rather an indicator of a common administrative thread. We will turn later to authorised beggars and the poor, but for the moment are concerned with the main 'various offences' punishable by statute: begging without cause when able to work, wandering without cause or obvious means of making a living, or in some other way engaging in activities deemed suspicious by relevant authorities. In other words, what do the punitive provisions of the vagrancy laws specifically tell us about attitudes towards women's work?

Edward III's *Statute of Labourers* (1349) is our legislative starting point. In the beginning it specified both men and women (*homo & femina regni*), demanded they labour for their living, and allowed for them to be 'committed to the next Gaol' if they refused to do so for what the master thought reasonable wages.[16] That twice in the same section women were explicitly mentioned draws our attention to the potentially significant role women played in the medieval English economy, especially in times of labour shortages or at points of the harvest cycle when excess labour was required.[17] Women, this emphatically tells us, were expected to work. Nor was this novel to the unique circumstances of post-Black Death England. Langdon's study of building wages in the late thirteenth century highlights how women can be identified working on major royal castle construction sites, apparently a response to a lack of men, and also suggesting the use of child labour, another thread in later vagrancy legislation.[18] In fact recent work on women's wages by Jane Humphries and Jacob Weisdorf highlights how women occupied a diverse range of occupations throughout the medieval and early modern period.[19] This leads us to be open to the possibility that women's work was not just limited to the domestic environment, to textile work, or to serving as a sort of husbandman's assistant, and the vagrancy regulations need to be seen in this light. Much later, in the 1520s, Sir Henry Willoughby made a couple of payments to 'wemyn that wesshed layd [washed lead] ore' and 'to wemyn that gaytherd layd [lead] ore', further highlighting the diversity of women's labour.[20] The notion of vagrancy legislation applied to women working in or at mines is a striking pointer to the broad application of the law, and the wide spectrum of activities that could constitute women's work.

When the parliament of Richard II introduced further vagrancy legislation, it did so without explicitly mentioning men and women in its general provisions, but through surprisingly inclusive language. The term used for beggars able to labour was 'chescun' (everyone).[21] Admittedly it is a masculine form of the word, but the point remains. For those wandering and perceived as suspicious, it simply used 'vagerantz' (vagrants).[22] However, it did draw attention to a specifically masculine issue, that is, 'they that feign themselves Men travelled out of the Realm' (essentially soldiers or sailors), doing so with explicitly masculine precision: 'hōmes' (men).[23] This linguistically gendered distinction between the general regulations about beggary and vagrancy (inclusive), and those that could really only apply to men (exclusive), continued in the next generation of vagrancy legislation under Henry VII.

Sadly neglected by historians, *11 Hen.VII.c.2* (1495), *An Acte agaynst vacabounds and beggers*, is one of the most important of the Tudor vagrancy acts, not only for the novelty of its provisions, but because it drew together the disparate issues of beggary and vagrancy into a single act for the first time in a developed way.[24] It, not the legislation of Richard II, gave us the term 'vagabond' in legislation for the first time, despite how the editors of the *Statutes of the Realm* translated 'vagerantz'. It enabled beggars and vagrants to be summarily punished, rather than processed through courts, expelled and sent to their home locality, rather than held in gaol until sessions; and, most importantly from the perspective of later legislation, it treated beggars and vagrants as the same for the purposes of initial punishment, with differences for secondary punishments. There is a particular irony in that the punishment for not working was to be placed in the stocks, where obviously one could not work.

11 Hen.VII.c.2 is also interesting for its apparent applicability to men and women. Initial clauses are largely gender-neutral in the Tudor sense: '*all suche* vagaboundes idell and suspecte p[er]sons lyvyng suspiciously, and *theym* so taken to sette in stokkes'. The following section's use of masculine terms, 'if eftsones [soon after] *he* be taken in suche defaute in the same Town or Township then *he* to be sette in the like wise in Stokkis', was corrected in the 1504 near-verbatim version of the statute and replaced with '*they* be taken' and '*then to* be sette', perhaps indicating a legislative concern to clarify that that section was likewise intended to apply to women.[25] Again there was a male-specific comment, with the requirement 'that *no man* be excused', but as with the earlier legislation this is used in reference to those pretending to have certain male professions: university clerk, soldier, and sailor. And if any officers of the realm had any doubts about punishing women, the final clause of both the 1495 and 1504 versions makes it unequivocally clear:

> Provided alwey that dymynucion [diminution] of punysshment of vagaboundes and beggers aforeseid may and shalbe had for *women greate with child*, and *men and women* in extreme sikenes.[26]

A legislator would presumably not need to note that pregnancy was a mitigating factor for magistrates to consider unless it was assumed that women would be punished.

A 'pregnancy proviso' was retained when Henry VIII issued a proclamation in 1530 that beggars and vagabonds ('be it man or woman') were to be 'bound and sharply beaten and scourged'.[27] When the punishment of whipping and expulsion was enacted in statute in 1531, again the criteria for punishment stipulated 'any *Man or Woman* beyng hole & mighty in body & able to laboure'.[28] And then in 1547 when the term 'vagabond' was first legislatively defined in a specific section, it included any '*man or woman* being not Lame Impotent or so aged or diseased wth sicknes that *he or she* can not worke', adopting the formula we have already seen.[29] When that act was repealed in 1550, the 1531 whipping provisions returned. Over subsequent statutory revisions of 1572, 1576, and 1598 the 'all persons', 'he or she', and 'his or her' constructions of vagabondage were reiterated to ensure that 'his or her body be bloudye', not just his.[30]

This, however, is not to say that there was an equal ratio of female vagrants to male vagrants, or that the authorities had no specific concerns about violent men. In fact, there are several examples of male groups being specifically singled out, although some confusion has been caused by the uncritical conflation of these particular male groups with the wider vagabond category. Royal proclamations are particularly instructive here. Common to the middle decades of the sixteenth century are proclamations ordering persons to leave the verge of the royal court (or household), which singled out 'masterless men', 'pages or boys', and 'boys and rascals'.[31] Here the threat of the vagrancy laws were specifically referenced to prevent 'assault or fray' by such persons, perhaps also to prevent politics by force in the tensions of the mid-1530s through to the early 1550s.[32] Later in the century returning soldiers were a particular group of concern to the Elizabethan court.[33] A final cluster of proclamations specifically regarding London, but also mentioning the court and soldiers, is also relevant to royal concerns about 'masterless men' in the environs of the court and government.[34] That various statutory provisions also specifically addressed the authority of the king's officers to enforce the laws within the verge of the royal court further highlights this very specific concern with a type of vagabond man, but also illustrates that this is a particular subset of the wider categories of 'vagabond' and 'mighty beggar'. The masterless man of the proclamation was not an unemployed ploughman. Rather, he was a masterless man-at-arms.

When Tudor royal proclamations railed against vagabonds they were usually a specific male-type loaded with kinetic potential for violence. But when towns and villages dealt with their local idlers, beggars, and vagrants, it was not necessarily this 'masterless man' variety. Certainly villagers will have—often rightly—feared and suspected strangers, but surely it was ever thus, and we should not see punishable beggary, idleness, and vagrancy as exclusively, or even principally, a male phenomenon. Surviving records of the punishment of female vagabonds highlights this quite clearly. A 1546 list of vagabonds in Norwich noted Jane Wyn being 'ponysshed [and] assigned to lyme [probably Lyme Regis]', and Agnes Howes 'to Berber in Warwickshire'.[35] In these instances women were being explicitly punished as vagabonds and recorded as such. Other major cities also punished women as vagabonds. For example, in Exeter in 1560:

> alice barrys was punysshed the 6 daie of June 1560 beyng of the Cown[t]e of Coryton and traveling the countrie as a vacabound and sent unto toryton agen wt a lettr testimonial of her ponyshmet according to the statute the daie & yere above writon.[36]

The careful notation that the punishment was accompanied with the provision of a letter, detailing that the punishment was performed 'according to the statute', would have authorised her to beg for alms on her way home. The letter of punishment was effectively a specific licence to beg. This serves to highlight the importance of law in regulating the treatment of vagabonds and beggars in Tudor England, and the diligence with which local authorities followed statutory regulations.[37] It also highlights how, conscious of that legal framework, the officials of Exeter saw no problem with punishing a woman. Yet they were not just punished. As far as these terse records reveal, these women all appear to have been punished in accordance with provisions of relevant national statute law as *vagabonds*.

Frustrating our chance to study female vagabonds in depth is the fact that from the end of the fifteenth century vagrancy was a summary offence. Few records needed to be made, and fewer would survive, detailing any punishment of vagabonds throughout the sixteenth century, excepting the begging letters themselves which were highly likely to be destroyed, intentionally or otherwise, and occasional notations of the sorts already quoted in town or parish records.[38] The whole framework of the statutory regime did not rely on extensive record keeping; instead it was the marks of whipping or branding that were used to identify prior punishments, and which were therefore treated in detail in statutory law.[39] The examples given may point to individual women like Alice Barrys of Exeter and Isabell Sudderon of Norwich individually being vagrant, but the relatively few records that exist seem to suggest the possibility that punishment was more likely when women were taken in a group and/or associated with men. This probably reflects the nature of the records, the circumstances of their production, and the particular dynamics of vagrant capture. For example, when a search for suspicious persons was undertaken in London and surrounds in 1519, Elizabeth Hammonde was 'taken at the buckler-maker's house', 'an old drab and a young wench' were found 'upon a sheet cast upon the ground' under a very crowded house, another woman was 'in a chamber underneath' yet another building, and in Chelsea was found 'in a barn a beggar and his wife'.[40] In two other cases in the same search women were taken in bed with men.[41] In all cases it seems to be the buildings that were being searched and the women were taken as vagrants as a result of their location. Some may have been prostitutes, but some were wives, and others clearly just destitute. But it was the search that produced the documentation, not the offences or offenders. The various searches for strangers and vagrants in the major towns of England throughout the sixteenth century probably netted similar results, with both men and women being rounded up for summary punishment and expulsion because of where they were, not where they had come from.

To have individually and specifically run afoul of the vagrancy laws probably required a greater prominence or nuisance-factor to any given town or village than simply wandering through or residing in an insalubrious dwelling-place. In 1588 the payments of the Plymouth city court reveal: 'Itm pd for a horse hire to draw the Carte when the Irish woman was Carted ... iiijd'. That this deserved and received special mention points to the rarity of the event. Similarly, while Exeter corporate records detail a few women punished in the late 1550s and early 1560s, they hardly constituted a tide of wandering vagrants. When in March 1560 Marion Barnes was 'whipped out of the Citie' of Exeter, it was 'for her incontynent lyffe'.[42] Further specifics of this case are unclear. Her husband Richard remained in the city, suggesting he, at least, was local. The vagrancy laws seem to have acted within towns as a useful umbrella package for social problems. A few months earlier, in December 1559, one John Smale of Trinity parish, Exeter (therefore a resident), was 'taken for a loyterer [loiterer] & vagrant p[er]son', imprisoned, released, and told to leave the city on pain of being whipped per the statute.[43] He was told he 'shall also take his wyffe and children wt him'.[44] So vagrants were not always men, and not always single. To suffer the effects of vagrancy law did not even mean having to be a vagrant; you could have been married to one. Nor did you have to be a stranger, as begging without authorisation was also prohibited. Illustrating this neatly, in the list of poor people named to receive relief in Exeter in 1565, Eleanor Marshal had a notation beside her name: 'to be whipped if she begs'.[45] Perhaps more interestingly, she is the only one out of 177 poor listed to receive relief in 1565 from Exeter with such a notation. For many poor, it seems, be they male or female, the vagrancy laws were a threat more often than an actuality.[46]

The records of the parish of Crondall, Hampshire, detail a series of persons punished as vagrants at the turn of the sixteenth and seventeenth centuries, which show women having a prominent statistical presence. 'Alice Whitewoode' from Dover, 'Elizabeth Harrys wydowe' from Cornwall, and 'Elizabeth Godfrye of St Gyles' were all taken for wandering and begging, then punished and sent to their respective homes.[47] So too 'Marye Elderton of the age fiftie two yeres [...] wth her child of the age of vij yeres was taken vagarant and begging within the p[ar]ishe', punished and sent back to 'the yle of wight'.[48] Similarly punished for beggary and vagrancy were 'Thomas Eastbrooke of the age of xxxviij yeres and his wyfe of the age of xxvj yeres and Kathernie Coulton a gerle of the age of x yeres', all returned to Cornwall.[49] As were 'Catheryin the wyfe of John Foster of East horshlye [...] wythe her doughter of the ages of eight yeres', 'Johan Lanwaye the doughtr of Robt Lanwaye of Compton'.[50] In the 1620s 'Edithe Lanwaye' and 'Alice Starke', aged 56 and 18 years respectively, attest to a diverse age profile of the female vagabond.[51] From pre-teens to their fifties, whether single, married, or widowed, from relatively nearby to further afield, females constitute about half of vagrants recorded in Crondall. Yet there are relatively few recorded instances all told, considering the years covered, and this serves to temper notions of an uncontrollable vagrant population, male or female.

In fact, in Crondall it was a woman who seemed a particular problem. The first of the vagrants recorded was 'Margarette Tyller al[ia]s Sansome late s[er]vant to Mr Osborne of Rye', 'taken begging and wandering' on July 19, 1598.[52] She was, 'for her rogishe lyfe punnyshed and the same daye sente [...] to the place of her birthe'. A subsequent note records that she was 'eight tymes' sent home, but that the inhabitants of her home-town Hasell 'brought her again'. Only with 'the eighth tyme beinge sent [did] they returne her nott'. Here then, we have a female vagrant being sent back and forth between two towns several times. The authorities did not seem to fear this vagabond, and had no compunction about punishing her. They do, however, sound a little smug at finally being rid of her.

Women's work: Chastisement and charity

Other than the overwhelming sense that women were expected to work or be supported in their own households, the vagrancy laws and their administration also draw attention to a few particular areas of women's work. Obviously, there is the work not being done by women, of which there survive some tantalising archival mentions of the sort already addressed, which suggests a broad range of economic activities. And while quantifying the range of women's work is beyond the scope of this chapter, it is worth noting that women's labour is sometimes discernible in surviving accounts. Building wages have been the main form of tracking daily wages, but the nuance of parish repair work allows for a closer look at some community dynamics.[53] For instance, extracting waged labour from the churchwardens' accounts for the parish of St Michael Spurriergate in York reveals that wives were sometimes paid for assisting their husbands. Although only a tiny fraction of the recorded payments, the payments demonstrably to women highlight a few useful elements. In 1526 a labourer was paid 2*s* 4*d* for seven days' work, and his wife 'for helping hym, vijd', or 1*d* per day.[54] Here the feminine contribution seems small, and the reward commensurate. In 1544 a labourer and his wife were paid 4*d* for a day of labour, the equivalent of a single male's standard daily wage.[55] The two, it seemed, were paid as a single economic unit. The most tantalising of the records is from 1542, when a labourer and his wife worked a day and a half and earned 12*d*.[56] The woman, this reveals, was paid the equivalent of a man's day wage. Because it was simply the fact of marriage which led to the specific notation, this suggests that other unnamed labourers may have been women.

Women who did not work, and did not have a legitimate reason for such 'idleness', were potentially subject to punishment under the vagrancy laws. The development, growth, and spread of workhouses, or 'bridewells', modelled on the London institution, is a well-rehearsed story not needing detailed repetition here.[57] From the mid-sixteenth century larger towns frequently established a local workhouse for the housing and putting to work of local beggars and poor, often using stocks of wool for their poor to work into cloth, which could be seen as attempts to remedy local economies as much as schemes specifically intended to support the poor. The city of York is typical in utilising some of its medieval hospitals to set the poor to work, and the following record from York in 1553 is fairly representative:

> the wardens [etc. ...] inquire which of the poore be hable eyther to spynne or doo any other work; and as they see cause to sett theym awork accordingly; and if any suche poor will refuse soo to doo then their releif to be taken from theym and spulsed [expulsed] the Citie.[58]

Here, drawing on statutory authority, York's magistrates felt comfortable with the poor being ordered to work. For the most part this seems to suggest the poor were to contribute towards the renewal of local manufacture of cloth. It is a little different from the penal labour espoused in later institutions, like the mills installed in St Anthony's hospital in York in 1577 'for setting of rogisshe and idle persones on work, hable to labour', but it is an application of the same legal notion.[59] On the basis of the York records, I suspect the transition from medieval hospital to early modern workhouse may have been smoother than some historians have considered.

Although putting people to work was allowed under earlier legislation, gleaning insights into whether and how those provisions were enacted in practice is frustrated by the summary nature of the proceedings and the apparent lack of institutional work programmes until the mid-sixteenth century. Evaluating what work women vagrants may have been put to therefore involves some guesswork. Contrary to some misconception, the initiative for the 1530s legislative authority to put vagrants to work was just as much about providing employers with workers, as it was with providing work for the unemployed.[60] Harvesting operations, harbour repairs, and other temporary or seasonal activities may have seen 'vagrants' being put to work by local justices of the peace, many of whom would of course be landowners. This could have been done quite summarily, was perfectly legal, yet would be extremely unlikely to leave any documentary trace.

Without excluding them from such public and communal activities as those discussed above, it is not unreasonable to suggest that many women punished as vagrants or beggars may have been placed into service, particularly domestic service. Although most records of punished vagabonds detail their being assigned to a place, sometimes the record may detail a vagabond being assigned to a named person, which rather suggests compulsory employment. A record from Norwich related how in 1546 'John Evans [was] punysshed & is assigned to John Petyber'.[61] This example is of a male, but at least suggests the possibility of women being similarly treated. Certainly, the law would have allowed it. Specific treatment of women in this regard is revealed in the way that children could be forcibly put into service and training. Under *27 Hen.VIII.c.25* (1536) all idle or begging children aged between 5 and 14 years old could be appointed 'to maisters of

Table 8.1 Ages at which vagrants were liable for service.

Statute (year)	*Age taken into service*	*Age completed service (women)*	*Age completed service (men)*
1536	5–14	16	16
1547	5–14	20	24
1549–50	5–14	15	18
1572	5–14	18	24
1597–98	Any children	21	24

Husbondrie or other craftes or labours to be taughte, by the whiche they may gette their livings whan they shall come to age'.[62] While that statute provided a vague sense that 16 years of age was the point at which this provision ceased affecting children, later statutes were more specific about the point of independence for women and men. The age parameters statutes provided for placing vagrant(s') children into service are given in Table 8.1. The constancy of women becoming independent ahead of men is significant, although possibly linked to notions of marriage norms and sexual maturity.

Finally, through the ways that women could be givers, collectors, or recipients of alms, the vagrancy laws provide a unique opportunity to explore other areas of women's work that might not normally be considered as 'work' because of the strong associations in modern society between 'work' and 'employment'. The first of these activities is begging, likely to have been extremely common, and rarely documented. Poorer women could beg for alms for a range of reasons from simple destitution or desperation, to opportunistic additions to personal or familial finances. This activity could take place in a range of places, whether typically public like church doorways and public streets, communal forms like funeral doles and daily distributions at religious houses, or private visits to fellow householders and the kitchens of lordly houses.

A reading of some of the relevant historiography of poor relief developments in sixteenth-century England might lead one to think that the parliament of England outlawed begging, or that stopping begging was one of its primary concerns. This, however, would be an oversimplification, for the Tudor state never outlawed begging, it only regulated it (although some towns temporarily banned begging entirely in times of plague crises).[63] A significant administrative shift occurred when parliamentary statute required all 'beggars' to carry written proof authorising them to beg from 1531 onwards.[64] Yet even this built on extant practices. Many towns had been giving 'their' beggars badges or tokens, which allowed them to beg.[65] And there is no reason to suppose that women were not a prominent feature of these cohorts of urban beggars. This, however, should not lead us to overplay the continuities in beggary throughout this period. Begging was allowed, but what was termed 'open begging', that is public begging, was increasingly discouraged, especially when the parish rate, a system of weekly charitable collection and distribution, was implemented.[66] Yet much authorised beggary survived.

Written 'licences' documenting a person's circumstance and authorising them to beg were used throughout the wider medieval to early modern period. Little documentation of authorised begging survives, but what does, like punishment records, generally points to conformity with the law and the presence of women. For instance, in 1463 the Beverley town Act Book records 'Littera testimonialis' allowing 'Agneti Herrison' to beg alms because of the death of her husband in war.[67] Similarly, in 1515 Joan Cressy was given a royal licence to beg alms to ransom her husband, and so could lawfully 'goo into what p[ar]ties of this our Realm for almoses and oder cheritable gyftes of cresten feythfull people for goddess sake to ask and gader' as she liked, the testimonial being protection against being placed in the stocks.[68] The household accounts of the Willoughby family from the Midlands highlight such begging in practice when in January 1543 4*d* was given 'to a woman of Lycetershyre that whent with a testymonyall for burning of hyr howse', highlighting that such migratory begging continued into the period of more intense regulations that the 1530s had ushered in.[69] Moreover, the regulations authorise persons who had been punished to be given begging letters for their journeys home, furthering the persistence of such practices.

The accounts of the Willoughby family are particularly useful for illustrating the range of begging practices and types. Within these, the full spectrum of the sixteenth-century begging scene can be found: friars, proctors (those who begged on behalf of churches, hospitals etc.), anchorites, men and women. Of the female beggars who appear in the accounts, a number were gathering money for religious uses:

> to the wemyn that gaytherd for Owre Lady's lyght att Mydylton ... iiij*d* [April, 1521].[70]
>
> to the wemyn of Wyllarton that gaytherd for Owre Lady's Lyght ... iiij*d* [1521].[71]
>
> in rayward [reward] to the wemyn of the toune that gathwrde for Saynt Stewyn ... iiij*d* [April, 1526].[72]

These women were clearly gathering alms for their churches, so they were possibly substantial women of the relevant towns and parishes, approaching the local worthies in small delegations. For those women able to devote some time to such gathering, perhaps due to the economic security offered by their husbands or independent wealth, this was sixteenth-century 'charity work'. Two of the examples noted above match the onset of spring weather, so these gathering expeditions may have been mini-pilgrimages inspired by the same circumstances that Chaucer described encouraging longer expeditions

('Whan that Aprill with his shoures soote').[73] And, like pilgrimages, the particular target of these alms-collecting expeditions, altar lights, disappeared from the English religious scene with the Reformation of the mid-century, so this sort of begging by women may have diminished.

But religiously motivated female beggars did not entirely disappear. Historians have noted that women were very prominent in the late medieval period as organisers of 'church ales', which were communal fund-raising efforts for charitable uses where ale was brewed and sold.[74] Similarly, historians have noted a shift from women playing a role in ales to being very active in early modern 'church briefs', where women would be authorised to go and collect money for specific charitable purposes.[75] Recognising the way that women collected on behalf of parishes discussed earlier helps reveal a greater continuity in women's charitable and parochial support work across the fairly arbitrary medieval and early modern specialist divide. The particular fund may have shifted, but the feminine activities associated with providing for that fund were relatively similar. Indeed, with the statutory advent of weekly parish and town collections for the poor from 1536 onwards, it is not unreasonable to suppose that women played some role in this form of charitable collection. Generally men were appointed to have charge of the actual fund and any written account, but they could and did appoint subordinates to do the actual collecting.[76] While rare, known cases of female churchwardens hint at further possible feminine participation in the administration of parish activities, particularly at the sub-documentary level in roles like those associated with charitable collections.[77] Certainly the legislation retained a general gender-neutrality in the sections regarding the appointment, accounting, and where necessary fining of collectors. J. Charles Cox uncovered some extraordinary cases from seventeenth- and eighteenth-century Derbyshire where some women's appointments as overseers of the poor, a more particular office than the sixteenth-century collectors, were challenged at quarter sessions on the basis that women could not serve in that role by virtue of their gender.[78] The courts initially agreed that women should not be overseers of the poor, in apparent contradiction of experience and statute law, yet subsequently the courts later seemed to ignore their own decisions and women continued to perform this role.[79]

At least impressionistically, however, surviving sources seem to point to a greater number of male beggars than female beggars among those authorised throughout the period. A surviving begging licence from 1576, for instance, shows one John Lawson, a labourer, being authorised to beg for a year because of the prolonged infirmity of his wife.[80] This may give us one explanation, being that the head of a household was recognised by authorities as the responsible provider, yet it also reminds us of the importance of a woman's contribution to household economies. Another explanation is that surviving sources tend to record more public exchanges of begging-almsgiving and the peculiarly masculine forms of authorised beggar. Parish records in St John's, Exeter, in the 1560s, and St Martin's Coney Street, York, in the 1570s, detail these parishes giving alms to persons begging at their churches. St John's only recorded money given to poor men, while of the at least eighteen recipients of alms from St Martin's, only two were women.[81]

This picture may also reflect other limitations of the sources about what sorts of beggary were tolerated in various localities. Some payments from the Willoughbys to poorer women may mask begging-almsgiving exchanges. Payments for posies of a penny each to 'mayddes' ('maids'), for example, might reflect mercantile 'cover' for what was in actuality a charitable exchange.[82] While this is suppositional, the fact that other payments in reward for gifts to Mrs Willoughby were suspiciously high may point to this being the case. Payments firstly 'to a pore woman that gave my Mrs. Nuttes', and another 'to a mayd of Nottingham for presenting my Mrs. With aples', netted the gift-givers 6*d* and 12*d* respectively, and might suggest these gifts were being rewarded at well above market value, especially when compared with the average day wage of 4*d*.[83] The same phenomenon is discernible in royal accounts where 'divers poor men, women and children' were given 'rewards' each new year's day for various gifts they brought.[84]

For those women in need of regular financial assistance, the development and implementation of the parish and town relief systems in the sixteenth century was a major innovation, albeit one increasingly thought to have had local and long-term precedents.[85] Nevertheless, following the statutory sanction for weekly relief systems, surviving records clearly show women to be overrepresented among the supported poor. This relative dominance of women is reflected in the Norwich Census of the Poor of 1570, which shows a higher proportion of women than men.[86] So too in Exeter, where the 'Accounts of the Poor' provide multiple lists of poor people, women outnumber men. About two thirds of the poor listed to receive weekly poor relief from the city were women across three separate lists.[87] Women were also much more likely than men to appear in multiple lists, suggesting longer periods in need of assistance.[88] Whether a function of old age, domestic duties and child care, absent or deceased spouses, or difficulties finding employment, the spectrum of possibilities and the relative dearth of evidence makes commentary on the relationship between worker and pauper difficult. The range of payments also complicates analysis.

However, isolating weekly alms payments in Exeter of 6*d* or higher—in other words, those payments which are significantly higher than the weekly average of 4*d* and which therefore potentially reflect those in greatest need of support—essentially erases the gender disparity from the Exeter data. The result of this analysis is presented in Table 8.2, where the number of persons who received 6*d* or more a week appears to demonstrate that there was no significant gender bias among the poorest of the poor.

Table 8.2 Number of persons who received weekly alms of 6*d* or greater.

Year of list	*Weekly almswomen >= 6d*	*Weekly almsmen >= 6d*
1563	10	10
1565	11	12
1567	8	7

There are some caveats with this data. In 1565 and 1567 Richard Martyn received money 'for a poor mayde', meaning the money was for a woman but given to a man. Similarly, one of the women in 1567 received her money for a 'boy'. Both cases reveal that payments could be for the benefit of a person at a remove from the actual accounts, possibly even taken into their care under the vagrancy provisions. In each case the figure has been tabulated according to the custodian of the money. Two names from 1565 and one from 1567, because of abbreviations or script, were considered too gender-ambiguous to include. Finally, almshouses have been excluded. Nevertheless, women and men receiving the greater sums did so in the same proportions. This, I rather suspect, is the group most dependent on the poor rate for their living.

Smaller sums like 2*d* or 4*d* complemented inadequate incomes. Eleanor Marshal who, as already noted was 'to be whipped if she begs', received 4*d* and yet still may not have had enough. This further suggests that the majority of payments were intended as supplementary funds rather than income replacements.[89] Therefore the greater proportion of women in poor lists suggests that their incomes were generally smaller than for men. Whether this was a function of unemployment, underemployment, or lower wages, is difficult to ascertain in the absence of wider evidence, but poses some interesting questions for further research.

On the other side of this charitable exchange, women were expected to contribute to poor relief, legislatively articulated through a vague but non-gendered gathering of the 'almes of the good christen people' in 1536, and from 1552 the annual asking 'of *everie man and woman* what they of charitie wilbe contented to give wekelie towards the relief of the Poore'.[90] In the Exeter poor relief system, women comprised at least 2–4 per cent of total contributors who supported the poor with weekly offerings in 1564/5, and 4 per cent in 1570.[91] This is a small proportion of contributors, but probably only reflects single women, and as such is not as insignificant as first appears. A number of the donors were listed as 'wydow', which further supports this, and also indicates that unsupported women were not always poor. Moreover, when it is thought that perhaps one out of every twenty-six contributors to the poor relief system was an independent woman, and that it was a weekly payment, it highlights the application of a presumption embedded in legislation that women's work was sufficient to justify contributing to the relief of the poor.

Conclusion

This brings us full circle, where just as the legislation was clear to stipulate that women who would not work should be punished as vagabonds, and that those who could not work should be provided with relief, so too it made clear that those who could contribute to the relief of the poor should do so, gender notwithstanding. This study has hopefully helped bridge a specialist divide, highlighting the considerable conceptual and practical continuities related to women's work at the cusp of the late medieval and the early modern. Women were expected to work; begging was often legitimate work, and so too was charitable gathering. It has certainly de-gendered perceptions of the notions of 'mighty beggars' and 'vagabonds', the scholarship of which has been relatively heavily influenced by Victorian and twentieth-century preconceptions and preoccupations. Modern stereotypes of late medieval and early modern women as housewives or domestic servants should be abandoned in light of contemporary images of the female vagabond and the assumptions pertaining to women's work that underlay those images. The cause of Isabell Sudderon's punishment may be obscured by time and distance, but it is entirely legal and plausible that she was put to work in a mine. The ramifications of that principle are legion, and deserve further exploration. Labour issues from slavery and convict transportation, to the application of summary communal justice, or the later growth of a Victorian understanding of female domesticity, all may derive in some part from England's vagrancy laws.

Notes

1 Norfolk Record Office (NRO), NCR Case 16a/5, fol. 429.
2 Although passed by parliament in 1547, the slavery provisions of the law were not due to come into force until 'after the first daie of Apryll next following', i.e., April 1548: 1 Edw.VI.c.3.1, *The Statutes of the Realm, Volume 4* (hereafter *SR* 4) (London: Eyre and Spottiswoode, 1819), 5. My emphases in italics throughout.
3 12 Hen.VIII.c.12.3, *The Statutes of the Realm, Volume 3* (hereafter *SR* 3) (London: Eyre and Spottiswoode, 1817), 329.
4 S. Webb and B. Webb, *English Local Government: English Poor Law History: Part I, the Old Poor Law* (London: Longmans, Green and Co., 1927); R.H. Tawney, *The Agrarian Problem in the Sixteenth Century* (New York: Longmans, Green and Co., 1912).
5 See, for instance, Paul Fideler, 'Poverty, Policy and Providence: The Tudors and the Poor', in *Political Thought and the Tudor Commonwealth: Deep Structure, Discourse and Disguise*, ed. P.A. Fideler and T.F. Mayer (Oxford: Routledge, 1992), and other publications by the same; see also works by Paul Slack, particularly *Poverty and Policy in Tudor and Stuart England* (London: Longman, 1988) and *The English Poor Law, 1531–1782* (Cambridge: Cambridge University Press, 1995), and the studies of A.L. Beier and Marjorie K. McIntosh cited below.

The focus on local experimentation seems to largely follow from E.M. Leonard, *The Early History of English Poor Relief* (Cambridge: Cambridge University Press, 1900). The tendency to focus on central government agency and ideas is largely a response to the work of Elton. See in particular G.R. Elton, 'An Early Tudor Poor Law', *Economic History Review*, new ser., 6 (1953).

6 Nicholas D. Brodie, 'Beggary, Vagabondage, and Poor Relief: English Statutes in the Urban Context, 1495–1572' (PhD Dissertation, University of Tasmania, 2010).

7 2 Thessalonians 3:10.

8 A.L. Beier, *Masterless Men: The Vagrancy Problem in England, 1560–1640* (London: Methuen, 1985).

9 Peter Clark, 'The Migrant in Kentish Towns 1580–1640', in *Crisis and Order in English Towns 1500–1700: Essays in Urban History*, ed. Peter Clark and Paul Slack (London: Routledge and Kegan Paul, 1972); Paul Slack, 'Vagrants and Vagrancy in England 1598–1664', *Economic History Review*, 2nd ser., 27 (1974). Slack's paper particularly poses a male vagrant dominance.

10 Jodi Mikalachki, 'Women's Networks and the Female Vagrant: A Hard Case', in *Maids and Mistresses, Cousins and Queens: Women's Alliances in Early Modern England*, ed. Susan Frye and Karen Robertson (Oxford: Oxford University Press, 1999), 53.

11 Nicholas D. Brodie, '"The names of all the poore people": Corporate and Parish Relief in Exeter, 1560s–1570s', in *Experiences of Poverty in Late Medieval and Early Modern England and France*, ed. Anne M. Scott (Farnham: Ashgate, 2012).

12 Susan Broomhall, 'Identity and Life Narratives of the Poor in Later Sixteenth-Century Tours', *Renaissance Quarterly* 57 (2004): 439–65.

13 For example: Lesley Silvester, 'The Experience of Single Women in Early Modern Norwich: "Rank Beggars, Gresse Maydes and Harlots"', in *Experiences of Poverty*, ed. Scott; Margaret Pelling, 'Old Age, Poverty, and Disability in Early Modern Norwich: Work, Remarriage, and Other Expedients', in *Life, Death, and the Elderly: Historical Perspectives*, ed. Margaret Pelling and Richard M. Smith (London: Routledge, 1991). See also how much the Norwich census supports aspects of several papers in Carol Rawcliffe and Richard Wilson, eds., *Medieval Norwich* (Cambridge: Cambridge University Press, 2004).

14 Marjorie K. McIntosh, 'Poverty, Charity, and Coercion in Elizabethan England', *Journal of Interdisciplinary History* 35 (2005), 463.

15 Sara Mendelson and Patricia Crawford, *Women in Early Modern England, 1550–1720* (Oxford: Clarendon, 1998), 256–97. The citations that McIntosh offered all point to studies of poor women. McIntosh, 'Poverty, Charity, and Coercion', 463; several papers addressing female poverty are cited, although these seem to relate to the later section of this paragraph.

16 23 Edw.III.3, *The Statutes of the Realm, Volume 1* (London: Eyre and Spottiswoode, 1810), 307.

17 On women in the English harvest, see: S.A.C. Penn, 'Female Wage-Earners in Late Fourteenth-Century England', *Agricultural History Review* 35 (1987); M. Roberts, 'Sickles and Scythes: Women's Work and Men's Work at Harvest Time', *History Workshop Journal* 7 (1979); M. Roberts, 'Sickles and Scythes Revisited: Harvest Work, Wages and Symbolic Meanings', in *Women, Work and*

Wages in England, 1600–1850, ed. Penelope Lane, Neil Raven, and K.D.M. Snell (Woodbridge: Boydell, 2004).

18 John Langdon, 'Waged Building Employment in Medieval England: Subsistence Safety Net or Demographic Trampoline?', in *Survival and Discord in Medieval Society: Essays in Honour of Christopher Dyer*, ed. Richard Goddard, John Langdon, and Miriam Müller (Turnhout: Brepols, 2010), 115–16.

19 Jane Humphries and Jacob Weisdorf, 'The Wages of Women in England, 1260–1850', *Journal of Economic History* 75 (2015).

20 Historical Manuscripts Commission (hereafter HMC), *Report on the Manuscripts of Lord Middleton* (London: HM Stationery Office, 1911), 336.

21 12 Ric.II.c.7, *The Statutes of the Realm, Volume 2* (hereafter *SR* 2) (London: Eyre and Spottiswoode, 1816), 58.

22 12 Ric.II.c.9, *SR* 2, 33; rather than the 'vagabonds' used by the translators of the *Statutes of the Realm* and most-often cited by scholars.

23 12 Ric.II.c.8, *SR* 2, 58: while this could be taken in a 'humankind' sense, later divisions seem to support a distinction between 'everyone' and 'men' being deliberate.

24 14 Hen.VII.c.2, *SR* 2, 569; its provisions were reiterated with the near-verbatim 19 Hen.VII.c.12, *SR* 2, 656–57.

25 11 Hen.VII.c.2, *SR* 2, 569; 19 Hen.VII.c.12, *SR* 2, 656.

26 11 Hen.VII.c.2.5, *SR* 2, 569.

27 Paul L. Hughes and James F. Larkin, eds., *Tudor Royal Proclamations Volume 1* (New Haven: Yale University Press, 1964), no. 128.

28 22 Hen.VIII.c.12.3 (1531 Act), *SR* 3, 329.

29 1 Edw.VI.c.3.1 (1547 Act), *SR* 4, 5.

30 3&4 Edw.VI.c.16 (1550 Act), *SR* 4, 115–17; 14 Eliz.c.5.5 (1572 Act) *SR* 4, 591; 18 Eliz.I.c.3.10 (1576), *SR* 4, 613; 39 Eliz.I.c.4 (1598), *SR* 4, 899.

31 Hughes and Larkin, *Tudor Royal Proclamations Vol. 1*, no. 141 (1533), no. 204 (1541), no. 371 (1551); Paul L. Hughes and James F. Larkin, eds., *Tudor Royal Proclamations Volume 2* (New Haven: Yale University Press, 1969), no. 396 (1553), no. 483 (1561).

32 Hughes and Larkin, *Tudor Royal Proclamations Vol. 1*, no. 141 (1533). But it is just as likely associated with the many proclamations ordering people to avoid court because of the plague, and may explain other specificities of the proclamations such as that requiring that 'no person keep any ferrets'.

33 Paul L. Hughes and James F. Larkin, eds., *Tudor Royal Proclamations Volume 3* (New Haven: Yale University Press, 1969), no. 716 (1589), no. 735 (1591), no. 740 (1591), no. 745 (1592).

34 Hughes and Larkin, *Tudor Royal Proclamations Vol. 1*, no. 250 (1545); *Tudor Royal Proclamations Vol. 2*, no. 416 (1554); *Tudor Royal Proclamations Vol. 3*, no. 796 (1598).

35 NRO NCR Case 16a/5, fol. 343.

36 Cornwall and Devonshire Record Office (CDRO), Act Book IV, fols. 9, 12v.

37 The subject of my PhD dissertation: Brodie, 'Beggary'.

38 Very few begging licences survived into modern times, and those that have were generally for specific causes like illness, property damage by fire, and such like. See Brodie, 'Beggary', 126–79.

39 For example: 22 Hen.VIII.c.12, *SR* 3, 330 (ears cut off for various specific offences); London, British Library, MS Royal 18 C VI, fols. 5v–6r (branding is

proposed for refusal to work, so that subsequent refusal could constitute felony); 27 Hen.VIII.c.25.10,11, *SR* 3, 560 (upper part of right ear cut off for specific offences; secondary punishment is felony); 1 Edw.VI.c.3.1, *SR* 4, 5 (offenders branded with a 'V' to denote prior punishment as a 'Vagabond').

40 John S. Brewer, ed., *Letters and Papers, Foreign and Domestic, Henry VIII, Volume 3 Part 1* (London: Eyre and Spottiswoode, 1867), no. 365 (July 8, 1518), 126–29.

41 Brewer, ed., *Letters and Papers, Foreign and Domestic, Henry VIII, Volume 3 Part 1*, no. 365 (July 8, 1518), 126–29.

42 CDRO Act Book IV, fol. 9.

43 CDRO Act Book IV, fol. 2.

44 CDRO Act Book IV, fol. 2.

45 CDRO, ECA Book 157, 'Accounts of the Poor', fol. 42; Brodie, '"The names of all the poore people"', 113.

46 See Brodie, '"The names of all the poore people"', 115 for details of numbers of poor in Exeter.

47 Surrey History Centre Archives, CRON/6/, fols. 78, 78v, 79. Thanks to Patrick Ball for this lead.

48 Ibid., fol. 81v.

49 Ibid., fol. 82.

50 Ibid., fols. 82–82v.

51 Ibid., fol. 83.

52 Ibid., fol. 78.

53 For instance: E.H. Phelps Brown and Sheila V. Hopkins, 'Seven Centuries of the Prices of Consumables, Compared with Builders' Wage Rates', *Economica* 92 (1956).

54 C.C. Webb, ed., *The Churchwardens' Accounts of St Michael, Spurriergate, York 1518–1548, volume I 1518–1537* (York: Borthwick Publications, 1997), 119.

55 Webb, ed., *Churchwardens' Accounts*. This exercise reveals some variation in day wages, but 4*d* is the most common by a significant margin.

56 Webb, ed., *Churchwardens' Accounts*, 249.

57 Paul Slack, 'Hospitals, Workhouses and the Relief of the Poor in Early Modern London', in *Health Care and Poor Relief in Protestant Europe, 1500–1700*, ed. Ole Peter Grell and Andrew Cunnigham (London: Taylor and Francis, 1997), 237.

58 Angelo Raine, ed., *York Civic Records Volume 5* (York: Yorkshire Archaeological Society, 1946), 84.

59 Angelo Raine, ed., *York Civic Records, Volume 7* (York: Yorkshire Archaeological Society, 1950), 148.

60 Nicholas D. Brodie, 'Reassessing 27 Henry VIII, c.25 and Tudor Welfare: Changes and Continuities in Context', *Parergon* 31 (2014).

61 NRO NCR Case 16a/5, fol. 343.

62 27 Hen.VIII.c.25.6, *SR* 3, 559.

63 For instance in York in 1550: Raine, ed., *York Civic Records Vol. 5*, 35; Brodie, 'Beggary', 162; David M. Palliser, 'Epidemics in Tudor York', *Northern History* 8 (1973).

64 1522 Hen.VIII.c.12, *SR* 3, 328–32.

65 Brodie, 'Beggary', 130–36.

66 Brodie, 'Beggary', 155–56.

67 HMC, *Report on the Manuscripts of the Corporation of Beverley* (London: H.M. Stationery Office, 1900), 141.
68 State Library of Victoria, Melbourne, Sticht Collection, 27, 'Royal licence [sic] issued to Joan Cressy to collect alms for ransoming her husband, Thomas, 23rd June 1515', STC 2nd ed. 14077c. 127.
69 HMC, *Lord Middleton*, 391.
70 HMC, *Lord Middleton*, 335.
71 HMC, *Lord Middleton*, 335.
72 HMC, *Lord Middleton*, 382.
73 Geoffrey Chaucer, 'The Canterbury Tales', *The Riverside Chaucer*, ed. Larry D. Benson, 3rd edn. (Oxford: Oxford University Press, 2008), Fragment 1 (Group A), line 1, 23.
74 Judith M. Bennett, 'Conviviality and Charity in Medieval and Early Modern England', *Past and Present* 134 (1993); Judith M. Bennett, 'Conviviality and Charity in Medieval and Early Modern England: Reply', *Past and Present* 154 (1997).
75 Robert A. Houston, *Bride Ales and Penny Weddings: Recreations, Reciprocity, & Regions in Britain from the Sixteenth to the Nineteenth Century* (Oxford: Oxford University Press, 2014), 45–46; Steve Hindle, *On the Parish? The Micro-Politics of Poor Relief in Rural England, c. 1550–1750* (Oxford: Oxford University Press, 2004), 59.
76 John A.F. Thomson, *The Early Tudor Church and Society, 1485–1529* (New York: Routledge, 2014; repr. 1993 edn.), 277–78.
77 J. Charles Cox, *Churchwardens' Accounts from the Fourteenth Century to the Close of the Seventeenth Century* (London: Methuen, 1913), 6–7; for a longer discussion and more examples, see K.L. French, *The People of the Parish: Community Life in a Late Medieval English Diocese* (Philadelphia: University of Pennsylvania Press, 2001), 87–88. Both give examples from the fifteenth to seventeenth centuries, in rural and urban areas. Where further identified, these women were often relatively well-to-do social matrons, widows, and such like, essentially substantial members of a parish community
78 J. Charles Cox, *Three Centuries of Derbyshire Annals, Volume II* (London, Bemrose and Sons, 1890), 137–38.
79 Cox, *Derbyshire Annals, Vol. II*, 138.
80 HMC, *Report on Manuscripts in Various Collections, Volume 2* (London: H.M. Stationery Office, 1903), 95–96.
81 CDRO DD 36772.
82 HMC, *Lord Middleton*, 331, 332, 333.
83 HMC, *Lord Middleton*, 432, 437.
84 For example see: J. Gairdner, ed., *Letters and Papers, Foreign and Domestic, Henry VIII, Volume 13, Part 2* (London: H.M. Stationery Office, 1893), 539 (no. 1280).
85 Christopher Dyer, 'Poverty and its Relief in Late Medieval England', *Past and Present* 216 (2012); and also Brodie, 'Beggary'; Brodie, '"The names of all the poore people"'; Brodie, 'Reassessing 27 Henry VIII'.
86 John F. Pound, ed., *The Norwich Census of the Poor* (Norwich: Norfolk Record Society 1971), 95.
87 CDRO, ECA Book 157, 'Accounts of the Poor', fols. 6–11v, 42r–v, 96v–97; Brodie, '"The names of all the poore people"', 113–24.

88 Brodie, '"The names of all the poore people"', 122.
89 CDRO, ECA Book 157, 'Accounts of the Poor', fol. 42; Brodie, '"The names of all the poore people"', 113.
90 27 Hen.VIII.c.25.4, *SR* 3, 559; 5&6 Edw.VI.c.2.2, *SR* 4, 131. Subsequent statutes maintain the 'Man or Woman' specificity in this section: 2&3 Phil.&Mar.c.5.2, *SR* 4, 280; 5 Eliz.I.c.3.2, *SR* 4, 411.
91 Thirteen women in 1564/5; twelve women in 1570, all identified by name or as 'wydow'. The 1564/5 list is highly annotated, so a range is an analytical necessity. Abbreviations mean the figures are necessarily minimal. For further details, see Brodie, '"The names of all the poore people"', 124–29; CDRO ECA Book 157, 'Accounts of the Poor', fols. 6–11v, 178–80.

Select bibliography

Beier, A.L. *Masterless Men: the Vagrancy Problem in England, 1560–1640.* London: Methuen, 1985.

Bennett, Judith M. 'Conviviality and Charity in Medieval and Early Modern England'. *Past and Present* 134 (1993): 19–41

——— 'Conviviality and Charity in Medieval and Early Modern England: Reply'. *Past and Present* 154 (1997): 235–42

Brodie, Nicholas D. '"The names of all the poore people": Corporate and Parish Relief in Exeter, 1560s–1570s'. In *Experiences of Poverty in Late Medieval and Early Modern England and France*, ed. Anne M. Scott, 107–31. Farnham: Ashgate, 2012.

——— 'Reassessing 27 Henry VIII, c.25 and Tudor Welfare: Changes and Continuities in Context'. *Parergon* 31 (2014): 111–36.

Broomhall, Susan. 'Identity and Life Narratives of the Poor in Later Sixteenth-Century Tours'. *Renaissance Quarterly* 57 (2004): 439–65.

Clark, Peter. 'The Migrant in Kentish Towns 1580–1640'. In *Crisis and Order in English Towns 1500–1700: Essays in Urban History*, ed. Peter Clark and Paul Slack, 117–63. London: Routledge and Kegan Paul, 1972.

Clark, Peter, and David Souden, eds. *Migration and Society in Early Modern England.* London: Hutchinson, 1987.

Hindle, Steve. *On the Parish? The Micro-Politics of Poor Relief in Rural England, c. 1550–1750.* Oxford: Oxford University Press, 2004.

Humphries, Jane, and Jacob Weisdorf. 'The Wages of Women in England, 1260–1850'. *Journal of Economic History* 75 (2015): 405–47.

Langdon, John. 'Waged Building Employment in Medieval England: Subsistence Safety Net or Demographic Trampoline?'. In *Survival and Discord in Medieval Society: Essays in Honour of Christopher Dyer*, ed. Richard Goddard, John Langdon, and Miriam Müller, 109–26. Turnhout: Brepols, 2010.

McIntosh, Marjorie K. 'Poverty, Charity, and Coercion in Elizabethan England'. *Journal of Interdisciplinary History* 35 (2005): 467–79.

Mikalachki, Jodi. 'Women's Networks and the Female Vagrant: A Hard Case'. In *Maids and Mistresses, Cousins and Queens: Women's Alliances in Early Modern England*, ed. Susan Frye and Karen Robertson, 52–69. Oxford: Oxford University Press, 1999.

Roberts, M. 'Sickles and Scythes: Women's Work and Men's Work at Harvest Time', *History Workshop Journal* 7 (1979): 2–28.

——— 'Sickles and Scythes Revisited: Harvest Work, Wages and Symbolic Meanings'. In *Women, Work and Wages in England, 1600–1850*, ed. Penelope Lane, Neil Raven, and K.D.M. Snell, 68–101. Woodbridge: Boydell, 2004.
Slack, Paul. *The English Poor Law, 1531–1782*. Cambridge: Cambridge University Press, 1995.
——— *Poverty and Policy in Tudor and Stuart England*. London: Longman, 1988.
Tawney, R.H. *The Agrarian Problem in the Sixteenth Century*. New York: Longmans, Green and Co., 1912.
Webb, S., and B. Webb. *English Local Government: English Poor Law History: Part I, the Old Poor Law*. London: Longmans, Green and Co., 1927.

9 Working at the margins

Women and illicit economic practices in Lyon in the late seventeenth and eighteenth centuries[1]

Anne Montenach

Historians of the medieval and early modern European economy have traditionally concentrated on the legalities underpinning economic activity, as shown, for instance, by the large body of work dealing with the corporate system in this period.[2] Recently, however, some historians have taken a great interest in the wide spectrum of activities existing beyond the regulated and legal economy, showing that irregular practices were a structural characteristic of early modern economies.[3] At the same time, women's work has been the focus of much research dealing with women and gender in the early modern economy. These studies have produced important results on the variety of female activities, ranging from business to petty trading.[4] Women played a prominent role in the regulated market, even if they were rarely mentioned in traditional source materials or relegated to a minor position by the guilds. Although the vast majority of women—as well as men—were not able to join guilds, they could nevertheless forge complex bonds with the corporate system. Women were thus omnipresent in a wide variety of informal or illegal work, a fact which blurred the boundaries between guild and non-guild worlds.[5] However, little scholarly attention has been paid to the dark or unofficial side of the pre-industrial economy from a gender perspective.

Women who were discriminated against in terms of rights to citizenship, property ownership, and access to work nonetheless played a key role in the early modern underground economy that was never completely separated from the rising market economy. The aim of this chapter is to explore female involvement in a wide range of illicit economic activities: from survival strategies for the poor to criminal activities such as smuggling. From this perspective, it concentrates on Lyon's textile trades, a highly feminised sector in the eighteenth century. At a time of strong demographic and economic expansion, women took advantage of the demand for consumer and luxury goods, especially in the garment sector, to find a niche for themselves in the cloth trades, in both licit and illicit ways. As elsewhere in Europe, the presence of guilds had a significant impact, both positive and negative, on the opportunities available to women. In March 1673 a royal edict required all unincorporated trades to form guilds. In several French cities, due to this reform, it was possible for women to create guilds in 'feminine' trades or to become members of mixed guilds.[6] However, in Lyon many corporations continued to exclude women—with the exception of widows—from a wide range of professions in the pre-industrial economy, thus relegating them to minor or marginal roles. This chapter therefore compares traditional source materials for the urban economy (guilds' archives) with specific documentation on practices, such as police ordinances and records of court proceedings relating to infringements and conflicts. Particular attention is given to the way women deliberately utilised, or circumvented, the systems in place in order to establish their economic identity in a gendered, and sometimes hostile, urban community. By interrogating the way in which women took advantage of loopholes in the law to rise above the restrictions on their lives, we can shed new light on their agency in the early modern urban economy.[7] The existing economic environment based on secrecy and solidarity, how women negotiated this environment, the ways in which women (and men) used the urban space as a resource to undertake their activities, both licit and illicit, and finally, the ambiguous attitude of social and political institutions towards female subversive work also need to be taken into account.

In order to understand the issues, modalities, and spatial configurations of informal and illicit forms of women's work in a major industrial city during the eighteenth century, the first part of this chapter will offer an overview of the official role available to women in the Lyon textile sector which was structured by the guilds and dominated by the *Grande Fabrique* (the term used for the regulatory body controlling much of Lyon's silk industry). We will then analyse the diverse options available to women in the black market by studying three different yet similar activities: informal activities (women working in sectors dominated by the guilds), a felony specific to the *Grande Fabrique* (*piquage d'once*, or theft of thread), and finally criminal activities (smuggling of printed cottons). In discussing these developments, we will also review attitudes towards the way in which women's work was seen by the women themselves and by the society in which they lived—was it permitted, tolerated, condemned, or expected?—and the nature of relationships that working women developed together and with men and city institutions (guilds, town councils), including the way women negotiated their presence in the urban space.

Women and the cloth trades in Lyon: An overview

In the eighteenth century Lyon was the second-largest city in France with a population that had grown from 100,000 to nearly 150,000 between the early 1700s and the end of the Old Regime. The textile sector, the city's largest industrial sector, was dominated by the *Grande Fabrique* which increased its female workforce tenfold during the eighteenth century.[8] Although indispensable, women working in the workshop or the shop still

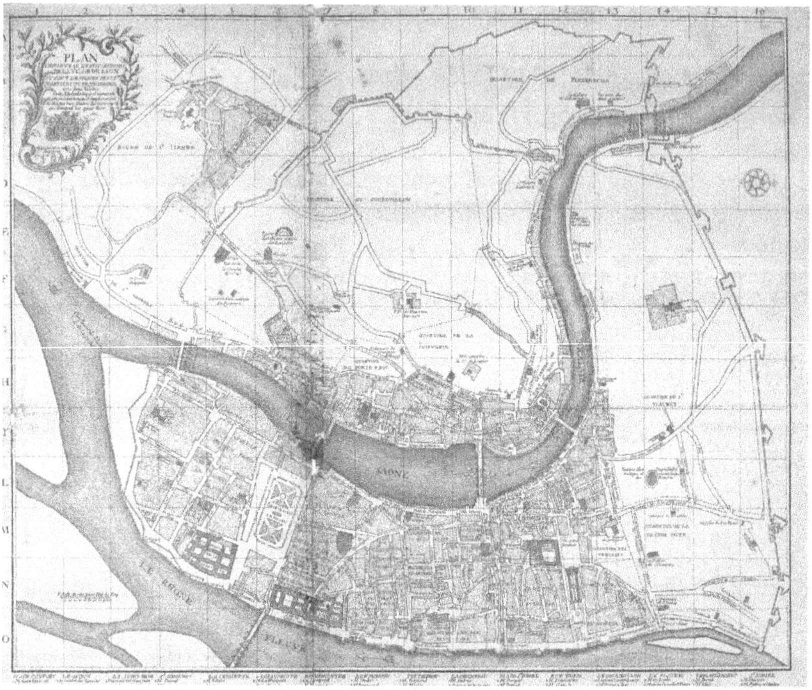

Map 9.1 Clair III Jacquemin, *Plan géométral et proportionnel de la ville de Lyon*, 1747. Photograph by J. Gastineau. Lyon, Archives municipales de Lyon, 3 S 693.

needed an authorisation from a master or their husband to be employed there.[9]

The kings of France regularly recognised and confirmed the freedom of Lyon's guilds until 1718, but in fact the statutes for their establishment had been issued during the medieval period and were constantly revised during the seventeenth and eighteenth centuries. Freedom here does not refer to free membership of a guild, but to the freedom conferred on the *consulat* (the city council) by the king to issue legislation for regulation of craft industries which, by the eighteenth century, had risen to seventy-two guilds.[10] These regulations, which placed the guilds under the supervision of the *consulat*, contributed to the division of labour into two distinct groups: professional craftsmen and journeymen, and 'unincorporated' workers, who were thus seen as 'usurpers'.[11] During the eighteenth century, Lyonnais guilds gradually closed their doors to strangers, then to men who were not sons of masters, and, in doing so, encouraged the emergence of oligarchies within the community. As this small and conservative elite developed, the number of conflicts multiplied and workers found new ways to resist domination by the guilds through barely disguised forms of fraud and unregulated or unauthorised work in the home.[12]

The role that women could play in the professions was closely linked to their marital status, since they could not be members in their own right. Regardless of the tasks they assumed as part of their husbands' activities, they were not entitled to any official status within the guild, with the exception of widows.[13] In Lyon, as in other cities, widowhood provided masters' wives with a status similar to that of their husbands, at least temporarily. As the rank of master was considered to be part of the family wealth, guild regulations gave widows the right, under certain conditions, to continue their husband's business. However, the guild officers placed restrictions on the membership of widows. Above all, guild regulations strictly limited widows' rights to membership to the period of their widowhood and forbade them from taking on new apprentices. There is evidence that remarriage with one of their husband's journeymen could, in some professions, facilitate his promotion to the status of master. Conversely, a widow who married a man from another guild automatically lost all her rights in her previous husband's guild. Widows of *passementiers* (makers of trimmings, buttonholes, decorations, etc.) nevertheless retained the right to keep a loom 'for themselves alone' (*pour elles seulement*) when their second husband worked in another profession.[14]

Similarly, while unmarried daughters could help their fathers carry on their business, in some crafts, such as tailoring, only boys could be accepted as apprentices.[15] On the other hand, women who married journeymen in the same guild as their father offered certain advantages for their husbands' accession to master status. Daughters, however, were totally banned from continuing to work for their father after marrying a man from a different profession. Thus, women appeared to be an important—but dangerous—link in the transmission of professional status, even though the skills that they acquired while working in their father's store or workshop were never explicitly recognised.

Marginalised by the guilds, women were also at a disadvantage in the world of legitimate paid work. Although Lyon was officially subject to Roman law, the city's tribunals came under the authority of the *Parlement de Paris* and legislation from the capital had precedence in Lyon's courts. Thus, according to common law, married women had no legal status in their own right and were considered to be permanent minors under the authority of their husbands. Once married, women were no longer legally autonomous (*capitis diminutio*)[16] and any contracts they might make without the permission of their husband were deemed to be null and void, with the exception of those made by the *marchandes publiques* (*feme sole* traders).[17] Deprived of the right to enter into contracts, they had very few options in the marketplace and were therefore relegated to unskilled work or illicit trading.

In addition, the way the *Grande Fabrique* had been organised during the sixteenth century is often presented as a demonstration of how women were excluded from all opportunities of obtaining financial autonomy. The term *Grande Fabrique* refers to the silk corporations which had grouped themselves into a large co-operative industry—it was in fact run along the same lines as a traditional craft organisation. These guilds handled different types of manufacture, the most prestigious consisting of silk weaving.[18] From 1596 all the guild regulations forbade women from working on the loom and only widows, wives, and daughters of masters were allowed to practise weaving.[19] As shown by Maurice Garden, apart from wholesalers (*marchands-banquiers*) and their staff (fewer than 100 persons in all), there were in the eighteenth century 350 master merchants (*marchands fabricants*) at the top of the pyramid who gave work to approximately 6,000 masters in silk weaving (*maîtres ouvriers en soie*) and master weavers (*maîtres à façon*).[20]

By the mid-eighteenth century the latter two groups had lost their right to sell their woven goods directly to consumers: the merchants had the exclusive control of sales. Together, they represented only a small proportion of the *Grande Fabrique*'s total workforce, which was estimated at more than 34,000 in 1789. A further 1,800 journeymen and apprentices were employed as members of the guilds and the rest of the workforce were lower-ranked labourers whose work was not covered by these regulations. Female workers made up a very large proportion of the 'true proletariat of the Lyon factory' ('véritable prolétariat de la fabrique lyonnaise')[21] and fell into two major categories. One group of labourers consisted of 3,900 masters' wives 'working in producing fabrics' (*occupées à la fabrication*),[22] 5,500 unsalaried sons and daughters of *maîtres façonniers*, and more than 1,000 waged female workers working on the loom: this last category was in fact clandestine work that was not recognised until September 1786 by a decree issued by the *Conseil d'État*. The second group covered 10,000 rope pullers or drawers (*tireuses de cordes*), unwinders of filament from cocoons (*dévideuses*), makers of warps (*ourdisseuses*), etc., who were in fact servants on very low wages with no opportunities for social mobility. Thus, inside the *Grande Fabrique*, two different hierarchies were interwoven: one covering the classic craft guilds of masters and journeymen; and the other covering commercial activities with the *marchand fabricant* dominating a mass of *maîtres façonniers* and a wide range of male and female workers working (sometimes clandestinely) at home or in huge workshops.[23]

Women's work at the margin of professional guilds

In this context, my approach seeks to understand the role and agency of women throughout the urban economy during the long eighteenth century. By comparing regulations and practices, I can go beyond the simple argument of exclusion and marginalisation by the guilds and explore, from the perspective of an entire city, the social, economic, political, and cultural issues that influenced the presence of women in various professions. Furthermore, the town offers a particularly pertinent perspective for highlighting the use and gendering of space at a micro-level. For this purpose, three types of workers will be analysed in particular: tailors and seamstresses, *passementiers*, and gauze makers (*guimpiers*), the latter two groups playing a key role in the *Grande Fabrique*'s production process. A review of the three guilds' regulations and records of infringements shows that the work of women, far from being marginal, was a real issue in power conflicts and can be analysed from a number of different perspectives: the couple and the family, relations within a given guild, relations with other similar trades, interactions between guilds and town officials, interactions between illicit activities and the urban environment. These conflicts shed light, in particular, on demands made by women, the gendered language used in court, and the image and spatiality of women's work.

Relations between tailors and seamstresses, and those between gauze makers and spinners (*fileuses*), illustrate the tensions caused by women's work and the ever-changing positions taken by the *consulat* concerning these triangular relationships. For example, masters appeared to be on the defensive with regard to women's work: in rules drawn up in 1667, master tailors prevented seamstresses from making clothes other than those for small children.[24] *Maîtres guimpiers*, on the other hand, sought to avoid using *fileuses* by establishing a monopoly in spinning threads of gold, silver, and silk for their wives and daughters. Behind these demands, we can clearly see gender issues in terms of attitudes towards work and of the 'master-*pater familias*' whose honour and prestige were linked, as Clare Crowston has shown, to their capacity to provide work for family members.[25]

On the other hand, women argued that there was, in Lyon, a tradition of freedom to work and that they needed to earn a living in order to survive; this led to calls for the right to work in the 1760s and 1770s.[26] On December 3, 1773 Demoiselle Verant was discovered making women's dresses with four friends in a fourth-floor bedroom in Place des Terreaux. She told the guild officers 'that she had no other right than that of working, that she did not consider that she needed to obtain anyone's authority [to do so]' ('quelle n'a d'autre droit que celui de travailler, qu'elle ne pense pas devoir être revêtue d'autre autorité').[27] Other testimony demonstrates this desire to work freely and perhaps explains the sometimes virulent reactions of women—and of men, in fact—to visits from, and seizures by, guild officers while also mentioning instances of solidarity from their neighbours, regardless of sex.[28]

At the centre of these questions was the *consulat*, which took a rather ambiguous position. Sometimes it opened up a limited range of areas in which women could operate: in 1682 it drew up a list of twenty-five named seamstresses who were authorised to 'work and make skirts and dresses for women and small children' ('travailler & faire des jupes & robes de femmes & petits enfants'), despite resistance by master tailors who made costumes for women.[29] The tailors complained about their inferior status within the guild and protested against both this decision by the *consulat*, which allowed seamstresses to compete directly with them, and the indulgence shown by guild officials to women infringing the rules who 'could offer better prices as they did not have to pay master's dues or any other fee to the guild' ('peuvent faire meilleur marché qu'eux ne payant ni maîtrise ni autres frais de communauté').[30] On other occasions, the *consulat* favoured the masters. In 1679 it banned the apprenticeship of girls to tailors, on the grounds that they 'would take work' (*ôtent le travail*)[31] away from masters and journeymen. In 1708, following complaints from *guimpiers*, the *consulat* finally agreed to a proposal that there would be no new nominations to the current list of 500 registered *fileuses* if any were to withdraw from the market during the next six years.[32] When new conflicts arose in the 1740s and 1750s, the *consulat* once again came to the defence of the *fileuses* taking into account essential considerations such as the 'naturally' feminine characteristics of a task 'which did not require an apprenticeship and had almost no need for training beyond a delicacy of touch and cleanliness' ('qui ne demande point d'apprentissage et qui n'a presque besoin que de delicatesse et de propreté'), and classic economic and moral concerns that, if they could no longer work away, there was a danger that they would be condemned to become prostitutes.[33] The somewhat ambiguous attitude adopted by the authorities towards women textile workers reveals the gap between social, economic, and repressive standards, in a global context of recurrent underemployment. It illustrates how the conservative city aldermen,[34] in assuming the paternalist role traditionally attributed to the king, were expected both to protect the masters' monopolies from illicit competition and to ensure survival for the poor women of the town.

In addition to measures regulating women's work, records of infringements of the guilds' statutes allow us to produce a more concrete analysis of the presence of women in the economy and to clarify the position taken by masters and city authorities with regard to illegal practices. Guilds' reports also reveal the existence, at the infra-urban level, of a shadowy world made of hiding places, clandestine workshops, inns, and peddling circuits, in which female actors discreetly operated. Irregular work appears to have been endemic and its principal actors were single women, either widows—who had to be particularly supervised by guild officers—or spinster 'girls' (*filles*): these two categories represent about 65 per cent of infringements recorded by officers of the guilds of tailors, *guimpiers*, and *passementiers* between 1670 and 1720.[35]

Living alone, and often in poverty, appears to have been a key factor in women's decisions to become involved in illegal activities. However, the situation was slightly different for seamstresses. 'Adult girls' (*filles majeures*) with professional skills and income may have simply chosen to remain unmarried and to practise their profession outside the restrictive framework of the tailors' guild. Most of them had one or more apprentices working for them or journeywomen, formally forbidden by the guild's regulations, but clearly demonstrating the importance of informal forms of female apprenticeships.[36] On the other hand, wives, daughters, or servants of masters found to be working illegally were, at first sight, rarely penalised, an indication of a certain tolerance of practices that led to the survival of numerous small workshops. Instances of couples arrested for illicit work refer mostly to practising a profession illegally or members of one profession encroaching on the activities of another: for example, the couple Besse made and sold braid 'as if they were master *passementiers*' ('comme s'ils étaient maîtres passementiers'),[37] while a master glove maker and his wife were arrested for making gold and silver thread.[38]

On occasion, women working illegally were part of a more complex system of subcontracts, involving masters and merchants with a good reputation in the town. In 1714 three masters and the widows of two others from the *passementiers*' guild were charged with having hired 'unqualified girls' (*filles sans qualité*) (i.e. those not authorised to work). The five offenders declared that they were themselves working for two other merchants from the same guild.[39] Another affair involved a former *fileuse* in 1700: a woman, who was living with her mother, had been banned from practice for bad workmanship but she employed a master *guimpier* (as he provided legitimacy for her workshop) and several 'girls' and was working for a *marchand fabricant* reputed to sell poor-quality silver and gold thread to other merchants.[40] Furthermore, records of infringements provide other evidence of women's entrepreneurship: often widows and spinsters lived together in the same home and set up clandestine workshops outside the guild system for making clothes, ribbons, and buttons that were later peddled throughout the town or sold in inns. In 1690 three women were arrested in an inn for selling lace pieces to 'foreign' merchants (*marchands étrangers*), an activity explicitly forbidden in the 1682 regulations.[41]

The relatively light sentences handed down by the *consulat* against these women could be interpreted as tolerance of activities that allowed them to escape poverty. In February 1715 a couple was fined 50 *livres* for hiring several women and 'girls' to make buttons in their homes, even though the husband was not a master button-maker. Two cases, heard on the same day, involved a widow and a spinster employing, respectively, six girls and five girls for making buttons with 'no right or authority' (*aucun droit ni qualité*); the first was fined eight *livres* and the second five *livres*.[42] In addition, the *consulat* and guild officers authorised certain women to practise their profession—on a case-by-case basis, and in complete contradiction of the professions' regulation—suggesting, once again, the inconsistencies in applying social and repressive standards. In the 1760s some women were officially accepted as *maîtresses passementières*, even though there was no mention in the guild's regulations of women becoming masters before 1779. However, all the women admitted were either sick or old and apparently spinsters who had worked for a long time as journeywomen. They were perhaps being offered a pension in their old age.[43]

Finally, some women were not content to take up the niche opportunities offered by the guilds' regulations. In August 1750 the Clair sisters, adult daughters of a master *guimpier*, were accused of working illegally by the guild's officers. This seems somewhat surprising since on July 17, 1748 the *guimpiers*' guild had decided to allow masters' daughters to have two spinning wheels or two looms on condition that they worked for guild masters. It seems that the sisters had decided to 'free themselves by setting themselves up in business' ('s'émanciper à travailler pour leur compte particulier') independently of the masters.[44] The circumstances of this case are indicative of a new attitude emerging in Lyon's guilds in the second half of the eighteenth century: while a minority of masters wanted to assert their authority and rigorously defended the existing regulations, a growing number of men and women—the latter being particularly numerous in the textile sector—sought to challenge the monopoly held by the guilds.[45] At the same time, the guild system in France encountered growing attacks from physiocrats—who believed that work was a basic human right—and the royal government stopped creating new guilds.[46] The master *guimpiers* also accused the Clair sisters of *piquage d'once* (stealing threads) by buying threads stolen by workers and servants from guild members.[47] There is no evidence that this accusation was made in order to condemn them more severely for their desire for independence, but the allegation does allow us to go beyond the simple facts of infractions of the guilds' regulations and learn more about illicit activities in the *Grande Fabrique*.

Women's work in the underground economy: The *piquage d'once*

The felony known as *piquage d'once* refers to the ability of the perpetrators (called *piqueurs d'once*) to buy 'both small and large quantities (ounces)' (*depuis le poids le plus petit jusques au plus haut*) of silks. Daryl Hafter has shown that Lyonnais female workers, because they were excluded from becoming masters in most professions in the silk industry, took advantage of their technical skills to steal and re-sell raw materials, sometimes to the masters themselves.[48] They developed, quite illegally, commercial practices that circumvented constraints placed on women workers by the *Grande Fabrique* which was heavily dependent on national and international markets and rigorously controlled its workforce.

Documents deposited at the City Archives in Lyon, covering some thirty cases over a little more than a century (between 1667 and 1773), provide more details for our study.[49] In fact, *piquage d'once* was far from being an exclusively feminine activity. On the contrary, a wide range of players throughout the production and distribution chain were actively involved in this illicit process, from the *marchand fabricant* to the *dévideuse*, including the *maître ouvrier* and the *marchande de modes* (milliner). Both men and women bought stolen silks which they gave to poor masters to make into clothing using stolen designs for later resale.

Regulations, reissued at steady intervals during the eighteenth century, bear witness to the ubiquitous nature of *piquage d'once*, but did not refer specifically to women. Rather than specify the identity of *piqueurs*, they appear to take greater interest in the neighbourhoods in which they operated, providing us with a map of a city immersed in a criminal, and thus frightening, obscurity even if this was probably quite imaginary. In 1711 *piqueurs d'once*, according to the masters specialising in silk sheets, 'avoid the sun's rays in all weathers'; 'they usually lived in dark houses and back alleys that are crowded and to be shunned by honest people. ... They have boutiques with low doors standing ajar along the street' and, 'in addition, ... several easy exits and backdoors always left open' for those who want to disappear discreetly after doing their business ('Ils devancent dans tous les temps les rayons du soleil ... Ils habitent ordinairement des maisons obscures, des rues retirées, remplies de peuple et impraticables aux honnêtes gens. ... Ils ont des boutiques dans le rez de chaussée dont la porte est toujours basse et à demi fermée [mais qui ont] en échange plusieurs sorties aisées et des portes de derrière toujours ouvertes').[50] Lyon's street layout, with its narrow, twisting streets and back passages on the peninsula and right bank of the Saône, make it easy for people to circulate without being seen and thus facilitated an underground economy.[51] Fabrics woven clandestinely from stolen silks were sold 'in hotels and private homes' ('dans les hôtelleries et les maisons particulières')[52] and also 'in basements, attics, and all sorts of boutiques run by craftsmen and small shopkeepers, including butter-makers, wine merchants, and haberdashers, and an infinity of other places that have several entries and exits' ('dans des lieux souterrains, dans des greniers, dans toutes sortes de boutiques d'artisans ou de petits marchands, chez des beurrières, des marchands de vin, des merciers, et dans une infinité d'autres endroits qui ont plusieurs entrées et plusieurs sorties').[53] In pursuing their illegal activities, *piqueuses d'once* thus made use of a range of private, public, and underground spaces. Furthermore, they may have moved between these places and thus constructed specific spatial configurations in their conduct of illicit work.

From these thirty or so cases, we can see the role played by women in the different phases of this illicit practice: production, distribution, and sale. Silk was usually stolen by *dévideuses*, the first workers to come in contact with the silk and then, moving up the production chain, by clerks, journeymen, and even *maîtres ouvriers en soie*. Sometimes, they stole waste silks, though these were supposed to be returned to the *marchand fabricant* who provided the raw materials. The threads, either silk or gold, were removed from the reels, the difference in weight being disguised by deliberately greasing or dampening the remaining threads before they were returned to the *marchand fabricant*.

In this first phase, it appears that the key factor was not so much the perpetrator's sex per se, as his or her easy access to the raw materials. Women played an essential role as peddlers or brokers, in the distribution of stolen silks: with their street knowledge and capacity for moving around without attracting attention, together with their inability to obtain skilled work or capital, they were essential in developing underground networks based on acquaintances and word of mouth. Networks created by *piqueurs d'once*, whether male or female, could be either direct or circuitous, usually involving several intermediaries in order to create further confusion. Records for 1761 provide two extreme examples. An accusation of stealing an ounce and 18 *deniers* from silk provided by a merchant made on July 4 involved a *dévideuse* who had sold it to the wife of a *maître ouvrier en soie* in whose house the officers had found scales and a loom for making handkerchiefs, thus proving that stolen raw materials were being re-used. In the second case, on May 25, a former silk worker's wife was arrested with stolen silk which she had bought from an upholsterer's wife. The upholsterer's wife, in turn, had acquired it from a *maître ouvrier*'s wife, who was given it by a comb seller. The comb seller, wife to a haberdasher, said that she earned a living 'any way she could' (*comme elle peut*) and claimed that she had bought it from a *marchand fabricant* who had given her an obviously fake invoice.[54]

Piqueurs d'once came from a wide range of social categories. Several worked as couples and in professions related to silk production: the husband might be a silk stocking maker, a folder of silk (*plieur de soie*), *guimpier*, or *passementier* and there are even two cases involving a *maître fabricant*. In other cases, we find the wives of a chair-porter and a scrap merchant among the culprits. Some deliberately turned to crime, including Pierre Terrasse, a former *guimpier* who was suspected of leaving his guild to avoid inspections by its officers. He then used his daughters to sell 'small foodstuffs and haberdashery as a form of free and independent commerce' ('de menues provisions de bouche et de mercerie qu'on regarde comme un commerce libre et indépendant'). At the same time, his girls discreetly asked their clients, male and female workers at the *Grande Fabrique*, whether they had silks to sell.[55]

Many different types of women were involved in this trade. One example is the female entrepreneur such as Widow Hérard, a *bourgeoise* and re-seller of fine clothes (*revendeuse à la toilette*), who was sentenced for repeated offences for *piquage d'once* in 1760.[56] Others were suppliers, both men and women: in 1763 Demoiselle Allard, a *marchande de modes*, was accused of paying an almost blind former silk journeyman for silks stolen by a *maître ouvrier* who had fallen on hard times '[and] had no bread for his children' ('n'ayant pas du pain à donner à ses enfants').[57] The wife of a Parisian merchant visited Lyon for a few weeks in order to buy silks, taffetas, satins, and other fabrics 'which she sold in her store in Paris' ('dont elle fait commerce à Paris'). She attracted a large number of brokers and peddlers to her lodgings in the Place des Carmes and this attracted the attention of the authorities.[58] At the other end of the social scale, a *dévideuse* was accused of *piquage d'once* in 1765: as she was separated from her husband who beat her and left her with only a spinning wheel, she was forced to earn a living as best she could. In her defence, she claimed that she was in fact covering for a *maître fabricant*'s wife who had already been convicted and wanted to hide her own illicit trade.[59]

Piquage d'once sometimes appears to offer the only alternative to poverty. A woman separated from a *maître ouvrier en soie* and having to feed 'five children and an aged mother' ('chargée de cinq enfants et d'une mère avancée en âge') explained that, after doing piecework for a widow, she began to produce 'a few fabrics herself in order to earn a living' ('quelques étoffes pour son compte particulier pour être en état de gagner sa vie'). Somewhat naively, she also said that 'with regard to the right to trade, after her husband left her to go to Spain fifteen years ago, she thought that women did not have this right' ('à l'égard du droit de marchand, son mari l'ayant quittée pour passer en Espagne depuis quinze ans, elle a cru que l'on n'accordait point ce droit aux femmes').[60] Poverty and ignorance were also used as an excuse. Ollard, a woman separated from her husband, a master silk worker, was arrested two years after her first conviction for *piquage d'once* for making handkerchiefs from stolen silk. She argued that, because she was illiterate, she had no ledgers for her purchases, sales, and bills for dyeing. But she was not as poor as she claimed, since she paid a 70-year-old widow to act as her cover and employed two country girls 'without qualifications' (*sans qualité*) and a girl from the Charity Hospital to work on her looms.[61]

Piquage d'once permitted not only feminine solidarity but also the exploitation of needy women by wealthier women and involved, we have seen, a number of male and female actors in an emerging world of working relationships based on mutual support and domination. In the final section, we will review a black-market activity with similar characteristics: the underground market for smuggled calicos, which was punished with much heavier penalties.

Smuggling inside the city: Women and the calicos trade

The fashion for printed, painted, or dyed cotton fabrics, originally imported from the Indies and later manufactured in Europe, spread quickly throughout France during the last decades of the seventeenth century.[62] However, following pressure from silk and wool manufacturers, bans on imports, manufacture, and wearing of cotton—whether bleached or coloured—were introduced into the kingdom between 1686 and 1759, as in most parts of Europe.[63] During the eighteenth century two regions, Dauphiné and the Lyonnais (the territory around Lyon), which lie on France's frontier with Savoy, provided smugglers with an ideal opportunity for bringing in cotton canvas produced in large quantities by factories in Geneva and the Swiss Cantons. Despite court orders and arrests, smuggling remained endemic, at least until 1759.[64]

Research into the fashion for calicos in Europe at the end of the seventeenth and eighteenth centuries has, until now, shown that women from all walks of life were the main customers for these light and coloured fabrics. The roles they played at the top of the chain, in terms of production and distribution of fabrics, are less well known. However, fashion and new tastes among a growing section of the population interested in calicos gave women opportunities to operate in the economy at various levels in the production and distribution of these fabrics. The archives of the intendant's office[65] in Lyon and Grenoble and of Lyon's customs office contain information on seizures of cotton textiles at the gates of, or even inside, these cities. These sources allow us to reconstruct, through the prism of gender, networks for smuggling and distribution of banned fabrics in the towns and to analyse the specific relationships that female smugglers developed with the urban space.

Unsurprisingly, given the restrictions on their legal status and their right to engage in economic activities under the Old Regime, few women appear in the group of major traders in contraband, who were often drawn from among the towns' leading merchants. One interesting example is Catherine Teillard, a merchant from Lyon and wife of a corrupt tax officer: together with her maid, she sold prohibited fabrics.[66] We find cases involving not only widows, but also women who were living in 'separation of property' (*séparation de biens*), that is, legally separated but still living with their husband. Both groups of women acquired greater social and financial autonomy, suggesting that poverty was not always the reason for women's involvement in illicit trade. In 1725 Widow Pattron appeared to take on the role of intermediary—perhaps to deflect interest from the principals—between Lyonnais merchants and their suppliers in Geneva.[67] In May 1748 Simone Assada, 'a merchant in fabrics in Lyon and separated from her husband Nicolas Gislain, erstwhile merchant in the said city' ('marchande de toile à Lyon & femme separée de biens de Nicolas Gislain, ci-devant marchand de ladite ville'), was banned from commerce 'for all time' (*pour toujours*), because she was involved in the smuggling of cottons and foreign textiles; she was sentenced again four years later as a repeat offender.[68] As shown by Julie Hardwick, separations of property 'depended legally on a husband's failure to maintain his wife'. These separations 'did not permit spouses to establish separate households'.[69] However, they were useful for a variety of reasons, for instance to shelter the household's assets from creditors, or from justice—as in this case, where the wife continued her husband's illegal trade.

The archives provide more information on the case of Widow Lescalier. For five years after her husband's death in 1713 she maintained her husband's partnership with his brother. Her sister had even invested 20,000 *livres* in the family enterprise, but was not involved in the management of the business. In 1718 Widow Lescalier was accused, together with her brother-in-law, of smuggling large quantities of calicos from Flanders, Germany, and Switzerland and from the East India Company. Moreover, false hallmarks, similar to those used by the East India Company, were found in their house, further proof that these were used in re-selling calicos to other merchants and clients in Lyon and elsewhere. The brother-in-law and five employees (*facteurs*) spent about three months a year travelling to Picardy, Champagne, Normandy, Flanders, and other countries to buy the merchandise, while the widow stayed in Lyon and managed the accounts: the judicial inquiry clearly shows that she was a full partner in the business, as was often the case for widows of merchants and traders who continued to exercise their husband's profession.[70] A clever woman, she made use of heavily gendered—and classic—arguments to wriggle out of false declarations 'because she was so troubled' during the search in their shop 'that she cannot remember what she might have said then' ('elle estoit si troublée lors de nostre transport qu'elle n'a aucune memoire de ce quelle peut avoir dit pendant notre recherche').[71]

Any attempt to analyse the geography and sociology of smuggling inside the city is limited by the low level of information available in the sources, which are exclusively documents from the judicial and police archives. However, these documents do at least provide some interesting information about the spatial and social environment in which the black market in Lyon and Grenoble operated. Official reports of seizures at Lyon's gates show that the town was a tightly controlled space and various actors of both sexes knew how to deploy tactics of varying levels of complexity. Some women and men were clearly receiving orders and operating as intermediaries, while others were acting on their own initiative and for their own purposes, for example women who hired poorer women to act as go-betweens, thus demonstrating real entrepreneurial skills. Magdelon Jardan, who was arrested at the Halincourt Gate on August 30, 1756 with five *coupons* (pieces) of calico under her dress, said that she came from Rives in Dauphiné, 'by profession washerwoman without residence here' ('de son talent lavendiere sans residence icy'). She explained that the calico had been given to her 'a little distance from the town, to be brought in with a promise of receiving a little something in return' ('à quelque distance hors de la ville, a entrer sous promesse de quelque chose'), and that 'necessity, as she was a poor girl, made her accept' ('la necessité, estant une pauvre fille, luy avoit fait accepter').[72] Claudine Sigeaux, 'not having for the present a fixed abode in Lyon' ('n'ayant par le present aucune demeure fixe dans Lyon'), had come from Vaise, where an unknown woman 'had given her the said calicos in order to carry them into Lyon for a salary' ('luy avoit remis lesdites indiennes pour les entrer dans Lyon moyennant salaire').[73]

Generally speaking, the police suspected several merchants, who were clearly involved in long-distance smuggling, of having clandestine 'shops' (*magasins*) where calicos were stocked prior to sale. In addition to these warehouses, they used inns and underground areas, including cellars, for storing clandestine stock.[74] According to a well-established delegation of responsibilities, women were allocated the task of peddling these fabrics around the town and even in the private homes of clients.[75] From the perspective of gender, we can see that, while very few women were involved at the macro level, their presence in these micro-spaces was dramatically more significant. This suggests that smuggling offered economic and social opportunities within the town as part of a multi-tasking household economy, but was also one of a single woman's strategies for survival.

Several records of arrests show that married women took responsibility for hiding, transforming, and selling smuggled calicos as a way of earning a living. Antoinette Renaud, a cook's wife, said she was a public hawker and 'sold clothes, china, furniture, and everything that she was given to sell, but did not have a boutique or a shop' ('elle revend des nippes de la vaisselle des meubles & tout ce qu'on luy donne pour revendre mais n'a ny boutique ny magasin').[76] Other women involved in hawking were dressmakers or wives of journeymen weavers, dyers, and tailors.[77] All said that they considered these activities to be a way of 'earning a living' (*gagner leur vie*): for instance, the wife of a Lyon canvas merchant, Claudine Billet was 'obliged to leave the trade because of the troubles and losses when he [her husband] went bankrupt' ('obligé de quitter le commerce par les malheurs et les pertes qui luy sont arrivés par le discredit des papiers dont il s'est trouvé chargé').[78] Fraud was clearly practised by couples, as can be seen from cases in Lyon where a shoemaker and a printer's boy and their wives were convicted.[79] In 1757 a couple in Grenoble was suspected of 'trading in banned calicos' ('faire un commerce prohibé d'indiennes') and of hiring Thérèse Caillat as a 'peddler' (*colporteuse*).[80] Trade in banned merchandise appeared to offer additional income for the households of craftsmen and town workers also involved in the textile sector. It developed into an intertwining of multiple licit and illicit activities within the family: smuggling was not a permanent source of income, but served as a fall-back plan frequently combined with legal forms of employment and resources. Husband and wife were often condemned and fined 'in collusion' (*solidairement*).

Finishing and re-selling banned fabrics could also offer widows and single women a survival strategy in combination with other forms of mutual support, such as shared homes. Several arrests involved widows and women who appear to have been spinsters, living in the same house: 'spinster clustering' was a common way to reduce the cost of heating and lighting, while offering a substitute family.[81] The type of fabrics seized—pieces or *coupons*, especially handkerchiefs—suggests that these women, who did not state their profession, were involved in finishing work as home-based and informal subcontracted work.[82] Sharing their resources and clandestine work in a typically feminine sector—sewing—was thus a survival strategy. Even if these activities were small scale, we can see that women were prepared to be enterprising, even with all the risks and uncertainties inherent in engaging in crime. Some widows set up clandestine workshops for manufacturing calicos in their homes, possibly managing a small cottage industry that would have served to employ other women: in September 1752 a raid on Widow Vaillet's house in Grenoble found twenty-one rolls of painted canvas, thirty-eight stencils for a variety of designs, twenty-one paintbrushes, and three platters filled with ground colours.[83] In the 'makeshift business' of smuggling, fraud was undoubtedly just another way of earning a living. Secrecy, confidence, solidarity with the network or with one's neighbours were essential elements in urban commercial activities, but more specifically in the case of these single women, neighbours and friends were important resources. Mme Sibut, a Lyon hawker accused of illegal trading in calicos, was protected by her neighbours who unanimously told the bailiff when he came to arrest her 'that the said Sibut had long ago moved to Trevoux' ('qu'il y a longtemps que ladite Sibut s'estoit retirée en la ville de Trevoux'); moreover, a month later, they all refused to sign the warrant in her name issued by the intendant.[84] Similarly, Claudine Billet, imprisoned while awaiting trial in January 1723, managed to escape from the archbishop's jail with the help of several women 'dressed in various ways' (*habillées de differentes façons*) who had come to visit her: 'she disguised herself by taking some of their clothes and headwear and left with them without being recognised when she was supposed to be in her bed' ('elle se deguisa en prenant partie de leurs habits et coiffures, et sortit entre elles sans être reconnues et la croyant dans son lict').[85]

Conclusion

These snapshots have highlighted the ways in which women's place, status, and influence within various types of social and economic configurations shaped their economic roles and their relationships to the urban space and environment. Although women appeared to operate in all sectors (licit and illicit) in the marketplace, the range of options available to them differed according to their social, legal, and marital status. Moreover, women's work was unequivocally positioned in an urban world of institutions, laws, regulations, customs, and ideologies. Town rules and customs, as well as police and guild regulations, affected women's participation in the urban economy and shaped their working experiences. For the most part, women were operating at just inside or just outside Lyon's guild structures. Here, Lyon seems to be out of step with other French cities where growth in several economic and manufacturing sectors, but particularly in the textile sector, favoured the entry of women in their guilds during the eighteenth century.[86] This was no doubt due to the influence of the *Grande Fabrique* and to the conservative position taken by the guilds' masters. Most Lyonnais women were excluded not from the workforce, but from positions of authority. This chapter draws attention to how women navigated these gendered terrains and found some niches for personal autonomy and freedom of action. Guild restrictions provide an example of the discordance between regulation and reality. Women could benefit from the contradictions inherent in moral and social unwritten norms and economic regulations, and this allows us to observe the divergences between official policy and real practice. In Lyon, the municipal authorities and guilds sometimes introduced flexible strategies for incorporating women and altered their rules to regularise female work.

Working women's experiences also differed according to marital status and to different phases in their life cycle. On the one hand, women did not operate alone, and often worked in partnership with husbands, family, employers, or other workers, since there was sometimes no clear dividing line between home and workshop. On the other hand, family and household were not always supportive structures for their members. Solitude, and more specifically widowhood, could thus, depending on circumstances, allow women greater freedom of movement in the economy or, on the contrary, push them into greater poverty and illegal ways for earning a living. These circumstances also forced them to develop, by necessity, a culture of solidarity to compensate for the fact that they were legally less protected. However, they initiated an entrepreneurial culture where those with greater skills or better positioned in the market did not hesitate to exploit the misery of those in need. In any event, the capital invested by women in family enterprises or, more modestly, the wages they earned from day to day were useful not only for the well-being of the family, but also for providing a better future in an uncertain present. Even if the archives are somewhat lacking in details, it is clear that their financial resources certainly contributed to, or allowed the development of, gendered interactions within the couple and the family.

From an urban and spatial point of view, we see that women did not necessarily operate in the same geographical spaces or in the same phases of craft, trade, theft, or smuggling as men; nonetheless, they were 'separate yet bound together' in networks of shared interests and complicities.[87] In the black market, for example, they acted as go-betweens in illegal and ephemeral networks and operated as intermediaries between the official and parallel markets. They were particularly present at the sales end of the smuggling chain: as peddlers and hawkers, they needed only a small financial investment to begin trading. Their knowledge of local neighbourhoods and of networks opened up opportunities for delivering stolen silk or banned merchandise and exchanging pertinent information. Women knew how to use the urban space as a resource in illicit trafficking. They made use of their knowledge of the town to find the most effective ways of operating and of increasing their daily earnings by greasing the wheel of the black market.

Women in Lyon were not the only women involved in illegal work or smuggling. They challenge the stereotypes which identify women as consumers and men as traders in the debate on luxury—and more specifically in the calico campaigns—in the late seventeenth and early eighteenth centuries. Detailed studies in other parts of Europe certainly demonstrate that women were broadly involved in this kind of illicit economy, as well as in the second-hand market for clothes and, more generally, in many grey areas of the urban economy that are often ignored by historians. Beyond the specific cases developed here, micro-analytical studies could therefore highlight the ways in which female activities contributed to both the construction of the urban space and the development of various and adaptive forms of work within European towns.

Notes

1 Translation by Caroline Mackenzie.
2 Two important studies, with further bibliography, are S.R. Epstein and Maarten Prak, eds., *Guilds, Innovation and the European Economy, 1400–1800* (Cambridge: Cambridge University Press, 2008); Jan Lucassen, Tine De Moor, and Jan Luiten van Zanden, eds., *The Return of the Guilds*, special issue of *International Review of Social History* 53, suppl. 16 (2008).
3 Laurence Fontaine, *Le marché. Histoire et usages d'une conquête sociale* (Paris: Gallimard, 2014); Laurence Fontaine and Jürgen Schlumbohm, eds., *Household Strategies for Survival 1600–2000: Fission, Faction and Cooperation*, special issue of *International Review of Social History* 45, suppl. 8 (2000).
4 Danielle van den Heuvel, *Women and Entrepreneurship: Female Traders in the Northern Netherlands, c. 1580–1815* (Amsterdam: Aksant, 2007); Merry Wiesner Wood, 'Paltry Peddlers or Essential Merchants? Women in the Distributive Trades in Early Modern Nuremberg', *Sixteenth Century Journal* 12 (1981).
5 Clare Crowston, 'Women, Gender, and Guilds in Early Modern Europe: An Overview of Recent Research', in *The Return of the Guilds*, ed. Lucassen, De Moor, and van Zanden; Dora Dumont, 'Women and Guilds in Bologna: The Ambiguities of "Marginality"', *Radical History Review* 70 (1998).
6 Elizabeth Musgrave's study of Nantes reveals an increased participation of women in the corporations as a result of economic growth (in 1728, for instance, the tailors' guild created a mistresses' section): Elizabeth Musgrave, 'Women and the Craft Guilds in Eighteenth-Century Nantes', in *The Artisan and the European Town, 1500–1900*, ed. Geoffrey Crossick (Aldershot: Ashgate, 2007). See also James B. Collins, 'The Economic Role of Women in Seventeenth-Century France', *French Historical Studies* 16 (1989); Clare Crowston, *Fabricating Women. The Seamstresses of Old Regime France (1675–1791)* (Durham, NC: Duke University Press, 2001).
7 Deborah Simonton and Anne Montenach, eds., *Female Agency in the Urban Economy: Gender in European Towns, 1640–1830* (London: Routledge, 2013).
8 Françoise Bayard et al., eds., *Histoire de Lyon des origines à nos jours* (Lyon: Éditions Lyonnaises d'Art et d'Histoire, 2007), 589.
9 Maurice Garden, *Lyon et les Lyonnais au XVIIIe siècle* (Paris: Les Belles Lettres, 1970), 594.
10 Garden, *Lyon*, 326.
11 Dean T. Ferguson, 'The Body, the Corporate Idiom, and the Police of the Unincorporated Worker in Early Modern Lyons', *French Historical Studies* 23 (2000): 551.
12 Françoise Bayard, 'Les conflits du travail portés en justice, Lyon, XVIIe–XVIIIe siècles', in *Le travail avant la révolution industrielle*, ed. Maurice Hamon (Paris: Editions du C.T.H.S., 2006), 79; Bayard, et al., eds., *Histoire de Lyon*, 605.
13 Scarlett Beauvalet-Boutouyrie, *Être veuve sous l'Ancien Régime* (Paris: Belin, 2001), 276–77; Janine M. Lanza, *From Wives to Widows in Early Modern Paris: Gender, Economy, and Law* (Aldershot: Ashgate, 2007).
14 Archives municipales de Lyon (AML), HH 168, March 16, 1682. See also AML, 304 326, June 21, 1668; 305 264, September 5, 1667, Art. XIV.
15 AML, 305 266, December 14, 1679.

16 While unmarried daughters under 25 (the legal age of majority) were minors under the authority of their father, adult spinster daughters were, theoretically according to common law, able to exercise their full legal rights.

17 The term *marchandes publiques* was adopted from Parisian common law and used exclusively for women who sold goods not produced by their husbands. A married woman could enter into contracts, under these conditions, 'for her wares' (*pour le fait de sa marchandise*), which would, given the notion of property held in common, specifically involve the responsibility of her husband. Brigitte Basdevant-Gaudemet and Jean Gaudemet, *Introduction historique au droit XIIIe–XXe siècles* (Paris: Librairie générale de droit et de jurisprudence, 2000), 270. On the very similar status of *feme sole* trader in England and the Netherlands, see Amy Louise Erickson, 'Coverture and Capitalism', *History Workshop Journal* 59 (2005); Amy Louise Erickson, *Women and Property in Early Modern England* (London: Routledge, 1993), 30–31, 140, 146; Nicola Phillips, *Women in Business, 1700–1850* (Woodbridge: Boydell, 2006), 18, 19, 27, 48–68; Van den Heuvel, *Women and Entrepreneurship*, 58–69, 84.

18 Daryl M. Hafter, 'Women Who Wove in the Eighteenth-Century Silk Industry of Lyon', in *European Women and Preindustrial Craft*, ed. Daryl M. Hafter (Bloomington: Indiana University Press, 1995), 47.

19 Jean-François Budin, 'Les ouvrières de la soie à Lyon au XVIIIe siècle', in *Le travail*, ed. Hamon, 117–18.

20 Maurice Garden, 'Ouvriers et artisans au XVIIIe siècle. L'exemple lyonnais et les problèmes de classification', in *Maurice Garden, un historien dans la ville*, ed. René Favier et al. (Paris: Éditions de la Maison des Sciences de l'Homme, 2008), 88–91.

21 Garden, 'Ouvriers et artisans au XVIIIe siècle', 89.

22 Garden, 'Ouvriers et artisans au XVIIIe siècle', 89.

23 Garden, 'Ouvriers et artisans au XVIIIe siècle', 89–91.

24 AML, 305 264, September 5, 1667; 305 266, December 14, 1679.

25 Clare Crowston, 'Engendering the Guilds: Seamstresses, Tailors, and the Clash of Corporate Identities in Old Regime France', *French Historical Studies* 23 (2000): 340–41.

26 At the same time, work was considered by the Minister Turgot to be a natural right (cf. Edict of 1776, preamble).

27 AML, HH 187, December 3, 1773. See also June 4, 1761; December 20, 1765; October 21, 1773.

28 A similar phenomenon was seen in Nantes during the second half of the eighteenth century: Samuel Guicheteau, *La révolution des ouvriers nantais: mutation économique, identité sociale et dynamique révolutionnaire, 1740–1815* (Rennes: Presses universitaires de Rennes, 2008), 111–13.

29 AML, HH 185, December 31, 1682. They were not allowed to take on apprentices or employ journeymen/women. Each woman had to pay the guild 9 *livres* as an 'entry fee' and an annual fee of 20 *sols*.

30 AML, HH 185 (n. d., early eighteenth century).

31 AML, 1 C 305 266, December 14, 1679.

32 AML, HH 92, September 10, 1708.

33 AML, HH 92, n. d. (probably 1703).

34 Garden, *Lyon*, 558.

35 Lanza, *From Wives to Widows in Early Modern Paris*, 139–47; AML, HH 96, HH 169, and HH 187.
36 See for instance AML HH 224, June 14, 1712 and March 28, 1713; HH 225, February 11, 1717.
37 AML, HH 171, April 27, 1757.
38 AML, HH 219, March 12, 1692.
39 AML, HH 170, June 4, 1714. See also HH 215, June 20, 1674; HH 170, August 28, 1713.
40 AML, HH 94, August 26, 1700–August 1, 1702.
41 AML, HH 218, August 23, 1690; HH 168, March 16, 1682, art. XXI.
42 AML, HH 225, February 20, 1715.
43 AML, HH 169, December 1, 1761, November 30, 1769; HH 260, January 16, 1770.
44 AML, HH 96, August 18, 1750.
45 Garden, *Lyon*, 561.
46 Crowston, *Fabricating Women*, 207–08.
47 AML, HH 96, August 18, 1750.
48 Daryl Hafter, 'Women in the Underground Business of Eighteenth-Century Lyon', *Enterprise & Society* 2 (2001).
49 AML, HH 147–55.
50 AML, HH 147, October 25, 1711.
51 Hafter, 'Women', 20.
52 AML, HH 147, October 25, 1711. See also Archives nationales (AN), F^{12} 764 B, June 19, 1744, art. X.
53 AML, HH 148, December 18, 1727.
54 AML, HH 150, May 25 and July 4, 1761.
55 AML, HH 147–48, 1727–28.
56 AML, HH 150, February 29, 1760.
57 AML, HH 151, July–October 1763.
58 AML, HH 150, January–August 1711.
59 AML, HH 153, August 1765–May 1766.
60 AML, HH 151, July–September 1763.
61 AML, HH 150, March 29, 1743.
62 For a review of the fashion for calicos in Europe, see Beverly Lemire, *Cotton* (Oxford: Berg, 2011); Giorgio Riello, *Cotton. The Fabric that Made the Modern World* (Cambridge: Cambridge University Press, 2013).
63 Beverly Lemire, *Fashion's Favourite: The Cotton Trade and the Consumer in Britain 1660–1800* (Oxford: Oxford University Press, 1991), 29–42; Beverly Lemire and Giorgio Riello, 'East & West: Textiles and Fashion in Early Modern Europe', *Journal of Social History* 41 (2008): 898.
64 The embargo was lifted in 1759 following a long debate on free trade, known as the *querelle des toiles peintes* (dispute over painted cloth). However, because calicos had to pay heavy taxes on entering France after 1759, they were still smuggled in the 1760s.
65 Intendants were the king's agents in the provinces. They were, *inter alia*, responsible for the repression of smuggling.
66 AML, FF 65, June 10 and 12, August 11, 1739. Olivier Le Gouic, 'La contrebande des indiennes à Lyon au temps de la prohibition (1686–1759)', in *Territoires*

de l'illicite: ports et îles. De la fraude au contrôle (XVIe–XXe siècles), ed. Marguerite Figeac-Monthus and Christophe Lastécouères (Paris: Armand Colin, 2012), 86–87.

67 Archives départementales du Rhône (ADR), 1 C 249, December 21, 1725.

68 Archives départementales de la Drôme (ADD), B 1304, May 22, 1748 and June 15, 1752.

69 Julie Hardwick, 'Seeking Separations: Gender, Marriage, and Household Economies in Early Modern France', *French Historical Studies* 21 (1998): 160–61.

70 ADR, 1 C 279, June–December 1718. See for instance Phillips, *Women in Business*, 118–19.

71 ADR, 1 C 279, December 13, 1718.

72 ADR, 5 C 12, August 30, 1756.

73 ADR, 5 C 12, April 26, 1756.

74 ADR, 5 C 12, March 11, 1756.

75 ADR, 1 C 277, July 3, 1722; 5 C 2, November 29, 1757; April 8, July 20, and August 17, 1758. The same phenomenon was found in Paris: Philippe Haudrère, 'La contrebande des toiles *indiennes* à Paris au XVIIIe siècle', in *Tisser l'histoire. L'industrie et ses patrons XVIe–XXe siècle. Mélanges offerts à Serge Chassagne* (Valenciennes: Presses universitaires de Valenciennes, 2009), 178–79.

76 ADR, 1 C 277, July 3, 1722.

77 ADR, 5 C 12, March 11 and 19, May 5, 1756.

78 ADR, 1 C 277, December 25, 1722.

79 ADD, B 1304, March 6, 1741 and June 10, 1752.

80 Archives départementales de l'Isère (ADI), 2 C 101, April 18, 1757.

81 Olwen Hufton, 'Women Without Men: Widows and Spinsters in Britain and France in the Eighteenth Century', *Journal of Family History* 9 (1984): 361; Garden, *Lyon*, 158 and 162.

82 ADI, 2 C 101, March 5, 1738; January 19, February 16, March 4, 1751; March 12, 1753; March 20, 1754; February 10, 1758.

83 ADI, 2 C 101, September 29, 1752. See also June 11, 1739.

84 ADR, 1 C 277, July 22 and August 26, 1722.

85 ADR, 1 C 277, January 6, 1723.

86 Crowston, *Fabricating Women*; Musgrave, 'Women'.

87 Claude Zaidman, 'Ensemble et séparés', Preface to Erving Goffman, *L'arrangement des sexes* (Paris: La Dispute, 2002), 9.

Select bibliography

Crowston, Clare. 'Engendering the Guilds: Seamstresses, Tailors, and the Clash of Corporate Identities in Old Regime France'. *French Historical Studies* 23 (2000): 339–71.

——— *Fabricating Women. The Seamstresses of Old Regime France (1675–1791)*. Durham, NC: Duke University Press, 2001.

Epstein, S.R., and Maarten Prak, eds. *Guilds, Innovation and the European Economy, 1400–1800*. Cambridge: Cambridge University Press, 2008.

Garden, Maurice. *Lyon et les Lyonnais au XVIIIe siècle*. Paris: Les Belles Lettres, 1970.

——— 'Ouvriers et artisans au XVIIIe siècle. L'exemple lyonnais et les problèmes de classification'. In *Maurice Garden, un historien dans la ville*, ed. René Favier,

Laurence Fontaine, Patrice Bourdelais, and Olivier Faure, 87–112. Paris: Éditions de la Maison des Sciences de l'Homme, 2008.

Hafter, Daryl. 'Women in the Underground Business of Eighteenth–Century Lyon'. *Enterprise & Society* 2 (2001): 11–40.

Hardwick, Julie. 'Seeking Separations: Gender, Marriage, and Household Economies in Early Modern France'. *French Historical Studies* 21 (1998): 157–80.

Heuvel, Danielle van den. *Women and Entrepreneurship: Female Traders in the Northern Netherlands, c. 1580–1815*. Amsterdam: Aksant, 2007.

Lanza, Janine M. *From Wives to Widows in Early Modern Paris: Gender, Economy, and Law*. Aldershot: Ashgate, 2007.

Musgrave, Elizabeth. 'Women and the Craft Guilds in Eighteenth-Century Nantes'. In *The Artisan and the European Town, 1500–1900*, ed. Geoffrey Crossick, 151–71. Aldershot: Ashgate, 2007.

Simonton, Deborah, and Anne Montenach, eds. *Female Agency in the Urban Economy: Gender in European Towns, 1640–1830*. London: Routledge, 2013.

Wiesner Wood, Merry. 'Paltry Peddlers or Essential Merchants? Women in the Distributive Trades in Early Modern Nuremberg'. *Sixteenth Century Journal* 12 (1981): 3–13.

10 Contested authority

Working women in leading positions in the early modern Dutch urban economy

Ariadne Schmidt

The recent debate on early modern women's work largely revolves around questions about access of women to the labour market, the opportunities of women to be economically active, and the contribution of women to the urban economy or to economic development. Careful reconsideration of the sources and the development of new methodologies have led to (re)assessments of female labour force participation rates. Broadening the perspective beyond women's employment opportunities and the inclusion of women's unremunerated work in family businesses has revealed the wide variety of ways in which women could be economically active.[1] By emphasising women's agency and their opportunities instead of restrictions, and by showing that notions of domesticity in practice had barely any impact on most working women's experiences—this notion did not, for example, lead to the withdrawal of a large number of women from the labour market, as the greater majority of women simply had to work for their maintenance—recent research has nuanced the interpretation of the early modern period as a time of reinforced patriarchy.[2]

The recent emphasis on the importance of the economic role of women does not alter the acknowledgement by historians that the position of women in the labour market or the family business was not equal to that of men. Women were economically active on a large scale, but, in general, their work was often lower skilled, lower paid, less esteemed, less visible, and more intermittent in nature than that of men.[3] Most women worked in subordinate positions. But women in the early modern period were not completely excluded from positions of authority; under certain circumstances they were able to gain access to positions in which they were in charge.

The most well-known example of women in leading positions are the widows who were granted the right to continue operating their husband's craft or trade after the death of their spouse. This was achieved by the written or unwritten rule that granted the widow the right to continue the work after her husband's death. But there were also women working in positions of authority who were apparently not widows, or who worked in other sectors of the economy. Women could be found as overseers at Dutch markets; in (very) rare circumstances they participated in administrative bodies of corporations, and women (co-)supervised welfare institutions in early modern Dutch towns.

This contribution examines the experiences of the numerically small, yet from a gender perspective very interesting, group of women, who worked in positions of authority in various sectors of the early modern urban economy. How did women gain access to positions in which they could exercise power? How was their authority legitimated in a society in which women were legally subordinate to men? What were the limitations of their authority? Did male colleagues, or subordinates, accept the authority of women in charge? To answer these questions I will analyse several case studies of seventeenth- and eighteenth-century women who worked in leading positions, and who, at a certain point in time, came into conflict with their male colleagues. These conflicts offer us an exceptional insight into the way in which their positions were legitimated. It reveals what restrictions were imposed on women, and, on the other hand, how women negotiated their power and defended their positions when their authority was contested. I will show that the symbolic analogy with the family played a crucial role in the legitimating of their authority.

The focus will be on the province of Holland in the period 1650 to 1800. Evidence is drawn from archival sources from Leiden and Gouda, combined with recent secondary literature about early modern women in the Dutch Republic. The sources include (fragmentarily preserved) guild membership lists and guild regulations, the archives of orphanages and especially the records of the administration of the orphanages' female boards. The most important evidence for the research presented here is, however, the petitions women submitted to the city council. Petitions were one of the appropriate instruments for city dwellers to come into contact with the urban authorities. With a standardised letter they asked the authorities for a favour, the resolution of a problem, or simply for justice in a situation in which they felt disadvantaged. Through the humble tone of the requests the subordinates affirmed the authority of the city council. The city council, in turn, could not ignore the petitions. The petition was the instrument par excellence through which burghers could exercise influence on the urban legislation. In fact, as Henk van Nierop has demonstrated, in Amsterdam almost all urban by-laws were made in response to petitions of individual burghers or corporations.[4] As the positive replies to petitions formed an essential part of urban legislation, these petitions were carefully recorded. Various Dutch city archives keep a complete series of such petitions covering the seventeenth and eighteenth centuries. Even though petitions were composed according to standardised forms, and often written by or with the help of professional writers, they do echo the voices of women,[5] and provide a unique insight into the problems women encountered and the solutions they brought to the fore themselves. Various of these problems were, in one way or another, related to issues about these women's authority, as we will see later.

As parties in conflicts about the authority exercised by women often referred to the law to sustain their arguments, I will first give a brief and general overview of women's civil legal status and their position in marital, property, and inheritance law.

The legal position of women in Holland

According to early modern Dutch law the legal relation between women and men was determined by the 'natural law'. The subordinate position of women in society was legitimated by their supposed inferior intellectual capabilities and their 'mental weakness'. The famous Dutch lawyer Grotius argued that the female sex was less capable of performing activities that required rationality or the ability to reason than the male sex, and therefore men were granted legal authority over women.[6] Women were similarly denied the administration of property and supervision over people. Women were deemed to be weaker than men; they were 'by nature' less suitable to judge and think logically and therefore excluded from government over people and over goods (*bestier van luijden en saaken*).[7]

As is well known, the marital status of a woman was of crucial importance in determining her legal position. A married woman fell under the legal authority of her husband. This implied that women had to obey their husbands and, in return, could count on the protection of their spouses. Furthermore, married women lost the right of disposal over their property. According to Dutch law the goods of both bride and groom became part of the joint property over which the husband had the right of disposal. Whereas in other regions in the Dutch Republic the husband was only allowed to dispose of his wife's movable property, in Holland he could alienate both movables and immovable goods without her consent. Finally, a husband represented his wife as her guardian in legal affairs, in court cases, when making contracts, or appearing before a notary.[8]

These rules applied to women who were married. The legal position of unmarried adult females in early modern Holland was different. According to the seventeenth-century Dutch lawyer Simon van Leeuwen, it was considered old-fashioned to place adult single women under permanent guardianship. He sustained his argument with a reference to the work of Johan van Beverwijck, the medical doctor who in 1639 had published his *Van de Wtnementheyt des vrouwelicken Geslachts* (On the excellence of the female sex). In this apology for the superiority of women over men, which has the character of a catalogue of learned women, Van Beverwijck described the virtues of women at length.[9] Van Leeuwen referred to this work when he argued that 'the innate character of women is not as weak as is often assumed' and that there could be found many women with a larger intellect (than men) and men with a smaller intellect (than women), 'indeed that many women exceeded man with respect to intellect and administration'. Therefore, the lawyer concluded, unmarried adult women were allowed to 'guide themselves' and dispose of their own goods.[10] In practice, when unmarried women and widows in the seventeenth and eighteenth centuries appeared before the court or entered into contracts they were assisted by a guardian, but these guardians were 'chosen' by the women themselves for the particular occasion and were thus not comparable with the permanent guardianship required for married women.

With respect to inheritances Dutch law may be characterised as remarkably egalitarian. In Holland, after the death of a spouse, the marital estate was divided in two equal parts. One half, representing the goods brought into the marriage, was taken out of the joint estate by the surviving spouse. The other half formed the inheritance of the spouse who had died and was divided among the heirs of the deceased, usually the children. Sons and daughters received equal parts or parts of equal worth. This equal inheritance practice implied that, at least in theory, the situation in which widows and widowers found themselves after the death of a spouse was exactly the same.[11]

In Dutch law, the subordinate legal position of women was legitimated with references to the supposed mental weakness of women and their incapability to judge. In practice, though, the fundamental legal inequality was not taken to the extremes. The marital status of women was a factor of importance, although there were some significant differences between the legal norm and legal practice, and, finally, inheritance law in Holland was relatively egalitarian. In the following we will examine if, and how, this legally subordinate status affected women working in positions of authority.

Guilds: Defining positions of authority

The impact of guilds on women's work is a much-debated issue in the historiography of women's work.[12] Initially many historians had a rather pessimistic view of the corporations and believed that the guild organisation had a limiting effect on women's economic role. The emergence of guilds was seen as one of the factors that excluded women from market production in the early modern period. Historians emphasised that craft guilds gradually imposed more restrictions on women's work.[13] In recent years, however, this perception has changed. Historians now emphasise the variations in the corporate status of women; they have shown that gendered patterns of inclusion and exclusion varied geographically and even from one guild to another. Another important finding was that the position of women in guilds was highly dependent upon a woman's marital status. In various guilds in cities in France and Germany marriage enabled women to access positions of authority and widows were often considered the legitimate successors of their deceased spouse.[14]

The evidence of Dutch guilds concurs with these findings. The impact of guilds on the position of women varied from one guild to another. Guilds did not necessarily exclude women from work—most urban craft guilds excluded unmarried and married women from membership, but allowed widows to continue their deceased husband's work. In the retailing and food sector, the segments of the urban economy that were usually more accessible to women, there were guilds that accepted women as members.[15] Within the guilds that regulated export industries, like the pipe-making industry in Gouda, women carried out work as wage labourers. And, last but not least, women quite often provided unpaid labour in the workshop or family business that was run in their husband's name or by the couple jointly.[16] Almost all guilds, though, excluded women from positions of authority. Women had no access to the guild's boards and had no right to vote. Even in the mixed-gender guilds, like the guilds of the innkeepers, of publicans, of schoolmasters or one of the shopkeepers' guilds that existed in many towns, the position of women was inferior to that of men.[17] Seamstresses formed an interesting exception.[18] In some Dutch cities they were assembled as a sub-division of the tailors' guild, and in Gouda they even had a board of their own, consisting of four female deacons (*dekeninnen*).That the position of this board was not equal to that of their male counterparts becomes clear from the stipulations that regulated the guild festivities: whereas female deacons received four guilders to celebrate their annual election, the male deacons were given up to eight guilders to spend.[19]

When it comes to the position of women in traditional artisanal guilds, marital status was of crucial importance. In her book *From Wives to Widows in Early Modern Paris*, Janine M. Lanza concludes that widows 'did not fit into the trajectory of loss and decline that other historians have laid out for women of Old Regime Europe'. It was precisely their position as masters' widows in the traditional artisanal guilds that set widows apart from other women. As Lanza argued, widows faced gender-specific challenges, and widows also functioned differently to men. Yet in eighteenth-century Paris, the period studied by Lanza, some women nonetheless still had access to 'well-paid, high-status work'.[20]

Many Dutch guilds or corporations acknowledged the so-called 'widows' right'.[21] This right—sometimes, though not necessarily, laid down in the guild regulations—gave women the opportunity to carry on their deceased husbands' work and to assume a formal position. The conditions under which widows were allowed to continue the work varied. Firstly, in most guilds widows were allowed to work as long as they were 'assisted' by a 'master journeyman' (*meesterknecht*). Secondly, a master journeyman was sometimes required to have passed his exam or to pass it within a limited period of time. A third condition found in various guild regulations was that widows were only allowed to continue work for a limited period of time. However, analysis of various guild regulations revealed that this was the period during which a widow was allowed to work *alone*. After the required time had passed, the widow had to hire a journeyman to assist her.[22] These restrictions imposed by the guild regulations upon widows' work served the same goal. Widows had often been active in the workshop or enterprise that was run in their husbands' name for years, but they had never had the opportunity to give proof of their expertise as they were excluded from official training. The presence of a (master) journeyman was required to ascertain the quality of the goods produced.[23]

Once a widow met the requirements she could work on the same conditions as her deceased husband had done, as was explicated in some of the guild regulations.[24] With respect to work, the status of a master's widow resembled that of a male master. She was bound by, or had the scope to exercise her work under, the same requirements as a male master. In Dutch records no restrictions concerning the hiring of apprentices or the quantity of goods produced in a widow's workshop are evident.[25] But the right to continue the work in her own name was restricted to the period of widowhood, until she remarried.[26] This illustrates how closely the status of a guild member was connected to the status of the head of the household—who represented the family, who was perceived to be the family's 'breadwinner', and who was usually male.

Guild regulations reflect the *norms* concerning the status of women. Women, however, sent petitions to the city council in which they asked for a flexible interpretation of the rules or for adaption of the regulations. In Leiden, only those petitions to which the city authorities responded positively survive in the records. Requests that were rejected were not always registered. Therefore, we do not know the frequency with which widows tried to alter their own situation; nor do we precisely know their chances of success. The petitions that were preserved do, however, shed a very interesting light on the position of women in guilds in daily practice. In some cases these women had worked for years in the family enterprise or workshop, as daughter or as a wife. Margriete van Eijck, widow of Tousseijn Barbarij, for example, when asking the local authorities in 1662 for permission to continue her husband's work as a coppersmith, emphasised that she was very experienced. During the frequent times her husband had been ill, all work had depended upon her, so she had 'thorough knowledge' of both the craft and of 'supervising the workshop', as she told the authorities. We do not know in detail how the authorities reacted, but apparently they were not prepared to allow Margriete the same rights as her husband had held. Initially Margriete received exemption from the rule for a limited period of time, but after two more petitions the widow had to close her shop, as will be shown below. The childless widow Johanna Cabeljauw argued in the petition she submitted in 1669 that she knew 'the art of dyeing' perfectly well, adding that she had always and continuously assisted her husband with his work when she was not burdened with children. Lysbeth Verborre, who worked in the Leiden textile industry in the 1620s, emphasised that she had assisted her parents in their workshop since her childhood, and had worked alongside her husband, thus demonstrating that she was able to serve the merchants to 'full satisfaction'.[27] Only as widows could Margriete,

Johanna, and Lysbeth claim the position in which they received a formal status and exercise supervision over the workshop.

In the absence of a man, a woman could take over the role of 'head' of the workshop, together with the accompanying responsibilities. Widows who married again lost this status. On some occasions a widow's new husband was allowed to take the place of his new wife and run the workshop in his name. The case of Laurens de Matter, who in the 1630s married Aeltgen Mourings, widow of the dyer Barent Claes van Paesschen, is remarkable in this respect. Laurens was allowed 'to swear the oath in addition to his wife' but was not admitted to the *actual* work of dyeing as he did not yet have the required experience.[28] Only after a year did the authorities grant him the right to carry out the work in his own name, 'as being married to the widow of Barent Claes van Paesschen'. In the intermediate year it was Aeltgen who both did the actual work and held the supervision.[29]

The enforcement of the rules concerning the application of the widow's right was not rigid. Some guilds without the so-called widow's right did accept widows as members after all;[30] other guilds extended the right to daughters. The Gouda wood merchants' guild, for example, in 1775 accepted Adriana Hooglandt, who wanted to continue the workshop of her deceased widowed mother, as a guild member. The married couple Dominicus van Luiten and his wife, who wanted to succeed Dominicus' mother-in-law into the guild, were granted permission to do so in 1764.[31] In Leiden three unmarried sisters, Anna, Margrieta, and Johanna, were allowed to run an apothecary. Judith Baes, Antoinette Vailliant, Hester Ongena, and Judith Huijgen were all unmarried daughters continuing the workshop of their father or mother in the textile industry producing serge.[32]

The widow's right was in practice not only extended to daughters; in very exceptional cases even divorced women were granted the right. For example, the Gouda blacksmiths' guild in 1771 granted Jannigje Kreek the right to run the blacksmith's shop in her own name under the condition that her (former) spouse would refrain from all rights as long as the couple lived apart.[33] The traditional artisanal guilds in cities in Holland applied rules with a remarkable flexibility, or adapted the regulation, sometimes in favour of women. By taking away some of the strictest conditions that hampered widows in their work, these guilds not only served the interests of the women and their families by enabling them to maintain themselves, they also prevented flourishing workshops closing and thereby served the interest of the wider local economy.[34] It is probably from this point of view that we should interpret the decision of guilds to choose the side of widows when they came into conflict with their journeymen, as we will see.

Conflicts in the workshop

Merry Wiesner was the first who, in her research into women's work in early modern Germany, discovered that journeymen frequently came into conflict with the widows working in guild shops. According to Wiesner the journeymen's hostility to women, motivated by both economic considerations and by an ideology of guild honour, developed into a gradual exclusion of women from guilds.[35] Janine Lanza also noticed that widows did not always get along with their master journeymen. In some cases widows met resistance to their authority in the workshop and these conflicts were often based on their gender.[36] Similar conflicts can be found in Dutch towns as well. Many masters' widows were experienced and had good knowledge of the work. The question of whether widows were actually involved in the production process was not relevant to their right to continue the work. Experience was not required according to guild regulations. The authorities' decision to grant widows permission to continue work was not related to the number of years a woman had provided 'assistance labour' in the workshop or family enterprise. Furthermore, it is possible that at least in some sectors, male masters were also not involved in the production process on a daily basis, but rather assumed managerial roles. These roles were not very different from the roles their widows assumed after their death, in which the actual work was left to journeymen. What was relevant, though, is that widows, whether experienced or not, were never given the opportunity to provide proof of their expertise. Even when they were experienced, and had good knowledge of the craft, like the above-mentioned Margriete van Eijck, Sophia Jans, Lysbeth Verborre, or Johanna Cabeljauw, these women were usually obliged to work in the presence of a journeyman. He was the one who formally had to guarantee the quality of the goods produced because he was the one who had been admitted to the formal training. This situation placed widows at a disadvantage in their relations with their journeymen.

The master journeyman who had to assist the widow in her work was a craftsman who had come close to finishing his training and who was often just one step removed from establishing an independent workshop. The knowledge that a widow was dependent upon him strengthened his bargaining position.[37] This becomes clear in a conflict between the widows of bakers and the bakers' journeymen. Widows of bakers were only allowed to keep the bakery open if they employed a journeyman who had been apprenticed for at least four years, two years of which he had to have served and lived with a Leiden master, and who had passed his exam. Master journeymen were well aware of the consequences of an untimely departure: the widow would have to close her bakery and lose her clientele. This happened often. The bakers' widows stated in a mutual petition directed to the city council in 1655 that journeymen left shortly after their employers had paid for the examination, only, as the widows claimed, 'to obstruct' their mistresses. The situation was repeated over and over again, and as a result the widows had to pay the costly exam fee for the journeymen several times within a short period. This behaviour was so 'impertinent' that it made them, as the widows claimed, 'merely the servants of their journeymen'.[38]

The behaviour of the journeymen who were supposed to assist the millers' widows was not much better. Well aware of the fact that the widow had to pay the guild admission fee of every new journeyman she hired, the journeymen were demanding excessively high wages, and threatened to leave if widows refused to pay. The millers' widows also sent a collective complaint to the city authorities. In 1673 they asked whether the guild regulation could be changed to bring the practice of blackmailing by the journeymen to an end. These collective petitions also reveal the shared occupational identity that could arise when female guild members, with their male colleagues, petitioned the authorities together to defend their common interests. Such was the case when the male and female sellers of vegetables, and the male and female rope makers of Gouda sought to counter competition from outside the town.[39] These joint petitions also indicated a preparedness for women and men to take the initiative collectively when their interests were threatened. Moreover, in these cases, the instrument of petitioning appeared to be effective. Both the bakers' and the millers' guilds decided to relax the rules. The bakers' guild stipulated that journeymen hired by widows no longer had to pass their exams. The millers decided that those widows who wanted to have a journeyman to work for them should pay the guild membership—and thus the admission fee—themselves, but only once.[40]

The widows of the bakers and millers complained that it was difficult to find qualified and reliable journeymen to assist them. Other widows petitioned the authorities for support because they were reluctant to hire journeymen beforehand. Sophia Jans, for example, a widow who had managed the apothecary of her husband for about ten years on her own, was summoned in the 1660s by the guild to meet its requirements and hire a master journeyman. Sophia refused to do so. Apart from the fact that she was very experienced, as she stated in her petition, Sophia emphasised that she was an old lady who did not look forward to the 'unfreedom of having a journeyman in her home'. Sophia was granted exemption from the guild regulation and was allowed to continue her work without a journeyman.[41] The above-mentioned Margriete van Eijck was also not inclined to hire a journeyman, but her grievances were more fundamental in nature. Margriete petitioned to the city council because, in her opinion, she had no need to be assisted by a master journeyman. During her husband's life Margriete had made 'much of the heavy work herself' and she had worked to the satisfaction of her customers. The widow argued that hiring a journeyman would lead to a 'incredibly inconvenient' situation. It would be 'inevitable' that she would get into conflict with a journeyman, which would harm her as well as the people around her. Margriete tried to convince the city authorities that she was very well capable of 'supervising her shop', that the supervision over the workshop could very well be trusted to her, and that she would inevitably lose 'the authority' over her workshop if she had to appoint a journeyman. Moreover, she continued, it would be impossible to find a journeyman who would be willing to submit himself to her authority.[42] Whereas Sophia Jans was allowed to continue her work without a journeyman, Margriete put her work at risk. She was granted exemption twice, but only for a limited period of time and she was summoned to leave the craft—and close her workshop—at the end of the term. What happened to the experienced coppersmith after she had closed her shop is unknown.

The loss of a husband brought a master's widow into a precarious situation. In many workshops where journeymen worked for their master, the wife of the master was also around. She even may have stood in for him once in a while. But the relations of authority had been clear to all: the male artisan was in charge and held the supervision over the workshop and the personnel. This changed when he was no longer present. The master journeyman, who had (almost) finished his education in an occupation that under normal circumstances was only open to men, was supposed to work under the supervision of a woman. This was a situation that was not readily accepted by all. The relationship between the master journeyman and the widow was, however, one of mutual dependency. The master journeyman, having completed his exam and acquired proof of his qualifications, enabled the widow to keep the shop open. The widow, on the other hand, owned the workshop in which he could bring his knowledge into practice. Costs for exams were expensive and establishing a workshop usually required the investment of a large amount of capital. It is no surprise that the cliché of the widow marrying her journeyman became reality for many. For those who did not, this mutual dependency did not necessarily ease the relations between the two.[43]

The decisions on the petitions Dutch widows submitted to their city councils indicate that the consequences of the conflicts between artisanal widows and their journeymen had outcomes different to those in the German cities described by Wiesner. There are no signs of an ongoing process of exclusion of women from guilds and widows were quite often supported by the guilds. Whether they were motivated by commercial reasons or by consideration for the broken family remains unknown, but it is telling that the guilds sometimes chose the side of the widow and enabled her to overcome the conflict with her employee and continue the work. Margriete van Eijck's loss of status suggests that her interests were only of temporary concern to the guild. But there are also examples in which the interests of women were given priority on a permanent basis. Apparently the patriarchal guild institutions prioritised the interests of these women out of concern for economic or social stability over gender ideology. Unwilling employees were rebuked or guild regulations were adapted in certain circumstances. That the interests of the widow were given priority must have strengthened her position of authority. The situation was, however, different when not journeymen but guild boards were the opponents. Even though, again, we do not know the precise frequency with which it occurred, in various cities widows came into conflict about their position with the board members. The records of disputes reveal on the one hand how widows tried to claim greater scope for autonomy and, on the other, how guilds defended their prerogatives, thus contributing to a fundamental inequality between the sexes.

Authority contested

Masters' widows may have been given the opportunity to work under the same conditions as their husbands had done, but their position within the corporation was by no means equal to that of men.[44] When economic motives were at stake, guilds were prepared to apply the regulations with flexibility. Thus the pipe-makers' guild decided that when a pipe maker's widow married a man from outside the guild, he—or the couple—was allowed to continue to use the trademark on *his* name when he would pay for it, and thus keep the workshop open.[45] The policy of the Amsterdam wine-merchants' guild was less flexible. In 1759 it forbade a widow who remarried outside the guild to continue the trade. It was directly against 'the natural order of things' if a married woman, 'who submitted herself to the marital power of a man, would be able to continue the trade or business in name and as if she was a widow of her deceased husband', as the guild justified its decision.[46]

It is not so much the decision as the justification of the wine-merchants' guild that strikes the eye. Such explicit references to marital law are not easily found in the decisions of authorities in the seventeenth century, although they appear to be more common in eighteenth-century rhetoric. The Gouda pipe makers may have been more flexible with regard to the position of women than the wine merchants, but only for practical reasons. By allowing the new husbands of remarried pipe-makers' widows to continue the work, they prevented the obstruction of the production in the industry that was of crucial importance for the local urban economy. That, however, the pipe makers shared the opinion that female guild members did not have the same status as their male guild counterparts becomes clear from the decisions on the petition of four remarried pipe-makers' widows, who in 1784 asked the city authorities for clarification on the inheritance laws.

In 1753 the pipe-makers' guild regulated the inheritance practices of the clay-pipe-makers' trademarks, which functioned as a licence to produce. After a pipe maker passed away, the ownership of his mark would devolve upon his widow and after her death, the (grand)children would inherit the mark. A possible second or third wife of a pipe maker could inherit the mark, but when the pipe maker had children from a previous marriage, this second or third wife did not acquire the ownership. In this case, she was entitled to use the mark as long as she lived, but she could not sell or bequeath the mark, as it would revert to the children of the first marriage of her deceased husband. In 1761, however, the regulation was changed and the guild stipulated that the master pipe maker was now allowed to bequeath his mark freely. A widow, by contrast, could only *use*, and not *bequeath* the mark. It was in 1784 that Sijna van Nierop, Lijsje van Berkel, Belighe Sliedrecht, and Geertrui van Vliet, all remarried pipe-makers' widows, asked the city council for the same right of the free disposal of their marks so that they could bequeath them to their second husbands.[47]

The four women remarked that the change in the regulation made in 1761 granted the right of free disposal only to the guild brothers, whereas women seem to have been deprived of the right to bequeath. As guild sisters (*gildezusters*) had the same obligations as guild brothers—they had to meet all requirements, they had to pay the guild—they also expected to receive the same rights. Such 'equal rights' would enable them to maintain themselves within the craft. The widows tried to convince the guild that the trademark should be considered as 'free property' which could be freely disposed of by the owner. They also told the authorities that their children tended to marry at a young age (at which moment they could demand their father's inheritance, including the trademark). By doing so, they deprived their stepfather, who until then had maintained his stepchildren with his work based on the mark, of his maintenance. The widows concluded their plea for equal rights by mentioning that it probably had never been the explicit intention to exclude the guild sisters of the right of disposal but that they must have been forgotten unintentionally, as, after all, there was ample reason to grant them the right to dispose of the mark as well.[48]

The members of the guild board, who were asked for advice by the magistrates, did not share this point of view. They refuted the arguments point by point: as the guild regulation made in 1753 only concerned male members of the guild, the subsequent amendment could also only concern men. Guild marks were not free property. Pipe making was a physically demanding craft for women and, therefore, many pipe-makers' widows remarried soon. Widows, however, had to be protected against the 'cunning flattery' of men who wanted to marry them and to whom they would too easily hand over their mark at the expense of themselves and their children.[49] In this the guild appealed to a universal notion that women as the weaker sex had to be protected against the outside world and that women were not capable of defending their own interests.[50]

The guild continued its argumentation with a remarkable consideration. It stated that the very fact that husbands had given proof of their expertise according to the guild rules, had obtained guild membership and thereby acquired the name of 'guild brethren' (*gildebroeders*) certainly did not imply that the wives of these guild brothers—as they would never be admitted to the proof of expertise—would be known under the name of guild sisters. Nor did it imply that they enjoyed the privileges and rights equal to those of their husbands.[51] 'No one with the slightest understanding of a guild—and especially of the guild of the pipe makers—would be able to maintain this.' This meant that:

> The pipe-makers' wives as a consequence cannot be considered other than just shareholders (*deelgenoot*) of the privileges of their husbands,

> as according to the decision of 1753, after the death of their husbands and during the period that they are widows, the guild's privileges are not granted to them as guild sisters, but as a special gift.[52]

The guild thus argued that widows of the pipe makers were not guild sisters. They derived their privileges from their deceased husbands, but only for the period of their widowhood. The magistrates followed the guild's advice and declined the widows' request.[53]

At the moment of the dispute between the guild and the widows the craft of the pipe making industry had been in serious decline. The loss of the importance of the industry for the local economy may have diminished the necessity for a flexible interpretation of the regulation. Similar authority conflicts arose in other areas of the eighteenth-century urban economy which illustrates that it was not only (the lack of) commercial motives that heated the debate.

Conflicts in the boards

Dutch lawyers denied (married) women the right to administer goods and people because they were considered to be unable to think logically, as we saw above. An important and noticeable exception to this general rule is offered by women who participated in the boards of welfare institutions and prisons or correctional institutions. Together with the male regents, the female regents supervised welfare institutions, the organisation of which resembled that of the family. The analogy becomes apparent in the occupational titles. Inside orphanages, hospitals, and prisons, an 'indoor-father' (*binnenvader*) and 'indoor-mother' (*binnenmoeder*), preferably though not necessarily a married couple, looked after the inmates (orphans, prisoners, the ill, or old-aged) and the staff (servants). The overall authority over the institution was held by the male and female regents, or 'outdoor-fathers' and 'outdoor mothers' as they were sometimes called. These male and female administrators were usually not related to each other and only had a business-like relationship.[54]

The female regents did not receive any form of compensation or emoluments for their work. The offices they occupied belonged to the so-called subaltern or 'serving' offices that were considered part of the civic duties that citizens, and in this case the most well-to-do citizens in town, were supposed to provide to the urban community. The subaltern officials, who formed the social layer just below that of the town councils and magistrates, were supposed to assist the senior administrative and judicial officeholders.[55] They were selected by the city authorities from the upper echelons of the urban community. The office of regent of a welfare institution was one of the lower rungs on the ladder a man might climb in order to pursue a long career of public service. Other, more prestigious positions might include treasurer, master of the Orphan Chamber, captain of the civic militia, and, possibly, the highest public offices of magistrate or city councillor.[56] For women, on the other hand, membership of the board of regents was the only area in which they could assume such a prestigious position of leadership.

The tasks of both the male and female board members were written down in instructions. The conceptual division of tasks is strongly reminiscent of the division between the public and the private sphere that became more sharply articulated in the eighteenth century, whereby the private sphere was increasingly promoted as a woman's domain and activities in the public sphere were more strongly promoted as the domain of men.[57] Male regents usually held the final responsibility over external affairs, finances, management of buildings and property, the admittance of inmates, and the employment of part of the personnel. Female regents in most institutions held the final responsibility over what was called the 'internal' affairs and domestic matters. They supervised the kitchen and the sewing room and sometimes also (part of the) female indoor staff.[58] The instructions were not always unambiguous. Relations were put to the test in such circumstances and on many boards conflicts arose about responsibilities and especially about the female regents' autonomy, as we will see.

Dutch female regents enjoyed a reputation of international fame.[59] They were portrayed as qualified leaders, full of confidence, by the famous Dutch painters of the seventeenth and eighteenth centuries.[60] In practice, however, their authority was far from self-evident. Willem Loran, orphan father from 1813 to 1845, wrote a history of the Utrecht orphanage. This account, written in retrospect, provides an interesting insight into a nineteenth-century male official's perspective on women in positions of authority. Loran characterised the female 'matronate' as 'a source of eternal discontent and quarrelsomeness'.[61] As Loran records, for most of the eighteenth century the Utrecht orphanage had functioned without a board of female administrators. Until the early seventeenth century, the wives of the male regents had fulfilled the task of female supervisors. But these women were 'burdened with children and their own household' and therefore in the beginning of the seventeenth century it was decided to appoint eight 'experienced and qualified women, above child-rearing age'.[62] In the first years these matrons worked under the supervision of the wives of the regents, who apparently still assumed an official role within the orphanage. This led to an unworkable situation. Whether this was caused by the 'imagined superiority' of the regents' wives, as Loran suggested, is unknown.[63] But in due course, the wives of the regents were excluded from involvement and the tasks of the matrons became autonomous activities. The matronate of the Utrecht orphanage functioned until 1702, when matrons ceased to hold office.[64] We are not informed about the reasons of this joint reassignment. Similar incidents in other cities suggest that conflicts over authority may have played a role.

The female regents of the house of correction in Gouda came into conflict with their male colleagues in the mid-eighteenth century because they demanded a say in the appointment of the new indoor-mother as this right had been granted to them in the regulations, and as they were the ones who had to work with her on a daily basis. As their protests were not heard, the female regents decided to resign. But even in this they were not heard, as the city authorities declined their request to be dismissed, without providing any further rationale for their decision.[65] Similar disputes arose in the boards of the Lutheran orphanage in Amsterdam in 1689, as well as in the orphanage in Middelburg in 1771. The Amsterdam female regents considered themselves independent and refused to give an account of their financial administration to the male regents. That the church congregation in the end accepted the women's claim of autonomy was unmistakably related to the fact that the board of female regents was established in 1680 with a special financial bequest and that the board could dispose of its own financial means.[66] The re-division of the tasks of the board of the Middelburg orphanage between the male and the female members was called 'a humiliating project' by the latter.[67] The female regents perceived themselves to be treated as 'housekeepers' who were allowed only some rather 'insignificant tasks'.[68] They refused to submit themselves to the supervision of the male regents, demanded a full say and responsibility over the orphan girls and the complete household, and wanted to appoint female staff and hold responsibility for the purchases of the household necessities. The last point was considered of special importance. The female regents believed that they were better equipped to plan the menu and to make the purchases as economically as possible. But what also played a role was that the possibility of favouring merchants with large orders and special assignments was incredibly important for consolidating social relations, and maintaining the social network-engendered status and social prestige within the local community. The regents, who wanted to assign their female colleagues a supporting rather than an executive role, did not give up the responsibility for purchasing that easily. The social importance of this task was simply too significant. The male regents appealed to the 'natural right' and argued that when a board consisted of both women and men, 'the management was reserved solely to men'. They explained to the female regents that:

> As was the case in the management of families in which one follows the natural order, men were granted the management and women the surveillance. For this very reason it was perfectly clear that the whole administration was given to the regents.[69]

As mediation was not of any help, the case was submitted to the city magistrates, who decided in favour of the male regents. The male regents held the overall supervision of the organisation and the right to appoint the employees to the higher echelons. The female regents retained supervision over the 'domestic matters', and were entitled to appoint the lower staff.[70]

That conflicts between male and female regents were not automatically settled in favour of the male officials becomes clear from the long-lasting dispute in the Leiden orphanage. Here, a disagreement between male and female board members led to a genuine management crisis. The female regents had punished a girl who had stolen clothes with a beating and five months' extra work.[71] The male regents were aggrieved about their actions, because they were not consulted, nor given notice of the incident. Moreover, as they argued, their female colleagues were not responsible for punishing the girls. They should have discussed this with the male regents, as the 'chief administration' belonged to them. The female regents resisted, arguing that they were appointed by the city council and thus that they only had to give account to the city council. They added that they would rather cede their functions than submit themselves to the authority of the male regents.[72]

As the boards could not come to an agreement, a committee was installed to examine the responsibilities and to mediate between the two. The committee—consisting of male regents—unsurprisingly supported the argument of the regents that they were the chief administrators, and that the moral education of the girls pertained to the responsibility of the male regents. The committee referred to the perceived fundamental inequality between women and men to sustain its argumentation. One member of the committee argued that he could not believe how the city authorities of Leiden entrusted the care of the poor and parentless girls—'whose welfare the committee considered to be equally important as those of boys'—to women. Another proposed that the male regents held the final responsibility with reference to the legal status of married women and argued that 'a married woman is not a [legal] person'.[73]

The female regents responded to each of the arguments separately. They acknowledged the authority and final responsibility of the male regents with respect to criminal conflicts, the property, finances, and the moral education of boys. Again we see that the fields of responsibility were made according the idea of public versus the private spheres informed by assumptions about gender, whereby the private sphere was seen as the domain of women and spheres of 'public' activity traditionally deemed masculine. Criminal behaviour had to be indicted by the criminal court, and thus outside the orphanage. Punishing a girl for less serious misbehaviour could be dealt with inside the house. It was part of the moral education of the girls, over which they held responsibility and they defended this responsibility with verve. They were the ones, the female regents argued in their response, who would educate the girls 'in all domestic tasks so that the girls, in due course, knew how to behave as good housekeepers and mothers'. Punishments were part of this. Moreover, there were issues that the women could not notify to men 'out of chastity' as the female administrators formulated cryptically. The female regents expressed their outrage over the imputation that the female regents could not take care of the girls. 'If the citizenry of Leiden shares the opinion of the members of the committee about the female regents, we, the female regents, would be made nothing, or little more than insignificant beings, or Machines, operated by the hands of others.' The argument that women were not legal persons was countered by the women as well. They responded that they knew very well that they fell under the marital power of their *husbands*, not under the marital power of the regents.[74]

The female regents demanded that the male regents acknowledge that the city council held the final say and that the responsibilities were to be divided as suggested in their petition. The male regents were incensed and stated that this would result in a fundamental change to the traditional organisational structure. Furthermore, they continued, it would imply a loss of unity in the governance of the orphans and this was a situation that 'even within the smallest household' would have 'lamentable consequences'.[75]

The mediation of the committee did not bring an agreement any closer. The female regents were accused of trying to counter the solid argumentation of the male regents solely with 'subtle expressions and insignificant rebuttals'.[76] The committee decided to instigate another committee, apparently also without success as the female regents finally presented the conflict to the city council. The city council asked both boards to make a draft for new regulations.[77] During the procedure the women were to maintain responsibility over the orphan girls and the men over the boys, which led the female regents to conclude that the council provisionally had decided in their favour.[78] According to the final regulations the female regents kept their authority.[79]

Conclusion

Whereas Dutch law denied women the right to govern on the basis of their supposed mental weakness and incapacity to judge, women could assume positions of authority in early modern towns. Law made a distinction between married and unmarried women whereby married women were placed in a subordinate position and unmarried women were legally capable of affairs. The dividing lines in the urban economy were different, though. Whereas law did not make clear distinctions between ever- and never-married adult women, the 'marital history' of women was of crucial importance when it came to access to work. It was through marriage that women gained access to positions of authority; literally, through marriage, as in the case of traditional artisanal guilds, or symbolically, as in the case of the boards of welfare institutions, where male and female regents acted as if metaphorically married, although in reality not to one another.

Women were granted formal positions as widows, as married women living alone because their husbands had left for work or were absent for other reasons, or even as divorced women who were considered substitutes of their (former) husbands. In some cases even daughters were allowed as stand-ins for their fathers in the artisanal sectors of the urban economy. Though in practice rules were applied with a remarkable flexibility, broadly speaking, the parallel with the patriarchal household as organising principle was dominant. The evidence from the two Dutch towns concur with the findings for other European cities, such as those in Germany or France. As Janine Lanza phrased it in her research on Paris, 'the shop itself, not the patriarch, constituted the central element of familial survival'.[80] The role assumed by women in charge was usually considered as that of the substitute of the patriarch. They were, in Wiesner's words, 'maintainers of the family unit'.[81] The work status of widows was conceptualised according their status within the broken family. They took over the role of the household head and could assume positions of authority, albeit temporarily, as long as a male household head was absent.

The analogy with the household was also paramount in the legitimisation of the authority of women in boards of administration. As has become clear in recent research, the frequently discussed notion of domesticity and the ideology of the separate spheres have little or no explanatory power in the work experiences of most women in the early modern period. The majority of women moved freely in the 'public sphere' and many participated actively in economic life.[82] The research presented here does not (aim to) challenge this notion. But it is interesting to see that the ideology of the separate spheres did play a role in the experiences of a very small group of women in urban society as it, paradoxically, was precisely the strictly gendered division of tasks that provided the conceptual basis for women to assume managerial roles in welfare institutions. The ideology of the gendered division of work may even have provided these women with a basis from which to claim authority, albeit in a very limited sphere of activity. Tasks between male and female overseers were divided between husbands and wives, according the *ideology* of the gendered division of work, along the lines of the public and the private spheres. The analogy with the household made it self-evident that women were in charge *in* the institution and men took care of external affairs.

The significance of the household as a structuring principle also became clear when conflicts arose. It seems as if masters' widows in Holland had little to fear from the opposition from journeymen who had difficulties with working under their supervision. That they found the guilds or city authorities quite often on their side in cases of conflict may indicate that journeymen were supposed to submit themselves to the authority of the household head, whether female or male. More fundamental were the discussions about the position of women that arose in the eighteenth century. The scattered information does not allow for a systematic analysis, but the records suggest that the authority of women became subject to debate more explicitly. Both in guilds and in boards, conflicts centred on the question of women's autonomy. The cases show that debates became particularly fierce when women tended to claim autonomy, or dared to demand a position that was equal to that of men. Male opponents tried to demarcate women's authority on the work floor with references to the 'natural order' and the law that placed married women in a subordinate position, or to the principle of inequality between the sexes. The conflict in the Leiden orphanage shows that female regents followed this line of reasoning, but not until the end. They accepted the gendered division of tasks according to which women held the responsibility over domestic matters, and men were responsible for external affairs, seemingly as self-evident. But the regents refused to subordinate themselves to the claimed, gender-specific authority of men to whom they were not married. They refused to relinquish power and thus refuted the analogy with the family in this respect.

Notes

1 This contribution is based upon earlier publications. The research was conducted for my dissertation and within the research project 'Women's Work in the Early Modern Northern Netherlands, *c.* 1600–1815', funded by 'Stichting Vrienden van het IISG', Netherlands Organization for Scientific Research (NWO) and 'Stichting Professor Van Winterfonds' at the International Institute of Social History. For this contribution, I reassessed the cases and analysed them from the perspective of women's access to positions of authority. See Ariadne Schmidt, *Overleven na de dood: Weduwen in Leiden in de Gouden Eeuw* (Amsterdam: Prometheus / Bert Bakker, 2001); Ariadne Schmidt, 'Gelijk Hebben, Gelijk Krijgen? Vrouwen en Vertrouwen in het Recht in Holland in de Zeventiende en Achttiende Eeuw', in *Het Gelijk van de Gouden Eeuw: Recht, Onrecht en Reputatie in de Vroegmoderne Nederlanden*, ed. Michiel van Groesen, Judith Pollmann, and Hans Cools (Hilversum: Verloren 2014); Ariadne Schmidt, 'Managing a Large Household. The Gender Division of Work in Orphanages in Dutch Towns in the Early Modern Period, 1580–1800', *History of the Family* 13 (2008).

See for example Jane Humphries and Carmen Sarasúa, 'Off the Record: Reconstructing Women's Labor Force Participation in the European Past', *Feminist Economics* 18 (2012): 39–67; Ariadne Schmidt and Elise van Nederveen Meerkerk, 'Reconsidering "The First Male-Breadwinner Economy": Women's Labour Force Participation in the Netherlands, 1600–1900', *Feminist Economics* 18 (2012); Nicola Phillips, *Women in Business, 1700–1850* (Woodbridge: Boydell, 2006); Hannah Barker, *The Business of Women: Female Enterprise and Urban Development in Northern England, 1760–1830* (Oxford: Oxford University Press, 2006); Danielle van den Heuvel, *Women and Entrepreneurship: Female Traders in the Northern Netherlands, c. 1580–1815* (Amsterdam: Aksant, 2007).

2 Schmidt and Van Nederveen Meerkerk, 'Reconsidering'. Cf. Merry E. Wiesner, '*Wandervogels* and Women: Journeymen's Concepts of Masculinity in Early Modern Germany', *Journal of Social History* 24 (1991).

3 Deborah Simonton, *A History of European Women's Work: 1700 to the Present* (London: Routledge, 1998), 68–69.

4 Henk van Nierop, 'Popular Participation in Politics in the Dutch Republic', in *Resistance, Representation and Community*, ed. Peter Blickle (Oxford: Oxford University Press, 1997), 286.

5 See for an elaborate discussion of this source Marcia Schmidt Blaine, 'The Power of Petitions: Women and the New Hampshire Provincial Government, 1695–1770', *International Review of Social History* 46, suppl. 9 (2001).

6 Hugo de Groot, *Inleidinge tot de Hollandsche Rechts-Geleerheid. Met de te Lund Teruggevonden Verbeteringen, Aanvullingen en Pomerkingen van den Schrijver en met Verwijzingen Naar Zijn Andere Geschreiften Uitgegeven en van Aantekeningen en Bijlagen Voorzien Door F. Dovring, H.F.W.D. Ficher, E.M. Meijers* (Leiden: Universitaire pers Leiden, 1965), 11. This is an annotated edition of Grotius' *Inleydinge*, first published in 1631.

7 Simon van Leeuwen, *Het Rooms-Hollands Regt* (Leiden / Rotterdam, 1664), 24.

8 Schmidt, *Overleven na de dood*, 55–59. For exceptions to these strict rules see Schmidt, *Overleven na de dood*, 59–61, 73–74. On the status of female public vendors, see Van den Heuvel, *Women and Entrepreneurship*, 58–69.

9 Lia van Gemert, 'The Power of the Weaker Vessels: Simon Schama and Johan van Beverwijck on Women', in *Women in the Golden Age. An International Debate on Women*, ed. Els Kloek, Nicole Teeuwen, and Marijke Huisman (Hilversum: Verloren, 1990), 39–41.

10 Van Leeuwen, *Het Rooms-Hollands Regt*, 24. Van Leeuwen's arguments and his (re)valuation of the intellectual capacities of women did not lead him to plead for a change in the legal status of married women. The intellectual capacities of women were defined *in relation to* men. When a man was present on a day-to-day basis, he was the one in charge. See also De Groot, *Inleidinge*, 11.

11 Schmidt, *Overleven na de dood*, 80–94.

12 For an excellent overview of the debate, see Crowston, 'Women, Gender, and Guilds'. The following is based on Ariadne Schmidt, 'Women and Guilds: Corporations and Female Labour Market Participation in Early Modern Holland', *Gender & History* 21 (2009): 170–89.

13 For example, Merry E. Wiesner, *Women and Gender in Early Modern Europe*, 2nd edn. (Cambridge: Cambridge University Press, 2000); Merry E. Wiesner, 'Guilds, Male Bonding and Women's Work in Early Modern Germany', *Gender & History* 1 (1989); Natalie Zemon Davis, 'Women in the Crafts in Sixteenth-Century Lyon', in *Women and Work in Preindustrial Europe*, ed. Barbara A. Hanawalt (Bloomington: Indiana University Press, 1986).

14 For example: Janine M. Lanza, *From Wives to Widows in Early Modern Paris: Gender, Economy, and Law* (Aldershot: Ashgate, 2007); Christine Werkstetter, *Frauen im Augsburger Zunfthandwerk: Arbeit, Arbeitsbeziehungen und Geschlechterverhältnisse im 18. Jahrhundert* (Berlin: Akademie Verlag, 2001); Anna C. Fridrich, 'Working Women in Guild Crafts: Female Strategies in Early Modern Economies', in *Female Agency in the Urban Economy: Gender in European Towns, 1640–1830*, ed. Deborah Simonton and Anne Montenach (New York: Routledge, 2013).

15 The textile industry was also a segment dominated by women, but this sector was usually outside the realm of guild control. Elise van Nederveen Meerkerk, *De Draad in Eigen Handen. Vrouwen en Loonarbeid in de Nederlandsetextielnijverheid* (Amsterdam: Aksant, 2007), 155–75.

16 Schmidt, 'Women and Guilds', 170–89. On guilds restricting women indirectly, see Danielle van den Heuvel, 'Guilds, Gender Policies and Economic Opportunities for Women', in *Female Agency in the Urban Economy*, ed. Simonton and Montenach.

17 Schmidt, 'Women and Guilds', 174; Van den Heuvel, 'Guilds, Gender Policies and Economic Opportunities for Women', 119.

18 For an elaborate discussion of the position of seamstresses in Dutch guilds, see Bibi Panhuysen, *Maatwerk. Kleermakers, Naaisters, Oudkleerkopers en de Gilden (1500–1800)* (Amsterdam: Stichting beheer IISG, 2000).
19 *Gildebrieven van alle de Gildens Binnen de stad Gouda, Kleer-maeckers* (n.p., 1713), 14-11-1614.
20 Lanza, *From Wives to Widows in Early Modern Paris*, 227–28.
21 The textile in industry in Leiden was not organised in guilds but in corporations called *neringen*. The city authorities held strict control over the industry that was so important to the city's economy. People who wanted to establish themselves as independent artisans in the textile industry had to ask for permission from the city council. Van Nederveen Meerkerk, *De Draad in Eigen Handen*, 159–63.
22 Schmidt, 'Women and Guilds', 175. See also Schmidt, *Overleven na de dood*, 146–47.
23 Schmidt, 'Women and Guilds', 175.
24 This was explicated in the guild letters of the surgeons and the schoolmasters. Schmidt, *Overleven na de dood*, 275
25 Simonton, *A History*, 49.
26 Schmidt, *Overleven na de dood*, 147.
27 Schmidt, *Overleven na de dood*, 146, 157–58.
28 In the textile industry—which was not organised in guilds but fell under the strict control of the urban authorities—people always had to ask the authorities for permission to start or to take over a workshop.
29 Schmidt, *Overleven na de dood*, 163.
30 Streekachief Midden Holland (SAMH), Oud Archief Gouda (OAG) no. 275, 17-10-1797.
31 SAMH, OAG nos. 215, 18-2-1775; 212, 12-6-1764.
32 Schmidt, *Overleven na de dood*, 153, 156. The sisters de Hoest were granted exemption from the rule that they had to work in cooperation with a master journeyman.
33 SAMH, OAG nos. 106, 21-8-1675; 214, 16-4-1771.
34 Ariadne Schmidt, 'The Profits of Unpaid Work. "Assisting Labour" of Women in the Early Modern Urban Dutch Economy', *History of the Family* 19 (2014): 19.
35 Wiesner, '*Wandervogels*', 767.
36 Lanza, *From Wives to Widows in Early Modern Paris*, 127.
37 The following examples are drawn from Schmidt, *Overleven na de dood*, 150–53.
38 Regionaal Archief Leiden (RAL), Stadsarchief van Leiden, 1574–1816 (SA II) no. 72, 1-4-1655, fols. 275v–277v.
39 SAMH, OAG no. 208, 8-2-1749, fols. 214–215; OAG no. 209, 21-7-1749.
40 RAL, SAII no. 84, 12-9-1673, fols. 16v–17.
41 RAL, SAII no. 77, 9-3-1662, fols. 260–261
42 RAL, SAII no. 78, 21-9-1662, fols. 39–40.
43 Schmidt, *Overleven na de dood*, 152–53.
44 This section is based upon Schmidt, 'Gelijk Hebben, Gelijk Krijgen?', 121–22.
45 Schmidt, 'The Profits of Unpaid Work', 17–18.
46 My translation. Cited in Maarten Prak, 'Individu, Corporatie en Samenleving. De Retoriek van de Amsterdamse Gilden in de 18de Eeuw', in *Werelden van Verschil. Ambachtsgilden in de Lage Landen*, ed. Catharina Lis and Hugo Soly (Brussels: VUB Press, 1997), 306.

47 SAMH, OAG no. 217, 29-12-1784.
48 SAMH, OAG no. 217, 29-12-1784, fols. 169–173.
49 SAMH, OAG no. 217, 29-12-1784, fols. 173–176v.
50 Simonton, *A History*, 14.
51 SAMH, OAG no. 217, 29-12-1784, fols. 173–176v.
52 SAMH, OAG no. 217, 29-12-1784, fols.175v–176.
53 SAMH, OAG no. 217, 29-12-1784, fol. 177.
54 This and the following paragraphs are based upon Schmidt, 'Managing a Large Household', 43–45, 51–54; Schmidt, 'Gelijk Hebben, gelijk Krijgen?', 123–24.
55 Manon van der Heijden, *Civic Duty. Public Services in the Early Modern Low Countries* (Newcastle: Cambridge Scholars Publishing, 2012).
56 Maarten Prak, *Gezeten Burgers. De elite in een Hollandse stad, Leiden 1700–1780* (Amsterdam: De Bataafsche Leeuw, 1985), 52–55.
57 Leonore Davidoff and Catherine Hall, *Family Fortunes: Men and Women of the English Middle Class, 1780–1850* (London: Hutchinson Education, 1987); Dorothee Sturkenboom, *Spectators van Hartstocht: Sekse Emotionele Cultuur in de Achttiende Eeuw* (Hilversum: Verloren 1998). This paradigm has been much criticised and seems to be inadequate to describe the experiences of the majority of women, although the ideology became more sharply articulated in moralistic literature.
58 Schmidt, 'Managing a Large Household', 45.
59 Els Kloek, 'De Geschiedenis van een Stereotype. De Bazigheid, Ondernemingszin en Zindelijkheid van Vrouwen in Holland (1500–1800)', *Jaarboek voor Genealogie* 58 (2004): 15.
60 Examples include Jacob van Loo, *Regents of the Almoners- and Poor- and Workhouse, Haarlem* (1659), Collection Frans Hals Museum; Frans Hals, *Regentesses of the Old Men's Alms House, Haarlem* (1664), collection Frans Hals Museum; Ferdinand Bol, *Three Regents of the Leprozenhuis in Amsterdam* (1668), Collection Rijksmuseum; Adriaan Backer, *The Regents of the Burgerweeshuis* (1683), Collection Amsterdam Museum.
61 Het Utrechts Archief (HUA),Geformeerd Burgerweeshuis (GBW) no. 1/II, 131.
62 A.J.M. Kunst, *Van Sint Elisabeths-gasthuis tot Gereformeerd Burgerweeshuis (1485–1814)* (Assen: Van Gorcum, 1956), 314.
63 HUA, GBW, no.1/II, 96.
64 HUA, GBW, no. 1/II, 129–30.
65 SAMH, OAG no. 210, 22-6-1756, fols. 199–203.
66 Simon Groenveld et al., *Wezen en Boefjes: Zes Eeuwen Zorg in Wees- en Kinderhuizen* (Hilversum: Verloren, 1997), 95.
67 Cited in J.L. Kool-Blokland, *De Zorg Gewogen. Zeven Eeuwen Godshuizen in Middelburg* (Middelburg: Koninklijk Zweeuwsch Genootschap der Wetenschappen, 1990), 381.
68 Cited in Kool-Blokland, *De Zorg Gewogen*, 380.
69 Cited in Kool-Blokland, *De Zorg Gewogen*, 382.
70 Kool-Blokland, *De Zorg Gewogen*, 384.
71 The following section is based upon Schmidt, 'Managing a Large Household'.
72 RAL, Heilige Geest Weeshuis (HGW) no. 197, 14-11-1796.
73 RAL, HGW no. 197, 22-11-1796.
74 RAL, HGW no. 197, 28-11-1796.
75 RAL, HGW no. 37, 12-12-1796.

76 RAL, HGW no. 37, 12-12-1796.
77 RAL, HGW no. 197, 11-2-1797, 13-2-1797.
78 RAL, HGW no. 197, 14-2-1797, 16-2-1797.
79 RAL, HGW no. 197, 11-2-1797; 13-2-1797; HGW no. 281, 1797.
80 Lanza, *From Wives to Widows in Early Modern Paris*, 224.
81 Wiesner, *Women and Gender in Early Modern Europe*, 90.
82 Simonton, *A History*, 87; Schmidt and Van Nederveen Meerkerk, 'Reconsidering'.

Select bibliography

Crowston, Clare. 'Women, Gender, and Guilds in Early Modern Europe: An Overview of Recent Research'. In *The Return of the Guilds*, ed. Jan Lucassen, Tine De Moor, and Jan Luiten van Zanden, special issue of *International Review of Social History* 53, suppl. 16 (2008): 19–44.

Heuvel, Danielle van den. 'Guilds, Gender Policies and Economic Opportunities for Women'. In *Female Agency in the Urban Economy: Gender in European Towns, 1640–1830*, ed. Deborah Simonton and Anne Montenach, 116–13. New York: Routledge, 2013.

——— *Women and Entrepreneurship: Female Traders in the Northern Netherlands, c. 1580–1815*. Amsterdam: Aksant, 2007.

Lanza, Janine M. *From Wives to Widows in Early Modern Paris: Gender, Economy, and Law*. Aldershot: Ashgate, 2007.

Panhuysen, Bibi. *Maatwerk. Kleermakers, Naaisters, Oudkleerkopers en de Gilden (1500–1800)*. Amsterdam: Stichting beheer IISG, 2000.

Schmidt, Ariadne. 'Gelijk Hebben, Gelijk Krijgen? Vrouwen en Vertrouwen in het Recht in Holland in de Zeventiende en Achttiende Eeuw'. In *Het Gelijk van de Gouden Eeuw: Recht, Onrecht en Reputatie in de Vroegmoderne Nederlanden*, ed. Michiel van Groesen, Judith Pollmann, and Hans Cools, 109–25. Hilversum: Verloren 2014.

——— 'Managing a Large Household. The Gender Division of Work in Orphanages in Dutch Towns in the Early Modern Period, 1580–1800'. *History of the Family* 13 (2008): 42–57.

——— *Overleven na de dood: Weduwen in Leiden in de Gouden Eeuw*. Amsterdam: Prometheus / Bert Bakker, 2001.

——— 'The Profits of Unpaid Work. "Assisting Labour" of Women in the Early Modern Urban Dutch Economy'. *History of the Family* 19 (2014): 301–22.

——— 'Women and Guilds: Corporations and Female Labour Market Participation in Early Modern Holland'. *Gender & History* 21 (2009): 170–89.

Schmidt, Ariadne, and Elise van Nederveen Meerkerk. 'Reconsidering "The First Male-Breadwinner Economy": Women's Labour Force Participation in the Netherlands, 1600–1900'. *Feminist Economics* 18 (2012): 69–96.

Simonton, Deborah. *A History of European Women's Work: 1700 to the Present*. London: Routledge, 1998.

Simonton, Deborah, and Anne Montenach, eds. *Female Agency in the Urban Economy: Gender in European Towns, 1640–1830*. London: Routledge, 2013.

Wiesner, Merry E. '*Wandervogels* and Women: Journeymen's Concepts of Masculinity in Early Modern Germany'. *Journal of Social History* 24 (1991): 767–82.

——— *Women and Gender in Early Modern Europe*, 2nd edn. Cambridge: Cambridge University Press, 2000.

Index

For Product Safety Concerns and Information please contact our EU representative GPSR@taylorandfrancis.com
Taylor & Francis Verlag GmbH, Kaufingerstraße 24, 80331 München, Germany

www.ingramcontent.com/pod-product-compliance
Ingram Content Group UK Ltd.
Pitfield, Milton Keynes, MK11 3LW, UK
UKHW011001180926
475701UK00004B/508
9781032401874